NATIONAL CONSUMER COUNCIL

Ordinary Justice

Legal services and the
courts in England and Wales:
a consumer view

LONDON HER MAJESTY'S STATIONERY OFFICE

Crown copyright 1989
First published 1989

British Library Cataloguing in Publication Data

A CIP catalogue record for this book
is available from the British Library

ISBN 0 11 701369 2

Other National Consumer Council reports published by HMSO include:

Consumers and the Common Agricultural Policy
1988, £11.95 ISBN 0 11 701370 6

What's Wrong With Walking?
1987, £4.95 ISBN 0 11 701271 8

Air Transport and the Consumer
1986, £7.95 ISBN 0 11 701268 8

HMSO BOOKS

HMSO publications are available from:

HMSO Publications Centre
(Mail and telephone orders only)
PO Box 276, London, SW8 5DT
Telephone orders 01-873 9090
General enquiries 01-873 0011
(queuing system in operation for both numbers)

HMSO Bookshops
49 High Holborn, London, WC1V 6HB   01 873 0011 (Counter service only)
258 Broad Street, Birmingham, B1 2HE   021-643 3740
Southey House, 33 Wine Street, Bristol, BS1 2BQ   (0272) 264306
9-21 Princess Street, Manchester, M60 8AS   061-834 7201
80 Chichester Street, Belfast, BT1 4JY   (0232) 238451
71 Lothian Road, Edinburgh, EH3 9AZ   031-228 4181

HMSO's Accredited Agents
(see Yellow Pages)

and through good booksellers

Contents

Chairman's foreword

Things are not perfect all the time. People make mistakes, and others suffer. Sometimes people set out deliberately to cheat or unfairly exploit each other. Individuals get themselves into muddles and cannot meet the obligations they have taken on.

In a free society we should have good systems for dealing with the disputes that inevitably result and for defining who has right on their side. That is the function of the courts and the legal services that give each of us as individuals ultimate access to the courts.

As consumers, of course, we have a direct interest in the way the law underpins the market place. If we are to go confidently about the daily business of exchanging money for goods and services then we must be sure that we can enforce the rights the law gives us if unscrupulous or careless traders take advantage of us. If we are injured, we need recompense. Our rights in our homes should be secure. Nor can traders with high standards prosper if unscrupulous competitors can get away with flouting the law. And if we get ourselves into trouble with money, we need systems to sort out the problem which are constructive and not destructive or obstructive.

Hence this book. We look both at the legal procedures for dealing with individuals' problems and at the way the courts, lawyers and advice services are organised. In this we consider them as a consumer service in their own right. The question is: how well do the courts and legal services serve those who need to use them?

Going to law can be a daunting experience for the lay man or woman. Many of us are justifiably put off by the worry, the delay and the cost.

Lawyers are already—and I welcome this—making changes to help with these problems in a new, more competitive environment. I hope our book will help them to put the needs of their clients—consumers—first.

Changes in legal services and changes in the courts must go hand in hand. I am heartened by the support for this approach from the Lord Chancellor's Civil Justice Review, whose findings we often return to in this book.

In the end, respect for the rule of law itself depends on its ability to protect the individual. If the processes of the law are seen as obscure, inaccessible and irrelevant, then people will not see the law as the protector of their rights and the arbiter of their responsibilities. I hope that what we have written will help to prevent this.

Sally Oppenheim-Barnes *Chairman, National Consumer Council*

Acknowledgements

This report is based on our previous policy papers and on a number of background papers commissioned by us in the course of our work. Our thanks are due to the following people who acted as our consultants: Enid Church, Craig Gardner, Ole Hansen, Elaine Kempson, Tim Kerr, Mark Mildred, Professor Alan Paterson and Dr Christopher J Whelan. We are grateful to the many others who commented on our draft report.

The work was overseen by a small working party chaired by Janet Graham (Vice-Chairman of the NCC), with John Nelson-Jones (council member), Robin Simpson (staff) and Guy Dehn (staff).

The report was written by Tamara Goriely, with research and assistance by Claudette Baker and Susan Foreman. It was prepared for publication by Steven Morris and typed by Rita Baptiste.

It takes account of events up to 1st October 1988.

Chapter 1
Summary and recommendations

Lawyers often seem to see our system of civil justice as a hand-tailored suit—too good for everyday use. This report is about off-the-peg justice. We want a legal system that is simple, quick, cheap and fair, and which can be used by ordinary people to sort out ordinary problems.

In this book we examine the civil legal system in England and Wales from the user's point of view. We define consumers of justice as all those who have reason to use lawyers and the courts in a personal capacity. Of particular concern are individuals who seek to enforce or defend rights against corporate opponents.

It is the job of the National Consumer Council to identify and represent the interests of those who use goods or services supplied by the public and private sectors. Whenever we are evaluating a product or service, we measure its provision against a number of consumer criteria—access, choice, information, price, redress and representation. How do these consumer yardsticks apply to lawyers and the courts?

★   access
A service cannot meet the needs of consumers if they are unable to use it. There is little point in parliament passing laws to protect consumers unless consumers are then able to pursue legal solutions to their problems and take advantage of legal safeguards.

For consumers approaching the law for the first time, the legal system can seem like a mysterious ritual whose language and ways are unfathomable and whose outcome is a high-risk gamble. We look at a number of ways of improving access both to legal advice and to court procedures.

★ choice

Not everyone wants to resolve their problems by going to law. But where the law provides a remedy consumers should have the option of using it. The Royal Commission for Legal Services in Scotland (the Hughes Commission) thought that the public's need for legal services fell into two parts:

"Firstly enabling the client to identify and, if he judges appropriate, to choose a legal solution; and secondly, enabling the client to pursue a chosen legal solution" (1)★.

We endorse this approach. Consumers should have the option of using legal remedies if they choose to do so.

Consumers also need a choice of legal services because not everyone will want the same service. We wish to see consumers able to choose the mix of price, specialist knowledge, convenience and friendliness which most suits them.

★ information

In order to make sensible choices, consumers need information—about legal rights and responsibilities; about court procedures; about which lawyer to choose; about legal aid; about solicitors' costs; and about what to do if things go wrong.

★ price

There is no doubt that cost is a major barrier to using the law. We need a legal system which consumers can afford to use. We look at ways in which the services can be made cheaper without sacrificing quality, and at how the risks associated with legal costs can be reduced.

★ redress

No product is perfect and no system is immune from mistakes. We wish to see accessible complaints systems which provide consumers with redress fairly, promptly and effectively when things go wrong.

★ representation

Often services cannot be left entirely to the market. The court system must be provided by the state and legal services are subject to a number of regulations and controls. Although everyone is now agreed that these controls should be made in the interests of consumers, consumers still have very little say in the

---

★ References and sources are given in full at the end of each chapter.

decision-making process. We want them to have a voice in the way that courts are run and in the process by which the professions are regulated.

Summary

In *Ordinary justice* we look in detail at five specific areas of law: obtaining compensation after an accident (chapter 11); getting redress for faulty goods and services (chapter 10); arguing with the landlord over repairs (chapter 12); being threatened with repossession as a result of rent or mortgage arrears (chapter 12); and being sued for an unpaid bill (chapter 13). These are all common problems in which ordinary people are in dispute with organisations—businesses, insurance companies, local authorities, banks, building societies or finance houses. In principle, the law provides the individual with a number of remedies or safeguards.

We have found that in practice, most individuals forego their rights. Individual consumers start at a disadvantage because they meet the legal system only rarely, have a limited understanding of how it works and limited resources in terms of money, time and energy. Their opponents use the courts frequently, have expert legal departments, and enough time and money to see the case through. The legal system does little to redress the balance. Most people do not even consider going to law. Of those who consider it, many reject it as being too costly or troublesome, and those who persevere have a number of obstacles thrown in their path.

In 1970, our predecessors, the Consumer Council, published *Justice out of reach* which looked at how far consumers were able to use the legal system. They concluded:

"individuals use the county courts very little for any matter at all, not simply consumer matters; they rarely sue and rarely defend if sued." (2).

Unfortunately this is still true today.

Claiming compensation after an accident (chapter 11)

In law, someone who is injured as a result of another's negligence can claim compensation. Compensation attempts, as far as money can, to put the victims back in the position they would have been in had the accident not occurred. The injured person may claim for loss of earnings, for the expenses of disability and for compensation for pain, suffering and loss of amenity.

The initiative lies with the injured person to make a claim and find sufficient evidence to prove his or her case. Naturally, it is only worth bringing a claim where the person who caused the accident is able to pay—either because they are insured or they have large resources. In practice, over 90 per cent of successful claims are met by insurance companies (3).

The Oxford Centre for Socio-legal Studies Compensation Study found that 85 per cent of accident victims did not make a claim for compensation (4). Around three-quarters of injured people did not even consider it; of those who did consider it, only half decided to take the first step. The trouble and bother of legal action, coupled with fear of legal expenses, problems in finding evidence and ignorance or confusion over rights were the most commonly cited reasons for not proceeding with a complaint.

Those who did claim generally received something. Eighty per cent of claimants in the study received a settlement. Only a tiny number—around 2 per cent—actually went to court. But people who settled waited a long time: the average time between the accident and the payment was 19 months (4). Cases that go to court take even longer. Research for the Civil Justice Review found that the average high court case took between five and six years, and the average county court case took between two and a half and three years (5).

People often settled for very small amounts: the full sum which a judge may have awarded had the matter proceeded to court is heavily discounted as a result of the problems claimants face. These problems include lack of skilled advice, uncertainty, and fear of legal costs.

Claimants need good solicitors: those who try to pursue claims without solicitors receive tiny sums. Solicitors differ markedly in their skills and experience of personal injury work and consumers have little information to go on when choosing lawyers. With a few exceptions, lawyers are not able to advertise that they specialise in any area of work.

Those without legal aid who fail to win their cases can be faced with very large bills from both their own and the defendant's solicitor. Research conducted in 1985 for the Civil Justice Review found that for cases in which court proceedings were started, average plaintiff's costs ranged from £1,500 in the county court to £6,800 in the high court in London. Defendants' costs were less in the county court but of an equivalent amount in the high court (5).

Redress for faulty goods and services (chapter 10)

The Office of Fair Trading consumer dissatisfaction survey shows that every year, people in the United Kingdom consider that they have cause to complain about 12 million significant purchases, such as furniture, household appliances, cars, car servicing, building work and holidays (6). Around eighty per cent of consumers who are dissatisfied with these things take action about their complaint—usually by contacting the supplier. Between a fifth and a third of consumers pursue the matter further—asking to see the manager, writing to head office, or contacting a third person such as an advice centre. Between sixty-five and seventy-one per cent of those complaining about furniture, cars and household appliances expressed themselves satisfied with the outcome, but the satisfaction rates fell dramatically for services. Only 20 per cent of people complaining about holidays and 26 per cent of people complaining about building work said they were satisfied with the outcome. In all, we give a very rough estimate of 4.5 million unresolved consumer complaints about high value goods in the United Kingdom per year—equivalent to around four million complaints in England and Wales.

It is remarkable how rarely people think of using the courts to resolve consumer complaints. Less than two per cent of people taking further action about their complaints threatened to go to the county court (6). Far fewer people actually did so. The small claims procedure, designed as an informal method of resolving consumer complaints within the county court, deals with less than 12,500 disputes about faulty goods or services each year.

The courts are not seen as a place where ordinary people can start cases. In 1979, when the Welsh Consumer Council asked people what the county court dealt with, more people thought (wrongly) that the court dealt with shoplifting and parking fines than with complaints about faulty goods (7). When people were asked what would worry them about going to court, 45 per cent mentioned costs, 31 per cent said the whole atmosphere of court action, and 24 per cent mentioned formalities. Twenty-seven per cent said they were worried about their name getting into the papers—for these people courts were associated with personal disgrace.

Getting housing repairs done (chapter 12)

The consumer concerns survey we conducted in 1980 revealed widespread concern about the way landlords carried out repairs (8). One-third of council tenants said that they suffered from damp or condensation, a third said that they needed repairs which had not been carried out, and a third complained about the time repairs took. Among private tenants the problems were worse—over half complained of damp and two-fifths said that they needed repairs which had not been carried out. The 1981 *English House Conditions Survey* found that 30 per cent of local authority homes and 60 per cent of privately rented homes required repairs of over £1,000. Almost 400,000 tenanted homes required repairs of over £7,000 and 437,000 tenanted homes were regarded as "unfit" (9).

Repairs are also a problem for leaseholders. In 1985, the committee of inquiry on the management of privately owned blocks of flats (the Nugee Committee) published its report (10). They found evidence of widespread problems: excessive delay in responding to requests for maintenance and repairs; difficulties in getting landlords to carry out their obligations; lack of information for lessees and dissatisfaction with the level of service charges and the quality of service provided.

In theory the law provides a remedy against disrepair. In practice, a tiny number of cases get to court. The Civil Justice Review considered a long list of housing cases—including disputes about repairs, service charges, mobile homes, homelessness, and the right to buy. They estimated that only 1,500 cases in England and Wales reached the county court each year and a further 100 cases were heard in the magistrates court (11).

People are often unaware of their rights, there is a shortage of housing advice and court action involves time, cost and worry. The Civil Justice Review carried out a small study of 65 people with housing problems who had not used the court (12). Unfortunately it was too small to draw firm conclusions but it revealed a very low awareness of legal aid. The interviewees showed considerable desperation in trying to sort out their problems—contacting councillors, MPs, social services and many other organisations—but they ruled out court action, usually on the grounds of cost.

Rent and mortgage arrears (chapter 12)

Possession actions for rent and mortgage arrears are a substantial part of county court business. In 1986, 153,870 possession actions were started in the county courts of England and Wales (13). Forty-six per cent were brought by mortgage lenders such as banks and building societies, and 38 per cent were brought by social landlords, such as local authorities and housing associations (13). Three-quarters involved unpaid rent or mortgage arrears (12).

The efforts of lenders and landlords to sort things out before taking court action were very variable. The Civil Justice Review research found that a third of banks and building societies and a fifth of local authorities did not enquire about the defendant's circumstances before the hearing. Three-quarters of local authorities did not follow the Department of Environment's advice and carry out checks to see if the tenant was receiving the right benefits (12).

In theory the law provides protection for those in financial hardship. In rent arrears cases, the court must be satisfied that it is "reasonable" to make an order, and the court cannot suspend possession on terms which cause "exceptional hardship". In mortgage cases, the court can give the borrower time to pay off the arrears.

In practice, court proceedings become a rubber stamp. The documents the court sends out are difficult to understand. The defendant is asked to fill in a form but it does not ask about the defendant's personal circumstances and no guidance is given on completing it. The returned forms rarely contain useful information.

Few defendants attend the court hearing. The Civil Justice Review research found that three-quarters of local authority tenants, half of private tenants and two-fifths of mortgage borrowers failed to go to court. Only a tiny minority—8 per cent—of defendants were represented at the hearing, even though where defendants are represented they are more likely to receive a favourable outcome (12).

Unpaid bills (chapter 13)

In possession cases there must be a court hearing. But most debt cases before the county court are dealt with by an administrative default procedure. Defendants are sent a summons and a form of reply. If they do not take steps to dispute the claim, judgement is entered and the creditor can then take steps to enforce the debt.

Two-thirds of defendants do not return the form, and only seven per cent defend the claim, although far more people think that they do not owe the money claimed (14). Generally, the debt system proceeds with little information about the debtor's circumstances. The Civil Justice Review study found that 67 per cent of creditors had no knowledge of the debtor's financial circumstances at the time of the original transaction, and 77 per cent did not obtain any further information before or during the proceedings (14).

The most common enforcement method—accounting for three-quarters of all enforcement in the courts—is the "warrant of execution" or threat to seize household goods. The first point of contact with the debtor will therefore usually be the bailiff at the door.

For the inexperienced debtor this can be a harrowing experience. In a study of 150 debtors by Queen Mary College, a third said that their health had suffered, just under a third said that their family's health had suffered and two debtors had taken drug overdoses following the bailiff's visit (15).

The debt recovery system is also confusing for individual plaintiffs. Consumers who win small claims are generally given little help in finding their way through the procedures (7).

Proposals for reform

In our view, there is a need to reform both court procedures and the way that legal advice, assistance and representation are provided, so as to make the law more accessible to individual consumers. In chapters 3 to 8 we discuss improvements to legal services, and in chapters 9 to 13 we discuss changes within the courts.

Our main findings are summarised below.

Legal aid (chapters 3 and 4)

Since the second world war it has been accepted that the state should provide support to those unable to afford to pay for lawyers. The legal aid scheme, first introduced in 1950, aims to put people of poor and moderate means in the same position as well-to-do paying litigants to obtain advice and pursue worthwhile cases before the courts. It operates by paying private lawyers on a case by case basis.

Legal aid in England and Wales compares well with legal aid schemes in other countries. It is relatively long-established; it provides the consumer with a wide choice of solicitor, with over 11,500 offices taking part; and it helps steadily increasing numbers of people. In 1986-7 around one and a quarter million people received help with civil matters through the legal aid scheme (16).

But despite its many strengths, a number of weaknesses are becoming increasingly apparent. These are:

★ *lack of knowledge about the scheme:* legal aid cannot help people unless they know it exists. The Oxford Compensation Study found that fewer than half the accident victims consulting a solicitor had heard of the legal aid scheme and only a quarter had heard of the green form scheme (4). Similarly low levels of awareness were found by the Civil Justice Review housing study (12) and by the Lord Chancellor's Department's research on the green form scheme (17);

★ *administrative delay:* in 1986-7 it took an average of 67 days to issue a non-contributory civil legal aid certificate and 124 days to issue a contributory certificate (16). During this time, all work on a case must be postponed;

★ *falling eligibility:* the government's figures for the number of people eligible for legal aid are inconsistent. The legal aid means test has not kept pace with either social security payments or earnings. Since 1979, the amount a family with two children can earn before becoming ineligible for help has dropped from 37 per cent above average male earnings to 6 per cent above average male earnings. The capital limits have also fallen in real terms. Meanwhile, the government is planning to increase contributions substantially;

★ *the statutory charge:* legal aid is only free for those who lose their cases. Where the legally aided litigant wins, the legal aid fund recoups its costs, first from the costs awarded against the loser, and secondly from any property "recovered or preserved" in the proceedings. This can cause hardship in matrimonial cases, where winners seldom recover all their costs from the other side. These difficulties are compounded by a lack of information to clients on how the statutory charge will affect them;

★ *fears that the number of solicitors in the scheme will fall:* until recently, the number of solicitors participating in the civil legal aid scheme has risen steadily. But in 1987, the number of solicitors ceasing to handle matrimonial legal aid exceeded those joining the scheme. Although the numbers undertaking non-matrimonial civil legal aid continue to increase, there are signs of unease about levels of remuneration (18);

★ *failure to provide a service in areas of social welfare law:* civil legal aid is dominated by traditional areas of lawyers' practice such as matrimonial and personal injury work. It is rarely used for social security, housing, debt, employment or immigration. Part of the problem is that legal aid is not available for representation before tribunals. Furthermore, the poor do not have a tradition of using solicitors: although legal aid aims to overcome the cost barrier, it does little to inform people of their rights, or make them less reluctant to use solicitors. Few solicitors are located in the areas where the poor have most need of them and very few are skilled in social welfare law.

The Legal Aid Act 1988 establishes a new framework for legal aid. Although the immediate effects of the change will be small, the Lord

Chancellor has stressed that it provides "an opportunity for some rigorous and adventurous thinking about the organisation and administration of the scheme" (19). In particular, the government aims to reform the green form scheme, which offers initial advice. The white paper on legal aid states that "the Government is attracted to the principle of using the skills of advice agencies" to deal with those areas of work in which their skills are greater than those of solicitors in private practice (20).

The National Consumer Council welcomes the opportunity to re-examine the relationship between private practice and the advice sector.

General advice

In our view, the first priority is to increase the provision of generalist advice, so that everyone has access to a local advice centre offering basic advice on any query raised. This must be done as an addition to, rather than a substitute for, legal aid. As we stated in 1977, the right to information and advice is a basic right of citizenship (21). As legislation and regulations become ever more complex, the need for information and advice becomes ever greater.

We are very concerned at the uneven distribution of advice workers. While in London there is one full-time equivalent advice worker (paid or volunteer) for every 3,750 people, in the East Midlands there is one advice worker for every 23,250 people (22). Overall, we estimate that provision is only a third of that needed.

The government will need to make resources available to local government to fund general advice and in chapter 4 we discuss what improved provision is likely to cost.

Recommendation 1: general advice

1.1 *The government should, as a first priority, make resources available to extend generalist advice to those areas of the country which are presently underprovided.*

1.2 *District councils and boroughs should be under a duty to provide general advice in their areas, by making grants to centres managed independently of the local authority. When deciding what provision to make they should pay special regard to the needs of disadvantaged groups within their areas. County councils should have a power to make additional funds available.*

1.3 *A central government department should be given primary respons-*
ibility for encouraging and advising local authorities on advice
provision.

Specialist advice

Once a network of general advice exists across the country, there are
advantages in providing legal advice and representation in areas of
social welfare law through advice centres rather than through
solicitors in private practice. Advice centres can take a more active
role in informing people of their rights; they are more likely to be
used; they have greater specialist skills in social welfare law; they place
greater emphasis on self-help; and they have developed more cost-
effective ways of handling large numbers of cases. There are also
significant administrative savings if applications do not have to be
approved on a case by case basis.

The case is clearest in social security. Very few solicitors have any
skills in this area and the number of welfare benefits green forms
submitted (29,000) is tiny compared with the two million cases
handled by existing advice centres (16). There is also a case for
providing help through salaried staff and volunteers in housing
possession cases, debt advice, consumer problems, employment and
immigration.

Although advice centres can offer a more accessible service, they are
not an easy or cheap option. The existing green form scheme is under-
used, and therefore costs less than it could. Advice centres would
generate much greater demands. Any transfer of resources from the
green form scheme to advice centres would need to be made on the
basis of an expanding budget. There needs to be very careful planning
and co-ordination, on a local and regional basis. We recommend
setting up regional legal services committees, along the lines of the
North Western legal services committee, to advise the Legal Aid
Board.

Recommendation 2: specialist advice

2.1 *The Legal Aid Board should take over funding those specialist*
advice centres where there is a conflict of interest between the centre
and the current funder.

2.2 *In transferring legal advice from private solicitors to advice*
centres, the Board should ensure that the following pre-conditions
are met.

★ *there must be an adequate level of general advice provision in the area;*

★ *the level of provision should be related to anticipated demand;*

★ *grants provided by the Legal Aid Board should not be used to cut existing advice provision;*

★ *there should be an adequate variety of centres to provide a choice;*

★ *centres should be able to provide the appropriate level of assistance and representation;*

★ *the quality of service provided should be monitored and centres should be financially accountable to the Board.*

2.3 *The Board should develop standards for advice provision. These should include resource standards laying down minimum numbers of staff and access points, and performance indicators measuring the service offered to consumers.*

2.4 *Legal services committees should be established to advise the Board on local and regional circumstances.*

2.5 *Part of the costs of specialist advice on debt matters should be borne by the credit industry, either through voluntary contributions or a mandatory levy.*

2.6 *Representation should be provided before tribunal hearings for complex cases, for people who have difficulties following proceedings or speaking for themselves, and for all cases before top-tier tribunals, including the social security commissioners and the immigration appeal tribunal.*

2.7 *The Legal Aid Board should evaluate the effect of new legislation on the need for legal advice, assistance and representation.*

Improving legal aid

Whatever the outcome of the government's proposals to transfer green form work, the bulk of civil legal aid in traditional areas such as matrimonial law and personal injury work will continue to be provided through private solicitors. There are a large number of tasks for the Board to tackle, which are listed below.

Recommendation 3: improving legal aid

We wish to see the Board:

3.1 *increase general awareness of the legal aid scheme through a publicity campaign;*

3.2 *decrease administrative delay;*

3.3 *establish an in-house research department;*

3.4 *conduct research into the present coverage of the legal aid scheme and the reasons for the high refusal rate for contributory legal aid;*

3.5 *set targets for the proportion of people to be covered by the legal aid scheme with the objective of reversing the reduction since 1979;*

3.6 *ensure that clients are fully informed about the effects of the statutory charge and increase the £2,500 exemption from the statutory charge in matrimonial proceedings;*

3.7 *increase the green form capital limits in line with income support capital limits;*

3.8 *permit telephone and postal advice to be given under the green form scheme.*

Choosing a lawyer (chapter 5)

Many people who could benefit from legal advice do not approach a lawyer for help. They may be unaware of their rights; they may not know that a solicitor could help; they may not know how to approach a solicitor or how to find one with the right skills. We wish to see consumers given more information in finding and choosing lawyers.

Referrals

The most common way in which people find solicitors is through personal recommendation, from family or friends, or from commercial organisations such as estate agents or banks. In many ways, businesses are in a better position than friends to assess a solicitor's ability. But solicitors who rely too heavily on commercial organisations to introduce business may compromise their independence. For this reason, until September 1988 "arrangements" between solicitors and others for the introduction of work were banned. Now solicitors may accept referrals and even provide "package" deals with local businesses, provided that they comply with the Law Society's code. This states that solicitors should carry out reviews every six months to check that they are not over-reliant on a limited number of sources of referral (23).

The code is full of admirable principles but we fear it will prove difficult to enforce. In our view the consumer's best safeguard against cosy deals among local firms is full disclosure. A record of those who make regular referrals should be available to consumers, preferably in a short brochure or leaflet describing the firm. In the event of a complaint, the record should also be produced to the Solicitors Complaints Bureau. In the long term we hope that greater advertising will mean that solicitors are less dependent on commercial organisations for referrals.

Recommendation 4: referrals to solicitors

4. *Records of who regularly refers clients to a firm of solicitors should be made available to clients, preferably within a brochure about the firm, and should be disclosed to the Solicitors Complaints Bureau in the event of a complaint.*

Advertising

Advertising is a new idea for this generation of solicitors. Press and radio advertisements were not permitted until 1984 and it was not until 1987 that solicitors were allowed to advertise on television and by direct mail. The National Consumer Council welcomed these relaxations of the rules on the grounds that advertisements can provide the public with more information and increase competition within legal services. Innovative ways of providing services are more likely to develop if consumers can be told about them.

In order to assess the usefulness of solicitors' advertising to consumers, in 1987 we carried out an analysis of 1,256 advertisements appearing in yellow pages and the local press (24). We concluded that advertising is a small step in the right direction. Advertisements tell consumers the type of work firms are willing to handle and whether they operate the legal aid scheme. Advertising has also helped make conveyancing more price competitive by providing some cost figures and encouraging clients to ring for quotes. But most advertisements only reach people who have already decided to see a solicitor. Very few draw people's attention to legal remedies, or explain about legal aid. Solicitors could be much more adventurous in telling people about the law.

The accident leaflet scheme

In 1978 the North Western legal services committee produced a leaflet which told people how they could claim compensation after an accident and offered a free initial interview with a solicitor. Research into the scheme found that it was very effective in reaching people who would not otherwise make a claim. Most people using the scheme were advised that they had a good claim (25).

We were very pleased that the Law Society decided to re-launch the scheme nationally in June 1987. Initial results are encouraging. We very much hope that solicitors will retain their enthusiasm for the scheme past the initial launch and that local law societies will ensure continuing publicity. We regret that some doctors and hospitals have refused to display posters on the grounds that they may encourage claims for medical negligence and we call on the British Medical Association to endorse the scheme.

Recommendation 5: the accident leaflet scheme

5. *We welcome the Law Society's decision to launch the accident leaflet scheme (ALAS!) and recommend that they continue to publicise the scheme; we call on the British Medical Association to endorse the display of leaflets in doctors' surgeries and hospitals.*

Specialisation schemes

Research into personal injury claims has shown that using a solicitor with specialist skills can make a significant difference to how the case is conducted. Yet it is often very difficult to find solicitors with the right skills. The regional directories list the categories of work undertaken but not solicitors' skills; solicitors are prevented from advertising themselves as specialists and although advice centres frequently recommend solicitors, most consumers approach solicitors without using advice centres.

A solution lies in the introduction of specialisation schemes, by which suitably qualified lawyers are recognised as specialists and are entitled to advertise their specialist status to the public. In our view, these have the potential to increase both access, by enabling consumers to identify lawyers with the right skills, and competence, by providing an incentive to lawyers to increase their skills.

We wish the Law Society to set up pilot schemes. We favour high-level schemes, covering broad areas such as personal injury or matrimonial work. Eligibility criteria should be applied flexibly, but could include attending courses, completing relevant tasks, and sitting practically based examinations. Specialisation schemes should be well publicised, so that the public is aware of what the particular qualifications mean. It is very important that solicitors without specialist qualifications are able to carry on doing the work. If schemes are made exclusive, access will be reduced and new monopolies will be created, which may raise prices.

Recommendation 6: specialisation schemes

6.   *The Law Society should establish a number of non-exclusive, high level specialisation schemes on an experimental basis.*

Paying for lawyers (chapter 6)

Cost is a major barrier to using the law. People are deterred by the level of solicitors' charges and the fear and uncertainty surrounding them.

Consumers lack information about how much a case will cost, about how costs are mounting and about how a bill has been drawn up. We wish to see the written professional standards on informing clients about costs better publicised within the profession. These contain useful guidance on giving estimates, and telling clients they may put an upper limit on the costs which may be incurred without further reference to them (26). Bills should be simplified so that the "expense rate" and "uplift" are covered by a single hourly rate. Where solicitors are charging by the hour they should be required to state the hourly charging rate of those dealing with the case at the initial interview. This will not give clients the whole story about how much a case will cost but it is a useful starting point. Solicitors should provide regular accounts to privately paying clients and those likely to be faced with a statutory charge, showing the costs which have been incurred to date.

In contentious matters, where the work involves a dispute, consumers who wish to challenge bills must ask the court to "tax" (i.e. vet) the bill. We wish to see taxation procedures radically simplified, so that consumers can represent themselves.

Recommendation 7: paying for lawyers

7.1   *Solicitors should disclose hourly charging rates, and should provide regular accounts to both privately paying clients and those who may be subject to the statutory charge. The written professional standards on informing clients about costs should be better publicised.*

7.2   *Taxation procedures should be simplified to enable consumers to represent themselves.*

Below, we examine alternative methods of paying for lawyers, to assess whether they can reduce uncertainty and worry for clients who do not qualify for legal aid.

Standard fees

With standard fees, the client agrees to pay a set amount for a particular item of work. This may cover a whole case, or a stage of a case. Standard fees are permitted but outside the field of conveyancing and criminal work they are not widely used. The government proposes to increase payment by standard fees in the civil legal aid scheme.

In America, "mass market" law firms have found a market for standardised services at fixed costs: like fast-food chains, mass market firms offer limited menus, quickly, economically and at a standard quality. They are able to reach consumers who would not normally think of using lawyers.

We support the use of standard fees in more routine cases: they enable consumers to know how much cases will cost, to budget in advance and to make price comparisons. We welcome the government's proposals to experiment with fixed fees within the civil legal aid scheme, and trust that information about the level of fees will be provided to those who may be subject to the statutory charge. In the long term, legal aid's experience of standard fees could be used to benefit paying clients.

Recommendation 8: standard fees

8.   *We support government proposals to introduce standard fees into the civil legal aid scheme; information about the fees should be provided for those likely to be subject to the statutory charge. If standard fees prove effective, they should be used to provide privately paying clients with more information about costs.*

Legal expenses insurance

In legal expenses insurance schemes, the consumer pays an annual premium or membership fee. If a legal dispute covered by the scheme arises during the year, the scheme pays the legal costs of taking or defending proceedings.

Legal expenses insurance is much more developed in the United States and in other European countries than in Britain. But the American and European traditions are very different.

In America, "pre-paid legal service plans" have usually been developed by trade unions and consumer groups, motivated by the desire to fulfil unmet legal need. Schemes often use in-house lawyers, or a limited number of nominated external lawyers.

The nearest British equivalents are the services provided by trade unions. Nearly all unions offer legal services for work accidents or employment disputes and a small number offer general legal advice, paid for by the union membership fee. They direct their business to a limited number of solicitors' firms. Motoring organisations and trade associations provide similar services.

We wish to encourage trade unions and other affinity groups to extend the legal services they provide. Group schemes should not automatically disentitle members to legal aid. Instead, schemes should be able to fill in the gaps of the legal aid scheme, by paying contributions or meeting the statutory charge, for example. We do not wish to see a ban on schemes providing initial assistance through in-house lawyers.

The European tradition is to provide legal expenses insurance on purely commercial lines. Thus schemes do not cover all the legal services which people might need but protect policy holders against unforeseen and infrequent events. In Germany, which has the most developed market, all schemes offer a free choice of lawyer.

In England and Wales, between three and four million people have some kind of commercially provided legal expenses insurance. In addition to meeting the expenses of a limited variety of court proceedings, most schemes include an advice line, where policy holders can get free telephone advice from staff employed by the insurers.

We have examined the policies on offer, and conclude that individual schemes provide a sensible way for relatively affluent families to meet legal costs arising out of unforeseen circumstances, such as accidents or dismissal.

They are not in any way an alternative to legal aid. We have heeded the warning of one of the leading American commentators against confusing business and social motives by developing schemes which redistribute "the high costs of justice among those who cannot afford it" (27). Insurance plans do not reduce costs: instead costs are increased to cover marketing and administration, and spread over more people. Insurance schemes are not appropriate for events (such as divorce) which are under the control of the policy holder.

We wish to see an expansion of legal expenses insurance, but consider that there is a need to prevent abuses and to provide consumers with clearer information. Different companies have different exceptions and present information in different ways. In 1983 the Advertising Standards Authority found some promotional information was misleading (28). Complaints systems leave much to be desired and only one company is a member of the Insurance Ombudsman Scheme.

We recommend that the main companies should develop guidelines to ensure that information about coverage is presented in a standard and comprehensible form and that there are fair procedures for dealing with disputes. The Department of Trade and Industry should monitor progress and be prepared to use its powers to make regulations if necessary. We are concerned that solicitors are being given commission to sell some schemes rather than others. The Law Society should issue guidelines to solicitors to ensure that they are able to give independent advice about the merits of different schemes.

Recommendation 9: legal expenses insurance

9.1 *Legal expenses insurance companies should develop guidelines to ensure that information about policies is presented in a standard and comprehensible form, and there are fair complaints systems. The Department of Trade and Industry should monitor progress and be prepared to use its regulation-making powers if necessary.*

9.2 *We wish to see trade unions and other groups extend the legal services they offer. Group schemes should be able to act as an addition to the legal aid scheme, by meeting contributions for example. We do not support a blanket ban on the use of in-house lawyers to conduct preparatory work. Insurance companies should be able to employ solicitors to give advice to the policy holders.*

9.3 *The Law Society should issue guidelines to solicitors to ensure that they are able to give independent advice about the merits of different legal expenses insurance policies.*

Contingent fees

Contingent fees involve lawyers assuming some of the risks of litigation: legal services are provided on the basis that the lawyer will receive no fee if the case is lost, in return for a higher fee if the case is won. They are banned here and in many other European countries, but are widespread in the United States of America where lawyers frequently receive a percentage of the award. Typical rates are 25 per cent if the case is settled early, a third if a writ is issued and 40 per cent in the event of an appeal.

Contingent fees are supported on the grounds that they enable people who cannot afford lawyers to go to court, and that the risks of litigation are more evenly spread over a number of cases, rather than falling directly on the individual litigant. They are opposed on the grounds that some of the fees charged are excessive, and that they create conflicts of interest because lawyers will have more incentive to settle a case for relatively little work rather than incur all the costs of preparing for trial. Contingent fees are also said to be responsible for a litigation explosion in the United States and to encourage lawyers to use unethical tactics to win cases.

Our conclusion is that there are no insurmountable problems with contingent fees. Safeguards can be enacted to control excessive fees: either maximum fees could be imposed or contingent fees could be "taxed" by the court. Nor do we have so little confidence in the legal profession to think that contingent fees will induce lawyers to abandon their ethical standards. The conflict of interest could be reduced if settlements made on a contingent basis needed the approval of a registrar or if contingent fees were calculated on an hourly basis, supplemented by a small risk premium.

Contingent fees, however, are unlikely to solve the problems consumers face. The rule that the loser must pay the winner's costs means that contingent fees will not eliminate risk, and generally damages in Britain are too low to leave much over for a contingent fee. We would prefer to see a mutual fund introduced, but if this does not prove possible the prohibition on contingent fees should be reconsidered.

Mutual funds

In recent years there have been two proposals for non-profit making funds to bear the risks of litigation. The claimant would approach the fund once a course of action had arisen and the fund would pay both the claimant and the other side's costs should the need arise. The Contingency Legal Aid Fund (CLAF), proposed by Justice, would work on a contingent basis by taking a percentage of damages (29); the Law Society's Fixed Costs Legal Services Fund would take a fixed non-returnable fee from winners and losers (30). Unlike CLAF, the fixed costs fund may not need substantial start-up funds.

There is clearly a need for such funds because they reduce the risks of litigation, especially in personal injury claims. We cannot say whether they are financially viable, but we would very much welcome further research and evaluation.

There is a need to keep costs as low as possible. Funds to finance personal injury litigation should not attempt to subsidise other cases, such as tribunal representation. Nor can such funds be expected to finance high-risk test cases.

If a fund is started it should be well publicised. Solicitors will need to give consumers clear explanations of the circumstances in which cover may be withdrawn.

Recommendation 10: mutual funds and contingent fees

10.1 *Proposals for non-profit making funds to assume the risk of personal injury litigation, paid for by either a contingent or fixed fee, should be actively pursued. If established, they should be well publicised to those who would not otherwise claim.*

10.2 *If it does not prove possible to establish such a fund, the prohibition on contingent fees should be re-considered.*

Complaints about lawyers (chapter 7)

Mistakes occur in any service. It is important that when they do, consumers can gain redress from an accessible, fair and effective complaints system.

The Solicitors Complaints Bureau

The Bureau started work in September 1986, as part of the Law Society but separated from it, and in January 1987 a new complaints procedure began. There are two committees: the adjudication committee, with a majority of solicitors, exercises the Law Society's statutory powers; while the investigation committee, with a lay majority, oversees the procedure and reviews complaints which the Bureau wishes to terminate but the complainant does not.

The Bureau offers many welcome improvements over the previous system. Complaints handling has been separated from pastoral care, and accommodation, staff morale and office organisation have improved. The Bureau can investigate "shoddy work" as well as misconduct, and can order solicitors to forego fees or take action to rectify mistakes. The investigation committee provides a welcome lay element and has worked hard to ensure greater openness, publishing an annual report and requiring both committees to give reasons for their decisions.

But many problems remain:

★ the Bureau refuses to handle cases of negligence, on the grounds that the matter must be pursued before the courts. Many consumers are reluctant to get embroiled in further litigation and are confused by the distinctions between misconduct, negligence and shoddy work. We wish to see a procedure which can award small amounts of compensation (up to £2,000) as an alternative to the courts;

★ clients find it difficult to recognise inadequate work because they don't know what solicitors are meant to do. We support the Civil

Justice Review's recommendation that the profession should produce written professional standards covering the principal types of litigation (31). Breaches should be investigated by the complaints procedure. Existing standards should be better publicised;

★ the Bureau has a high attrition rate. The great majority of complaints do not reach either committee. We agree with the investigation committee that the standard of service provided in such cases should be investigated. We recommend that the Bureau commissions an independent research study;

★ the present procedure is too centralised. Expanding the interview panel is an important first step towards providing a local element but the role of panellists should be widened. They should conciliate as well as report to the Bureau;

★ the dual committee structure is complex and difficult to understand. Much of the investigation committee's time is taken up with monitoring cases going before the adjudication committee, and there is too little time to examine the procedures used in the great majority of complaints which do not go to the committee;

★ consumers are confused by having to distinguish between overcharging which is unreasonable—where the Law Society vets the bill and issues a "remuneration certificate"—and overcharging which involves misconduct, which is the responsibility of the Solicitors Complaints Bureau. We wish to see a single point of entry for both complaints and remuneration certificates.

In 1985 we recommended an independent legal council because our research had led us to the conclusion that the public had lost confidence in complaints handling by the Law Society (32). We wish to see the Bureau procedure substantially improved. If it is not, public concern over the Law Society's multiple roles is likely to continue. In this event, the Lord Chancellor should take the initiative in drafting legislation for an independent legal council.

Complaints against barristers

Complaints against barristers can be investigated by the Bar Council's professional conduct committee. Serious cases are referred to an independent disciplinary tribunal. The Bar is considering changes to the procedure but the complaints system will remain concerned with disciplining barristers rather than providing consumers with redress.

There is no power to award compensation to clients and although the disciplinary tribunal can order barristers to repay or forego fees, it does not appear to have done so in the last three years. We wish to see a complaints system which can award compensation, and remit fees for minor cases.

In the long term, public confidence would be increased if complaints against barristers were investigated by an independent body. If an independent legal council were established, it should cover both solicitors and barristers. This would lead to much needed simplification because it would be up to the council, rather than the consumer, to decide whether the solicitor or barrister were to blame.

The Bar has not yet implemented the Benson Commission's recommendation to produce written professional standards (33). We agree with the Civil Justice Review that these have an important role in providing clients with information about the standard of service they may expect.

Where undue costs have been incurred due to poor quality representation, courts can penalise solicitors by refusing their claim for costs, or by ordering them to pay the other side's costs. We wish to see courts have similar powers against barristers.

Barristers and solicitors who have been negligent in the way they present cases in court cannot be sued. The law offers special protection for work closely connected with court proceedings. We are not convinced that there are special reasons for protecting advocates and we wish to see the immunity abolished.

Recommendation 11: complaints

11.1 *We endorse the Civil Justice Review's recommendation that the professions should produce written professional standards, to be enforced through the professions' complaints procedures.*

11.2 *The solicitors complaints system should have:*
   ★ *the power to investigate negligent work, as an alternative to the courts, and award compensation of up to £2,000;*
   ★ *a single point of entry for requests for remuneration certificates and complaints of misconduct and shoddy work;*
   ★ *locally based conciliation;*
   ★ *independent research commissioned by the investigation committee into complaints which do not reach the committees.*

11.3 *The barristers complaints system should have the power to award*

*compensation for negligent advisory and court work, and remit fees
in minor cases.*

11.4 *If improvements are not introduced to both complaints systems, the
Lord Chancellor should draft legislation to establish an independent
legal council.*

11.5 *The courts should have the power to penalise barristers in costs.*

11.6 *Advocates' immunity from the law of negligence should be
abolished.*

The structure and training of the legal profession (chapter 8)

Restrictions on advocacy

As a general rule, clients who wish to be represented in trials in the
high court or appeal courts must use a barrister. In the county courts,
they may use either a barrister or a solicitor.

These rules have been the subject of considerable debate between
barristers and solicitors. In 1979 the Benson Commission accepted the
Bar's arguments in favour of the status quo (33). The Marre
Committee, reporting in July 1988, recommended that only barristers
should be allowed to appear in the high court and court of appeal, but
that solicitors who have been recognised by a new rights of audience
advisory commission should be able to appear in criminal cases in the
crown court (34).

The Benson Commission argued that in an adversarial system of
justice, advocates are there not just to help clients: they also help the
judge to bring out the facts of the case, test the evidence and refer to
the relevant legal authorities. Judges share a common outlook with
barristers, and this makes trials quicker and more efficient. Judges are
entitled to insist that litigants use barristers to represent them to
ensure that cases are argued in the way judges would wish.

From the litigant's point of view there are two problems with a
strictly adversarial system. First, many litigants cannot afford to pay
for the appropriate advocates. Secondly, the more specialist the
advocate, the greater the barriers between the consumer and the
judicial process. When both barristers and solicitors are used, the
litigant is kept at two stages removed from the trial. Litigation appears
a remote and mysterious process.

We are not suggesting that the adversarial system should disappear
overnight, but the Civil Justice Review's recommendations for
reforming the courts are a cautious step towards less remote, more
investigative justice (31). As courts become less formal, a wider range

of representatives should be allowed to appear. Litigants should have the right to be represented by lay people in small claims, housing and debt cases. The proposals to move more cases to the county court will mean that in middle-range trials litigants will have a choice between being represented by barristers or solicitors.

The effect of the changes should be monitored. If it is clear that solicitors are representing clients well in substantial county court cases, the restrictions on solicitors appearing in the high court and appeal courts should be relaxed. Changes in the crown court are outside the scope of this report.

Solicitors offering representation should give estimates of how much it will cost, so that clients may make price comparisons with barristers. Disciplinary rules should specify that where clients ask to be represented by a barrister, their wishes should be respected.

Recommendation 12: restrictions on advocacy

12.1 *The effect of the Civil Justice Review's proposals to transfer cases from the high court to the county court should be monitored, and if solicitors are representing clients well in substantial county court cases, the restrictions on solicitors appearing in the high court and appeal courts should be relaxed.*

Restrictions on forms of practice

Solicitors are only allowed to practice as sole practitioners or in partnership with other solicitors. Law Society proposals permit solicitors to form limited companies, provided that all the directors and shareholders are solicitors. The present restrictions prevent mixed, or "multi-disciplinary", practices between members of different professions and they have been the subject of considerable debate. Consumers' demands for new services are growing. Restrictions inhibit consumer choice, may prevent the development of new services, and can cause duplication, delay and extra costs. Our starting point is that there should only be restrictions on forms of practice if these are clearly needed to protect consumers.

There appears to be a demand for "one stop" house transfer. If consumers wish, they should be able to obtain a mortgage, survey, help with selling a house and conveyancing services in one place.

Building societies should be able to employ solicitors to provide conveyancing to their borrowers but a number of safeguards are needed to prevent them from exploiting their market position. No mortgage offer should require a borrower to use a particular conveyancing service and all the different parts of a house-purchase package should be costed separately. Where building societies are prepared to add their own conveyancing fees to the mortgage, they should also be willing to increase the mortgage to cover similar independent conveyancing costs. They should account for commissions and carry adequate professional indemnity insurance. They must not act for both buyers and sellers and should tell consumers about potential conflicts of interest. We wish to see a duty placed on the Director-General of Fair Trading to monitor anti-competitive practices in the conveyancing market.

Solicitors' firms should also be free to offer house-transfer packages. If they wish they should be able to employ surveyors and allow them to become partners. There may also be a demand for mixed practices with accountants. In some circumstances, solicitors may wish to go into partnership with those who do not have professional qualifications, but who have management expertise. We do not see any strong reasons to forbid such practices.

But consumers should know what they are getting and where they should go if they have a complaint. If a practice is called "solicitors" it should have a majority of solicitor partners, and should be bound by the solicitors' account rules, insurance and compensation arrangements; it should disclose and account for any commissions received; and should be subject to the solicitors complaints procedure.

There will be problems where different professional rules clash but we do not think that these are insoluble. We wish to see the Office of Fair Trading convene a liaison committee between representatives of consumers and the various professions to sort out any problems.

Barristers must practise as individuals: they are not permitted to form partnerships, even with other barristers. This rule does not offer significant protection to consumers and we recommend that it should be abolished.

Recommendation 13: restrictions on forms of practice

13.1 *The Lord Chancellor should use his powers under schedule 21 of the Building Societies Act 1986 to permit building societies to offer conveyancing services to their borrowers, subject to safeguards to prevent them from exploiting their market position; the Law Society should permit employed lawyers to provide the service.*

13.2 *Solicitors should be able to enter into partnerships with non-solicitors, provided that firms calling themselves "solicitors" are controlled by solicitors, account for commissions and are subject to solicitors' accounts, insurance, and compensation rules and complaints procedures.*

13.3 *The Bar's practice rule preventing partnerships between barristers should be repealed.*

13.4 *The Office of Fair Trading should convene a liaison committee between representatives of consumers and the professions to resolve conflicts between different professional rules in mixed practices.*

Training solicitors

We are concerned that solicitors receive little training in social security, housing, debt, employment and immigration law. All the subjects on the solicitors' vocational course are compulsory. As the scope of work dealt with by solicitors increases, it becomes more difficult to fit new areas of law alongside conveyancing and business law. We recommend that the solicitors' final course should be restructured to allow for optional subjects, including social welfare law.

There is general agreement that lawyers often have difficulties communicating with clients. The Law Society's written professional standards set out the basic principles but more needs to be done to publicise them to students and to practitioners.

We agree with the Benson Commission that the importance of good communication should be stressed at an early stage. We have examined the solicitors' final examination course to see how it approaches oral and written communication skills.

There is no incentive for students taking the course to be interested or skilled in interviewing clients. Teaching staff who are aware of the importance of oral communication fit it in as best they can. We recommend that the Law Society considers how practical exercises can be built into the course to train solicitors to interview clients and provide clear explanations of the law and procedure in simple problems. The Solicitors Complaints Bureau should be involved in the course, telling students the pitfalls to avoid.

The course notes include many examples of badly drafted documents, written in long, poorly punctuated sentences, using obscure words. There are too few examples of good documents in plain English. We recommend that the College of Law reviews all the materials used on the final examination course, to ensure that students are given examples of good legal drafting. Students should be examined on their ability to draft documents and write letters in plain English.

Publishers of legal precedents should also review their materials to make sure they are in plain English.

Recommendation 14: training solicitors

14.1 *The solicitors' final examination course should include options in social welfare law.*

14.2 *The Law Society should consider how practical exercises in oral communication can be included in the course; the Solicitors Complaints Bureau should be involved in telling students the pitfalls to avoid.*

14.3 *The College of Law should review the course materials to ensure that students are given examples of good legal drafting in plain English.*

14.4 *Students should be examined on their ability to write documents and letters in plain English.*

14.5 *The Law Society should publicise its written professional standards on communicating with clients to students and to the profession.*

14.6 *Publishers of legal precedents should ensure that their precedents are clearly drafted in plain English.*

The courts: their organisation and facilities (chapter 9)

Reform of the courts needs to go hand in hand with reform of legal services. We very much support the thrust of the Civil Justice Review published in June 1988 to make the courts more accessible to ordinary people (31).

Generalist courts or specialist tribunals?

We do not recommend setting up new consumer or housing tribunals. Instead, we wish to see the problems of formality and inaccessibility tackled at source, within the county court. Separate tribunals would not only be expensive, they would also lead to more overlaps, gaps and jurisdictional disputes. We have not, however, examined the proposals for a unified family court.

High court and county courts

The Civil Justice Review states that its "leading objective" is that cases should be handled at the lowest appropriate level (31). We agree that at present too many cases are dealt with in the high court. Two-thirds of money claims in the Queen's bench division are for less than £5,000. The high court is more formal, slower, more expensive, less accessible, and more intimidating than the county court. We regret that the Review stopped short of recommending a unified civil court in which all cases were begun in the same way and allocated to the appropriate level of judge. Instead, they recommended a variety of different measures to deal with more cases in the county court. We support the recommendation that the implementation plan should specify a date and criteria for reviewing the success of the changes. If the high court is continuing to deal with large numbers of minor cases, a single civil court should be reconsidered.

The plan must be adequately resourced or high court delays will be transferred to the county court. At present court staff are paid for by court fees but the Treasury does not automatically permit increases in staff to be paid for out of increased fees. Excess fees are paid to the exchequer and courts are subject to rigorous expenditure and staffing controls. There is a strong case for reviewing this accounting procedure.

The Review proposes that full county court trials should be held at a limited number of trial centres. It is important that sufficient trial centres are provided and that they have adequate facilities for people coming from a distance.

Investigative justice

The Civil Justice Review recognises that the British adversarial system causes injustice where unrepresented litigants are opposed by experienced organisations. They recommend that cases where individual litigants tend not to be represented should be conducted on an interventionist basis. The registrar should explain legal terms and procedures, and ask questions to find out the facts. We very much support this key recommendation.

This requires a new approach to judicial training. Judges have no experience of dealing with unrepresented litigants before they are appointed and interventionist justice requires great judicial skills. The present Judicial Studies Board is run on a shoe-string budget. We recommend that the Board should be restructured and provided with its own teaching staff. Priority should be given to developing courses for registrars and circuit judges in civil matters.

We agree that the increased role of registrars should be recognised and that they should be referred to as judges. We favour the term "district judge".

Court facilities

We agree with the Review's recommendation that court facilities should be improved. As the Welsh Consumer Council's survey of county courts in Wales has shown, many of the most important improvements involve more thought than money (35). Court buildings and offices within the court should be well signposted; signs on court counters should state that a private room is available; leaflets and booklets should be displayed; public telephones and drinks machines should be installed; and pictures and information posters could brighten up bare walls.

We do not wish to see a morning's cases blocklisted for a single time. Instead, listing in "batches" at intervals is used effectively in many courts.

Lay involvement in the courts

Lay people have very little involvement in the way courts are run and this shows in the language and procedures used.

We recommend that membership of committees involved in drawing up procedural rules should be expanded to include representatives of court users and lay people with a good knowledge of plain English.

The Review recommends that judges and court administrators should take steps to see that practitioners' views are heard at circuit and local level. We wish to see representatives from consumer groups and advice centres included in these consultative arrangements.

Recommendation 15: reforming the courts

15.1 *We do not recommend specialist housing or consumer tribunals; instead, reforms should aim to make the county court more accessible.*

15.2 *We support steps to transfer cases from the high court to the county court but regret that the Civil Justice Review did not recommend a unified civil court. The plan for implementing the Review should include a date and criteria for reviewing the changes. If they do not prove effective, a unified civil court should be reconsidered.*

15.3 *The county court must be adequately resourced in terms of judges and staff to deal with the increased work load; there should be sufficient trial centres with adequate facilities.*

15.4 *We very much support the Civil Justice Review's recommendation that cases where individuals are rarely represented should be conducted on an interventionist basis.*

15.5   *Judicial training in the civil field should be substantially increased.*

15.6   *Court facilities should be improved.*

15.7   *The rule committees should include lay representatives.*

15.8   *Lay representatives should be included in consultative arrangements at local and circuit level.*

Small claims (chapter 10)

In 1973, the small claims procedure was established within the county court. The rules state that defended claims of not more than £500 may be referred to arbitration before a registrar; the hearing should be informal; strict rules of evidence do not apply; and the registrar has discretion to modify normal procedure. Legal representation is permitted but discouraged by the costs rules. Normally, only legal costs connected with the issue of the summons may be claimed.

Fifteen years on, it is clear that the small claims procedure has several advantages: it is quicker, cheaper and simpler than standard procedures, and litigants generally consider it to be fair. On the other hand, there are a number of problems:

★   the procedure is rarely used by individuals for consumer disputes. The great majority of cases are brought by businesses pursuing debts;

★   there is considerable variation between registrars: many approach arbitration in much the same way as a formal trial. Just under half of unrepresented litigants complained that the registrar had not helped them put their case (36);

★   the majority of litigants attend court more than once. This causes difficulties for people in work, over half of whom lose pay. Fifty-nine per cent of litigants did not feel that the preliminary hearing had been useful (36);

★   many of the forms used by local courts are confusing, poorly produced, and use legal jargon. One in five people found the legal words very difficult or impossible to understand (36);

★   the variation between different registrars is confusing. Litigants do not know what to expect;

★   the procedure is still too slow. Almost two-thirds of cases took

more than three months, and half took more than five months
(36);

★ attempts to discourage legal representation have failed. Around
a third of litigants use lawyers, and one or both parties are
represented in just under a half of cases. Large organisations are
much more likely to be legally represented than individuals.
Twenty-eight per cent of unrepresented litigants commented
that this made their case more difficult to prove (36);

★ individual plaintiffs who win their cases find it difficult to
enforce judgements. They receive little help or advice about this
(7).

We very much welcome the Civil Justice Review's proposals to extend
and improve the procedure. We wish to build on good practice to
ensure a nationally consistent procedure, which is accessible, simple,
cheap, quick and fair, and can be used by ordinary people without
lawyers.

The main changes we recommend are:

Recommendation 16: small claims

16.1 *The small claims limit should be increased to £1,000 and the
procedure improved. In particular:*
*(a) The Lord Chancellor's Department should publicise the
procedure, and take steps to improve the image of the court;*
*(b) court forms should be produced centrally; the Lord Chancellor's
Department should design and pilot claim forms for common
consumer disputes;*
*(c) as far as possible, small claims should be dealt with by specially
designated staff, trained to advise the public;*
*(d) link officers liaising with advice centres should ensure that
literature about the scheme is properly distributed and displayed;*
*(e) consumers claiming for faulty goods or services should be able to
serve their claim on the shop where the goods or services were bought;*
*(f) preliminary hearings should not normally be held; the
Department should provide a notice and accompanying leaflet to
give advice on preparing for the hearing;*
*(g) the court rules should be contained in a short, self-sufficient code,
written in plain English;*
*(h) the registrar should explain the law and procedure, and should
question the parties to elicit the facts. The parties should not be
allowed to cross-examine witnesses;*
*(i) the Judicial Training Board should provide training and discus-
sion for all serving and new registrars on the conduct of*

small claims; courses should be supplemented by a registrar's manual;

(j) registrars should have the power to ask for experts' reports paid for out of public funds;

(k) experimental evening hearings should be held;

(l) lay representation should be permitted.

16.2 *The Legal Aid Board should provide resources to enable people to seek advice about the small claims procedure, and to be accompanied by lay advisers in complex cases or where litigants have particular difficulties in expressing themselves.*

Reforming personal injury procedures (chapter 11)

In most personal injury cases, litigants will continue to need skilled legal advice and representation. Given the present substantive law, it is difficult to reduce costs but much can be done to reduce delays. We make a number of recommendations to this effect below.

At present, parties to litigation are able to keep most of their evidence secret until the trial. The Review recommends that parties should exchange witness statements well before a case is set down for hearing. We support this proposal. It would encourage solicitors to gather evidence at an early stage, and plaintiffs would be able to see the defendant's evidence before reaching a settlement. The additional costs of early investigation would be justified by more informed settlements. Police reports and factory inspectors' reports should also be released at the earliest opportunity.

We are disappointed that the Review recommends no change to the "payment-in" rule, which, in our view, puts unacceptable pressure on plaintiffs to accept low offers. The rule effectively asks plaintiffs to play "double or quits" with their compensation money: either they accept an offer which appears to be considerably less than the court would award, or they go ahead in the knowledge that there is a small chance that the court may award less and they will be faced with a very large bill to pay. We wish to allow a margin of error. We recommend that successful plaintiffs should only be liable for defendants' costs where payments-in exceed the eventual award by at least 25 per cent. In small cases (involving less than £2,000) it should exceed the award by at least £500. Plaintiffs should not have to decide whether to accept payments-in until after they have seen defendants' witness statements.

We agree with the Review that, at present, trials place too great an emphasis on oral evidence and argument. We would support proposals to shorten trials, provided that the evidence referred to but not read out in trials is made available to the public.

These proposals go some way towards reducing delays and risk. But very serious problems remain. Accident victims are unlikely to receive payment when they most need it, in coping with the after-effects of the accident. The onus will remain on victims to fight their claims, and those without knowledge and stamina will continue to be disadvantaged. The system will remain extremely expensive. In 1978, the Pearson Commission estimated that for every £1 given to injured people, a further 85p was spent on administration and legal fees (3). The issue of no-fault schemes should be returned to the political agenda.

Recommendation 17: reforming personal injury procedure

17.1　*The Law Society should produce written professional standards for personal injury work. These should specify that solicitors should start proceedings within a year of being consulted.*

17.2　*Writs should be served on defendants within two months of being issued.*

17.3　*The court should monitor cases to ensure that they are set down for trial within nine months of the defendant giving notice of an intention to defend.*

17.4　*Courts should provide a hearing date within three months of a case being set down for trial; the Lord Chancellor's Department should publish targets for both the high court and county courts, together with information about how well the targets have been met.*

17.5　*We support the Civil Justice Review's proposals to exchange witness statements before cases are set down for trial; police and factory inspectors' reports should be released quickly.*

17.6　*The Lord Chancellor should consider how no-fault schemes should be established.*

Multi-party personal injury claims

The problems of personal injury claims where many plaintiffs pursue similar claims have recently been brought to public attention by the Opren litigation, in which around 1,500 plaintiffs claimed compensation for injuries alleged to have been caused by a defective drug. The plaintiffs faced many of the problems common to all personal injury claimants; they also faced some additional problems, unique to multi-party claims.

Each claimant issued an individual writ in the high court, but it soon became clear that 1,500 separate claims would be unmanageable. The high court judge grouped the cases together into a scheme, in which pre-trial proceedings issued in the name of one plaintiff could be used for the benefit of the whole group.

One problem is that there is no explicit power in the high court rules to deal with cases in this way. The scheme went ahead on the basis that both the plaintiffs and the defendants agreed to it. If one of the parties had strongly disagreed with a court order, the scheme could have fallen apart.

The most serious difficulties concerned costs. The nominal plaintiffs were legally aided, but the government (a defendant in the action) argued successfully that the 500 or so plaintiffs who did not qualify for legal aid should not be given a free ride on the back of the legal aid fund. The judge made an order that the costs of the action should be shared equally between all the plaintiffs. Thus if the plaintiffs lost, the non-legally aided plaintiffs would be liable for 1/1,500 of the total bill of both plaintiffs and defendants (37).

The costs of the action threatened to be more than the plaintiffs could afford. If an outside benefactor had not stepped in, nearly all of the non-legally aided plaintiffs would have been forced to withdraw. Even if the costs had not been so great, there would still have been serious problems. The plaintiffs alleged a number of different symptoms, and some claims stood a higher chance of success than others. If some plaintiffs had won and some had lost, the winners would share the costs of the losers. Even successful claimants who were legally aided would pay towards losing cases out of their compensation through the legal aid statutory charge. This made the liability of each plaintiff very difficult to predict and set up serious conflicts of interest among the plaintiffs.

On the other hand if costs had fallen entirely on the legally aided "lead" plaintiffs, this would also have also caused problems. In such complex litigation there could easily have been a substantial shortfall between the successful plaintiffs' costs and the costs recovered from the defendants, and this would be paid out of the "lead" plaintiffs' compensation through the statutory charge.

The problems raised by the Opren litigation have led to calls for class actions. Although we support an enquiry into how class actions can help with other forms of litigation, the problems raised by Opren affect a number of other multi-party personal injury claims and are too urgent to await the outcome of a lengthy study. Less sweeping and controversial changes should be made immediately.

New rules of court should be introduced formalising the existing voluntary system of lead actions. These changes in procedure should be accompanied by changes in legal aid. We recommend that in multi-party claims which have a reasonable prospect of success, which have been certified by the court, and which could not be brought without legal aid, the Legal Aid Board should waive the upper income and capital limits. No plaintiff should be liable to pay more than a total of £1,000 in contributions or statutory charge.

Recommendation 18: multi-party personal injury claims

18.1 *The supreme court rules committee should introduce a new court order giving the court power to establish group schemes for multi-plaintiff claims.*

18.2 *In appropriate multi-party claims, the Legal Aid Board should waive the upper income and capital limits and require plaintiffs to pay no more than a total of £1,000 in both contributions and statutory charge.*

Reforming housing possession procedures (chapter 12)

Too many housing possession cases are decided without adequate information. We endorse the Civil Justice Review's conclusion that "there should be reforms in procedure and forms to provide the court with fuller evidence on the basis of the claim and the circumstances of the defendant".

The main changes we wish to see are listed below. These will enable courts to make more careful decisions about possession. Inevitably, cases will take longer, and the courts will need more resources to do their work. But we are conscious of the need to keep expenditure to a minimum. Greater training will enable some courts to transfer business from circuit judges to registrars. We also wish to see fewer cases brought to court. Local authorities should carry out benefit checks, and should not require families with serious mortgage arrears to wait for possession proceedings before qualifying under housing the homeless legislation. The Review recommends a simpler default procedure for rent arrears where possession is not sought. Landlords who ignore this procedure and seek possession, but receive a money only judgement, should be penalised in costs.

Recommendation 19: reforming housing possession procedures

19.1 *We endorse the Civil Justice Review's recommendation that "there should be reforms in procedure and forms to provide the court with fuller evidence on the basis of the claim and the circumstances of the defendant''. In particular:*

(a) plaintiffs in housing possession cases should, where reasonably practicable, provide the court with details of defendants' circumstances;

(b) landlords should state whether the property is in good repair;

(c) the summons and form of reply should be redesigned and tested;

(d) plaintiffs should be prohibited from telling defendants not to attend court;

(e) courts should specify plaintiffs' costs, and these should be in accordance with guidelines given by the Lord Chancellor's Department;

(f) costs should be awarded against landlords who receive money-only judgements;

(g) the Judicial Studies Board should provide both registrars and judges with systematic training in housing work;

(h) lay representation should be permitted.

19.2   *The Legal Aid Board should work with regional legal services committees to develop court representation schemes for possession cases in county courts.*

19.3   *Local authorities should be given guidance under housing the homeless legislation that families forced to sell their homes by mortgage arrears should be accepted as homeless.*

The "housing action" procedures (chapter 12)

The Civil Justice Review recognised that tenants often forego their rights rather than use the county court. They recommend a new "housing action" which would operate as a small claims procedure for housing matters, such as service charges, repairs, the right to buy, leasehold enfranchisement and mobile homes (31).

We agree that there is a need for cheaper, simpler procedures which consumers can use to resolve disputes about repairs and service charges without using lawyers. The Southwark arbitration unit, established in 1983 to deal with disputes between the London Borough of Southwark and its 60,000 tenants, has demonstrated that if the right procedures are available, tenants will use them.

A new informal "housing action", however, is not an easy or cheap option. The substantive law is complex, and a procedure that can be used without lawyers will involve substantial changes not only in court rules, but in the training and attitude of court staff. We strongly recommend an experimental scheme along the lines of the Dundee small claims experiment (38). Legal aid should not be withdrawn for housing disputes until the housing action has been shown to be accessible to unrepresented litigants. We are pleased that the Review has recommended that expert assessors should be available, paid for out of court funds. We would not wish the experiment to go ahead without access to expert assistance.

The experimental scheme should be well-publicised, and the local authority should send details about it to all their tenants. The Lord Chancellor's Department should produce a guide to procedure. The registrars in the scheme will need an understanding of both the law and the practical aspects of repairs problems, and court staff will need special training in advising litigants. The Legal Aid Board should be involved in monitoring the advice implications of the experiment.

We wish to see reforms in court procedures go hand in hand with a simplification of the substantive law. As a first step, the Law Commission should prepare a repairs code covering the most common disrepair difficulties.

Recommendation 20: housing action

20.1 *An experimental housing action procedure should be established along the lines of the Dundee small claims experiment. It should have access to expert assessors, paid for from court funds. Legal aid should not be withdrawn from housing disputes until the housing action has been shown to be accessible to unrepresented litigants.*

20.2 *The Legal Aid Board should be involved in monitoring the advice implications of the experiment.*

20.3 *The Law Commission should produce a repairs code, covering the most common disrepair problems.*

Debt (chapter 13)

People who can pay their debts should pay them, and the court system must ensure that recovery is quick, simple and cheap. But it also needs to be sufficiently sensitive to distinguish between those who won't pay and those who can't pay, and make sensible arrangements for those who genuinely need time to pay. It should not subject debtors and their families to unwarranted fear, hardship or humiliation.

At present, multiple debtors often face enforcement from a bewildering variety of different courts and procedures. We wish to see all debt enforcement against individuals brought together into the county court. We recommend that no case against an individual involving less than £25,000 should start in the high court. Imprisonment for unpaid rates or poll tax should be abolished and rates and taxes should be enforced through normal county court procedures. As long as fuel and water boards retain their right to disconnect consumers, disconnection should only be allowed on the express authority of the county court, after the debtor has failed to keep to repayment arrangements.

A tough approach is needed to prevent harassment of debtors. The protection offered by section 40 of the Administration of Justice Act 1970 needs to be strengthened. A duty should be placed on trading standards departments to enforce the legislation and, where debtors can show that they have been the victims of unreasonable pressure, the debt should not be enforceable.

The Lord Chancellor's Department has produced plans for a central, computerised county court "claims registry" to send out summonses (39). It is important that the forms sent to defendants state clearly that advice can be sought from the local county court, and include the address and telephone number of the local court and advice centres. Returned forms must be carefully scrutinised by trained staff so that legitimate defences are not missed, even if defendants have used the wrong part of the form, or put forward offers to pay. An advantage of a central claims registry is that it would allow creditors to obtain more information about debtors. We recommend that judgement creditors should have access to the full file on debtors before deciding which enforcement method to use.

We agree with the Civil Justice Review that the bailiff's role should be redefined. In our view, bailiffs' first duty should be to investigate debtors' circumstances, and arrange and collect payments. They should explain procedures to debtors, tell them where to go for further advice and report information to creditors.

We consider that the "warrant of execution" (an authority to seize goods) should only be granted after a hearing before a registrar. We envisage hearings in which courts would have a flexible range of sanctions including instalment orders and attachment of earnings orders. The seizure of goods would no longer be seen as the principal method of enforcement but only as one among many. Where no enforcement was appropriate, the court would be able to make an order of unenforceability, which would be published to other creditors.

We wish to see an increase in the categories of goods exempt from seizure. Small county court debtors, like bankrupts, should be able to retain enough clothing, bedding, furniture and household equipment to satisfy the basic domestic needs of the family.

The administration order is the only procedure which enables the court to deal with all a person's debts together. The Civil Justice Review follows the Cork Committee by recommending that a reformed administration order should act as a "poor man's bankruptcy" (40).

We agree that administration orders should be made more widely available and that they should be shorter. The research found that a third of orders are expected to run for more than ten years, and the longest ran for 70 years (14). These provide debtors with little incentive to pay. We agree with the Review that no order should last more than three years. Where the debtor is unable to pay off the debt within that time, the registrar should make a composition order for repayment of less than the full amount. The only exceptions would be where debtors behaved dishonestly or recklessly.

At present fuel and water boards can subvert the effect of an order by threatening disconnection unless the debtor pays them more than the pro-rata rate paid to other creditors. We are very pleased that the Review recommends that where utilities are scheduled to an administration order they should only be able to disconnect essential services with the leave of the court.

The success of these measures depends crucially on the availability of good money advice. The Review recognises the importance of money advice and recommends that lay representation should be permitted in debt cases. The Legal Aid Board must take immediate steps to improve provision, paid for by both central government and the credit industry.

The terminology used to describe debt recovery is particularly obscure. We are pleased that the Review body has recommended that phrases such as "warrant of execution" and "writ of fifa" should be replaced by clear modern terms.

Individual creditors are also confused by the system. We recommend that court staff should assist small claims plaintiffs to enforce judgements.

Recommendation 21: debt recovery

21.1 *All debt cases against individuals involving less than £25,000 should start in the county court.*

21.2 *Recovery of unpaid rates and taxes should be dealt with through the county court; imprisonment for unpaid rates should be abolished.*

21.3 *As long as fuel and water boards retain the right to disconnect consumers, it should only be permitted on the authority of the court.*

21.4 *A duty should be placed on trading standards departments to enforce the legislation against harassment of debtors, and debts should not be enforceable where debtors can show that they have been subjected to unreasonable pressure to pay.*

21.5 *Summonses sent to debtors from a central claims registry should include the address and telephone number of the local court and local advice centres.*

21.6 *Judgement creditors should have access to the claims registry's file on debtors.*

21.7 *The bailiff's role should be redefined, to include investigating debtors' circumstances, and arranging and collecting payments. The authority to seize goods should only be granted after a hearing before the registrar.*

21.8 *The categories of goods exempt from seizure should be increased.*

21.9 *We support the Civil Justice Review's proposals to reform the administration order procedure.*

21.10 *Debt recovery procedures should be renamed with clear, modern terms.*

21.11 *Court staff should assist small claims plaintiffs to enforce judgements.*

21.12 *The Legal Aid Board should take immediate steps to improve the availability of money advice, paid for both by central government and the credit industry.*

References to chapter 1

1. Royal Commission on Legal Services in Scotland (Chairman: Lord Hughes), *Report*, Cmnd 7846, HMSO, 1980.
2. Consumer Council, *Justice out of reach: a case for small claims courts*, HMSO, 1970.
3. Royal Commission on Civil Liability and Compensation for Personal Injury (Chairman: Lord Pearson), *Report*, Cmnd 7054, HMSO, 1978.
4. Harris, D. and others, *Compensation and support for illness and injury*, Oxford Socio-legal Studies, Clarendon Press, 1984.

5. Inbucon Management Consultants, *Study of personal injury litigation*, conducted for the Civil Justice Review, Lord Chancellor's Department, November 1985.

6. Office of Fair Trading, *Consumer dissatisfaction: a report on surveys undertaken by the Office of Fair Trading*, February 1986.

7. National Consumer Council/Welsh Consumer Council, *Simple Justice: a consumer view of small claims procedures in England and Wales*, 1979.

8. National Consumer Council, *An introduction to the findings of the consumer concerns survey*, August 1981.

9. Department of the Environment, *English House Conditions Survey*, HMSO, 1982 and 1983.

10. Department of the Environment, *Report of the Committee of Inquiry on the Management of Privately-owned Blocks of Flats* (the Nugee Committee), 1985.

11. Civil Justice Review, *Housing cases*, consultation paper no.5, Lord Chancellor's Department, January 1987.

12. School for Advanced Urban Studies, University of Bristol, *Study of housing cases: final report to the Lord Chancellor's Department*, produced for the Civil Justice Review, Lord Chancellor's Department, 1987.

13. Department of the Environment, Scottish Development Department and Welsh Office, *Housing and construction statistics 1976-86*, HMSO, 1987, table 11.10.

14. Touche Ross Management Consultants, *Study of debt enforcement procedures*, carried out for the Civil Justice Review, Lord Chancellor's Department, December 1986.

15. Cotterrell, R. and others, "The recovery of judgment debts in the county court", in ed. Ramsay, I., *Debtors and creditors*, Professional Books, 1986.

16. *Legal aid*, 37th annual reports of the Law Society and the Lord Chancellor's advisory committee, 1986-87, HC 233, HMSO, 1988.

17. Baldwin, J. and Hill, S., *The operation of the green form scheme in England and Wales*, Lord Chancellor's Department, March 1988.

18. Law Society, *Survey of legal aid provision*, April 1988.

19. *Hansard* 15 December 1987, col. 610.

20. Lord Chancellor's Department, *Legal aid in England and Wales: a new framework*, Cm 118, HMSO, March 1987.

21. National Consumer Council, *The fourth right of citizenship: a review of local advice services*, 1977.

22. Kempson, E., *A survey of current advice and law centres provision*, Advice Services Alliance, September 1986.
23. Law Society, *Solicitors' Practice Rules 1988*, rule 3 and *Solicitors' Introduction and Referral Code 1988*.
24. Taylor Nelson Media, "An analysis of solicitors' advertising", prepared for the National Consumer Council, October 1987.
25. Genn, H., *Meeting legal needs?: an evaluation of a scheme for personal injury victims*, Centre for Socio-legal Studies, Oxford and Greater Manchester Legal Services Committee, 1982.
26. Law Society, *The Professional Conduct of Solicitors*, appendix C/7, "written professional standards".
27. Pfennigstorf, W. and Kimball, S.L., ed., *Legal services plans: approaches to regulation*, American Bar Foundation, Chicago, 1977.
28. Advertising Standards Authority, case report 98 (29 June 1983).
29. Justice, *CLAF: proposals for a contingency legal aid fund*, 1978.
30. Law Society contentious business committee, *Improving access to civil justice: the report of the Law Society's working party on the funding of litigation*, July 1987.
31. Civil Justice Review, *Report of the Review Body on Civil Justice*, Cm 394, HMSO, 1988.
32. National Consumer Council, *In dispute with the solicitor: consumers and the professions: a review of complaints procedures*, Spring 1985.
33. Royal Commission on Legal Services (Chairman: Sir Henry Benson), *Final report*, Cmnd 7648, HMSO 1979.
34. Committee on the Future of the Legal Profession (Chairman: Lady Marre), *A time for change*, presented to the General Council of the Bar and the Council of the Law Society, July 1988.
35. Welsh Consumer Council, *Courting the consumer*, October 1988.
36. Touche Ross Management Consultants, *Study of the small claims procedure*, produced for the Civil Justice Review, Lord Chancellor's Department, 1986.
37. See *Davies v. Eli Lilly and Co. and others*, *The Independent*, 10 December 1987, upheld by the court of appeal at [1987] 1 Weekly Law Reports p.1136.
38. Connor, A. and Doig, B., *A research-based evaluation of the Dundee small claims experiment*, Central Research Unit, Scottish Office, 1983.
39. Lord Chancellor's Department, *The claims registry: computerisation of county court procedures in debt cases*, consultation paper, July 1987.
40. Review Committee on Insolvency Law and Practice (Chairman: Sir Kenneth Cork), *Report*, Cmnd 8558, HMSO, 1982.

Chapter 2
Who provides legal services?

People with problems turn to many different places for advice: their family, friends and colleagues, the media, local councillors, MPs, social workers, doctors, charities, self-help groups, trade union officers or religious leaders. Where it appears there may be a legal solution to the problem, the next step is usually to seek legal advice and assistance by approaching an advice centre or solicitor. A few people (about 5 per cent of those consulting solicitors) also go on to use a barrister (1).

Most people seek legal advice and assistance at some stage in their lives. But most approach lawyers rarely and only after much thought and discussion. A study of accident victims found that 90 per cent of those approaching a solicitor to claim compensation had discussed the matter with someone else first, and three-quarters reported that the idea had first come from someone else (2). In 1977 the Benson Commission found that 57 per cent of people had used a solicitor for their personal business at least once. By 1986, the proportion had increased following the rise in home ownership. A survey by Research Surveys of Great Britain found that 65 per cent of people had used a solicitor at some stage, but use tended to be infrequent (3). Half of those using solicitors had last done so more than three years ago. A survey by the BBC in the same year (1986) found that just under a quarter of people had used a citizens advice bureau at some stage (4), though the total using some form of advice centre will be higher.

Solicitors and advice centres tend to attract different sorts of customers for different sorts of problems. Those most likely to use a solicitor are owner occupiers and those with above average incomes (1, 3), while advice centre users are more likely to be out of work and to live on low incomes (5). Single parents, disabled people and members of ethnic minorities are also more likely to use an advice centre than the general population (5). Table 2.1 shows the reasons why respondents to the RSGB survey had last used a solicitor.

Table 2.1: services for which a solicitor was last used, 1986

Service	Proportion of all those who had ever used a solicitor
conveyancing/property matters	51%
wills/trusts	16%
divorce/separations	9%
settling disputes	5%
negotiating claims/compensation	5%
motoring offences	4%
witnessing signatures	1%
preparing/enforcing contracts	1%
other law and order matters	2%
settling matters of debt	1%

Source: Research Surveys of Great Britain Limited *Awareness, usage and attitudes towards the professional services and advice provided by solicitors*, February 1986.

In comparison, table 2.2 shows the six main categories of advice given by citizens advice bureaux in 1987/8:

Table 2.2: number of enquiries to citizens advice bureaux in England and Wales in 1987/88 (six largest categories)

Category	No. of enquiries (000s)	Percentage
social security	1,710	24.2%
consumer, debt etc	1,410	20%
housing, property and land	820	11.6%
family and personal	678	9.6%
employment	633	9%
administration of justice	511	7.2%
others	1,284	18.4%
Total	7,045	100

Source: National Association of Citizens Advice Bureaux, *Annual Report 1987-88, p.26* (figures for Northern Ireland have been removed from totals).

Despite the clear differences, there are many areas of overlap between advice centres and solicitors. Although the "housing, property and land" category in the CAB statistics covers rented housing and homelessness rather than conveyancing, "family and personal" includes help with the practical problems following bereavement, separation and divorce. The "administration of justice" category includes legal aid, court procedures, claims for compensation for personal injuries and complaints against solicitors (6).

In this chapter we describe in turn the main suppliers of legal advice, assistance and representation: advice centres, solicitors in private practice, and barristers; how many are there, where are they, and how are they organised? In subsequent chapters we make recommendations for reform.

Advice centres

Advice centres can be defined as organisations whose primary function is to give information, advice and help free of charge to members of the public.

The number of advice centres is growing. In 1983 we calculated that there were 1124 main advice centres and extensions in England and Wales, excluding directly-run local authority centres (7). In 1986 we counted 1617 (8). The numbers, however, have not kept up with the increased demand for advice brought about by increased poverty, unemployment and marital breakdown, complex legislative changes and growing consumer awareness. The National Association of Citizens Advice Bureaux reports a 59 per cent increase in enquiries between 1981/2 and 1987/88, compared with a 10.1 per cent increase in the number of bureaux (6). Other advice centres also report a growing demand for their services (9).

Advice centres can be divided into two broad types: general and specialist. General advice centres offer basic advice about any query raised, and where possible will refer complex questions to a solicitor in private practice or to a specialist agency. Some general advice centres, such as citizens advice bureaux, offer advice to all comers, while others, such as disablement information and advice lines, provide a general service to groups with special needs. Specialist centres, on the other hand, develop a higher level of expertise in a limited number of areas—such as housing, debt, welfare benefits, immigration or consumer problems. They often take referrals from a general centre and are expected to possess a level of expertise comparable or superior to solicitors in private practice. They frequently employ specialist lawyers. A number of centres straddle this divide. Some general centres may have developed a capacity to give specialist advice in areas of law where local needs are not catered for elsewhere—they may have been helped by regional resource centres, or have employed specialist staff.

In recent years advice-giving has become much more sophisticated. Areas such as social security, in which people need detailed advice about legal rules and entitlement, have increased in importance; queries about local buses or leisure services, which involve no legal knowledge, have decreased and now account for a very small proportion of the work done (6). In 1986, Shelter Housing Aid commented that their work has become more legalistic in recent years: "repairs may be less a case of contacting the right person and 'oiling the wheels of bureaucracy' but more likely advising on options for legal actions" (10). Although general advice centres cover more than legal advice, it is becoming increasingly difficult to discuss legal services without taking into account the important contribution made by general advice centres in improving awareness of legal remedies and providing advice and assistance in legal matters.

There is remarkably little government co-ordination or interest in the advice sector as a whole. One result of this is that statistics about advice centres and their funding are very difficult to obtain. In this chapter we describe the main types of advice centres, drawing on a report by Elaine Kempson commissioned by the Advice Services Alliance in 1986 (11).

Citizens advice bureaux (CABx)

In 1988 there were 683 main bureaux and 209 extensions in England and Wales (12). They are the longest established network, having started as an emergency measure in response to the second world war. They offer general advice to all sections of the public. Although provision of CABx is better in London and the major cities, bureaux are more evenly spread over the country than are other advice agencies. Country bureaux, however, tend to have fewer paid staff and offer a less specialised service than their urban counterparts (11).

Each bureau is run by a local management committee, and must meet certain minimum standards in order to affiliate to the National Association of Citizens Advice Bureaux (NACAB). Bureaux are largely dependent on local authority funding, which is estimated to be about £15 million a year (6). Additional funding of £1.9 million is paid to bureaux by NACAB out of its grant of £8 million from the Department of Trade and Industry (6). In addition, the bureaux receive the benefit of NACAB's central services, which include training, information, field support and policy work.

Bureaux estimate that 90 per cent of their workers are volunteers, who between them donate around 7 million hours per year to the service (6). Each new worker undergoes a training programme and must now work a minimum of 4 hours per week. The number of paid staff is increasing, however, and the great majority of bureaux have a paid manager, full-time or part-time. Kempson estimates that bureaux rely on 2,500 full-time equivalent workers, of whom around half are paid (11).

In addition to offering a general service, CABx are becoming increasingly involved in providing specialist help. There are now 46 paid staff who provide tribunal representation, 8 community lawyers who give legal help to bureaux staff and members of the public, and 17 specialist consumer advisers. One hundred and eighteen bureaux have specialist money advisers (13). Many bureaux also offer specialist legal or financial sessions either run by lawyers, accountants and other professionals outside the bureau, or by bureau staff with a particular skill.

There is a high awareness among the public about citizens advice bureaux. The BBC survey showed that 92 per cent of people questioned had heard of them (4).

Citizens advice bureaux also aim to "exercise a responsible influence on the development of social policies and services, both locally and nationally" (6). They therefore make recommendations to improve procedures and laws, in order to improve their clients' access to services and to the courts.

Independent advice centres

The directory published by the Federation of Independent Advice Centres (FIAC) lists around 390 independent advice centres in England and Wales (14). A few are national agencies such as the British Refugee Council or the Disability Alliance but many have grown out of local voluntary groups, such as community associations, self-help, pensioners or tenants' groups, and combine advice giving with a community centre or practical help. Such centres have strong links with the communities they serve, enabling them to reach people who do not usually seek legal advice. More than half of independent advice centres provide advice in one or more minority language (15) and FIAC's directory provides details of fifty-three languages spoken by advisers (14).

Fifty-five per cent of independent centres provide advice to the general public, while the others provide advice to particular groups, such as ethnic minorities, the elderly, young people and those with disabilities. Over eighty per cent of centres provide help with welfare benefits and housing, and over half deal with debt and employment (14).

Independent advice centres place greater reliance than CABx on paid staff. In 1986, Kempson estimated that there were around 1,400 full-time equivalent staff (11), of whom 750 were full-time paid staff and 430 were part-time paid staff (15). In 1988 there were over 1,000 full-time paid staff (14). Research by Gillian Borrie into advice agencies in selected London boroughs which we published in 1982 suggests that independent advice agencies provide a more in-depth service than CABx (16). While CABx spent about half their time dealing with "one-off" enquiries, independent neighbourhood centres spent a quarter of their time on "one-off" enquiries: the rest of their time was used in taking action on behalf of clients and in dealing with repeat calls. Generally, interviews and telephone calls took longer in independent centres (16). A recent analysis of independent centres shows that fifty-nine per cent provide some form of tribunal representation. Over half of centres represented clients at social security tribunals and seventeen per cent provided some court representation (14).

Although it is difficult to be precise about funding, it is probably around £10 million (15). An analysis of the funding of London centres in 1986 showed that out of 189 centres, 75 received some funding from London boroughs, 33 received some from the London borough grants scheme, 28 received some from trusts and charities, 9 received some from Urban Aid, 5 received some from central government, and 5 received some from the Manpower Services Commission (17).

FIAC is presently seeking to increase its membership among the many advice centres that do not belong to any national network, and are therefore rarely counted in the official estimates of advice-giving.

Young people's counselling and advisory services

Young people are much less likely to use an advice centre or solicitor to cope with their problems. To meet their needs a network of centres has been set up to give advice—some concentrate on therapeutic counselling, while others have a more practical bent. In 1986, Kempson counted 70 centres in England and Wales which provide advice and information, employing the equivalent of 220 full-time staff (11). They are mostly members of the National Association of Young Peoples' Counselling and Advisory Services, which has a small secretariat funded by a grant of £49,000 from the Department of Education and Science (18).

Disablement information and advice lines

In 1988, there were 65 advice lines in England and Wales affiliated to DIAL U.K. (Disablement Information and Advice Lines). They concentrate on providing advice and assistance to people who are disabled or who have a disabled relative (19). Each is staffed by people who have direct experience of disability. Most staff are volunteers but a few advice lines do have paid staff. Each service is organised independently and has developed its own method of working and area of expertise. Some concentrate on a telephone service, while others include a centre at which people can call. DIAL UK estimates that the network receives around half a million enquiries a year (15).

Law centres

In 1988 there were 57 law centres in England and Wales, most of which are based in large conurbations (20). They all employ solicitors as well as general advice workers, community workers and sometimes barristers. Each centre provides a full legal service and is able to conduct cases on behalf of clients before the courts. Kempson estimated that in 1986 law centres employed around 450 full-time equivalent staff (11). They varied in size from 3 to 17 paid staff (15).

The first law centre opened its doors in North Kensington in 1970, in response to increasing concern about unmet legal need. In 1978 there were 27 law centres and the Royal Commission commented:

"The impact of law centres has been out of all proportion to their size, to the number of lawyers who work in them and to the amount of work it is possible for them to undertake. The volume of work they have attracted has shown how deep is the need they are attempting to meet. It has dispelled the possibility of complacency over the institution of the legal aid scheme, has emphasised the importance of a wider distribution of legal services and has shown the desirability of enabling and encouraging lawyers to take up work elsewhere than in their traditional areas of activity and types of practice." (1)

An agreement with the Law Society prevents law centres from working in traditional areas of solicitors' practices, such as conveyancing, divorce, personal injury litigation and adult crime. Instead they concentrate on areas inadequately served by traditional practices: housing, welfare rights, employment, immigration, child care and juvenile crime. They also advise tenants' and community groups, and take up public interest and test cases. Pressure of work means that most law centres are selective about the cases they undertake: unlike CABx, they will not advise everyone who comes through the door but set priorities among cases. However, like CABx, they use their clients' experiences to improve procedures and practices, especially at a local level.

Initially, a substantial proportion of law centre funding came from central government, mainly from the Lord Chancellor's Department and the urban programme. Now only seven law centres are funded by the Lord Chancellor's Department. Most are largely dependent on local authority funding. Total funding for law centres is estimated at around £7 million, of which about £1 million comes from central government, £700,000 is earned through legal aid, and around £5 million comes from local government. A small amount of money is received from trusts and charities (20).

Law centres are members of the Law Centres Federation, which employs six and a half staff in London and Birmingham. The Lord Chancellor's Department provides a grant for two posts (20).

Housing aid

The first housing advice centre was opened by the Catholic Housing Aid Society in 1956. By 1986, there were fifty-five access points operating independently of the local authority, staffed by 179 full-time equivalent workers (11). Ten centres are run directly by the Shelter Housing Aid Trust. They cover wide areas of the country and organise surgeries in around twenty different locations. There are a further 15 centres in England which are either funded or associated with Shelter, and four offices run by Shelter (Wales). These are financed partly from Shelter's campaign, partly by a grant from the Department of the Environment and partly by local authorities and housing associations (21).

1986 figures show that about half the people consulting a housing aid centre are homeless or facing homelessness, and over a quarter have homes in a serious state of disrepair (10). The range of services offered differs from centre to centre, but usually includes advice about harassment, eviction, repairs, homelessness, housing benefits and mortgage problems.

In addition, many housing advice centres are run directly by local authorities. The service they provide to private tenants is often similar, but they are constrained in the help they can give to local authority tenants and homeless applicants because they cannot fight legal battles against the local authority. They often handle applications for improvement grants and local authority mortgages, and give advice about council house waiting lists.

Money advice

In 1982 we identified sixteen money advice centres in Britain and argued for their expansion (7). In 1988 a study by the Policy Studies Institute identified nearly a hundred specialist money advice services, all but four of them in England and Wales (22). Most consist of single specialist money advisers located in citizens advice bureaux. Four CAB advisers work in the courts. In addition, NACAB is in the process of setting up six regional centres to give specialist back-up to other bureaux. There are a handful of independent specialist centres offering advice direct to the public and most other provision is run directly by local authorities (22).

So far, local authorities are the main funders but recent initiatives have concentrated on obtaining funding from the credit industry. NACAB has secured around £750,000 over three years from commercial sources and has set a target of £2 million a year (6).

Immigration advice

In 1986, there were 14 service points offering specialist immigration advice and tribunal representation, employing the equivalent of about ninety full-time staff (11). The United Kingdom Immigrants Advisory Service (UKIAS) runs 11 units in England and Wales, which in 1986-87 gave advice in over 60,000 cases, and represented clients in 2,000 hearings before adjudicators (23). Although UKIAS is attempting to raise funds from a variety of different sources, the great majority of its funding comes direct from the Home Office (23).

Local authority advice centres

In addition to the independent advice services we have described, some advice centres are run directly by the local authority. Specialist centres are common in the fields of housing advice (see above), welfare benefits and consumer advice. Some local authorities also run general information and advice desks, or employ advisers to work in neighbourhood offices.

In 1986 the Policy Studies Institute estimated that there were 65 local authorities in the United Kingdom which provided welfare benefits advice directly to the public. Eight English authorities ran full-time welfare benefits advice centres (24). Consumer advice centres were common in the late 1970s, when a grant was provided by central government. At one stage there were 126 centres in operation (7). In 1980 central government withdrew funding and many centres closed. In 1986 there were 29 consumer advice centres run by the trading standards departments of 20 local authorities (25).

There are no national figures on the number of general advice services run directly by local authorities. Gillian Borrie's research into advice agencies in selected London boroughs looked at six local authority bureaux, and compared their work with that of independent advice centres (16). She found that local authority centres did a very different type of work. They spend much more time than other centres giving information and referring callers elsewhere, rather than providing support and explanations or taking action on behalf of callers. Callers were much less likely to return for further help with the same problem. Three-quarters of centres' time was spent handling "one-off" enquiries. Callers appreciated the help they received and were not worried about the centres' lack of independence but there was a general feeling that certain types of problem were unsuitable for council help and that in these cases it was better to use an independent advice service (16).

It appears that local authority advice bureaux perform a useful function in making local authority services more accessible. But in areas where the caller and the local authority have conflicting interests—such as housing, housing benefit and social services—they are no substitute for independent advice centres.

Advice services in rural areas

Country-dwellers often have particular problems in gaining access to advice. The need for advice is as great in rural areas as elsewhere (26) but solicitors' offices and advice centres tend to be concentrated in cities (11). The problem of a lack of solicitors is compounded by the long distances which people have to travel to visit solicitors and the statutory services, and people's low awareness of legal rights. The Lord Chancellor's legal aid advisory committee has commented that in rural areas:

"A crucial element of the problem is the lack of awareness of rights and the low expectations of both individuals and institutions. Low income, poor housing, inadequate information on entitlement to welfare rights and geographical isolation often become accepted norms and, combined with an innate conservatism in the enforcement of statutory rights, prevent many people from seeking access to legal services" (27).

A considerable number of experiments have demonstrated different ways in which advice and information can be provided in areas where the population is too sparse to support even a part-time advice centre (28). Mobile advice centres, telephone services and "village contact" schemes have a part to play.

A number of mobile advice centres have been set up, run by a variety of different groups including rural community councils, citizens advice bureaux, local authority departments and voluntary groups (28). In some a van is equipped as a mobile office and makes a regular schedule of visits. One of the first mobile centres was Gwynedd mobile CAB, established in 1973, which continues to make a weekly tour of small towns in the Bangor area of North Wales. It is used in the same way as part-time static centres, and deals with around 100 enquiries a month. Alternatively, advice workers can travel to a variety of different sites on a regular basis. Mobile vans have the advantage of being conspicuous and people are more aware of when they call. The use made of a mobile centre depends on how frequently and regularly it calls. The Gwynedd research recommended that the van should call at least once a week and should stop for at least half a day. This makes mobile centres an attractive option in communities of 4,000 people or more. Recent technological innovations such as the citizens advice bureau microfiche briefcase (which provides the equivalent of a filing cabinet of information in a portable form) and the cordless telephone have made mobile advice easier.

The use of telephone advice was pioneered in 1978 by the Northumberland rural citizens advice bureau, which attracted some 75 to 90 enquiries per month from a rural population of 70,000 people. The bureau organiser commented that the scheme demonstrates "how much can be dealt with over the phone...the rural CAB is gaining useful experience in dealing with telephone queries which may, in itself, have ramifications for all CABx" (29). In 1979-81, the Scottish Consumer Council set up an experimental scheme to provide freephone advice in the Western Highlands, one of the most sparsely populated areas in Britain (30). Calls were answered by the Inverness and District citizens advice bureau, which already dealt with a large number of telephone enquiries. The service was well used: overall it attracted around 569 enquiries in the first 18 months, equivalent to a rate of one enquiry per 23 households per year, of which 17 per cent concerned social security. The bureau did not find that providing telephone advice caused any special difficulties. It was vital, however, that the scheme was adequately publicised. The level of enquiries rose substantially after leaflets about the scheme had been delivered (30).

"Village link" schemes were started by the community council in Shropshire in 1973, and have now been run by citizens advice bureaux in Montgomeryshire, Cambridgeshire, and in Dumfries and Galloway, among others. The Scottish Consumer Council has also established and monitored a scheme in the Grampian region (30). Volunteers are recruited from each village and are provided with information, training and back-up. In some schemes, the volunteer's role is limited to providing information and signposting people to other agencies; in others, they provide advice and practical assistance. Village link schemes can draw a relatively high level of enquiries—one per eleven households per year in the Dumfries and Galloway scheme. But the level of enquiries depends crucially on the standing and personality of the contact and on the publicity about the scheme. The Scottish Consumer Council found that contacts who worked from established advice points rather than from home, or who had an established position in the community, drew much greater levels of enquiries. The local contacts were valued for their local information, but were used less frequently for personal and family problems than more established advice centres. Again, social security enquiries were the largest category. The Scottish Consumer Council concluded that there was a strong argument for link schemes to be formally associated with an established advice centre in the locality, which would provide training and support and reassure users that good, confidential advice would be provided (30).

In recent years, rural libraries have become more involved in providing information and advice. Much can be achieved by close co-operation between different agencies. In South Molton, for example, different organisations have combined to turn the library into an "information centre".

The success of rural advice schemes relies on two crucial factors. Firstly, they need considerable publicity, preferably on an ongoing basis. This need is much greater than for urban "shop front" centres which have a clear physical presence in the community. Secondly, they need to have access to specialist, back-up resources. In rural areas these are less likely to be provided by private practice. Arguably there is a greater need for specialist salaried services in rural areas than in urban areas where there are more specialist solicitors in private practice. Up until now, however, specialist law and advice centres have been largely confined to urban areas.

Other advice centres

In addition there are a large number of voluntary legal advice schemes which run part-time surgeries in which local solicitors provide their services free of charge. Many such schemes have strong links with local advice agencies, who provide premises and refer clients to them. The free representation unit in London is staffed by volunteer trainee barristers and provides free tribunal representation in cases referred by London advice agencies. It is financed by a small grant from the Bar Council. The Equal Opportunities Commission and Commission for Racial Equality also provide legal advice and representation in significant cases.

There are also a number of outreach services providing advice to people who are poorly served by existing services. In 1987-8, thirty-one citizens advice bureaux provided services inside hospitals, and twenty-three worked in prisons (6). The Springfield legal advice project is a law centre based in a mental hospital.

Advice centre funding

A major weakness of the advice sector in England and Wales is that it has never been recognised as a part of a national scheme to ensure access to justice. Centres have relied on local initiatives and short-term funding.

Local government is under no statutory duty to provide money for advice. Under section 142 of the Local Government Act 1972, local authorities can make grants to voluntary organisations which give information about local and central government services, but this does not cover taking action in a case or providing legal services. Most councils rely on a general power under section 137 of the Local Government Act 1972 which enables them to spend a limited amount of money on matters not otherwise authorised but which are in the interests of their area or their inhabitants.

In *The fourth right of citizenship* published in July 1977 we described the funding of advice centres as "chaotic" (31). Cash came from a bewildering variety of sources. Almost every central or local government department could, and did, provide funding but in many areas no cash was available. Advice agencies wasted time that could have been spent giving a service to consumers in making applications for funds. Often potential funders recognised a need for an advice agency but delayed funding it in the hope that some other department would step in. There was no central government co-ordination of advice provision and co-operation between departments was minimal.

In 1986 we found that the funding situation had deteriorated. The abolition of the Greater London Council and metropolitan authorities left a question mark over the future of all advice centres funded by them; rate capping endangered local authority funding; and changes in the urban programme withdrew funding from new agencies.

Central government refused to accept responsibility for law centres. In a six month period we were told of closure threats hanging over fourteen agencies (8).

Few centres did in fact close but the uncertainty took its toll. In 1986 the legal aid advisory committee commented, "the experience of Paddington Law Centre this year demonstrates only too vividly the results that the present tortuous and unpredictable arrangements can produce" (27). Paddington, one of the first law centres in London, had been funded by the Greater London Council (GLC). When the GLC was abolished in March 1986, funds were forthcoming from neither Westminster city council nor the London grants committee and the law centre closed. Staff were dismissed and clients were told to go elsewhere. Three months later, the centre was successful in its appeal against the London grants committee original decision and it re-opened. This is an extreme example, but each closure threat leaves clients uncertain whether they will be represented when their cases come to court, and makes it very difficult to retain experienced staff, train new ones or plan for the future in such circumstances.

There is little co-ordination between the various government departments with an interest in advice centre funding. These departments include the Department of Trade and Industry, which provides funds to the National Association of Citizens Advice Bureaux, the Lord Chancellor's Department which provides £750,000 towards law centres, and the Department of the Environment which is responsible for the urban programme. The Home Office and Departments of Health and Social Security also have some interest in advice provision.

Geographic distribution

The government has recognised the value of law and advice centres but has repeatedly stressed that the existence or level of provision must be a matter of local decision and initiative (32). The direct consequence of this is a very uneven distribution of advice provision, where some people have no access to a general advice centre and the majority of people are outside the catchment area of a specialist centre.

The geographic inequality of advice provision is more serious than that of private solicitors. Table 2.3 shows the number of people per full-time equivalent advice worker (paid or unpaid) in either a general or specialist centre in 1986. Most centres are in London and the major conurbations. London has one advice worker per 3,750 people, and Merseyside has one worker per 9,250. At the other end of the scale is the East Midlands with one per 23,250 people, and East Anglia and the Southern legal aid area with one per 17,750.

Table 2.3: population per advice worker, for each legal aid area, in 1986.

Legal aid area	Population per advice worker
South Eastern	13,250
Southern	17,750
South Western	16,250
South Wales	12,250
West Midland	11,750
North Western	11,250
Northern	10,750
North Eastern	15,750
East Midland	23,250
Eastern	17,750
Chester and N. Wales	12,000
London South ⎫ London East ⎬ London West ⎭	3,750
Merseyside	9,250
Total	10,150

Source: Kempson E., *A survey of current advice and law centre provision*, vol. 2, table 14, September 1986.

Advice centres are overwhelmingly concentrated in cities. Local authorities with particularly poor provision of general advice centres included shire counties such as Lincolnshire, Derbyshire and Gwynedd and metropolitan districts adjoining big cities such as Barnsley, Bolton, Gateshead, Solihull, Sandwell and Walsall (11).

There are so few specialist centres that it is invidious to pick out particular badly provided authorities. In 1986, out of 47 shire counties, 22 had no law centre or independent housing or money advice centre. Out of 36 metropolitan districts, 21 were without such centres. Even in London, which is by far the best provided area, 14 out of 33 London boroughs had no independent specialist centres. Over a third of all shire counties and metropolitan districts had no tribunal representation service of any description (11).

The role of advice centres

There is a growing awareness of the value of the work done by advice and law centres. Tributes have been paid by the Royal Commission on Legal Services (1), the Lovelock report on citizens advice bureaux

(33), the government's efficiency scrutiny of legal aid (34), and the Lord Chancellor's Civil Justice Review (35). The Lord Chancellor's legal aid advisory committee has repeatedly stressed their importance (36).

There is also a growing demand for their services. But the increases in recognition and demand have not led to better planning or more secure funding. Advice is still seen as a marginal activity, dependent on local circumstances and initiatives. As a result, whether you receive the advice you need depends on where you live. Centres continue to be threatened with closure for reasons unconnected with the value of their work, and important new developments are failing to get started.

In its 34th report, the Lord Chancellor's legal aid advisory committee stated:

"No longer can the work of law centres, Citizens Advice Bureaux, neighbourhood advice centres and the like be regarded as peripheral to the statutory legal aid schemes. They provide services which are complementary to the statutory schemes and, in terms of providing initial access to the justice system, they are often vital to those schemes. The importance of their role must be recognised not merely in theory but by taking them fully into account in the development of legal services policy" (37).

We agree. In chapter 4 we make proposals to integrate advice centres into the planning and funding of public legal services.

Solicitors in private practice

There are around 39,000 solicitors in private practice in England and Wales, operating from 7,800 separate firms (38). The last fifteen years has seen a dramatic increase in the number of solicitors. In 1971 there was one solicitor in private practice for every 2,418 people while in 1985 there was one solicitor for every 1,324 people (39). The expansion of tertiary education during the 1960s provided more law graduates, anxious to meet an increased demand for legal services, fuelled by increased home ownership and higher rates of crime and marital breakdown. Nearly every category of solicitors' work has increased, including that financed by legal aid. The number of lawyers in England and Wales tends to be similar or higher than the number in other European countries, but significantly smaller than in the United States of America (40). Cross-country comparisons are fraught with uncertainties, however, and should be treated with caution.

Size of firms

The solicitors' profession is one in which small, generalist practices continue to play a very important part. A 1985 survey carried out on behalf of the Law Society found that 81 per cent of firms are small, in that they are either sole practitioners or have fewer than five partners. Seventeen per cent of firms have between five and fourteen partners and two per cent of firms are large (ie fifteen partners or more) (41). The proportions have not changed substantially since 1976, when research was carried out for the Royal Commission on Legal Services (1).

Overall, small firms account for 37 per cent of all work but they carry out more than half of all conveyancing, matrimonial and criminal work. Large firms concentrate on company and commercial work, including commercial conveyancing, and litigation. Large central London firms play a significant role in the profession, and account for 17 per cent of all solicitors' earnings. But outside London there are relatively few large firms—provincial firms of 15 partners or more are responsible for only 6 per cent of work (41).

Type of work

Table 2.4 shows the proportion of total fee income earned by private practitioners from different categories of work:

Table 2.4: analysis of total fee income for different categories of work, for all firms of solicitors in private practice.

domestic conveyancing	29%
company and commercial	25%
probate and wills	9%
other non-contentious work	5%
matrimonial	7%
criminal	5%
other contentious work	20%

Source: Law Society special committee on remuneration: *Survey of the structure and finances of the profession in private practice*, Peat Marwick, 6th January 1986.

Domestic conveyancing continues to be the most important source of work. It is especially important for small firms, where it accounts for over 40 per cent of earnings. It appears to have declined in importance over the last 15 years, though direct comparisons are difficult: previous studies have looked at domestic and commercial conveyancing together, while the 1985 survey puts commercial conveyancing in the "company and commercial" category. In 1968 conveyancing as a whole accounted for around fifty-six per cent of solicitors' incomes (42) and in 1976 the figure was put at 47 per cent (1). The change is due to increases in other forms of work, notably criminal, matrimonial and litigation work, rather than to any decline in conveyancing.

The category "other contentious work" covers many different areas including commercial litigation, personal injury, housing and consumer work. A survey carried out among solicitors in Devon and Cornwall in 1985 gives an idea of the comparative importance of each of these areas (43). Firms and individual solicitors were asked to rank their five most important categories of work out of twenty categories used by the Law Society. Again, residential conveyancing dominated the list, for both individuals and firms, in terms of both time and earnings. It was generally regarded as more profitable than other areas of work. Next came wills and trusts, family, and general litigation— with wills being regarded as more profitable than matrimonial or litigation. One respondent put it bluntly: "litigation is not very profitable but it is a client getter" (43).

The middle ranking categories included agricultural property, general crime, commercial property, business affairs and accident and personal injury litigation. Solicitors were split about whether personal injury work was profitable.

At the bottom of the list were those categories where expertise was lacking. The authors commented: "on the one hand they include those highly specialist areas, like bankruptcy and taxation, which are technically complex; on the other they encompass areas, such as welfare, housing, planning, juvenile crime, employment, child care and consumer problems, which often have a large social welfare element and tend to be unprofitable, because those likely to be affected by them are relatively poor" (43). Child care, juvenile crime, employment and welfare were each mentioned by only one firm out of 83 in the survey.

A survey of 45 citizens advice bureaux in South Wales confirms that there is a shortage of skills in employment, housing and welfare rights matters (44). Twelve bureaux reported difficulties in referring clients to solicitors on employment matters, 10 had difficulties in housing cases and 8 had difficulties in welfare rights matters. Eight bureaux also expressed lack of confidence in referring clients to solicitors in matrimonial cases, though this related more to the way solicitors dealt with distressed clients, and to their lack of knowledge about related welfare rights issues, than to shortages of solicitors willing to do this work.

Geographic distribution

A study by Exeter University has shown wide regional differences in the numbers of solicitors. As table 2.5 shows, the South East and South West have high concentrations of solicitors while the North and East Midlands do relatively badly (39).

Table 2.5: regional variations in the number of persons per solicitor in England and Wales in 1985

Region	No. of persons per solicitor
South East	924
South West	1,261
East Anglia	1,550
North West	1,638
Wales	1,731
West Midlands	1,826
Yorkshire and Humberside	1,876
East Midlands	1,998
North	2,119
England and Wales	1,324

Source: Watkins C., Blacksell M., and Economides K., *The distribution of solicitors in England and Wales,* University of Exeter, March 1986, p.12.

On a county basis, Northumberland and Durham have the lowest numbers of solicitors. Durham has one solicitor per 3,237 people while Northumberland has one solicitor per 2,985 (39).

The study showed that, excluding inner London, there is a high correlation between the number of solicitors and the proportion of owner occupied households and elderly people. This reflects the importance of both conveyancing and probate work. Solicitors are also concentrated in town centres—districts without clear administrative centres have particularly low numbers of solicitors. Blaby and South Cambridgeshire are the districts with the lowest number of solicitors (one solicitor per 76,610 people and one solicitor per 53,659 people respectively), but Bolsover, Torfaen, Cleethorpes, South Ribble and Rhondda are also among the twenty worst provided districts. Out-of-town council estates are particularly unlikely to be served by solicitors. Among the twenty best provided districts are Norwich, Oxford, Bournemouth, Cheltenham and Bath. Large cities, including Manchester, Newcastle, Nottingham and Bristol also do well (39).

The organisation of the profession

Solicitors are a highly regulated profession. The broad framework has been laid down in successive acts of parliament, now consolidated into the Solicitors Act 1974. This gives solicitors a monopoly over certain work and provides the profession's private association, the Law Society, with wide ranging powers over membership, training, discipline and business structure. Solicitors' charges are subject to control by the courts (see chapter 6).

Not all solicitors need to be members of the Law Society. Solicitors may choose whether to pay a subscription to join either their local or the national Law Society. But all solicitors are subject to the Law Society's regulation and discipline. When solicitors complete the required training they are admitted and their names are placed on the Law Society's register or "roll". A person on the roll is not entitled to practise, however, without a practising certificate, which must be renewed every year. Applicants must provide an accountant's certificate showing that their clients' accounts are in order, and newly qualified solicitors must show that they have undergone the required course of continuing education.

The Law Society requires that solicitors in private practice operate as individuals or in partnership with other solicitors. It requires all solicitors to carry insurance against negligence claims and to contribute to a compensation fund to reimburse the clients of dishonest solicitors. It also runs and finances the Solicitors Complaints Bureau which receives and investigates complaints against solicitors.

The Law Society is governed by a council of up to seventy members who meet once a month. The majority are elected by members of the Society to represent 31 constituencies in England and Wales and a few are co-opted "on account of their distinction and eminence" (45). The Council chooses a President and Vice-President. The profession is thus self-governing. Abel-Smith and Stevens in writing a history of the profession comment:

> "The extent of self-government which Parliament granted to solicitors was exceptional. While the legislature had insisted on introducing non-professional members on the bodies responsible for the education and discipline of doctors, nurses, midwives, dentists, pharmacists and architects, no non-lawyer could interfere with the affairs of solicitors" (46).

Work reserved for solicitors

In many areas of work, such as advice on tax matters, solicitors compete with other professions. There are some areas of work, however, which only solicitors are allowed to undertake. Under the

Solicitors Act 1974 it is a criminal offence for a non-solicitor to imply that "he is qualified...to act as solicitor" (47).

It is a criminal offence to act as a solicitor by starting, continuing or defending any court proceedings. Only solicitors or barristers may "draw...or prepare any instrument relating to...any legal proceeding" for reward (48). Generally, non-lawyers are not permitted to act as advocates in the civil or criminal courts, though they may accompany people, "take notes, (and) quietly make suggestions and give advice" (49). In some cases, registrars have discretion to permit lay representatives to appear in minor matters before the county court.

Solicitors, along with parliamentary agents, patent agents, trade mark agents and other employed barristers, are able to instruct barristers. Solicitors also have a monopoly in probate matters. It is a criminal offence for non-solicitors "in expectation of any fee, gain or reward" to take "instructions for a grant of probate or a grant of letters of administration" or to "draw or prepare any paper on which to fund...such a grant" (50). Exemptions are given to unqualified people working in a solicitor's office provided they work at the direction and under the supervision of the solicitor.

The ending of the conveyancing monopoly

From 1804 until the passing of the Administration of Justice Act in 1985, solicitors enjoyed a virtual monopoly over conveyancing transactions. After prolonged public debate, legislation was passed to establish a new profession of "licensed conveyancers", permitted to compete with solicitors in the field of domestic conveyancing. Their activities are regulated by a new statutory body, the Council for Licensed Conveyancers. Like solicitors, licensed conveyancers are required to carry compulsory insurance, keep separate clients' accounts, contribute to a compensation fund and be subject to a disciplinary code and complaints procedure. But unlike solicitors, the Council is a statutory body, with a majority of lay members rather than a professional association.

Licensed conveyancers are required to take examinations of a level equivalent to the conveyancing papers in the solicitors' final examinations. The transitional exams held in December 1986 proved tough: out of 399 candidates sitting, only 176 candidates passed the subjects they needed (51). In May 1987 the first licensed conveyancers were given licences and by December 1987 there were 200 practising licensed conveyancers.

Solicitors will face a further competitive challenge when the provisions of the Building Societies Act 1986 are brought into effect. Under schedule 21, the Lord Chancellor may make rules to permit "recognised institutions", such as building societies and banks, "to undertake the provision of conveyancing services". It is for the Lord Chancellor to lay down conditions for recognition which may include rules to protect customers against conflicts of interest, and to provide compensation in the event of negligence or dishonesty.

A new competitive climate

Traditionally, the Law Society has been suspicious of competition on the grounds that consumers are incapable of exercising sensible choices about which lawyer to use. It is argued that unless the services available are carefully regulated, standards will fall. This attitude is changing. In their green paper on restrictive trade practices, the government argued that the professions should no longer have blanket exemptions from competition law. The paper states:

"Whilst open to argument about retaining any exemption, the Government intend to end as many as possible and to make sure all sectors of the economy operate as far as possible under the incentives of competition" (52).

The rising numbers in the profession, together with a changed political climate and the ending of the conveyancing monopoly, have led to a new climate among solicitors. In 1986, a Law Society discussion paper declared that "restrictive practices can only be justified if they exist for the protection of the public" and that the starting point for any discussion must be "the needs of the consumer" (53). The profession is reconsidering almost every aspect of its practice rules. Most of the restrictions on advertising have been removed, and the Law Society has circulated discussion papers on specialisation schemes, mixed practices, greater rights of audience and mutual litigation funds.

Barristers

In 1987 there were 5,642 barristers practising in England and Wales, an increase of over 2,000 since 1974. Seventy per cent of all barristers work in London, while the rest work in major provincial centres (54).

Consumers may not approach barristers directly: they must first use a solicitor who will instruct the barrister on their behalf. The Benson

Commission estimated that barristers were consulted in around 5 per cent of cases where the solicitor took some action (1).

The difference between solicitors and barristers is largely historical and can be traced back to the practitioners who appeared before the medieval and Tudor law courts. At the beginning of the 19th century, the division became institutionalised. A professional pressure group, the Gentlemen Practisers Society, campaigned vigorously to increase the standing of solicitors and to control unethical practices. This led eventually to the establishment of the Law Society to regulate their activities. Meanwhile the four Inns of Court in London became the exclusive preserve of barristers. A compromise was arrived at between the two branches of the profession: in return for a rule that no member of the public was to approach a barrister except through a solicitor, barristers were given the exclusive right to appear in the higher courts, including the high court, court of appeal and House of Lords. When, however, the county courts were founded in 1846 as accessible local courts to deal with small claims, both barristers and solicitors were given equal rights to act as advocates.

This compromise provoked criticism at the time and continues to be controversial today (55). In chapter 8 we examine whether it is in the interest of consumers. The division has, nevertheless, survived largely intact and continues to govern relationships between the two branches of the profession. Barristers do not deal with conveyancing or uncontested probate, which forms a large proportion of the work of solicitors. Barristers act as advocates in the higher courts and give opinions about difficult points of law. In some respects the work of barristers and solicitors overlaps: both appear in magistrates and county courts, both draft documents to put before the court and both give legal advice.

Some barristers are generalists, working in "common law" chambers doing a mixture of crime, divorce, contract, personal injury and landlord and tenant work. Other barristers concentrate on just one of these areas. Chancery barristers deal in tax, trusts, probate and company matters, while some specialise in just one area of law, such as libel, planning, patents or local government.

Research for the Royal Commission in 1977 found that barristers are heavily dependent on public funds, which account for 46 per cent of their income. Twenty-one per cent of barristers' gross fees came from criminal legal aid, 16 per cent came through criminal public funds for prosecution, and 9 per cent came from civil legal aid (1).

Barristers are not allowed to form partnerships or companies. In theory, each barrister is a sole practitioner. In practice, barristers work from "chambers", in which a number of independent practitioners band together to share office costs and to employ a clerk. The clerk is responsible for bringing work into the chambers and for negotiating fees with solicitors. Barristers are limited in the type of offices they can use—if they propose to practise from a London address outside the four Inns of Court, they require special permission from the Bar committee. Outside London, the consent of the circuit committee is needed.

Organisation of the profession

Every barrister must belong to one of the four Inns of Court. The Inns started as medieval teaching colleges, and they have been described as the "true survivors of the medieval Guild system" (56). They still preserve many of their old traditions. They are extremely rich institutions, owning land worth several hundred million pounds (1). In the past much of their accommodation was let to barristers' chambers at less than its market value, but the policy has now changed: the Inns are increasing their rents so as to be able to buy suitable accommodation in nearby areas (57).

The Inns of Court provide their members with libraries and social facilities, and organise some lectures and mock-trials for students. They are governed by "benchers" who are chosen for life by other benchers. Around a third of benchers are practising barristers. The rest are mainly judges.

There is a conflict for control of the profession between the Inns which are governed by judges and the most senior members of the profession, and the Bar Council. Until 1st January 1987, rules for practice, discipline and training were the responsibility of a body called "The Senate of the Inns of Court and the Bar", which was composed of representatives of both the Inns and the Bar Council. In January 1987, a new compromise was reached. The governing body of the Bar was declared to be the General Council of the Bar, which is largely elected by the profession. Thirty-nine members of the Council are elected by practising barristers, 12 are elected by the regional circuits, 12 are elected by employed barristers and only 12 are appointed by the benchers of the Inns. The Inns agreed that, for the time being, they would implement the policy of the General Council, provided that they were consulted first. A new institution, the Inns' Council, was established to represent their interests. Where the Inns' Council and the General Council disagree, the General Council's policy will be implemented, provided it has the support of two-thirds of the profession (58).

The Inns retain a major influence over training: a barrister's education continues to be run by the Council of Legal Education, which has a majority of members appointed by the Inns. We examine this in greater detail in chapter 8.

This change in structure heralds a period of other change. The code of conduct has been redrafted and changes have been made to training and complaints handling.

Queen's Counsels and juniors

In 1987 there were 584 practising barristers who carried the title "Queen's Counsel" (QCs) (54). QCs are appointed by the Queen after consultation with the Lord Chancellor. The selection procedure does not depend on interviews or examinations. Instead the Lord Chancellor carries out private consultations with judges and leading members of the profession. QCs tend to charge more than ordinary "junior" barristers. Traditionally, QCs were not permitted to appear in court without a junior barrister being present. Although this rule has now been relaxed it is still unusual for QCs to appear alone.

Reliable information about barristers' income is hard to come by because surveys of barristers' earnings tend to have a very low response rate. But there appears to be a great difference between the earnings of barristers at the top of the profession and those at the bottom. The Top Salaries Review Board estimated that in 1985 the top quarter of QCs earned around £95,000 (59), while a survey commissioned by the Bar the same year suggested that a barrister specialising in criminal law, of over 10 years experience could be receiving a modest £8,620 (60). QCs do not necessarily earn the highest incomes. Some very successful "juniors" may find that when they become QCs their fees increase but the volume of work falls.

A "gentleman's profession"

Traditionally, the Bar has been a "gentleman's profession". Barristers are not meant to get involved in the commercial aspects of their work but should leave the clerk to arrange and collect fees. The polite fiction was that barristers did not work for a fee but for an "honorarium" and the rule that barristers cannot sue for their fees continues. The solicitor who fails to pass on a fee, however, may be guilty of professional misconduct.

Barristers were largely drawn from the upper and middle-classes. In 1977 the Royal Commission found that three-quarters of all new barristers came from professional or managerial families and eight per cent of entrants had fathers who were lawyers (1). Even today it is a predominantly male profession. In 1987, only 14 per cent of practising barristers were women (54).

The barrister's profession is dominated by traditions, and by quaint customs which may amuse or infuriate clients. In court, wigs and gowns must be worn and out-of-court clothes are expected to be dark. Wigs and gowns are traditionally carried about in special bags—junior barristers use blue bags, but a QC may award a junior a red bag as a special honour. Clients are expected to meet their barristers in chambers or at court, not in the solicitor's office, and to be accompanied by someone from the solicitor's firm while they do so. These and other similar customs help to cement camaraderie between barristers and at the same time exclude non-lawyers who are unaware of the etiquette.

On the other hand, links between judges and barristers are very close, and are maintained by the social activities of the Inns in London and circuit committees in the provinces. High court and appeal court judges must be barristers: solicitors may not be appointed even if they are experienced circuit judges. This contributes to a definite atmosphere in the higher courts—the judge and opposing barristers "belong", the solicitor is tolerated and the client is an outsider.

References to chapter 2

1. Royal Commission on Legal Services in England & Wales (Chairman: Sir Henry Benson), Cmnd 7648, HMSO, 1978.
2. Harris, D. and others, *Compensation and support for illness and injury*, Oxford Socio-legal Studies, Clarendon Press, 1984.
3. Research Surveys of Great Britain Limited, *Summary report: awareness, usage and attitudes towards the professional services and advice provided by solicitors*, prepared for Charles Barker City Limited, February 1986.
4. Broadcasting Research Department, *Citizens advice bureaux: the price of advice*, a survey of 1,736 people carried out by the BBC in week 41, 1986.
5. Childs, D., Hickey, A. and Winter, J., *Citizens' advice; a study of who uses London's Citizens Advice Bureaux and the services they receive*, Greater London Citizens Advice Bureaux Service, October 1985; Kempson E., *Advice Services in Oldham: a review of current provision and patterns of use*, Social Development Unit, Oldham Metropolitan Borough Council, 1987.
6. National Association of Citizens Advice Bureaux, *Annual Report 1987-88*.

7. National Consumer Council, *Information and advice services in the United Kingdom*—report to the Minister of State for Consumer Affairs, April 1983.

8. National Consumer Council, *The reform of publicly funded legal services in England and Wales*, a consumer response to the Scrutiny Team, September 1986.

9. National Consumer Council, *Good advice for all: guidelines for local advice services*, 1986, p.8.

10. Shelter, *Housing aid 1986*, a report of the work of Shelter's Housing Aid Division.

11. Kempson E., *A survey of current advice and law centre provision*, Advice Services Alliance, September 1986.

12. NACAB's annual report, see reference 6, records that there are 712 main bureaux and 213 extensions in England, Wales and Northern Ireland. Of these, 29 main bureaux and four extensions are in Northern Ireland.

13. Personal communication with NACAB.

14. Thackeray, A. and Jones, M., *The FIAC directory of independent advice centres*, Federation of Independent Advice Centres, 1988.

15. Kempson, E., *Welfare benefits work by non-statutory advice and law centres*, unpublished report prepared for the Policy Studies Institute, January 1986.

16. Borrie, G., *Advice agencies: what they do and who uses them*, National Consumer Council, 1982.

17. Figures supplied by the Federation of Independent Advice Centres.

18. National Association of Young Peoples' Counselling and Advisory Services, *Annual Report 1987-88*.

19. List of affiliated and non-affiliated groups supplied by DIAL UK (Disablement Information and Advice Lines), 3 May 1988.

20. Figures supplied by the Law Centres Federation.

21. Figures supplied by Shelter.

22. Hinton, T. and Berthoud, R., *Money advice services*, Policy Studies Institute, 1988.

23. United Kingdom Immigrants Advisory Service, *Annual Report 1986-87*.

24. Berthoud, R., Benson, S., and Williams, S., *Standing up for claimants: welfare rights work in local authorities*, Policy Studies Institute, October 1986.

25. Compiled from a list of centres provided by the Institute of Consumer Advisers 1987.

26. A study published in 1980 of five rural parishes in north Lincolnshire found that nearly half the people interviewed had

needed information and advice in the preceding six months, see Clarke D. and Unwin K., *Information services in rural areas: prospects for telecommunication access*, GEO Books, 1980; a similar study in the Upper Coquetdale area of rural Northumberland in 1976-77 found that over half (97) of the 167 households studied had been faced with a problem in the previous few months. The main areas were housing, income maintenance and consumer matters, and problems were frequently long-standing and complex (see Richards J., *Rural advice and information; the proof of need; the Coquetdale experiment*, CAB occasional paper no.2, NACAB, 1978).

27. *Legal aid*, 36th annual reports of the Law Society and the Lord Chancellor's advisory committee, 1985-86, HC 87, HMSO, 1987.
28. See Kempson, E., and Moore, N., *The development of advice services in rural areas*, Acumen, September 1983.
29. Northumberland rural CAB, unpublished report prepared by D. H. Elliot, Organiser, August 1980 (quoted in *A call for advice—* see reference 30 below).
30. Scottish Consumer Council, *A call for advice—an evaluation of two rural advice experiments in Scotland*, 1983.
31. National Consumer Council, *The fourth right of citizenship, a review of local advice services*, 1977.
32. See *Hansard* 24th July 1987 columns 653 and 654, *Hansard* 14th January 1988 col. 1394.
33. Review of the National Association of Citizens Advice Bureaux (Chairman: Sir Douglas Lovelock), HMSO, 1984, Cmnd 9139.
34. Lord Chancellor's Department, *Legal aid efficiency scrutiny*, 2 vols, June 1986.
35. See Civil Justice Review consultation paper no.4 *Enforcement of Debt* and no.6, *General issues*, Lord Chancellor's Department, 1987.
36. See 34th, 35th & 36th Legal Aid Annual reports.
37. 34th Legal Aid Annual Reports 1983-84, HC 151, HMSO, 1985.
38. Law Society, *Annual statistical report 1987*.
39. Watkins, C., Blacksell, M., and Economides, K., *The distribution of solicitors in England and Wales*, Access to Justice in Rural Britain Project, working paper 8, University of Exeter, 1986.
40. See Podmore, D., *Solicitors and the wider community*, Heinemann, 1980, p.13.
41. The Law Society special committee on remuneration, *Survey of the structure and finance of the legal profession in private practice*, Peat Marwick, January 1986.

42. National Board for Prices and Incomes, report no.54, *Remuneration of solicitors*, Cmnd 3529, HMSO, 1968.

43. Blacksell, M., Economides K., and Watkins, C., *Solicitors and access to legal services in rural areas: evidence from Devon and Cornwall*, Access to Justice in Rural Britain Project, working paper 6, University of Exeter, 1986.

44. Beale, D. and Stow, B., *CAB and access to legal services in South Wales*, CAB occasional paper 17, NACAB, 1986.

45. The Law Society, *Royal Charter and Supplemental Charters*.

46. Abel-Smith, B. and Stevens, R., *Lawyers and the courts; a sociological study of the English legal system 1750-1965*, Heinemann, 1967, p.192.

47. Solicitors Act 1974, section 21.

48. Solicitors Act 1974, section 20 and section 22 (1)(b).

49. *McKenzie v McKenzie* [1970] 3 Weekly Law Reports, p.472.

50. Solicitors Act 1974, section 23.

51. *Observer*, 21 June 1987.

52. Department of Trade and Industry, *Review of restrictive trade practices policy: a consultative document*, Cm 331, HMSO, March 1988.

53. The Law Society's contentious business committee, *Lawyers and the courts: time for some changes*, a discussion paper, 1986.

54. Figures provided by the General Council of the Bar, 1988.

55. See Reeves, P., *Are two legal professions necessary?* Waterlow, 1986, p.104.

56. General Council of the Bar, *A career at the Bar*, 1987.

57. *The Times*, 17 June 1987.

58. General Council of the Bar, *Introduction and Constitutions of the General Council of the Bar, the Council of the Inns of Court and the Council of Legal Education*, 1987.

59. Review Body of Top Salaries, *Eighth report on top salaries*, report no.22, Cmnd 9525-i, HMSO, 1985.

60. Coopers and Lybrand, *Study of remuneration of barristers carrying out criminal legal aid*, commissioned by Senate of the Inns of Court and the Bar, September 1985.

Chapter 3
Legal aid: the present system

The principle that everyone should have access to the law has no meaning if people who are unable to afford lawyers cannot use it. Since the second world war, it has been accepted that the state should provide support for those unable to afford legal assistance. In this chapter we describe and analyse the existing system of civil legal aid. In chapter 4 we comment on recent proposals for reform, and make our own recommendations to the government and to the Legal Aid Board.

How the legal aid scheme started

The present system has its origins in the report of the Rushcliffe Committee, established in 1944 (1). The previous system for helping poor litigants in which lawyers provided free services on a charitable basis had broken down. The committee recommended a legal aid system in which lawyers were paid for their services out of public funds. The aim was to put people of poor and moderate means in the same position as well-to-do paying litigants, enabling them to obtain advice and pursue worthwhile cases before the courts.

From the first, a distinction was made between legal representation in court proceedings and legal advice. The Rushcliffe Committee recommended that while representation should be provided by lawyers in private practice, initial legal advice should be given by full-time salaried lawyers in area offices. In rural areas private solicitors could be paid on a sessional basis. Although these proposals were enshrined in legislation, they were never implemented. The first scheme, introduced in 1950, was confined to representation before the high court and appeal courts; in 1956 it was extended to the county court. In 1959, when legal advice was included for the first time, it was decided that advice, like representation, should be provided on a case by case basis through private solicitors. In fact, a distinction is still preserved between legal advice and assistance and full civil legal aid: initial advice and assistance is provided under a special scheme, known as the "green form" scheme. Criminal legal aid is administered separately.

The three main schemes

The present legal aid provisions are complicated. There are five separate schemes, covering civil and criminal legal aid, each with its own rules about eligibility, assessment and payment. There are also several important areas of work that are not covered by legal aid, including representation at most tribunals. Nor is legal aid provided for assistance with private prosecutions. Initial advice on these subjects, however, may be provided under the green form scheme.

The three schemes which are most significant in the field of civil law are full civil legal aid, legal advice and assistance (known as the green form) and "advice by way of representation" or ABWOR. Each is described below. In broad terms, in 1986-87, out of a net legal aid budget for civil and criminal legal aid of almost £300 million, full civil legal aid accounted for £104 million, the green form budget for £50 million and ABWOR for £11.5 million. Almost £25 million is spent on administration (2).

1. Full civil legal aid

This covers assistance with legal proceedings before the county court, high court and appeal courts. Consumers apply to the legal aid area office, usually with the help of the solicitor they have chosen. If the application is granted, a certificate is sent in the name of the chosen solicitor. Work cannot start on a case until a certificate has been granted although in urgent cases there is an emergency procedure. The consumer cannot change solicitor without the approval of the area office.

A legal aid certificate not only provides help with meeting one's own legal costs but also provides protection against having to pay the other side's costs should the case be lost. Under section 8 (1)(e) of the Legal Aid Act 1974, a legally aided party only has to pay the other side's costs as far as is reasonable, "having regard to all the circumstances, including the means of all the parties and their conduct in connection with the dispute". In practice, the courts limit cost orders against legally aided litigants to the amount of the legal aid contribution.

For successful litigants, legal aid acts as a loan rather than a grant. Where a legally aided litigant succeeds in a claim, the legal aid fund recoups its costs by means of the "statutory charge", both from the costs awarded to the assisted party and from any property recovered or preserved in the proceedings. We discuss the implications of this later in the chapter.

In order to qualify for a certificate, the consumer must meet both a merits test and a means test. The merits test is administered by the legal aid area office. Staff decide whether there are reasonable grounds for taking or defending the action and whether the outcome will be sufficiently important to the applicant to justify the expenditure. Legal aid is not normally granted for small claims, unless the claim is particularly important. In some cases legal aid is limited to certain steps—for counsel's opinion or up to a case being set down for trial for example—and the applicant must re-apply when that stage is reached. The area office must be informed if the client rejects an offer to settle which the solicitor considers reasonable, and the certificate may be revoked if the area office thinks that the client is acting unreasonably (3).

Where legal aid is refused, the applicant may appeal to the legal aid area committee. Appeals are usually heard by a committee of three or four solicitors or barristers in private practice.

The second hurdle is the means test, which applies separately to both income and capital. Where spouses are living together, their means are aggregated, but in divorce and family disputes against the other partner, each income is assessed separately. Thus, many more people are eligible for legal help with disputes against their spouses than with other forms of legal proceedings.

In order to apply the income test, it is necessary to calculate "disposable" income by taking actual income and deducting work expenses, housing costs, and fixed "allowances" for dependants. Discretionary allowances may also be given by the Department of Social Security assessment officers. Details of discretionary allowances have never been made public—they are contained in a confidential manual known as the "L code". They include school fees, unusually high hire-purchase payments for necessities and capital earmarked for specific use in the near future, such as house purchase.

There is an upper and lower income limit. An applicant whose disposable income is at or below the lower limit is entitled to free assistance, without having to pay a contribution from income. An applicant who is above the upper limit is not entitled to assistance at all. Those whose income falls between the upper and lower limits must pay a contribution out of income, equal to one-quarter of the amount by which their disposable income is above the lower limit. At present contributions must usually be paid in twelve monthly instalments, irrespective of the length of the case.

In calculating capital, the legal aid scheme disregards the value of a person's house, personal possessions and tools of trade. Savings and life assurance policies are included. In 1988, the upper capital limit was £5,000 and the lower limit was £3,000 (4). An applicant with capital of less than the lower limit is entitled to assistance without a contribution out of capital, while an applicant with more than the lower limit is asked to pay the whole of the excess as a contribution. An applicant with more than the upper limit is refused legal aid if the probable costs of the proceedings are not likely to exceed the maximum contribution payable (5). This provision normally means that in order to obtain legal aid an applicant above the upper capital limit would have to show that the likely costs of the action would be more than the contribution payable. A special exception applies to applicants on income support who are granted non-contributory legal aid irrespective of capital. Capital contributions must usually be paid in a single sum before legal aid is granted. Applicants who are assessed as being liable for both capital and income contributions have to pay both.

Table 3.1: what is full civil legal aid granted for?

	New certificates granted in 1986/87	Percentage of new certificates in the year in each category
matrimonial	126,883	51.6%
adoption, custodianship, guardianship and wardship	12,639	5.1%
trust, contentious probate, Inheritance Act	2,138	0.9%
contract	18,855	7.7%
negligence		
— to plaintiffs	55,842	22.7%
— to defendants	1,877	0.8%
landlord and tenant	9,700	3.9%
company and partnership	1,195	0.5%
land	2,830	1.1%
bankruptcy	2,430	0.1%
employment appeal tribunal	212	0.1%
miscellaneous	12,063	4.9%
House of Lords and court of appeal	1,186	0.5%
Total	245,663	

Note: in addition, 431 new civil legal aid certificates were granted for proceedings in magistrates courts.

Source: Legal aid, 37th annual reports of the Law Society and the Lord Chancellor's advisory committee, 1986-87, HC 233, HMSO, 1988, appendix 2C and 2D, pp. 53-55.

Applicants may be reassessed if their income increases or decreases within the first year. Reassessments will also take place if an applicant's capital increases but no reassessment is made as a result of a reduction in capital.

The means assessment is carried out by the Department of Social Security, who liaise with legal aid area offices. In 1986 the Legal Aid Scrutiny Team suggested that the means test was unnecessarily complex, and contributed to the serious and growing delays in providing certificates (6).

As table 3.1 shows, matrimonial problems and negligence cases dominate civil legal aid, accounting for around three-quarters of all certificates. This reflects both the type of work solicitors traditionally do and the legal aid eligibility criteria. In divorce matters, a wife's income is not aggregated with that of her husband, and thus wives without full-time jobs will normally qualify for legal aid. Victims of serious accidents who are unable to work are also likely to qualify for full legal aid. On the other hand, legal problems affecting those in full-time work, including building and consumer disputes and leasehold problems, figure much less prominently in the scheme.

2. The green form scheme

The green form scheme covers initial legal advice and assistance on any area of English law. Solicitors are permitted to provide up to £50 worth of advice (which pays for around 1 hour 20 minutes of a solicitor's time (2)) without seeking the approval of the legal aid authorities. A special limit of £90 applies to divorce cases.

The solicitor checks whether the consumer is eligible. Consumers are asked to sign a (green) form which the solicitor submits to the area office at the end of the case. If the advice needed comes to more than the limit, the solicitor can apply for an extension to the area office. The green form scheme can be used for experts' reports as well as legal advice.

Eligibility for green form advice on the basis of income is calculated in a broadly similar way but the limits are considerably lower than for civil legal aid. The Scrutiny Team calculated that in 1986 a married couple with two children aged 5 and 9 on an average income would not qualify under the green form scheme. The same family on two-thirds of average income would qualify, but would pay a contribution of £38 towards the cost of their advice (6). In theory, solicitors collect contributions, but research into the green form scheme found that many solicitors have difficulty enforcing payment and that a substantial minority do not bother to collect contributions (7).

Capital is dealt with differently. In assessing disposable capital, dependants' allowances are deducted. Those with over £850 disposable capital remaining are excluded from the scheme, while those with less than £850 are eligible on capital grounds. No capital contributions are payable. The green form capital limit, unlike the full legal aid one, is applied to applicants on income support, and means that not all income support claimants are eligible for green form advice. As with civil legal aid, the "statutory charge" applies to any money received as a result of the solicitor's action. Table 3.2. shows the use made of the green form scheme in 1986-87 by the type of problem.

Table 3.2: use of green form scheme by type of problem

Type of problem	No. of bills paid	Percentage of bills paid in each category
divorce and judicial separation	222,956	22.7%
other family	175,111	17.9%
crime	226,168	23%
landlord and tenant and housing	60,672	6.2%
hire-purchase and debt	57,529	5.8%
employment	19,924	2.0%
accidents and injuries	44,575	4.5%
welfare benefits	28,823	2.9%
immigration and nationality	7,823	0.8%
consumer problems	21,138	2.0%
other matters	115,788	11.8%
Total	980,507	

Source: Legal aid, 37th annual reports of the Law Society and the Lord Chancellor's advisory committee, 1986-87, HC 233, HMSO, 1987, appendix 1F, p.42.

Despite the intention of the green form scheme to provide low-income clients with initial advice about a wide range of problems, the scheme is heavily weighted towards family and criminal work which accounts for almost two-thirds of all bills paid. The number of welfare benefit cases grew by 32 per cent between 1985-86 and 1986-87, but remain a tiny part of the scheme, with only 29,000 cases. Although advice agency enquiry figures are collected in a different way and are not directly comparable with legal aid figures, it is clear that the numbers of cases dealt with by advice centres are much greater. We estimate that in 1986 advice centres received over two million welfare benefit enquiries (8), around one and a quarter million housing enquiries (compared with only 61,000 green form bills) and 135,000 immigration enquiries (compared with 7,823 green form bills) (9).

Many employment queries result in payment of unfair dismissal compensation or final wages, to which the statutory charge applies. Where this occurs, the solicitor does not submit a bill to the legal aid office and the case does not appear in the legal aid statistics. Even allowing for this, it appears that advice centres will deal with more clients: an estimated 650,000 enquiries to advice centres (9) compared with a grossed-up figure of 100,000 employment cases under the green form scheme (10). Most people with consumer problems do not meet the green form means test, but again the number of cases is low compared with over 600,000 cases reported to trading standards departments and advice agencies (11).

John Baldwin and Sheila Hill, who carried out research into the green form scheme for the Lord Chancellor's Department commented:

> "It may be thought that, in response to this growing demand, solicitors might be induced to expand their relatively narrow spheres of interest and grapple with issues such as welfare or employment rights with which most of them are at present unfamiliar. There is, however, little evidence in the study we have conducted to suggest that this is happening on any scale at present. In tackling the legal problems of poorer members of the community, it has been left largely to Law Centres, Citizens Advice Bureaux and a handful of private practitioners to fill the void beyond matrimonial and criminal work." (7)

The study found that in most legal aid areas there appeared to be one or two firms of solicitors which attracted clients with problems which were not crime and family matters. But generally employment, welfare benefits, immigration and consumer problems featured among the green forms of only a minority of firms in the sample, and then at a very low level (7).

3. Assistance by way of representation ("ABWOR")

This is a hybrid scheme, half way between the green form and full legal aid. It is mainly used for representation in domestic proceedings before the magistrates court but it also covers representation before mental health tribunals and the prisons' board of visitors. The eligibility limits are more generous than the green form scheme, but less generous than for full legal aid. The ABWOR income limits are similar to those of the green form, but the capital limit is higher. In

March 1986 it was increased to £3,000. Table 3.3 shows what the scheme is used for.

Table 3.3: what is ABWOR used for? Bills paid in 1986/87

Type of problem	No. of bills paid	Percentage
family proceedings in magistrates courts—includes maintenance, protection orders, custody/access, affiliation, guardianship and child care proceedings	56,372	96.1%
other magistrates court work	301	0.5%
mental health review tribunals	1,900	3.2%
prisons' board of visitors	58	0.1%
Total	58,631	

Source: *Legal aid*, 37th annual reports of the Law Society and the Lord Chancellor's advisory committee, 1986-87, HC 233, HMSO, 1987, appendix 1k, p.45.

Some civil proceedings before the magistrates courts, such as care proceedings, are covered by criminal legal aid.

Awareness of the legal aid scheme

One problem with the legal aid scheme is that very few people know about it. The Oxford Centre of Socio-legal Studies survey of accident victims found that of those who had consulted a solicitor, fewer than half had heard of the legal aid scheme and only a quarter knew of the legal advice scheme (12). Baldwin and Hill interviewed 124 clients who had been given advice under the green form scheme. They found that two-thirds of people had no idea about legal aid and did not know that financial assistance was available when they approached a solicitor (7). It is reasonable to assume that the level of the awareness among those who did not seek advice was lower. Research for the Civil Justice Review into potential housing litigants found that out of 65 people with housing problems who had decided not to go to court, 22 (43 per cent) said that they did not know about the legal aid scheme, even though they had sought advice about their problems (13). Most had contacted several different agencies.

In 1986-87, the legal aid administration spent £94,000 publicising the legal aid scheme, a small reduction on the previous year. For this, they were able to print and distribute 650,000 leaflets about the scheme entitled *Getting legal help*, and 325,000 free thirty-page booklets, entitled *The legal aid guide*. They also sent out some 17,000 posters. Distribution was largely through advice centres, libraries, local authorities and the courts (14). Unfortunately, leaflets are not generally available in post offices, job centres or doctors' surgeries, and are not usually sent out by courts with summonses (15).

In the last few years the legal aid administration has made several welcome improvements to its publicity. Asian language versions of *Getting legal help* have been printed and distributed. Translations are available in other minority languages, including Welsh, Arabic and Vietnamese for other organisations to reproduce and distribute. The legal aid administration is also planning to produce a third leaflet designed for people such as social workers and religious leaders who give advice to others. A video for school children is being produced in co-operation with the Law in Education Project.

An evaluation of the effectiveness of legal aid publicity commissioned by the legal aid administration suggested that the leaflets are useful for people who are literate, who already have some awareness of their rights and of the scheme, and have taken steps to find out more (15). But the leaflets are not a suitable medium for increasing general public awareness of legal aid. Advice workers commented that people do not generally read leaflets, and that many clients would have difficulties in working their way through *Getting legal help*. Advice centres and libraries do not always display the most up-to-date version of the leaflet, and the report comments that the leaflets may take a while to find in libraries.

Administering legal aid

It is estimated that, in all, over £30 million is spent on administering civil and criminal legal aid (6). This includes a £25 million grant to the Law Society, £3.5 million spent by the Department of Social Security in carrying out means tests and over £1 million in vetting legal aid bills in the county court. These figures do not include the administrative costs borne by solicitors themselves.

The government's reaction to rising administrative costs has been to impose stringent cash limits on the legal aid offices. In 1985-86, the Law Society, as administrator of the legal aid scheme, commented:

"The dominant issue for legal aid administration this year has again been Government restrictions on staff numbers and legal aid expenditure... Because of restrictions on staff recruitment and training in previous years the volume of work has progressively outstripped the numbers of people available to process it, so that throughout the year there were backlogs of work in most legal aid offices." (16).

In 1986-87 there have been slight improvements but delays are still serious. It takes an average of 67 days to issue a non-contributory certificate, and 124 days to issue a contributory certificate (2). Work cannot start until the certificate is granted. The legal aid advisory committee has commented that:

"from the point of view of the ordinary consumer, who uses the legal aid system perhaps only once in his lifetime, the delay in obtaining legal aid must seem quite staggering." (2).

The worst delays occurred in the London (South) Office which took an average of 231 days to issue contributory certificates in 1986-7 (2). The office was the subject of an unsuccessful microfiche experiment, which has now been abandoned. The office is in the process of being converted back to paper.

Any system which relies on case by case approval is bound to be costly in administration and the present one is particularly complex. An application for a full legal aid certificate is usually submitted with the help of a solicitor and must be scrutinised by two separate public agencies, one looking at the merits of the case and one looking at the applicant's means. The area office monitors settlements as the case progresses. When a case is finished, bills are frequently prepared by cost draftsmen, at a fee of around five per cent of the bill, and vetted by the county court, which takes another five per cent. The solicitor then submits the paperwork to the legal aid area office, which checks it over and sends the bill for payment some four to twelve months after the case is finished (6). The Law Society has suggested that delays in payment have caused concern about the economic viability of some firms specialising in legal aid work (16).

One objective in any reform of the legal aid system must be to reduce administrative costs and delays.

Who does legal aid work?

The Law Society's annual report on legal aid records that in 1986-87 payment was made to 11,560 offices (2), an increase of 60 offices since 1985-86 (16). Unfortunately, it is not possible to compare this figure with the total number of solicitors' firms because some firms manage their accounts centrally, while in others, each branch is paid separately. It is clear, however, that most high street firms will do some legal aid work. The Exeter University study of solicitors in

Devon and Cornwall found that almost all did some legal aid work, but for two-thirds of firms it only provided between 10 per cent and 40 per cent of their income (17). Nevertheless, there are a few firms who carry out a significant amount of legal aid work. According to the 1986-87 annual legal aid reports, half of all expenditure went to only 1,250 firms (2). This compares with 1,029 firms who received 45 per cent of all expenditure in 1985-86 (16).

Despite these figures, there have been several reports in the last two years that the number of solicitors providing legal aid is falling as a result of low levels of remuneration (16). A 1988 survey by the Law Society showed that this is a significant problem in criminal legal aid, and it is beginning to affect matrimonial legal aid (18). In 1987, the numbers of solicitors ceasing to handle matrimonial legal aid exceeded those joining the scheme, and the volume of legally aided matrimonial litigation showed a small decline. At present the numbers of solicitors undertaking non-matrimonial legal aid and green form work continues to increase but there are signs of unease. The survey showed that 14 per cent of participating solicitors were seriously considering giving up non-matrimonial civil legal aid work, and 16 per cent were seriously considering giving up green form work (18).

The numbers of people eligible for legal aid (19)

The Rushcliffe Committee recommended that legal aid should not be confined to "those normally classed as poor" because middle-income groups also had difficulties in gaining access to justice. It recommended a scheme in which the poor were provided with free legal aid, and those who could afford to pay something made a contribution (1). Their recommendations were accepted. When the first Legal Aid Act was introduced in 1949, it was entitled "an Act to make legal aid and advice... more readily available for persons of small or moderate means". Since the scheme began, legal aid has been available to the poor, but the position of those of moderate means has been more problematic. The number of people eligible for legal aid has fluctuated markedly over the last 38 years.

Traditionally, governments have approached the question of eligibility for legal aid by calculating the percentage of the population falling within the scope of the scheme. However, all the calculations made since 1950 have been on the basis of income alone. Very little information is available about individual capital holdings, and none of the calculations has attempted to take into account the effect of the capital limits. Thus all the official estimates have overestimated the numbers of people covered by legal aid. An unknown number of people qualify on income grounds but are excluded by their capital holdings.

Generally, the figures quoted are for the numbers of people eligible for full civil legal aid, on either a full or contributory basis, for non-matrimonial litigation. More people will get help with divorce, where husbands' and wives' income is assessed separately.

Coverage of the legal aid scheme 1950-1979

In 1950, when the legal aid scheme was introduced, it covered over eighty per cent of the population. The years between 1950 and 1974 saw a steep decline and by 1973 only forty per cent of the population were eligible. The decline was particularly acute for married couples with children: in 1964, over sixty per cent were covered, but by 1974 the figure was just over twenty per cent. The reason was that while the eligibility limits had kept pace with inflation, earnings had risen faster and many more wives, in particular, had begun to earn money (20).

The Lord Chancellor's advisory committee expressed grave concern about these changes. In their 26th annual report (1975-76) they pointed out that because the cost of civil litigation had been rising faster than earnings, the position of people outside the scheme had become worse since 1950, despite the general increase in affluence. They also drew attention to the effect of declining eligibility on the types of problems covered by the scheme:

"the diminution of the proportion of the population which is eligible for legal aid, coupled with the fact that for matrimonial proceedings the resources of married couples are usually assessed separately, while for other proceedings they are usually assessed together, has reinforced the tendency of matrimonial litigation to dominate the scheme" (20).

In 1974, the position stabilised. The legal aid limits and allowances were increased annually in line with increases in supplementary benefit levels which, in turn, increased in line with average earnings.

In April 1979, all the legal aid limits were substantially increased. The lower income limit was increased from 21 per cent below the long-term supplementary benefit level to 50 per cent above it. Dependants' allowances were also raised to 50 per cent above the dependants' allowances in the supplementary benefit scheme. An increase in the upper income limit made 70 per cent of the population eligible for legal aid. This restored eligibility to something approaching 1950 levels. The increases were intended to be paid for out of changes in the undefended divorce procedure.

The position since 1979

Since 1979, the value of the means limits has not been maintained. No increases took place in November 1980 and 1981. As a result, between April 1979 and November 1981, the lower limit fell from 50 per cent to 11 per cent above the supplementary benefit long-term rate. An increase in the legal aid limits in April 1982 failed to make up the ground lost, and only brought the limit up to 20 per cent above supplementary benefit. After the supplementary benefit increases in November 1982, the relative value of the lower limit fell to 8 per cent above supplementary benefit. Since then, with increases in April and November 1983, November 1984 and 1985, July 1986 and April 1987, the lower limit has held steady at about 16 per cent above the long-term supplementary benefit rate. Throughout this period, the upper income limit has remained 240 per cent higher than the lower limit, and has therefore fluctuated in the same way as the lower limit in relation to supplementary benefit allowances.

Since April 1988, the comparison with the long-term supplementary benefit rate is no longer possible. Supplementary benefit was replaced by income support, which does not have a long-term rate but a number of premiums for different groups. After the 1988 legal aid upratings, the lower limit was 4.8 per cent above income support with the pensioner premium.

The income limits show an even greater fall in relation to earnings. Between January 1980 and January 1988 average earnings rose by 107 per cent (21), while the legal aid limits increased by only 37 per cent. Even after the April 1988 uprating, the increase since January 1980 is only 41 per cent.

Eligibility is not only affected by the income limits: the dependants' allowances which are used to calculate disposable income are also significant. In April 1986, dependants' allowances were cut from 50 per cent to 25 per cent above supplementary benefit rates. This was the first time since the introduction of the legal aid scheme that a government had reduced eligibility for legal aid in money terms. It had the greatest effect on families with children. The Lord Chancellor's Department estimated that 1,200 applicants per year would be made ineligible, while others would be asked to pay more in contributions. The department estimated that the reduction in allowances would save around £7.5 million a year (22).

The 27th report of the Lord Chancellor's advisory committee

identified two-parent families with children as a core group, substantial coverage of which would indicate substantial coverage of the population as a whole (23). In table 3.4 we plot the minimum income which would cause such families to become ineligible for the scheme against average male earnings from 1979 to 1988.

Table 3.4: minimum family income causing ineligibility for legal aid compared with average male earnings 1979-1987

Date of change in legal aid limits	Minimum income making ineligible	% above average male earnings
married couple with three children aged 4, 8, and 13		
November 1979	£9,843	52% (1980)
November 1983	£14,305	53% (1984)
November 1985	£15,543	44% (1986)
March 1986	£14,402	33% (1986)
April 1987	£14,631	27% (1987)
April 1988	£14,717	17% (1988)
married couple with two children aged 4 and 8		
November 1979	£8,890	37% (1980)
November 1983	£12,922	39% (1984)
November 1985	£13,943	29% (1986)
March 1986	£13,024	21% (1986)
April 1987	£13,258	15% (1987)
April 1988	£13,323	6% (1988)

Note: the minimum income at which applicants become ineligible is that published by the Law Society whenever a change takes place in limits or allowances. It is supplied by the Lord Chancellor's Department and based on Department of Social Security information.

Average male earnings are for the full calendar year mentioned in brackets and are taken from the *Employment Gazette.* The figure for 1988 is based on a 1987 average male earnings increased by 8.5 per cent for the year, which is the underlying rate of increase according to the index also published in the *Employment Gazette.*

The average male earnings are simply a bench mark against which to measure the income limit. One cannot conclude from these figures that any particular proportion of families is eligible for legal aid. Such a calculation would involve taking into account tax and housing costs, the number of two-earner households, the wages for married women and unemployment rates, in addition to earnings and household composition. But as the upper limit approaches the level around which most family incomes are distributed, any reduction in eligibility limits has a particularly serious effect on the numbers covered by the scheme.

Cyril Glasser is the former special consultant on legal aid to the Lord Chancellor's advisory committee who was responsible for the figures in the 26th and 27th reports. He has attempted to estimate the number of people covered by the scheme using principally the *Family Expenditure Survey* and *General Household Survey* published by the Central Statistical Office. He concludes:

"Between 1979 and 1986 it can be estimated that just over a quarter of all households and of the population, went out of eligibility for legal aid. The failure to up-rate the limits properly has also had a marked effect on those within the scheme. By 1986, the estimated proportion of two parent families with children eligible for free legal aid had halved to 15% compared with the position in 1979. The rest faced a growing proportion of their income being taken by way of contributions. Since 1986, the position has certainly deteriorated further. The gross income levels at the upper limit for aid have increased by only 1.5-2.5 per cent, yet average earnings over the period March 1986-October 1987 have risen by 11 per cent, suggesting another fall in eligibility, perhaps involving another million people. It is probable that under 60 per cent of households and only just over half of the population are now eligible for civil legal aid" (22).

The legal aid statistics themselves provide further evidence of the decline in eligibility among those in work. As the eligibility of the working population goes down, the more the scheme is limited to the poor and unemployed. Those who formerly paid a contribution no longer qualify, and the proportion of contributory certificates decreases. The legal aid statistics show that the scheme has become increasingly non-contributory since 1979. In 1979-80 the proportion of non-contributory certificates was 73.3 per cent, compared with 80.1 per cent in 1986-87 (2).

The government's figures

The number of people covered by the legal aid scheme depends on a wide variety of factors, including changes in the limits and allowances, changes in earnings, tax, housing costs, income distribution and household composition. There are few reliable figures about the current coverage of the legal aid scheme. In January 1983 the Solicitor-General told parliament:

"of wage earners with a non-working spouse and two children aged under 11, it is estimated that at least 75 per cent of such families were eligible on income grounds for civil legal aid in 1979-80, at least 70 per cent in each of the years 1980-81 and 1981-82, at least 75 per cent this year" (24).

Since 1983, it is clear that the proportion of this particular group who are covered by the scheme has fallen sharply, as dependants' allowances have been reduced, and the maximum limit has fallen from 39 per cent above average male earnings to 6 per cent above average male earnings.

Despite this, the government claims that the proportion of the population covered by the scheme has remained broadly constant since 1979. In March 1986 the then Lord Chancellor, Lord Hailsham, told the House of Lords that about 70 per cent of the population had remained eligible "ever since the 1979 reforms" (25). He claimed that the result of reducing the allowances would be "practically unobservable" (25). The legal aid white paper, published in March 1987, states that "at present, it is estimated that some 70 per cent of households qualify for legal aid" (26). The change from population to households as the basis of calculation has not been explained. As larger households of families with children are less likely to be eligible for legal aid on income grounds than smaller pensioner or one-parent households, the white paper statement implies that considerably less than 70 per cent of the population is eligible for legal aid. Cyril Glasser suggests that the difference between population and households excludes 10 million people from the scheme (22).

In a written parliamentary answer in July 1987, the Attorney General stated:

> "It is not possible to calculate with precision the percentage of the population eligible for legal aid. The figure of 70 per cent, which has remained broadly constant throughout the past eight years, is an estimate only. It is based on a comparison between the qualifying levels of income for legal aid for different compositions of households and figures published by the Department of Employment for household incomes. This method has been used throughout the last eight years" (27).

It is difficult to understand why the figures should have remained constant despite the clear reduction in eligibility limits against both supplementary benefit and earnings and the calculations made by Cyril Glasser. It would appear that the government's figures are inaccurate.

In his evidence to the Public Accounts Committee in April 1986, the Lord Chancellor's Department Permanent Secretary, Sir Derek Oulton, acknowledged that "the calculations are, frankly, crude" (28). During the committee stage of the Legal Aid Bill, the Lord Chancellor, Lord Mackay, commented:

"If one uses households generally, still the best estimate that I have from the department is that 70 per cent of households are still covered. However, I would be the first to acknowledge... that these figures are very difficult to attach any real weight to at all, and I am not clear that there are very good figures that can be used for this purpose..." (29)

Calculating what proportion of the population is eligible for legal aid requires detailed and specific statistical information about income and expenditure in different population groups. This information is not available, even to government, on a routine basis. The figures in the 26th and 27th annual reports of the legal aid advisory committee, which formed the basis for the 1979 reforms, were collected in a special exercise by the DHSS. Since then, the task of calculating eligibility has become more complex—particularly because of a greater variation in housing expenses. No special exercises to estimate eligibility have been carried out since the mid-seventies. Such an exercise is needed.

The capital limits

Despite the absence of hard information, considerable concern has been expressed that the capital limits may operate unfairly towards people on low incomes with savings, particularly the elderly. The Royal Commission on Legal Services in Scotland recommended that capital should be wholly disregarded, while the Benson Commission thought that it should continue to be assessed but on very much more generous terms. The Opren case has brought the debate about capital limits to the fore. Out of 1,500 mostly elderly claimants, a third were excluded from the legal aid scheme, largely by the operation of the capital limits.

One problem is that capital limits have failed to keep pace with other social security means tested benefits. The 1988 upper limit of £5,000 is below the capital cut-off for income support (£6,000) and considerably below the cut-off for housing benefit (£8,000). The Lord Chancellor has specifically rejected any link between income support and legal aid limits:

"While I agree that it is useful to use changes in the qualifying limits for social security benefits as a starting point for considering changes in the legal aid limits, I do not accept that it is necessarily right that they should always coincide... Income support and legal aid are two entirely different things; and it does not necessarily follow that because one limit is right for income support it is necessarily right for legal aid. That is particularly true where capital is concerned. While it may well be unreasonable to expect someone to use up capital resources for everyday living—which is what the income support allowance is for—it may not be at all unreasonable to expect them to use that capital for one-off expense of particular legal proceedings'' (30).

Problems with the capital limits occur when elderly people are using relatively small amounts of carefully invested capital to supplement low incomes. In these circumstances funding litigation involves the risk of a permanent reduction in living standards. In 1984, in its 34th report, the Lord Chancellor's advisory committee commented on the operation of the civil legal aid capital limit:

"our chief concern, and the most common concern of those who submitted evidence to us, has been the plight of persons, particularly widows, on very low income who depend for much of that income on interest from investment capital. Though their resources are small, they may technically be ineligible for legal aid or be eligible only on payment of a large capital contribution, which will have the effect of diminishing an already exiguous future income.'' (31)

The committee suggested that where a person's earned income falls below the lower income limit the lower capital limit should be increased by the amount of capital necessary to generate an income equivalent to the deficiency.

The green form limits are particularly low. In 1978, the advisory committee commented:

"there is considerable evidence that people, particularly pensioners who have saved a little capital, are thereby taken outside the scope of the scheme, and we do not think that this was intended. Again we think that no smaller amount than exists for supplementary benefit purposes should be available here.'' (32)

This call has been echoed in subsequent reports.

Setting the level of contributions

Although twenty per cent of recipients make a contribution and seven per cent pay over £300 (2), contributions actually raise very little revenue. The Legal Aid Scrutiny Team estimated that in 1984-85, £10.4 million was collected, of which £7.5 million was retained. But net income, after allowing for the estimated cost of assessment and collection was only £4.9 million (6).

The Team argued that contributions should nevertheless be retained on three grounds. First, they enable the legal aid financial limit to be graduated, rather than have a single cut off point. Secondly, they do raise some funds, however limited, to be used elsewhere in the system. Thirdly, they impose financial discipline on applicants, by preventing them from proceeding with cases for which they would be unwilling to pay a reasonable amount of their own money.

In fact, the refusal rate for contributory offers is high. One in five applicants receiving an offer of contributory civil legal aid decides not to proceed with the case (6). Of those who do accept contributory offers, 29 per cent are in arrears (2). These figures suggest that the level of contributions may already be set too high.

The Scrutiny Team recommended that income contributions should be extended, so as to become payable throughout the case, rather than stop after the first year. The recommendation has been accepted by the government. The 1987 legal aid white paper states:

"The Government wishes to strengthen the incentives for applicants for legal aid and legal advice and assistance to consider the cost, both to the taxpayer and, potentially, to themselves, of the actions in which they are involved.

In line with this aim, the Government intends to make a change in the arrangements for collecting contributions towards civil legal aid. At the moment, applicants for civil legal aid are required to pay their contribution in 12 monthly instalments. If an applicant is assessed as being able to afford a particular amount each month, there is no reason why he should not continue contributing that amount throughout the case. This would bring legal aid into line with what happens in privately funded cases, and would instil in legally aided litigants a better sense of the cost of litigation" (26).

Provision for this change has been made in the Legal Aid Act 1988 (33). If an applicant's means change, the case may be reviewed, and no one will be asked to pay more than the costs of the case.

The Law Society's legal aid committee estimates that the average legal aid certificate runs for between two and two and a half years (34). Thus the effect of the government's proposal would be to double, or more than double, the amount of contributions applicants are asked to pay.

The statutory charge

For successful litigants, legal aid often acts as a loan rather than a grant. As far as possible, the legal aid fund seeks to recoup the legal costs paid out on an applicant's behalf, firstly from costs paid by the other side, secondly from contributions paid by the applicant, and thirdly, from any property which the applicant has "recovered or preserved" in the proceedings.

The last rule is known as the "statutory charge", and its effects are wide. It covers money, houses and other forms of property obtained through court orders and settlements in the proceeding for which legal aid has been granted, whether or not court action has been started. Where property is "in issue" in the case, and it is successfully claimed by the plaintiff, the property will be "recovered". Where the defendant successfully resists the claim, property has been "preserved" (35).

There are a number of exemptions from the statutory charge which are contained in regulation 96 of the Legal Aid (General) Regulations 1980. These include means tested benefits and awards (or settlements) from the employment appeal tribunal. All maintenance payments to spouses or children are exempt, as is the first £2,500 of lump sum payment in matrimonial and inheritance disputes.

Proponents of the statutory charge give two reasons for it. Firstly, it is said to mitigate some of the undoubted advantages given to legally aided clients in litigation, and to put them more into the position of non-legally aided litigants. It ensures, for example, that successful legally aided clients ask for their costs from the losing party and are subject to the same pressures as unaided clients to accept payments into court. Secondly, it is said to prevent "unreasonable conduct of legally aided litigation" (36).

The statutory charge operates very differently in matrimonial and non-matrimonial litigation. In 1986-87, in non-matrimonial cases, the statutory charge raised £3.79 million, an average of £121 in each case to which it applied. In matrimonial cases on the other hand, it raised £16.87 million, or an average of £712 per case charged (2). The reason for this difference is that in most successful non-matrimonial cases, the legal aid bill will be paid out of costs recouped from the other side (in unsuccessful cases, the charge cannot apply at all). The statutory charge will only come into play in a few circumstances; when there is a question of a payment-in, for example, or where the other side does not pay the costs awarded. The statutory charge may also apply when solicitors incur unusual expenses, by instructing leading counsel for instance. Even if the expense is approved by the legal aid fund, it will not necessarily be approved by the taxing master or registrar for payment by the losing party. If it is not paid by the other side, it would normally be paid for out of money recovered or preserved in the proceedings.

The most serious problems occur in matrimonial cases where costs are not automatically awarded against the losing party. In these circumstances, the statutory charge can operate harshly and arbitrarily. The consequences can be particularly severe when the property preserved or recovered is intended to provide a home in which the children can live. If the property is a house, the legal aid fund will not require the house to be sold by enforcing the charge straightaway. Instead, they will register the charge against the property and recoup the legal costs when the house is sold. Where a legally aided client wishes to sell the original house and buy another one, the legal aid fund has a discretion to substitute a charge on the new house for the original charge. Under guidelines issued by the Law Society, this will be considered where the second house is to be occupied by a child, or where it is necessary for the family to move for reasons of "health, disability or employment". There must be sufficient equity in the new house to cover the amount of the charge and the area committee must be satisfied that hardship would be caused if the substitution did not take place (36). The legal aid statistics for 1986-87 show that out of 38,425 registered charges held by the legal aid fund, substitutions were permitted in 135 cases. Most registered charges on property are paid within two years, with an average payment of £1,024 (2).

Until recently there was no possibility of a postponement where the assisted party receives not a house but a lump sum payment which is intended to provide the family with the resources to buy somewhere to live. The government has announced that this rule will be changed: the legal aid administration will be given a discretion to postpone the operation of the charge on lump sums. This change will be paid for by charging interest on postponed charges (both on houses and lump sums) at the mortgage rate.

Difficulties about the statutory charge are compounded by lack of information and explanation to clients. According to a Law Society leaflet "the operation of the legal aid charge, particularly in matrimonial proceedings, causes more misunderstanding than any other part of legal aid" (36). Some of these misunderstandings are revealed in a survey of divorced people in Newport and Bristol conducted in 1983. The researchers did not ask questions about the statutory charge but they found that divorcees often raised the subject, complaining that they had not been warned about the consequences (37). The following comments show the problems:

> "It came as a shock to me when, after I'd been forced to sell the house, the statutory charge applied and I had to pay back all the £5,800 legal aid fees... I wish that a little more attention could have been paid by my solicitor to my situation—he never emphasised how the statutory charge would affect me."

> "[The statutory charge] has only come to light recently... Only once I can remember I did ask him [the solicitor]. I said 'who will be paying for all this?'. He said 'the taxpayer'. That was the only time it was raised."

The Law Society has repeatedly stressed to solicitors that they must explain the effects of the statutory charge to clients, both at the start of the case, and before a settlement or final order is reached. In July 1985, they published a leaflet aimed at solicitors to explain the effect of the charge, stressing the need for a personal explanation to clients (36). The legal aid form also contains a tear-off slip which applicants are handed, explaining the effect of the statutory charge.

In divorce cases, the statutory charge will usually include the full costs of the proceedings, including disputes over custody and access. Thus partners who reach a reasonably quick settlement to sell the house, can end up paying for disputes over children out of the proceeds of the home. The following is an example of how one consumer viewed the matter.

> "People are led to believe that it's all on legal aid—until the property's sorted out. Then it comes as a hell of a shock, having to pay all that. And it was all through no fault of mine—I had to have a solicitor and a barrister because my husband had them and he was fighting to take my kids away. I had to pay £2,000..." (37).

The statutory charge can also distort the type of settlements reached. Maintenance payments are wholly exempt, and spouses may well be better off arguing for a maintenance order than for a lump sum. This flies in the face of the principle of a "clean break" between divorcing couples.

Conclusions

From this analysis, it is possible to identify a number of problems with the legal aid scheme from the consumer point of view. These include:
* lack of knowledge of the scheme;

* administrative delay;
* falling eligibility levels, coupled with increased contributions for those who are eligible;
* the harsh effect of the statutory charge in matrimonial litigation;
* an inadequate service in the field of social welfare law;
* fears of a possible reduction in services if solicitors withdraw from the scheme.

We describe these problems further in chapter 4, and discuss recommendations for reform.

References to chapter 3

1. *Report of the committee on legal aid and legal advice in England and Wales* (Rushcliffe Committee), Cmd 6641, HMSO, 1945. See also Abel-Smith, B. and Stevens, R., *Lawyers and the courts*, Heinemann, 1967.

2. *Legal aid*, 37th annual reports of the Law Society and the Lord Chancellor's advisory committee, 1986-87, HC 233, HMSO, 1988.

3. Legal Aid (General) Regulations 1980, regulations 68 and 74 (No. 1894).

4. Legal Aid (Financial Conditions) Regulations, April 1988 (No. 667).

5. Legal Aid (General) Regulations 1980, regulation 28 (No. 1894).

6. Lord Chancellor's Department, *Legal aid efficiency scrutiny*, 2 vols., June 1986.

7. Baldwin, J. and Hill, S., *The operation of the green form scheme in England and Wales*, Lord Chancellor's Department, March 1988.

8. See Kempson, E., *Welfare benefits work by non-statutory advice and law centres*, Acumen, 1986. It is estimated that in addition to the 1.2 million citizen advice bureaux enquiries, independent advice centres handled half a million cases; disablement information and advice lines gave welfare rights advice to 200,000 disabled people; advisory and young people's advisory services helped 24,000 young people with welfare benefits problems and law centres handled 5,000 cases in the field of welfare rights plus an unspecified number of general enquiries. There are also 65 local authority welfare rights services in the UK which give advice direct to the public, eight of which run full-time advice centres in England.

9. Estimates were compiled in 1986 by Elaine Kempson and are based on the annual reports provided by the Law Centres

Federation, National Association of Citizens Advice Bureaux, Shelter Housing Aid, United Kingdom Immigrants Advisory Service, and the Federation of Independent Advice Centres' database.

10. Figures produced by the Central Office of Industrial Tribunals show that of cases started, around eighty per cent result in a payment of compensation; see "Industrial tribunals in England and Wales: fact sheet", March 1986. If one assumes that 80 per cent of all queries result in a payment, this gives a total of 100,000 cases dealt with under the green form scheme.

11. Office of Fair Trading, *Annual Report of the Director General of Fair Trading 1987*, HC 6, HMSO, 1988.

12. Harris, D. and others, *Compensation and support for illness and injury*, Clarendon Press, Oxford Socio-legal Studies, 1984.

13. School for Advanced Urban Studies, University of Bristol, *Study of housing cases, final report to the Lord Chancellor's Department*, produced for the Civil Justice Review, Lord Chancellor's Department, 1987.

14. Personal communication with the Law Society.

15. Wood, G., "The effectiveness of legal aid publicity brought out by the Law Society", unpublished MSc thesis, Department of Information Science, City University, September 1987.

16. *Legal aid*, 36th annual reports of the Law Society and the Lord Chancellor's advisory committee, 1985-86, HC 87, HMSO, 1987.

17. Blacksell, M. and others, *Solicitors and access to legal services in rural areas; evidence from Devon and Cornwall*, Access to justice in rural Britain project, working paper 6, University of Exeter, 1986.

18. Law Society, *Survey of legal aid provision*, April 1988.

19. This section is based on an unpublished background paper, Hansen, O., "Legal aid eligibility", commissioned by the National Consumer Council in 1987.

20. *Legal Aid*, 26th annual reports of the Law Society and the Lord Chancellor's advisory committee 1975-76, HC 12, HMSO, 1977.

21. *Employment Gazette*, April 1988.

22. Glasser, C., "Legal aid eligibility", *Law Society Gazette*, 9 March 1988, pp.11-13.

23. *Legal aid*, 27th annual reports of the Law Society and the Lord Chancellor's advisory committee, 1976-77, HC 172, HMSO, 1978.

24. *Hansard*, 26 January 1983, col. 428.

25. *Hansard*, 18 March 1986, col. 921.

26. *Legal aid in England and Wales: a new framework*, Cm 118, HMSO, March 1987.
27. *Hansard*, 13 July 1987, col. 316.
28. House of Commons Committee of Public Accounts, *Minutes of evidence*, Lord Chancellor's Department, HC 330-i, HMSO 1986.
29. *Hansard*, 14 January 1988, col. 1365.
30. *Hansard*, 18 January 1988, col. 70.
31. *Legal Aid*, 34th annual reports of the Law Society and the Lord Chancellor's advisory committee 1983-84, HC 151, HMSO, 1985.
32. *Legal Aid*, 28th annual reports of the Law Society and the Lord Chancellor's advisory committee 1977-78, HC 5, HMSO, 1978.
33. Legal Aid Act 1988 section 16.
34. *Legal Aid*, 35th annual reports of the Law Society and the Lord Chancellor's advisory committee, 1984-85, HC 156, HMSO, 1986.
35. Legal Aid Act 1974 section 9 (6).
36. *Legal aid handbook*, HMSO, 1986, pp.253-274.
37. Davis, G. and Bader, K., "Client costs: a failure to inform", *Legal Action*, February 1985, pp.9-11, and "The legal aid clawback", *Legal Action*, April 1985, pp.7-8.

Chapter 4
Legal aid: proposals for reform

The Legal Aid Act 1988 establishes a new Legal Aid Board to administer publicly funded legal services, with a view to "helping persons who might otherwise be unable to obtain advice, assistance or representation on account of their means" (1). The immediate effects of the 1988 Act are small, but it provides an opportunity for radical reforms of the legal aid system in the future. The Lord Chancellor has commented that "the change to the Board will provide an opportunity for some rigorous and adventurous thinking about the organisation and administration of the scheme" (2). In this chapter we take advantage of the opportunity. First we look at the strengths and weaknesses of the present system; secondly we describe the government's own proposals; lastly we put forward our own recommendations for reform including our proposals for expanding the role of the advice services.

Strengths and weaknesses of the present system

Along with other Western European countries, Britain has adopted what the Americans call a "judicare" system of legal aid. In their international survey of access to justice, Cappelletti and Garth describe "judicare" as:

> "a system whereby legal aid is established as *a matter of right* for all persons eligible under the statutory terms, with *the state paying the private lawyer* who provides those services. The goal of judicare systems is to provide the same representation for low income litigants that they would have if they could afford a lawyer. The idea is to make a distinction only with respect to the billing: the state, rather than the client, is charged the cost." (3).

This is different from a salaried system, in which lawyers are employed specifically to provide a service to the less affluent. According to Cappelletti and Garth, the English and Welsh legal aid system compares relatively well with the "judicare" systems of other countries. It is relatively long established (4); has extended eligibility limits beyond the poor; and provides the consumer with a wide choice of solicitor, with over 11,500 offices taking part in the scheme (5).

They comment: "its results have been impressive: aid over the years has been given to steadily increasing numbers of persons" (3). In 1986-7 around one and a quarter million people received help with civil legal matters (5).

Despite the many strengths of the legal aid scheme in England and Wales, the analysis in chapter 3 revealed a number of weaknesses from the consumer's point of view.

The first problem is **lack of knowledge** about the scheme. Research studies suggest that a significant number of people with problems do not know that help is available. This is a significant factor in preventing people from seeking legal advice.

The second problem is **administrative delay**. It now takes an average of 17 weeks to issue a contributory certificate, during which time work on the case is delayed (5). This is an unacceptable wait.

The third problem is **falling eligibility**. Fewer people are eligible for help with their legal costs, and those who are eligible are paying more. The government's policy towards uprating the income and capital limits is inconsistent. Its figures do not enable it to ensure that a given proportion of the population is covered by the scheme; the limits are not uprated in line with earnings; and the Lord Chancellor has recently rejected an overt link with supplementary benefit or income support levels (6). Without any clear commitment to uprate the means test, we fear that eligibility for legal aid will continue to fall, and the service will fail to help those of moderate means.

The fourth problem is the **statutory charge** in matrimonial litigation. Consumers are often unprepared for the size of the charge, which may seriously affect the parties' ability to provide a home for their children. It may also distort the settlements that are reached.

Fifthly, there are fears that the **number of solicitors participating in the scheme may fall**, leading to reduced availability. This is a particular problem for matrimonial work. The situation requires monitoring.

The sixth problem is more fundamental and is one which is inherent in all "judicare" systems. Legal aid **fails to provide a service in areas of social welfare law**. It does not give the poor and deprived accessible help in those fields of law which are of most concern to them, such as social security, housing, debt, employment and immigration. Although legal aid aims to overcome the cost barrier, it does not overcome any of the other barriers which people encounter in using lawyers. It does very little to inform people of their legal rights, and it does not prevent them from being intimidated by the idea of going into a solicitor's office. Few solicitors' offices are located in deprived areas where the poor have most need of them, and solicitors receive little training in social welfare law. The problem is circular—the poor do not think of using a lawyer for advice with their problems, hence lawyers do not develop skill and expertise in these areas, and a service is not available for those wishing to use it.

Tables 3.1, 3.2 and 3.3 show that the legal aid scheme is dominated by traditional areas of lawyers' practise such as matrimonial and personal injuries work. Although welfare benefit and debt cases are growing fast, the numbers of people helped in social welfare law under the green form scheme are tiny in comparison with those helped by advice centres.

The problem is compounded by the fact that legal aid does not cover representation before the majority of tribunals, including industrial tribunals, and both first and second tier tribunals dealing with social security and immigration. Solicitors' experience in this area is likely to be confined to representing employers in unfair dismissal and redundancy cases. Without the experience of seeing cases through, they rarely give advice about these matters under the green form scheme. The idea is perpetuated that social security and immigration are not proper "legal work". In preliminary research carried out into the green form scheme one solicitor commented on this dilemma:

> "The issue was raised in 1984 about whether welfare benefit work or immigration work was proper solicitors' work. It's related to the question of why solicitors don't do certain types of work. It becomes a self-defining and self-perpetuating definition which rests entirely upon the status quo: it's proper solicitor's work because solicitors do it." (7).

In 1977, the National Consumer Council published *Why the poor pay more* which looked at ways in which the poor received less value for money from both private and public services (8). We concluded that despite the legal aid scheme, legal services were not readily available to the poor. The poor lived in neighbourhoods with a smaller choice of solicitor, and solicitors had less knowledge of the areas of law that most concern them. The poor had little access to information about their legal rights, and were unlikely to be familiar with using a solicitor's office. There was little empirical evidence on whether legally aided clients received a service of equivalent standard to fee-paying clients, but it was likely that the ignorant and inarticulate demanded and received less from their solicitors. The legal aid scheme of itself did little to address inequalities in knowledge or use, or to encourage solicitors to provide new services. We concluded that there was a need to make lawyers more accessible through salaried services in law centres and community agencies.

Although the detail has changed in the last twelve years, we consider that the essential analysis of *Why the poor pay more* continues to apply to legal services provision.

The salaried model

An alternative approach to a "judicare system" is what Cappelletti describes as the "public salaried attorney model" of legal aid (3). This system of providing legal aid for the poor has been pioneered in the United States of America. Cappelletti describes the objectives of the Legal Services Programme which was first introduced in the USA in 1965:

> "Legal services were to be provided by 'neighbourhood law offices', staffed with attorneys paid by the government, and charged with furthering the interests of the poor as a class. As one commentator observed, 'The objective was to use taxpayers' money in the most cost-effective way—to obtain, in Department of Defense terminology "the most bang for the buck"...' In contrast to existing judicare systems... this system tends to be characterized by major efforts to make poor people aware of their new rights and willing to use lawyers to help pursue them. In addition, offices were small and typically located in poor communities to facilitate contact with the poor and to minimize the barriers of class. Attorneys were supposed to learn firsthand about these barriers and thus be able to attack them more effectively. Finally, and perhaps above all, the staff attorneys sought to extend the rights of the poor by test cases, lobbying and other law reform activities on behalf of the poor as a class." (3).

This approach has many advantages. The law office can take an active approach to informing people of their rights. Salaried lawyers can become experts in the problems that most affect the poor, and are able to offer a more skilled service. Such schemes do not suffer from the administrative problems involved in making payment on a case by case basis. Many advice centres use volunteers to keep down unit costs, and are quick to explore the most cost-effective means of providing services. They do this by producing self-help leaflets for simple problems, by educational work, by working through community groups and by advising several people with the same problem at the same time.

The North American experience shows that there are also some disadvantages. Campaigning and lobbying activities may become associated with a particular political viewpoint and law offices are therefore vulnerable to political changes. Individuals cannot be given an entitlement to legal assistance with their particular case: instead, lawyers decide on a day-to-day basis how to allocate their scarce resources. Lawyers may pursue the "glamorous" test case at the expense of important but mundane matters.

Since 1975, the American Legal Services Corporation has moved towards a mixed system for delivering legal services to the poor. Instead of relying entirely on staff attorneys, many more projects now involve private practice. A major research study completed in 1980 demonstrated the need for local flexibility in providing services. It measured services against four criteria—cost, client satisfaction, quality and "impact". "Impact" was defined in terms of improvements or avoidance of deterioration in the living conditions of significant segments of the eligible population. Schemes which combined staff attorneys with private practice scored well, while pure judicare systems failed the "impact" measure (9).

In Britain, law centres have more or less consciously emulated the American "staff attorney" model. But the advice sector in England and Wales is more varied than in the United States and there are many different models of what an advice centre should be like. The advice sector as a whole has not become associated with any particular political viewpoint, which has made it much more resilient to political change. Nor have advice centres in England and Wales been dominated by lawyers: volunteers and lay people have played the major part. One result is that advice centres have dealt with a large number of routine cases in addition to glamorous test cases.

The advantages of a mixed delivery system were recognised by the Rushcliffe Committee. It wished to see legal advice provided by a salaried service run by the Law Society. In 1970, the advisory committee's proposal for the green form scheme also included a salaried "advisory liaison service" to supplement private practice. Although both these proposals were incorporated in legislation, financial constraints meant that the proposals were never implemented. Despite the many strengths of the British advice network, it has never been recognised as an integral part of legal services provision, nor has it received funding on a national, long-term basis.

The government's proposals on legal aid

The Scrutiny Team's proposals for reform

The present reforms originated in the report of the Efficiency Scrutiny Team. In 1986 four officials from the Treasury and Lord Chancellor's Department carried out a 90-day investigation of the legal aid scheme and their report was published in June 1986 (10). Their most radical proposal was that there should be a reappraisal of the relationship between private solicitors working under the green form scheme and the advice sector. They concluded that the present arrangements do not work well:

"In particular, they do not ensure equal access to advice nor do they make effective use of the resources available. There is a real danger that problem areas are not fully explored before specialist advice is given on a particular aspect of a case. CAB advisers are trained to interview clients and to establish precisely the areas on which advice is needed, but that is not always the case with solicitors. Some solicitors do not communicate well with their clients, and we have heard from a number of CABx that they frequently deal with enquiries from clients who could not understand the advice given by their solicitor. Furthermore, there are some areas of law—particularly welfare benefit and housing matters—where expertise is concentrated in CABx and other advice agencies rather than among private practitioners." (10).

They recommended a new relationship between advice agencies and solicitors in giving initial advice. They suggested that:

★ publicly funded advice under the green form scheme from solicitors should no longer be available for wills, probate, conveyancing, defamation and non-imprisonable offences;

★ advice on other criminal matters should continue to be directly available from a solicitor in private practice;

★ in family matters, initial advice should be provided by an advice centre rather than a private solicitor. The advice centre would give advice on housing and welfare benefits, outline what the courts are likely to decide about maintenance, property and the children, and tell clients about local conciliation services. The centre should then refer clients to a private solicitor to provide detailed advice, negotiation and representation under the legal

>   aid scheme. For clients not on state benefits there would be a £10
>   fee to consult a solicitor about family matters;
>
> ★   in all other areas of civil law, all initial advice should be provided
>   through an advice centre. Clients would only be referred to
>   private practitioners once it became clear that court proceedings
>   should be started. Clients who go direct to a solicitor for full legal
>   aid without first obtaining advice from an advice centre would be
>   charged a £10 fee.

The Scrutiny Team estimated that these changes would free around
£25 million from the green form budget. The same quantity of advice
could be provided by solicitors and trained lay advisers working in
advice agencies for around £16 million. Legal aid area directors would
be provided with a budget to spend on advice centres in their own
area. The Team envisaged that they would seek tenders from citizens
advice bureaux, from other advice centres and from consortiums of
local solicitors to provide the best service for the money available. The
remaining £9 million could be put into providing better tribunal
representation and an out-of-hours advisory service through the
advice network (10).

The legal aid scheme would no longer be providing legal advice
exclusively through private practices. It would therefore be
inappropriate to leave the administration with the Law Society. The
Team recommended establishing a new Legal Services Board which
would be responsible for strengthening the advice sector and for
administering the legal aid scheme to private practice.

The National Consumer Council, together with most lawyers and
advice centres, was critical of many of these proposals (11). The
scheme to provide green form advice through advice centres would
only work if there was a well-provided general advice centre in every
area. The additional funding proposed by the report was intended to
enable advice centres to provide an additional service, replacing
specifically legal advice currently provided by solicitors under the
green form scheme. It would not have turned the existing patchy
provision of advice centres into a national network covering all areas.
The Team criticised the lack of co-ordination of the work of advice
agencies where "the availability of suitable advice depends very much
on where a client lives or can reach easily" (10). Yet the report did
not directly challenge existing government policy which states that
advice services are a matter for local government and local priorities.
It was not intended that the Legal Services Board would replace
existing funders. Instead there was a real danger that the Board would

become yet another player in the game of "pass the parcel" through which advice centres are currently funded.

There was a widespread fear that provision of advice agencies would be inadequate and that long waiting lists would develop. The requirement that consumers should visit an advice centre before seeing a lawyer would become a way of rationing access to the legal aid scheme. In rural areas, consumers would have to make unnecessary journeys to the advice centre in a large town before they were allowed to see a local solicitor.

We do not consider that it is right to separate initial advice from court work. In personal injury work, for example, very few people visit an advice centre before seeing a solicitor. The Oxford Centre for Socio-legal Studies Compensation Study found that most referrals were made by trade unions, or by the victim's family or friends. Out of 248 people, only four had been referred to a solicitor by a citizens advice bureau (12). Although we wish to see more information about the right to claim damages, this is not exclusively a matter for advice centres. Accident victims should continue to be able to go direct to a solicitor's office.

In the field of family law there are difficulties in expecting advice workers to give accurate advice on the approach courts are likely to take to property, custody and access matters when they have no direct experience of representing clients in court. Social security and housing matters are often integral to a matrimonial dispute. There are real dangers if solicitors consider that these have all been dealt with in the initial interview, and they need no longer take them into account in negotiating a divorce settlement. In our view, the divide between matters best handled by an advice centre and those which should be handled by a private solicitor is dictated not by the stage the case has reached but by the type of problem.

Nevertheless, despite these criticisms of the detailed proposals, there is a strong case for re-examining the relationship between advice centres and legal aid provided through private practice. We support the basic premise that in some areas of law, advice and assistance can be provided better, more cheaply and in a more accessible way through advice centres than through solicitors in private practice.

The white paper

The Scrutiny report was followed by a white paper, published in March 1987 (13). The government decided that it was no longer appropriate for the legal aid scheme to be administered by the Law Society, and that a new board should be set up. While the Scrutiny

Team recommended a "Legal Services Board", the white paper talked of a "Legal Aid Board". It describes the Board in the following terms:

> "The Board will act under the Guidance of the Lord Chancellor. The Lord Chancellor will appoint the Chairman and members, who will act in a non-executive capacity, and will concur in the appointment of some key staff in senior positions. The Board will comprise both lawyers and non-lawyers, all of whom will be chosen for their particular experience and skills." (13).

The Board begins by taking over the functions currently carried out by the Law Society. It is envisaged that in the future it will assume other functions, including the assessment of means currently carried out by the Department of Social Security.

The government was attracted to the idea of providing more legal services through the advice sector but it rejected the specific proposals on advice put forward by the Scrutiny Team. The white paper outlines the following proposals:

> "The Government believes that the present green form scheme can be improved to provide better service at lower cost. The Government is attracted to the principle of using the skills of advice agencies, especially to deal with those areas of work in which their special experience is likely to be greater than that of many solicitors in private practice...

> "The Government will require the Board, as an early task, to consider the most cost-effective way of providing advice and assistance, including specifically whether better arrangements might be made by making use of advice agencies. Once the Board has set up suitable arrangements for contracting with agencies and other organisations for the provision of advice in the specified areas of work—for instance, advice on welfare benefits—these will be excluded altogether from the green form scheme. The detailed arrangements could well involve tenders being sought for the provision of advice in the geographical areas covered by the Board's area offices, and the form of coverage may well be different in different geographical areas." (13)

According to the white paper there would be no general extension of publicly funded tribunal representation, at least until research into the effectiveness of representation at tribunals is completed. This research is being carried out by Queen Mary College and is due to be completed in March 1989 (14).

The Legal Aid Act 1988

The white paper was followed by legislation, introduced into the House of Lords in December 1987. The main provision is part II section 3, which establishes a board of between 11 and 17 people, appointed by the Lord Chancellor. Two members must be solicitors, appointed after consultation with the Law Society. The new Board is charged with administering the present scheme and is expected to advise the Lord Chancellor on improvements. The Lord Chancellor has commented that the second task is of "extreme importance" (15). The Legal Aid Act does not lay down a blueprint for the reform of legal aid; instead it is "for the board, in consultation with all who have an interest, to look at all the possibilities and to come up with workable, worthwhile proposals" (15).

In the short term, the Board is to take over the administration of legal aid from the Law Society. In the longer term it may be responsible for other aspects of administration, such as the means test. The Lord Chancellor described the relationship between the Board and the Department in the following terms:

> "The Legal Aid Board is not going to be free to do what it likes, when it likes and how it likes with the legal aid scheme, any more than the present legal aid administration has that kind of freedom. The Government will continue to set the broad framework of the legal aid arrangements and will retain their present role over such matters as financial eligibility limits" (16).

Section 16 permits the Lord Chancellor to extend contributions throughout the duration of the case. The government also retains control over fees to be paid to lawyers.

Section 4 gives the Board wide powers to provide advice, assistance or representation "by means of contracts with, or grants or loans to, other persons or bodies". Different arrangements may be made in different areas in England and Wales and in different fields of law. These powers may only be exercised if the Lord Chancellor so directs. The Act appears to go further than the white paper by including representation as well as advice and assistance in these provisions. The Lord Chancellor has explained that it will allow the Board to take over the funding of those seven law centres presently supported by the Lord Chancellor's Department, and will enable those law centres to continue to represent clients. He states that there is also a second reason:

> "if at some stage in the future (and I must emphasise that we have no current plans for this) publicly-funded representation were to be

extended to more tribunals, it might well be more convenient for the same agency that has provided advice also to provide representation." (15)

Section 35 retains the legal aid advisory committee, at least for the time being. Its position will be reviewed after the first year.

Our recommendations

The National Consumer Council welcomes the opportunity to re-examine the relationship between private practice and the advice sector. In this section we make recommendations to improve the provision of both generalist and specialist advice, and to improve the legal aid scheme. These fall into three parts:

★ the first priority is to increase the provision of generalist advice, so that everyone has access to a local centre, offering basic advice on any query raised. This must be done as an addition to, rather than as a substitute for, legal aid. We see general advice as useful in itself and as a vital point of contact with the legal system. We estimate how much it would cost to extend the existing network to provide a national service, and look at how responsibilities for advice should be allocated;

★ when a network of general advice centres exists across the country, there are advantages in providing specialist advice and representation in such fields as social security, housing, debt counselling and consumer problems through salaried and voluntary services rather than through legal aid to private practice. Although this can be partially financed by savings in the legal aid budget, services must be provided on the basis of need rather than on what is currently spent through legal aid. Specialist centres are cost-effective but they are not necessarily cheaper than private practice, because by being more accessible, they generate greater demands for their services;

★ we wish to see private solicitors continue to provide a service through legal aid in the traditional areas they do best, such as matrimonial law and personal injury work. Solicitors give a widely available service, offering a good choice to consumers. We examine the changes which we wish to see the Board implement to improve the civil legal aid scheme for consumers.

Access to general advice centres

In our view, the first priority is to ensure that everyone has access to a general advice centre, rooted in the local community. These should provide information, leaflets, advice, practical assistance and mediation on a wide range of different issues.

In 1977 we described the right to information and advice as the "fourth right of citizenship". We commented that:

> "People will not be able to get their due as citizens of present day society unless they have continuous access to the information which will guide them through it, and where necessary the advice to help them translate that information into effective action; and unless they get their due they are unlikely to recognise the reciprocal obligation that all citizens have to society" (17).

If the right to information and advice is regarded as a right of citizenship, it follows that advice should be available to everyone, irrespective of means, class, or race. It is true that, in practice, the poor and disadvantaged have a greater need for advice, and make greater use of advice centres than the more prosperous middle-classes. However, we do not see advice services as a service for the poor alone. The middle-classes are less likely to have problems with housing or welfare benefits but when they do have problems they still need advice about their rights and obligations. According to the survey of users of citizens advice bureaux in Greater London, five per cent of users had household incomes of over £200 per week, which represents over 54,000 enquiries from such people in London per year (18).

In an increasingly complex society, the need for information and advice becomes greater. Changes in legislation concerning social security and housing have created enormous needs for information and advice. The courts, the Office of Fair Trading and the Department of Social Security increasingly rely on advice centres to inform people of their rights: their leaflets frequently tell people to consult a citizens advice bureau or local advice centre for more information. People who do not have a local centre are left high and dry and find it increasingly difficult to use services, find out their rights or gain access to justice.

General advice centres act as access points for specialist centres, sorting out which queries need specialist advice and which do not and referring people to the appropriate place. Sometimes clients will be given an appointment to see a specialist within the centre, at other times staff will contact a regional resource centre for more advice on dealing with the problem themselves, and some clients will be referred to a separate specialist centre. Without general advice centres, there is a danger that specialist centres will use their scarce resources dealing with mundane enquiries and consumers will be baffled about where to turn.

Costing general advice

It is not easy to define the amount of advice people need. It often appears to be infinite—the better the service that is offered, the greater the demands made upon it. Academics have stressed the difficulties of defining "legal need" in objective terms and have pointed out that the level of resources devoted to legal and advice services must be a matter of political judgement.

We agree that the question of what amounts to an adequate level of service must be decided by a debate between consumers, tax payers, advice providers and politicians at both local and national level. However it is a debate which should be based on objective research into existing patterns of need and use.

For this reason, in 1986 we published a discussion document, *Good advice for all*, which sets out guidelines on standards for local advice services (19). The report envisages a service based on a network of general neighbourhood advice centres able to offer advice, practical assistance and mediation on a wide range of subjects. In practice, the majority of enquiries will relate to social security, housing, fuel, consumer, money and family matters. The precise way in which these centres work will reflect the communities they serve. In densely populated areas it is likely that there will be a range of different centres, including citizens advice bureaux and other independent advice centres. Where there is a sufficiently high level of need, some workers will concentrate on the advice needs of specific groups such as young people, disabled people, and members of particular ethnic communities. The staff may work for a general advice centre, from a community centre which meets other non-advice needs of a particular group, or from an agency, such as a disablement information and advice line, which concentrates on providing advice to a particular group.

Good advice for all was based on research evidence collected about the level and pattern of use of advice centres in a range of different geographical locations—inner city, urban, market town, and rural. We chose centres which were relatively well provided for and were acknowledged to be examples of good current practice. We looked at the catchment areas they served, and the demand which was generated from within the catchment area. We also studied the level of service which could be provided by given staffing levels. This enabled us to publish suggested standards for staff and access points per population, to serve as a basis for further discussion. A very similar exercise was carried out for public libraries in 1962 and most libraries now meet the required standard (20).

The research showed that the nearer consumers live to the centre, the more likely they are to use it. Half of the users of general advice centres live within half a mile of the centre and only ten per cent of users travel more than two miles. The catchment area of advice centres is very similar to that of public libraries. As a general principle, neighbourhood advice agencies serve a catchment area of up to one mile radius, though in less densely populated communities this increases to two miles. Rural areas, which cannot support part-time advice centres, need special provision, such as mobile centres, telephone services, outreach workers or village contacts (19).

Good advice for all recommends that there should be one generalist advice worker (paid or unpaid) for every 4,000 people. In deprived or low-income areas, sparsely populated areas, and areas with large black and ethnic minority communities, additional staff are needed. The levels also need to be reviewed to take into account social changes and changes in legislation.

The level of staffing envisaged in our report is much greater than the number of people presently working in advice centres in either a paid or an unpaid capacity. In her 1986 survey of advice provision Elaine Kempson estimates that as of September 1986 there were 4,300 paid or unpaid full-time equivalent staff working in citizens advice bureaux, independent advice centres, youth counselling and advice centres and Dial groups (21). Taking *Good advice for all* staffing levels and allowing that 15 per cent of the population live in areas requiring additional resources (25 per cent above the basic level), we calculate that a total of 12,810 staff would be required in England and Wales. This leaves a shortfall of 8,510 (22). Overall, the number of generalist advice staff is a third of the number we recommend but some parts of the country are much worse off than others. Fifteen shire counties and eleven metropolitan districts and boroughs have less than a fifth of the recommended staffing levels (21).

In 1986 we used these figures to calculate the cost of implementing the guidelines (22). We estimate that 38 per cent of the work in general advice centres is currently carried out by unpaid staff and we assume that this proportion of voluntary work will continue. On the basis of salary levels recommended in *Good advice for all* and allowing 50 per cent on-costs to cover premises, equipment and training, we calculated a total additional expenditure in England and Wales of £70 million, compared with an estimated £25 million currently spent. If one assumes that the new staff will be employed on existing salary levels, with the current on-costs of around 43 per cent, expenditure is estimated at £50 million (22).

Although these figures appear large when compared with what is currently spent on advice, they are very small in comparison with other areas of local government expenditure: £480 million on arts and public libraries, and £2,738 million on social services in England (23). The figures are also much lower than the estimates of staffing costs used by the Scrutiny Team, which were based on civil service expenditure levels. Advice is very good value for money, relying as it does on extensive voluntary effort, and cost-effective, non-bureaucratic methods of working.

Our resource guidelines are not the final word on the service that should be implemented, or the amount that should be spent. But they do provide the best available empirical evidence on the cost of a national network of generalist advice. In our view, extending generalist advice is a priority. We recommend that resources should be found within the lifetime of this parliament.

Responsibility for general advice

In our view, general advice is a service in its own right. Although it is often vital in providing access to legal services, it is not in itself a part of the legal aid system. The service is currently suffering through disputes about who is responsible for funding it. Resolving who is responsible will require legislation. We consider that the responsibility should be placed on local authorities, who already provide the bulk of the funding. They should be enabled to do this through specific ear-marked grants from central government.

We wish to see local authorities provide grants to advice centres which are managed independently of the local authority. Local authority run centres can be a useful part of advice provision, especially in areas such as social security or consumer law where the local authority is not a party to the dispute. But local authority agencies are not a substitute for independent centres and they are not used in the same way for the same type of problems. In our view everyone should have access to a centre which is independent of the local authority. It is unusual for a local authority to be given a statutory duty to fund a service that it does not manage but we do not think that this would cause insuperable problems.

We have considered whether responsibility should be placed on counties or on district authorities. It is important that responsibilities are clearly allocated and disputes between authorities reduced. Counties are better placed to plan a service, by consulting existing centres, assessing advice needs, and encouraging local initiatives. On the other hand, district authorities presently provide the bulk of funds to generalist centres. The catchment area of general advice centres is relatively small, and it is important that every district should have one. On balance, our view is that the responsibility for generalist advice should be placed on district councils. Counties should be given a power to provide additional funding, but should not be under any duty to do so.

It is important that general advice should be accessible to the most disadvantaged groups. Disabled and housebound people are often in the greatest need of advice, and yet they have the most problems visiting and queuing at an advice centre. Research by the Greater London Citizens Advice Bureaux Service showed that young people, aged under 20, are under-represented among the users of traditional advice centres (18). It also showed that members of ethnic minorities have a particularly high need for advice. Advice should be provided in the languages spoken by users. We recommend that local authorities should pay special regard to the needs of disadvantaged groups in their areas when deciding what type of provision to make.

In order to improve advice provision it is vital that central government should advise and encourage local authorities in their task and provide them with financial assistance. This means that a decision must be taken about which central government department is responsible for advice. There are several possible candidates—the Department of the Environment, the Department of Trade and Industry, and the Lord Chancellor's Department, but none have been anxious to take on the task. The Lord Chancellor's Department would appear to be the most logical candidate in order to integrate the provision of legal services. On the other hand, the Lord Chancellor's Department has never seen itself as a major spending department and has little experience of working with local government. A decision is required by central government.

The central government department selected should endorse resource standards to act as a guide about the level of service required. We trust that *Good advice for all* will act as a basis for further discussion and research. We do not see the resource standards as mandatory, at least at first. But the standards should offer clear guidance to local authorities about what they are expected to achieve.

Once minimum resources have been provided, it becomes possible to measure the output of services, rather than the input of resources. There is a need for the financial management of advice centres to be monitored by funders to see that the public is getting good value for money. The first step is to set clear objectives for the centre. The next step is to gather a range of statistics rather than relying on crude overall numbers of enquiries. These may include figures on the level and type of enquiries, on who uses the centre, and on the policy comment and research work which has been carried out. In some cases, independent researchers could be asked to assess the views of clients and others in the community about the work of the centre and how it could be developed.

Specialist advice

Once a network of general advice centres exists across the country, it can be used to provide access to specialist advice and representation provided by salaried staff and volunteers rather than by solicitors in private practices. In many fields of social welfare law there are advantages to providing specialist assistance in this way. The advice sector can take a more active role in informing people of their rights; advice centres are more likely to be used; they have greater skills in social welfare law; and they have developed more cost-effective ways of handling large numbers of cases. There are also significant administrative savings if applications do not have to be approved and payments made on a case by case basis. We look at each of the main advice areas in turn: social security, housing possession, debt, consumer, employment and immigration law.

★ social security

The case for specialist advice through advice centres is clearest in the field of social security. Very few solicitors have any skills in this area, and the number of cases undertaken through the green form scheme (29,000) is tiny compared with around two million cases handled through existing advice centres (24). Few people think of seeking advice from a solicitor about benefit problems and our advertising survey found that only two per cent of advertisements mentioned welfare benefits or social security as an area of work which solicitors were willing to undertake (25).

The service that can be provided under the legal aid scheme excludes representation before tribunals—even before the social security commissioners, who hear appeals from social security appeal tribunals on points of law. Yet the evidence suggests that representation at the tribunal significantly increases the claimant's chance of success. According to the social security statistics for 1986, claimants who neither attend nor are represented before a social security appeal tribunal have a 9 per cent success rate; claimants who attend on their own are successful in 32 per cent of cases; where a representative attends without the claimant, the success rate rises to 37 per cent, and in cases where both the claimant and representative attend the success rate is 51 per cent (26). Partly this is because representatives "weed out" cases with very little chance of success (itself a useful function), but this is not the whole story. In an experiment in Wandsworth, representatives were offered to all claimants coming before the tribunal. The success rate increased from 18 to 29 per cent, at a time when the comparative national success rate for represented clients was 32 per cent (27).

Social security tribunals decide cases on the basis of detailed regulation, rather than because they believe there to be a genuine need. Yet research in Birmingham found that over half the appellants did not understand that decisions would be made on this basis. None of the 54 people interviewed understood the case papers they had been sent before the hearing and six people found the case papers so daunting that they had stopped even trying to read them (28). Since the research was conducted, single payment appeals have been abolished, but the rest of the appeal system remains intact.

Ideally, the procedure before tribunals should be sufficiently clear and simple to allow people to represent themselves, after receiving advice and assistance about their case. But however much tribunals are improved, not everyone will be able to represent themselves. Representation before social security appeal tribunals should be available both for complex cases and for those applicants who find it particularly hard to speak for themselves. Representation should also be available as of right before the social security commissioners, where all cases turn on disputed points of law. There are relatively few cases: in 1986 the commissioners heard 1,782 appeals, compared with around 90,000 cases decided by social security appeal tribunals (29).

★ housing possession

In their 34th report the legal aid advisory committee drew attention to a number of lay representation schemes which operated within the county court to give advice and representation to tenants and borrowers at risk of losing their homes (30). These included a scheme which trained lay volunteers in Bristol and Manchester, a welfare officer employed in Birmingham county court and duty representative schemes run by law centres and citizens advice bureaux in Coventry.

Representation by a solicitor through legal aid is available where it might not be reasonable for the court to make an order. Yet there are many advantages to representation offered through advice centres and lay organisations. Representatives who are present at the court see people who would not normally make their way into a solicitor's office; lay advisers often take a wider view of the problems and offer much needed skills in debt counselling and the welfare system; and representation can be offered much more cost-effectively to many more people. The lay schemes described by the advisory committee were also able to bring general problems to the attention of the local authorities and the courts, and worked with them to improve their procedures. We wish to see an extension of representation schemes using lay advisers, though there is a case for continuing representation under the legal aid scheme where the defendant has a defence involving a point of law.

★ debt

Debt is one of the fastest growing problems of the 1980s. The credit society which has brought benefits for many has been characterised by a growing toll of casualties, as fuel debts, rent, rates and mortgage arrears and consumer debts increase (31). Although the number of hire-purchase and debt cases dealt with under the green form scheme has increased from 52,392 to 57,529 over the last year (5), this is a drop in the ocean. It is advice centres which have responded to the growing need. In 1982 we identified 16 money advice services (32); by 1986 the Policy Studies Institute identified nearly one hundred services, ranging from specialist agencies to single specialist workers employed in other types of service. They counted around one hundred and ninety staff working in the field (33).

The Policy Studies Institute report demonstrated that in-depth advice to multiple debtors is labour intensive, taking an average of one and a half days work, spread over nine months to a year. The help provided by money advisers goes further than the help given by solicitors under the green form scheme. It involves defending clients against immediate sanctions, ensuring that debtors are receiving all the benefit due to them, drawing up an expenditure plan, and negotiating a stable repayment plan with creditors. Where court proceedings are involved, advisers will accompany debtors to the hearing.

Advice centres provide a service which is seen as accessible and free. The green form and legal aid means tests are often not appropriate to those with debt problems. Debtors may have an income which is over the green form limit without being able to afford to pay for a solicitor. They are deterred from seeking advice from a solicitor through fear of costs.

★ consumer problems

People are much less likely to contact a solicitor about a problem with goods and services than to go to a trading standards department or advice centre. The Royal Commission estimated that around 73,000 people a year visited a solicitor with problems over the purchase of goods or services (34). This figure is now out-of-date, but it still appears low when compared with over 600,000 complaints received by trading standards officers and advice centres (35). Workers in advice agencies and trading standards departments will usually have more experience of consumers' problems and of the practices of local traders.

The service provided by solicitors is not suitable for small value claims. Often consumers do not need a full legal service, but information, advice and someone to accompany them to a hearing if they are likely to have problems putting their own case. Advice centres are more used to encouraging clients to do what they can for themselves rather than taking over the case. There is a danger that the widespread use of solicitors in small claims proceedings would introduce too much formality in a procedure designed for ordinary people to use for themselves. The survey of litigants conducted for *Simple justice* (1979) found that 40 per cent of those using solicitors for small claims proceedings were very or fairly satisfied with the help they had received, compared with 58 per cent of those using advice centres (36).

★ employment and immigration

Similar arguments apply in employment and immigration work. Solicitors handle relatively few immigration cases and have little knowledge of immigration law. Their experience of employment law tends to be on behalf of employers rather than on behalf of employees. Legal aid is not available for industrial tribunals, immigration assessors or the immigration appeal tribunal, despite the increasing formality of the procedure and the complexity of the law they administer. One possible solution would be to extend the legal aid scheme to cover the most formal tribunals, including industrial tribunals and the immigration appeal tribunal. An alternative would be to channel additional resources through advice and law centres, who would place greater emphasis on self-help, giving advice and assistance, and accompanying clients in cases of special difficulty. Advice and law centres may be able to provide a more cost-effective service, using paid specialist staff and volunteers where this is appropriate. It would not be necessary to incur the high administrative costs of approving bills on a case by case basis.

Expanding specialist advice

Generally, we wish to see an expansion in specialist services provided through advice and law centres in areas where solicitors' expertise is low. Such specialist services should take a more active approach to informing people of their rights and responsibilities. They would place emphasis on self-help, but would also be able to represent clients where this was required. They would work closely with general advice services, training general workers, and taking referrals from them. They would also act for clients in test cases and actions affecting groups of people.

Specialist services offered through advice and law centres are not an easy or cheap option. Any expansion in specialist services is dependent on the establishment of a national network of general advice. Specialist services will also require very careful planning at a local and regional level to ensure access throughout the country. The existing green form provision is comparatively rarely used, and therefore costs comparatively little. It is likely that specialist services will generate much greater demand and therefore cost more overall. Any transfer of resources from the green form scheme will need to be made on the basis of an expanding budget.

Good advice for all examined the demand for specialist advice. It envisaged a network of services providing expert help in the fields of social security, housing, consumer, money and immigration matters. These represent the major areas of work at present, and may need to be added to as new needs arise. The service would include specialist advice and assistance and would extend to representation in cases of special complexity or need—in tribunals, in small claims and in debt and possession cases. Also included would be a home visiting service for disabled people, legal assistance for community groups and access to independent public health inspectors. Public health inspectors would produce reports on disrepair and other housing problems for use in negotiation and court proceedings. Specialist services should also be able to carry out research, education and project work to inform people of their rights and to exercise a responsible influence on the development of laws, policies and procedures at a local and national level (19).

There are a number of ways in which salaried specialist services can be provided, including local law centres, housing aid and money advice centres, or specialist staff located within general centres. In less populated regions, specialist units could provide back-up services to a number of different general advice centres. The choice is one that should be made locally. Generally, we wish to see a variety of different advice agencies based on local needs, rather than a single national model. One of the advice movement's great strengths is its ability to experiment and adapt to new demands. This flexibility should be preserved.

The staffing levels suggested in *Good advice for all* are:

★   one money advice case worker per 12,500 population
★   one law centre/legal case worker per 12,500 population
★   one housing advice case worker per 30,000 population
★   one consumer adviser per 30,000 population (19)

These levels are very much higher than those provided at present, as can be seen in table 4.1.

Table 4.1: shortfall in full-time equivalent posts in specialist advice agencies in England and Wales

Type of advice agency	Actual staffing levels (1)	Recommended staffing (2)
law centres	442	4,120
money advice	170	4,120
housing advice	180	1,715
consumer advice	257	1,715
Total	1,049	11,670

Notes:

1. Staffing figures provided by the Advice Services Alliance member networks and set out in detail in E. Kempson, *A survey of current advice and law centre provision*, September 1986. Consumer advice figures are supplied by the Institute of Consumer Advisers, and in E. Kempson, *The cost of providing a comprehensive advice and law centre service*, a report commissioned by NCC, 1986.
2. Based on the levels recommended in *Good advice for all* with an allowance for 15% of the population living in areas that require an additional 25% increase in staffing.

In 1986 we calculated the cost of implementing these guidelines. Using recommended 1986 salary levels, with 50 per cent on-costs, and all paid staff, the cost amounts to £163 million, compared with £12.5 million currently spent. If one assumes that the new staff will be employed under the same salaries and conditions as existing staff the figure for new expenditure is £138 million (22).

There is no doubt that these figures are large. We do not recommend that the guidelines should be implemented in their entirety. But they do give an indication of the likely demand for specialist advice and assistance, and we put them forward as a basis for discussion.

The demand for legal advice is growing in response to increasingly complex legislation and growing consumer awareness. We stress that it is not possible to keep expenditure at current levels, without substantial cuts in eligibility limits for legal aid and in the range and scope of legal services. The legal aid bill for social welfare law is expanding particularly rapidly: between 1985/6 and 1986/7 social security green form advice grew by 32 per cent, and debt grew by 10 per cent (5,37). It is far preferable that expenditure should be planned and used to produce the most effective service, than spent in the current unplanned and inefficient way.

Our figures include £61 million to be spent on money advice. In our view, the credit industry has some responsibilities towards the casualties of the credit boom. We consider that it should bear some of the cost of money advice, either through voluntary contributions or through some form of levy administered by the Office of Fair Trading.

Specialist advice and the Legal Aid Board

The Legal Aid Board has wide discretion to reform the provision of specialist advice. In particular, it has the power to provide advice and assistance currently available under the green form scheme through contracts, grants or loans to advice centres or consortia of local solicitors. We set out our proposals for how the Board should set about its tasks.

★ funding existing centres

In a tidy world, the Legal Aid Board would assume primary responsibility for funding specialist advice and would gradually take over funding existing centres from central and local government. In the real world, this is unlikely to prove either practicable or desirable. Such an exercise would cause administrative confusion and may stifle new developments and initiatives. However, we do recommend that the Legal Aid Board should take over funding those centres where there is a conflict of interest with present funders. It will also need to develop new centres where none exist at present.

A conflict of interest would appear to exist where local authorities fund law centres whose work consists of bringing legal action against themselves as employers or landlords or in care proceedings. The government's current policy is that law centres and other advice agencies are largely a matter of local need to be provided by local authorities. Although we recommend that general advice should be a local government responsibility, this is a less appropriate way of funding specialist advice. There is also a conflict between the United Kingdom Immigration Advisory Service and the Home Office which funds it.

★ regional planning

The Legal Aid Act 1988 envisages that the Board will make different arrangements for specialist advice in different areas. As the advisory committee pointed out, it will need many local contacts and expertise:

> "We think that the task of assessing needs for legal services and allocating resources to meet them will be a demanding task calling for a wide range of skills. The need to co-ordinate a wide range of providers suggests that a co-ordinating forum such as a regional legal services committee composed of consumers, providers of services and other interested bodies as individuals would be essential and that a separate post of Legal Services Co-ordinator should be created for each area" (5).

We endorse the advisory committee's recommendation for a legal services co-ordinator in every area.

Regional legal services committees have been pioneered by the North Western legal services committee. This began in 1977 as a pilot project in Greater Manchester, with representatives of the legal profession, advice centres, social and welfare services and the courts' administration. In 1982 it expanded its work to cover the whole of the North West legal aid area. The Lord Chancellor's Department pays for a liaison officer.

Its work has been documented by the legal aid advisory committee and includes publishing directories of existing services, co-ordinating the work of advice centres and local solicitors, promoting new services, such as law centres and prison advice services, and running training courses in areas where local expertise is low. The legal services committee pioneered the accident leaflet scheme which is now being applied nationally (5).

The North Western model has been followed in the North East, where a committee is established but unable to obtain funding, and in South Wales, where a steering committee is established (5).

The Legal Aid Act 1988 gives the Board power to fund regional services committees. We wish to see the Board provide immediate funds to those committees which are already established in the North

West, North East and South Wales. If these experiments prove successful, regional services committees should be encouraged in other areas, to advise the Board in the exercise of its functions.

★ setting standards

Before green form advice can be replaced by contracts or grants to advice centres it will be necessary for the Board to establish standards for advice provision. The advisory committee has commented:

> "We hope that in tendering for contracts, details about the numbers and qualifications of staff who are to provide advice will be required and that the Board will monitor the standard of service which is being provided and be required to review such new arrangements as are made after a reasonable period of operation" (5).

In our view, two distinct exercises are required. The first is the setting of *resource standards*, which lay down the minimum level of staff and access points for a given level of population. These will need to be adjusted for areas of social deprivation and for areas of sparse population. *Good advice for all* provides a first attempt at such an exercise (19).

Figures on staffing levels and access points measure input, not output. The Board will also need to develop a series of *performance indicators* to measure the services actually offered to consumers. These can be used to ensure that adequately resourced centres provide the expected level of service. The National Consumer Council has been involved in developing performance indicators to be used in measuring local government services and the health service but we are not aware of any performance indicators developed in Britain to measure the quality of legal services. Developing quality controls for legal and advice services breaks new ground.

★ "contracting out" green form advice

The replacement of green form advice by arrangements with advice centres or consortia of solicitors is one of the most controversial subjects which the Board is invited to consider. In principle we support the provision of advice in areas like social security and debt through advice centres rather than private practice. We believe that such centres can provide a more accessible service, more cost-effectively.

We stress, however, that this is not a cheap option. Green form advice is presently rationed through ignorance. People who need green form advice do not use it because they do not know it is there. The demands the public will make on advice centres will be much greater and will therefore cost more to meet. The switch can only be made in the context of an expanding service.

In our view there are a number of pre-conditions to the effective transfer of green form advice. We set these out below in the form of a series of questions which the Board will need to ask for each geographic area and field of law under consideration.

(i) *Is there an adequate level of general advice provision in the area?* We stress that a transfer should only be considered in areas of the country where the level of general advice provision is adequate. If specialist centres are established in areas where general advice is lacking, they will be bombarded by clients seeking answers to general queries. They may squander scarce specialist resources in answering low-level general queries, or develop a "siege mentality", keeping users away by very short opening hours, long queues in the waiting rooms, or constantly engaged telephones.

In our view, the full implementation of the contracting out provisions will only be possible if the government undertakes a separate initiative to expand the provision of general advice nationwide.

(ii) *What is the demand for advice, assistance and representation in this field of law?* In our view, the level of provision must be related to anticipated demand for advice, assistance and representation rather than to the quantity of advice presently provided by the green form scheme. The Board will need to measure demands by looking at the number of queries generated by centres which are well-resourced and are acknowledged to provide a good service. *Good advice for all* provides guidance on this (19).

(iii) *What effect will our plans have on existing advice provision?* The Board will need to ensure that other advice centres in the area are securely funded and that the grants or contractual payments they provide will not be used as a reason for other grants to be cut.

(iv) *Is there an adequate variety of provision?* No-one should be forced to use a particular advice source. The Board will need to fund a sufficient variety of different centres to provide some form of choice. There may be many reasons why an individual has no confidence in a particular centre: the centre may have advised someone with whom they are in dispute, they may have had a bad experience with the centre, or they may have personal ties with a member of the centre's staff. Where centres may be called on to advise both parties to a dispute, the variety of different organisations will need to be greater.

(v) *What level of assistance should be provided?* We do not consider that all clients with tribunal cases need to be represented. But we have identified three categories of consumers who do require representation: those with cases before the higher tribunals (such as the social security commissioners, and immigration appeal tribunal); those with complex cases; and those who have difficulties in following proceedings or speaking for themselves.

In such circumstances, specialist centres should be able to provide representation in addition to advice and assistance. Providing some representation is also important in maintaining the expertise of staff. We do not consider it possible to provide skilled advice and assistance without experience of how tribunals or courts administer the law. Unless centre staff regularly represent clients, they are unlikely to develop sufficient specialist skills or experience.

(vi) *How will the quality of service be monitored?* This will depend on providing clear objectives to the service and developing effective performance indicators. Defining the quality of legal services is not an easy task—time will have to be provided for a number of experiments. Controls will also have to be placed on a centre's financial management.

★ commenting on the advice implications of legislation

Demand for advice will alter as new laws are brought onto the statute book. Too often new rights are introduced without sufficient attention being paid to the need for advice and legal assistance which the legislation will generate. We wish to see the Legal Aid Board advise the government on the advice needs generated by legislation. Provision for advice should be made before Bills become law.

Improving legal aid

The development of new forms of specialist advice will have only a limited impact on the legal aid scheme. The great majority of consumers seeking advice about matrimonial or personal injury problems, or starting court cases, will continue to use solicitors in private practice.

In this section we set out what we see as the main tasks facing the Board to improve the civil legal aid scheme, both in terms of administering the present scheme and in advising the Lord Chancellor on making regulations.

★ publicity

As we discussed in chapter 3, present publicity is useful for those who already know that legal aid may be able to help them, but it does little to help those who do not consider seeking advice. We consider that general awareness of the legal aid scheme should be increased by using other publicity media and increasing the publicity budget.

Ideally, if resources permitted, publicity would include a full national advertising campaign of the type recently used by the Department of Trade and Industry for its enterprise schemes. Even if this is not possible, there are other cheaper media which could be explored such as radio advertisements, public service announcements and the post office video and leaflet service. Press releases stating how legal aid can be used could be issued when the limits are uprated. Posters could also be developed for different situations, drawing attention to the fact that legal aid can help with different legal problems: those for doctors surgeries could concentrate on compensation for accidents for example. Another suggestion for increasing awareness among minority communities is advertisements placed on videos of minority language films.

* decreasing administrative delay

The present time taken to grant certificates is unacceptable and reducing it must be a priority. The Scrutiny Team recommended a number of changes to simplify the means test: the function should be transferred from the Department of Social Security to legal aid area offices, discretionary allowances should be abolished and a simplified form should be introduced (10). We hope that the Board will investigate these suggestions sympathetically. We fear that it will not be possible to make improvements without relaxing the present stringent controls on staffing and resources. The manual given to assessment officers should be made public.

In chapter 5 we discuss the advantages of solicitors' specialisation schemes. Once they have been established certified specialist solicitors could apply the merits test on behalf of the Board, saving both staff and time.

★ research and development

The Board is entrusted with the task of considering a number of new proposals. In our view it is vital that proposals are adequately researched before they are implemented. In the past neither the Law Society nor the Lord Chancellor's Department have seen research into the legal aid scheme as a priority and this has led to the present highly regrettable situation in which we do not know how many people are covered by the scheme or how a change in the eligibility limits will affect expenditure or take-up.

We recommend that the new Board should establish an in-house research department. Its first task should be to consider legal aid eligibility limits and contribution levels, with a view to advising the Lord Chancellor on the setting of eligibility limits. We discuss this below.

★ establishing the coverage of the scheme

The white paper states that "at present, it is estimated that some 70 per cent of households qualify for legal aid. The Government does not intend to extend this proportion." (13)

We agree with the objective of the 1979 reforms—that legal aid should cover around 70 per cent of the population. But we fear that it no longer does. There is an urgent need for more accurate figures on the coverage of legal aid. We recommend that the Legal Aid Board's research unit works with the Department of Social Security to conduct a special exercise from which accurate estimates of legal aid coverage can be made. These can then be used to form appropriate targets and performance indicators which will enable the Board to monitor the effectiveness of the legal aid scheme in terms of the number of people eligible for help.

Traditionally, legal aid coverage has been measured by looking at income limits only. We are concerned that the capital limits exclude many elderly people on low incomes. The upper capital limit is below the income support capital cut-off and substantially below the housing benefit cut-off.

If it proves too expensive to study legal aid coverage among all sections of the population, it may be possible to isolate "core groups", substantial coverage of which indicates substantial coverage of the population as a whole. This was the approach taken in 1978 by the advisory committee who concentrated their efforts on two-parent families with children. This group will give a good indication of the effects of the income limits. We would also wish to see a study conducted to measure the effects of the capital limits on retired people.

★ contributions

The National Consumer Council agrees that contributions should be retained because we do not wish to see a single cut-off point. Instead, graduated help should be provided for those who are not poor but who cannot afford the full cost of a complex court case.

Setting the level of contributions involves a difficult balancing act. On the one hand, people should not enter into litigation lightly or frivolously, and should not use public money in a way in which they would not be prepared to use their own. On the other hand, the level of contributions should not be so high that people are deterred from using the courts through lack of means.

In our view, the present balance is tipped towards contributions being too large. This is shown both by the high refusal rate and the high level of arrears. One-fifth of contributory offers are refused (10) and 29 per cent of accepted contributory accounts are in arrears (5). The proposals to extend contributions throughout the length of the case will effectively double contributions, and is likely to lead to an even higher level of refusals and arrears.

There is a need for more information about why applicants refuse contributory offers and why so many are in arrears. We wish to see the Legal Aid Board carry out research among those who refuse legal aid and among those who accept but fail to pay. The research could then be used to establish optimal contribution levels. It should be stressed that contributions raise very little revenue (the Scrutiny Team estimated a net £4.9 million (10)). Spending time and effort in collecting contributions which are set too high is unlikely to be a cost-effective use of resources.

★ the statutory charge

In non-matrimonial cases, the statutory charge appears to meet its objectives without causing undue hardship to those affected. But in matrimonial cases it causes real problems. There have been a number of calls for radical reform. The National Association of Citizens Advice Bureaux has recommended that the charge should not apply in matrimonial cases. They point out:

"in other cases where costs do not normally follow the event—such as appeals to the Employment Appeal Tribunal—the statutory charge does not apply. That, presumably was also one of the reasons it did not apply to matrimonial cases before 1977'' (38).

The Legal Action Group has commented that the statutory charge reveals how "important and urgent is the need to take a thorough look at the rules in relation to costs in matrimonial proceedings and how they operate in practice" (39). Any such inquiry is outside the scope of this report. We have not looked in detail at matrimonial law or procedure, and are not in a position to make long-term recommendations for how the costs of matrimonial proceedings should be allocated. Nor does such radical reform fall within the ambit of the Legal Aid Board.

There are some actions, however, which the Board could take to mitigate against the most harsh effects of the statutory charge.

The first, and most important task, is to ensure that clients are fully informed, not only about the statutory charge but about the legal costs they incur. This will involve constant monitoring by the Board. The Law Society has stressed the need to provide information at the start of the case, and before a final settlement is reached. But clients need to be able to control the costs and conduct of the case throughout the proceedings. We recommend that clients who will be affected by the charge should be provided with regular accounts (at no less than three monthly intervals) showing the costs incurred to date. We discuss this in more detail in chapter 6. A move towards standard fees will also help clients predict and budget for their legal costs.

The £2,500 exemption in matrimonial proceedings has remained at the same level since 1976. It is now too low to represent a down-payment on a new home. We recommend that it should be raised. This can be financed, at least in part, by the revenue raised from charging interest on postponed charges—a change which is calculated to raise £1 million after three to five years (10).

★ the green form scheme

Even if social welfare law is excluded from the green form scheme, the scheme will continue to play a major part in other areas, including matrimonial and personal injury work. If the green form is to meet its original objective of providing initial advice to those on low income with minimal administrative delay a number of reforms will need to be negotiated with the Lord Chancellor's Department.

In 1979 the Benson Commission recommended that the green form limit should be raised in line with the hourly rates paid to lawyers under the scheme, so that it would always cover 4 hours work (34).

The recommendation was not followed, and the limit has depreciated markedly in the last few years. The £50 limit for non-divorce work now covers less than one hour 20 minutes (5).

Where it appears that the cost of giving advice and assistance is likely to exceed £50, solicitors can apply to the legal aid office for an extension. But they may not give the advice before the extension has been granted. The regulations state that the office should grant an extension where "it is reasonable for the advice and assistance to be given" and "the amount of the costs to be incurred...is fair and reasonable" (40). In 1986-87, there were 171,059 applications for extensions, an increase of around forty-five per cent since 1983-84. About eighty per cent of applications are granted (5).

Baldwin and Hill's research found that solicitors' most common criticism of the green form scheme was that the initial limits were too low. The researchers commented that "making applications for an extension is widely regarded as irksome in that it is time-consuming, causes delay and raises difficulties with clients" (41). They recommended that the limits should be raised immediately:

"Raising these limits would be better for clients who may be seriously inconvenienced and distressed by delays in dealing with their cases. It would be fairer and simpler for solicitors who presently do work unpaid rather than be restricted by the requirement that they seek permission to exceed the prescribed limit, and it would ease the burden on Area Office staff who would be likely to be faced with somewhat fewer applications for extensions." (41)

In October 1988 the government announced that the limit (ie the maximum amount which can be paid without an extension) would be increased and updated regularly so as to cover two hours of advice in most cases and three hours of advice in matrimonial cases (5). We welcome this improvement.

We also fear that the green form capital limit is much too low and has the effect of excluding single people on income support with savings of over £850. A couple with over £1,050 are similarly excluded. We wish to see the capital limit raised, and all those on income support given an automatic entitlement to green form advice.

Another problem with the legal advice and assistance scheme, or green form, is that it does not cover the needs of the housebound or those living without transport in remote areas. Solicitors are not permitted to give advice by telephone or post, or to travel out to see housebound clients. The regulations require that advice is only given in a face to face interview, after the client has signed the form in the presence of the solicitor. The only exception is that proxies are allowed to attend on the client's behalf.

Telephone and postal advice has been the subject of a prolonged debate between the Law Society and the Lord Chancellor's advisory committee. The advisory committee argues that although a face-to-face interview is usually preferable for people who are able to visit a solicitor's office, telephone or postal advice or home visits are often the only means by which people who are housebound, disabled, or without transport in rural areas can obtain any assistance under the green form scheme (37).

We support these arguments. The experience of telephone advice services, such as those run in Northumberland and Inverness, has shown that they can provide useful advice (42). Elderly and housebound callers and those in remote areas appreciate the savings in time and travel which the telephone can bring.

We wish to see the Legal Aid Board implement the recommendations made by the Lord Chancellor's advisory committee in their 36th annual report, to permit postal and telephone advice where this is suitable, and the difficulties of the client preclude an interview in the solicitor's office (37). Where telephone or postal advice is not suitable, but the client is unable to travel, the green form should permit the solicitor to make a home visit.

In chapter 11, we comment on the particular problems created by multi-party claims.

References to chapter 4

1. Legal Aid Act 1988, section 1.
2. *Hansard*, 15 December 1987, col. 610.
3. Cappelletti, M. and Garth, B., ed., *Access to justice*, vol.1, Sitjthoff Giuffre, Milan, 1978.
4. Although the Germans introduced the first state payments to lawyers for services to the poor in 1919, in France legal services continued on a charitable basis until 1972, see Cappelletti, M., above.
5. *Legal aid*, 37th annual reports of the Law Society and the Lord Chancellor's advisory committee, 1986-87, HC 233, HMSO, 1988.
6. *Hansard*, 18 January 1988, col. 70.
7. Baldwin, J. and Hill, S., "Research on the green form scheme of legal advice and assistance", *Civil Justice Quarterly*, 1986, pp.247-259.

8. Williams, F., ed., *Why the poor pay more*, National Consumer Council, 1977.

9. American Legal Services Corporation, *The delivery systems study*, June 1980.

10. Lord Chancellor's Department, *Legal aid efficiency scrutiny*, 2 vols, June 1986.

11. National Consumer Council, *The reform of publicly funded legal services in England and Wales; a consumer response to the report of the Legal Aid Scrutiny Team*, September 1986.

12. Harris, D. and others, *Compensation and support for illness and injury*, Clarendon Press, Oxford Socio-legal Studies, 1984.

13. Lord Chancellor's Department, *Legal aid in England and Wales: a new framework*, Cm 118, HMSO, March 1987.

14. Lord Chancellor's Department, "Research programme 1987-88", Press notice (87.40), 6 April 1987.

15. *Hansard*, 15 December 1987, cols 611-612.

16. *Hansard*, 15 December 1987, col. 608.

17. National Consumer Council, *The fourth right of citizenship: a review of local advice services*, 1977.

18. Childs, D., Hickey, A. and Winter, J., *Citizens advice: a study of who uses London's citizens advice bureaux and the service they receive*, Greater London Citizens Advice Bureaux Service, October 1985.

19. National Consumer Council, *Good advice for all; guidelines on standards for local advice services* (a discussion paper), Summer 1986.

20. Bourdillion standards in the report of the working party on standards of public library service in England and Wales, 1962.

21. Kempson, E., *A survey of current advice and law centre provision*, Advice Services Alliance, 2 vols, September 1986.

22. Kempson, E., "The cost of providing a comprehensive advice and law centre service", National Consumer Council, October 1986.

23. Autumn statement, HC 110, HMSO, November 1987.

24. Kempson, E., *Welfare benefits work by non-statutory advice and law centres*, Acumen, 1986.

25. Taylor Nelson Media Ltd, *An analysis of solicitors advertising*, prepared for the National Consumer Council, October 1987.

26. *Social security statistics 1987*, HMSO, 1988.

27. Wadham, J. and Page, R., "Tribunals duty advocates", *Legal Action*, October 1983, pp.9-13.

28. Farnelly, M. and Storey, O., "I only want justice", *The Advisor*, June/July 1987.

29. Council on Tribunals, *Annual Report 1986/87*, HC 234, HMSO, 1988.

30. *Legal aid*, 34th annual reports of the Law Society and Lord Chancellor's advisory committee, 1983-84, HC 151, HMSO, 1985.

31. Parker, G., *Consumers in debt*, background paper, National Consumer Council, January 1986.

32. National Consumer Council, *Information and advice services in the United Kingdom: report to the Minister of State for Consumer Affairs*, April 1983.

33. Hinton, T. and Berthoud, R., *Money advice services*, Policy Studies Institute, 1988.

34. Royal Commission on Legal Services (Chairman: Sir Henry Benson), *Final report*, Cmnd 7648, HMSO, 1979.

35. Office of Fair Trading, *Annual Report of the Director General of Fair Trading 1987*, HC 544, HMSO, 1988.

36. National Consumer Council and Welsh Consumer Council, *Simple justice: a consumer view of small claims procedures in England and Wales*, September 1979.

37. *Legal aid*, 36th annual reports of the Law Society and Lord Chancellor's advisory committee 1985-86, HC 87, HMSO, 1987.

38. National Association of Citizens Advice Bureaux, *Legal aid scrutiny—the response of the CAB service to the legal aid scrutiny report*, September 1986.

39. *Legal Action*, "The statutory poverty trap", February 1984.

40. Legal Advice and Assistance Regulations, no.2, 1980, section 15.

41. Baldwin, J. and Hill, S., *The operation of the green form scheme in England and Wales*, Lord Chancellor's Department, March 1988.

42. Scottish Consumer Council, *A call for advice: an evaluation of two rural advice experiments in Scotland*, February, 1983.

Chapter 5
Choosing a lawyer

A number of empirical studies have shown that a large proportion of people who could benefit from legal advice do not approach a lawyer for help. The Oxford Centre for Socio-legal Studies survey of accident victims (the Compensation Study) found that three-quarters of people did not even consider making a claim for compensation, and even among those who did, only about half took the next step and consulted a solicitor (1). Research for the Civil Justice Review suggests that this problem is not confined to personal injury claims, and that defendants in debt and housing possession actions rarely obtain advice, even when they risk losing their homes (2). As we see in chapter 12, the vast majority of people with consumer disputes would sooner "lump it" rather than use the law.

One particular difficulty about using lawyers is that consumers are often unaware of their rights, or may not know that a solicitor can help. They may not know how to approach a solicitor, or how to find one with the right skills. In this chapter we examine the main ways in which people find solicitors—through referrals and advertising. We then look at ways in which people can be given more information about approaching solicitors. We describe the fixed fee interview scheme and the successful accident leaflet scheme, which offers accident victims a free initial interview. Lastly, we examine proposals for specialisation schemes which allow consumers to find out about solicitors' particular skills.

Referrals

The most common way in which people find solicitors is through personal recommendations, usually from family or friends. People also ask estate agents, building societies or banks to recommend solicitors. A poll in February 1986 by Research Surveys of Great Britain Limited found that 38 per cent of people using solicitors had been recommended by friends, relatives and colleagues, and 18 per cent had been recommended by a bank, estate agent or other professional. In conveyancing cases, 24 per cent had been recommended by other professionals. Six per cent of clients had seen the office, and very few (2 per cent) had been attracted by advertisements (3). In a 1985 survey of solicitors in Devon and Cornwall over half the solicitors interviewed considered that building societies and estate agents were very important sources of referrals. A third considered that banks were very important, and just under a quarter thought that the police were very important. This compares with only 13 per cent who thought that the citizens advice bureaux were very important sources of referrals and only 4 per cent who mentioned the courts (4).

In many ways, people who are actively involved in buying and selling houses, such as estate agents and building societies, are in a better position to assess solicitors than friends. But if solicitors rely too heavily on other commercial organisations to introduce business they may feel unable to offer entirely independent advice. A solicitor who advises a client not to proceed with a house purchase, for example, may well annoy the local estate agent acting for the seller. It is possible that a solicitor may feel reluctant to do this where the estate agent is an important source of new clients. Solicitors may be tempted to recommend estate agents or mortgage companies, not on the basis of merit, but because they are returning a favour.

It is for this reason that the *Solicitors' Practice Rules 1987* sought to ban any "arrangement" for the introduction of clients. Rule 3 stated:

> "A solicitor may not enter into an arrangement with another person for the introduction of clients to the solicitor" (5).

The only general exceptions were arrangements with other lawyers, though some solicitors working for trade unions or law centres obtained waivers from the Law Society.

Rule 3 did not stop commercial organisations from referring clients, but solicitors were not permitted to discuss or acknowledge referrals. In practice it was hard to enforce, because tacit arrangements are difficult to define or prove. Many highly beneficial arrangements were clearly in breach of the rule. For example, a scheme in which a housing aid centre or self-help group monitored or trained solicitors before referring work to them broke the practice rules. The rule also stopped the development of one price conveyancing or tax "packages" in which different professionals worked together to provide a service.

The Law Society brought in new rules in September 1988. The new rule 3 states that "a solicitor may accept introductions and referrals of business from another person and may make introductions and refer business to another person" provided that it does not compromise the solicitor's independence or integrity, and it complies with a new code, drawn up by the Law Society (6).

The code states that solicitors "should not allow themselves to become so reliant on a limited number of sources of referrals, particularly a single source, that the interests of the introducer affect the advice given by the solicitor to his client" (7). It provides that every six months each firm should carry out a review of where the firm's business comes from. Where more than 20 per cent of a firm's income arises from a single source of introduction, "the firm should consider whether steps should be taken to reduce the proportion" (7).

The code prevents solicitors from paying commission to introducers, but "normal hospitality" is allowed (7). They may refer clients to the introducer, where this is in the client's best interests, but they may not enter into arrangements where they are only permitted to refer clients to particular firms.

The most radical effect of the code is that it allows "packaged" services. The solicitor may not only give the estate agent a price list to hand to the client, but may also do work as part of an inclusive deal in which the agent charges the seller a fixed price and pays the solicitor at a fixed or hourly rate for the conveyancing service. The terms of such agreements must be set out in writing and made available to the Law Society and Solicitors Complaints Bureau. Deals of this sort, however, may not be made with lenders or developers (7). We discuss the issue of packaged services further in chapter 8.

The 1987 rule was certainly too narrow. The introduction and referral code is full of admirable principles, but we fear that it may prove difficult to interpret and enforce. Whether a solicitor is fully "independent" is very much a matter of degree and judgement. As Hazel Genn's research into personal injury negotiations shows, many solicitors feel that it is best to adopt a reasonable and conciliatory approach to negotiations while others adopt an adversarial technique (8). Neither technique is necessarily better, but it may be more difficult to adopt a highly adversarial stance if one is dependent on one's reputation among local businesses or with the local police to receive work. A client charged with a crime who alleges malpractice against the police may feel that it is very important that the firm does not rely on the police to bring in business, while a house purchaser who has already agreed a purchase and arranged a mortgage may have no qualms about using a solicitor who has a close relationship with local building societies or estate agents. A 20 per cent rule is difficult to apply rigidly in all cases.

In our view, the best safeguard the consumer has against cosy deals among local firms is full disclosure. The results of the six month review should be recorded in writing and made available to clients, preferrably as part of an introductory leaflet or brochure. Consumers will then be in a position to judge for themselves how independent their solicitor is. The Law Society and Solicitors Complaints Bureau should also be able to call on solicitors to produce records of their reviews, to check that the code is being complied with.

In the long term, the development of advertising is likely to reduce the importance of introductions by local businesses and thus increase solicitors' independence. So long as the advertising carries useful and accurate information on which selections can be made, it should be advantageous to consumers.

Advertising by solicitors

For around fifty years, between the 1930s and 1980s, advertising by solicitors was prohibited. Rule 1 of the *Solicitors' Practice Rules 1936-72* forbade any attempt to obtain professional business by advertising. Publicity was confined to referral lists, discreet door plaques, and corporate advertising by the Law Society. The prohibition was criticised by the Monopolies Commission in 1970 and 1976. They considered that it prevented new entrants to the profession, deprived the public of information about the service offered, reduced competitiveness and efficiency and encouraged less open methods of attracting business (9). In 1979 the Benson Commission repeated the Monopolies Commission's call for liberalisation of the advertising restrictions (10).

It was not until 1984, however, that the rules on advertising changed in the wake of the threat to the conveyancing monopoly. Rule 1 was abolished and advertising in the press and on radio was allowed. In February 1987 the rules about advertising were further relaxed. There are no longer any restrictions on advertising media: solicitors may advertise on television, by direct mail, on tee shirts or by sky writing if they wish. The solicitors' publicity code prevents solicitors from making unsolicited visits or telephone calls, claiming to specialise, criticising their competitors or mentioning success rates or clients in their advertisements. Any information about fees must be clearly stated, and advertisements cannot say that a fee is from or upwards of a certain figure. The code also states that "publicity must not be inaccurate or misleading in any way". Serious or persistent breaches of the code can be dealt with by the Solicitors Complaints Bureau (11).

The changes to the rules on advertising have provoked very little controversy compared to the battles that have occurred in the United States of America. In 1977, in the *Bates* case (12), the supreme court found that absolute prohibitions on lawyers' advertising were unconstitutional. Advertisements for lawyers' services now appear on television. Traditional lawyers thought that their worst fears had been realised when Ken Hur, an attorney in Wisconsin, appeared on television to promise clients who used his services in drink/drive charge cases a ten-speed bicycle if they lost their licences (13). But large scale advertising is still very much a rarity in the USA. Surveys suggest that over two-thirds of American lawyers do not advertise at all, and those who do are most likely to use local directories and yellow pages (14).

In 1987, the first television advertisements for solicitors' services in England and Wales appeared. Burnetts of Carlisle ran a series of thirty-two 20-second advertisements on Border Television, and were reportedly pleased with the outcome (15). Television is not heavily used, however, because it is an extremely expensive way of reaching the narrow band of potential clients. Solicitors with commercial clients may send out brochures advertising their services, and, as in the USA, directories, yellow pages and the local press are the most common way of reaching the general public.

The solicitors in Devon and Cornwall interviewed by the Access to Justice in Rural Britain Project expressed very little interest in advertising (4). Half of all firms said that they would not advertise at all, and a quarter said that they would advertise only if other firms did so. About ten per cent thought they would advertise specialist services or produce a brochure, and another ten per cent were considering the possibility of advertising. Only one per cent of the sample said that they would definitely take advantage of their new found freedom. Several solicitors thought that advertising was unprofessional. One commented "it's making the profession into a retail trade. I don't like it at all" (4).

A survey quoted in the *Solicitor's Journal* in June 1987, however, suggests that Devon and Cornwall solicitors are unusually cautious (16). Out of 350 firms questioned, 55 per cent said that they had placed press advertisements, mostly in the local paper or in business magazines. Just over a half of those who had tried advertising said that they would continue to do so, either regularly or sporadically.

The National Consumer Council has welcomed the relaxation of the solicitors' advertising rules on the grounds that advertisements can increase awareness of legal remedies, inform consumers about the services a solicitor can offer, help them make an informed choice of solicitor and increase competition within legal services. Innovative ways of providing services are more likely to develop if consumers can be informed about them. Whether these benefits will materialise, however, depends on the quality of information contained within advertisements.

Our own survey of advertisements

In order to assess the usefulness to consumers of solicitors' advertisements, the National Consumer Council commissioned a market research company, Taylor Nelson Media, to carry out an analysis of 1,256 advertisements appearing in yellow pages and the local press (17). We looked at a random sample of 20 out of 57 volumes of 1986 yellow pages, and 95 out of 1,273 local papers appearing in one of the first two weeks of September 1987. Yellow pages appears to be the most popular medium. We estimate that around 3,500 solicitors' adverts appear in the yellow pages for England and Wales, and around 460 advertisements appear each week in the local press. Yellow pages advertisements accounted for 97 per cent of all the adverts in the survey.

Most of the information contained in the advertisements was about the areas of work the firm was willing to carry out. In all, 79 per cent of adverts specified areas of work, and most listed several areas: the average number per advert was 4.4. The areas of work are given in table 5.1.

Not surprisingly, conveyancing was by far the most common area, followed by family law, wills, personal injury, crime, commercial work, litigation and employment. All other subjects appeared rarely. On average, there was one advertisement for advice on welfare benefits per volume of yellow pages. Only a few adverts (7 per cent) indicated the age of the firm, and very few (1.5 per cent) gave its size.

Forty-five per cent of advertisements stated that the firm operated the legal aid scheme, or reproduced the legal aid logo. We found no advertisements which described the scope of the legal aid scheme, or gave any indication of the eligibility limits. Someone who did not already know about legal aid would be little the wiser after seeing the advertisements.

Table 5.1: areas of work mentioned in advertisements

conveyancing	59%
divorce/family/matrimonial	46%
wills/probate/trusts	44%
personal injury/accidents/negligence	32%
crime	31%
litigation/court work	29%
business/commercial	29%
employment/redundancy/dismissal	17%
landlord and tenant/repairs	8%
debt/money worries	8%
consumer problems	5%
planning	4%
personal/unspecified tax problems	3%
care proceedings/wardship	3%
welfare benefits/social security	2%
immigration	2%
medical negligence	1%
neighbour disputes	1%
all legal work/general	29%
none specified	21%

Base: total advertisements 1,256

Source: Taylor Nelson Media, "An analysis of solicitors' advertising", 1987.

Five per cent of advertisements offered a free first interview, and 2 per cent offered a fixed fee first interview. Otherwise, price claims were generally confined to conveyancing. Forty-nine per cent of advertisements said that quotations were available, and two per cent mentioned specific prices; these ranged from £90 to £200 for a house conveyance. Around twelve adverts offered "conveyancing packages", of which the following examples are typical:

"Moving house? The complete service. Solicitors do it all at one fixed cost—arrange your house sale; fix your mortgage; advice on insurance and survey; all the legal work: for free quotation ring..."

"At last there is a one stop selling plan available through a firm of qualified solicitors. Homeplan means no more guessing when it comes to the costs involved in selling your house—for a fixed fee of only two and a half per cent + VAT of the sale price Homeplan makes selling your property as straightforward as you could wish...

* Estate Agents instructed
* Estate Agents fee included
* All legal work and fees included

* No hidden extra charges
* No fees without sale." (17)

The solicitors' publicity code states that "no claim may be made that a solicitor is a specialist, or an expert in a particular field", unless the solicitor is a member of a recognised scheme. But it is not improper for a solicitor to claim experience in a particular field, provided that this is true (11). Despite the rules we found seven advertisements which used the word "specialist", apparently in breach of the code. In some of the advertisements it was difficult to tell whether the firm claimed to specialise in all the subjects listed or only in the subjects listed most prominently. For instance:

"WE SPECIALISE IN ACCIDENT AND INJURY CLAIMS
DIVORCE AND FAMILY MATTERS
HOUSE SALES AND PURCHASE (WRITTEN ESTIMATES
AVAILABLE)
CRIMINAL CASES
consumer problems, debts and many more"

"Professional and friendly advice: specialists in

* CONVEYANCING * WILLS AND PROBATES
* legal aid * divorce and matrimonial *
  accident and insurance claims..."

One firm simply claimed to be "the friendly specialists" without listing any area of work (17).

The great majority of advertisements are aimed at people who are already looking for a solicitor. Most press advertisements appeared in the property pages or classified section rather than in the editorial pages. Generally, solicitors who listed consumer law said that they dealt with "consumer disputes", rather than stating that if you had a problem with a faulty good or service a solicitor could help. We found only four adverts which could be said to contain information about legal rights. The following are examples:—

"In trouble with the police? Need help quickly?

* speak to us before making a statement to the police!
* arrested—insist that the police ring us—we will come and advise you—at the police station—even after hours
* use our emergency telephone number after office hours and at weekends..."

"Accident? Injured? you may be able to claim compensation as the victim of a...

* motoring accident * violent crime * fall in the street * accident at work * industrial disease. You may be able to claim compensation for your injuries as well as loss of earnings, legal and other expenses. To arrange a FREE appointment, home or hospital visit dial 100 and ask the operator for FREEPHONE..." (17).

This last advertisement was also unusual in giving a photograph of the solicitor concerned.

Our conclusion is that solicitors' advertising is a small step in the right direction. It tells consumers the type of work a firm is willing to handle, and whether the firm operates the legal aid scheme. It has also helped to make conveyancing more price competitive by encouraging potential clients to ring for a quote. The fact that some adverts give a costs figure provides a point of comparison. We are pleased that a fair number of firms are now advertising that they deal with employment law and landlord and tenant and that some are advertising an interest in consumer law. We hope that the ability to advertise will encourage more firms to offer these services. But solicitors are missing the opportunity to reach new clients who do not know that a solicitor can help them. Advertisements rarely draw attention to legal remedies which people do not know about, or explain who and what the legal aid scheme covers.

There are several breaches of the rule against advertising specialisation. This emphasises the need to introduce specialisation schemes of the sort discussed below.

Fixed fee interview scheme

The fixed fee interview scheme was designed to overcome people's reluctance to visit a solicitor. Solicitors may advertise that they will offer an interview of up to half an hour on any subject for a fixed fee. In 1976 the fee was £5 and it has remained at the same level since then. Unfortunately, the scheme has not been successful. John Baldwin and Sheila Hill interviewed 115 solicitors, as part of a research project on the green form and related schemes (18). They found that the fixed fee scheme was "almost invariably characterised by simple apathy". Although 84 per cent of solicitors said that they were willing to give a fixed fee interview if a client specifically asked for one, only two solicitors made a point of offering one. Most solicitors said that they gave fixed fee interviews less than once a week. Several firms displayed Law Society notices about the scheme in their reception areas, but otherwise the scheme was given very little publicity. The researchers concluded that "only the CAB network was keeping the scheme alive and that ignorance of the scheme beyond this network was almost total". Solicitors were split about what they thought should happen to the scheme. Four out of ten thought that it should be ended; almost a quarter thought that the fee should be increased, but a substantial minority (22 per cent) thought that the scheme should be continued without a fee.

In our view, a well advertised free interview scheme offers the best way of overcoming consumers' reluctance to enter a solicitor's office. We discuss this in more detail below.

The accident leaflet scheme

The accident leaflet scheme was started by the North Western legal services committee in 1978. Concern was expressed by the lay members of the committee about the large number of accident victims who were unaware of their right to claim, or were reluctant to contact a solicitor. The committee produced a leaflet giving simple information about personal injury claims and suggesting sources of help, such as solicitors, trade unions and advice centres. The leaflet also offered a free interview with a solicitor. All the client had to do was to complete and return the tear-off coupon to the committee. The committee sent the coupon to a local solicitor who had agreed to participate in the scheme, who then contacted the client (19).

The scheme proved a success and soon overcame the initial reluctance of the legal profession. Solicitors were willing to offer the initial interviews as a "loss leader" to further work. An evaluation of the scheme carried out by the Centre for Socio-legal Studies found that it was very successful in encouraging claims from people who would otherwise be unlikely to visit a solicitor (20). Nearly two-thirds of accident victims using the scheme had never consulted a solicitor before. The Compensation Study found that, in normal circumstances, elderly people, housewives and those injured elsewhere than at work or on the roads were particularly unlikely to claim (1). However, a high proportion of housewives and elderly people used the free interview scheme, and well over a third of scheme-users had accidents other than on the road or at work. Forty-two per cent of users said that they would not have thought about claiming had they not seen a leaflet for a free interview. Scheme-users tended to have suffered serious injuries, and most were advised that they had good claims. Over half of victims had been ill for over 2 months, and almost ten per cent had suffered permanent disability. In all, eighty per cent of people given free interviews were advised to make a claim. Both victims and solicitors spoke well of the scheme and thought that it had been helpful (20).

One problem that the scheme ran into was opposition from the medical profession. Many doctors thought that the scheme would encourage claims for medical negligence and refused to carry the leaflets. Eventually, the hospitals in Greater Manchester agreed to display the leaflets but it did not prove possible to distribute the leaflets to doctors' surgeries. In practice, half of all those returning coupons had obtained the leaflet from a citizens advice bureau.

After the initial experiment in the North West, the Law Society decided to launch the scheme in other regions through local law societies. At first, the response from solicitors was disappointing. Out of 120 local law societies, around 40 started schemes, and about 30 continued with them. Many law societies gave up in the face of opposition from doctors.

In June 1987 the Law Society relaunched the scheme on a national basis, under the new title ALAS! (Accident Legal Advice Service). The scheme has been much better publicised than before. The Law Society distributed half a million leaflets and posters to local authorities, regional health services and the Department of Health and Social Security, and produced a 30 second video shown on the post office video service. The scheme has also received substantial publicity in both the national and local press. Accident victims in other areas can return the forms to a central freepost address or ring a freephone number to be referred to a local solicitor.

The relaunch of ALAS! is very encouraging. Figures from the Law Society suggest that in the first few months 5,000 people used the scheme, of whom 3,000 made claims (21). It is clear that the scheme can significantly increase access to the law. The next step is to overcome the reluctance of the medical profession. It is regrettable that the British Medical Association still expresses concern about advertisements encouraging people to come forward if they believe they may have a claim for medical negligence or other personal injury (22).

Success will depend on how far interest in the scheme continues after the initial enthusiasm. Carolyn Schofield, secretary to the North Western legal services committee who originated the scheme, has commented: "without someone locally to check on distribution and encourage the proper display of posters, the spread of information is likely to be patchy... The new scheme, like the earlier one, will depend upon the involvement of local law societies" (19). We hope that the Law Society will continue to fund national publicity and that local law societies will ensure that the scheme works on the ground.

If the accident leaflet scheme continues successfully, thought could be given to developing similar schemes in other fields of law.

Specialisation schemes (23)

Choosing the right lawyer is often crucial to the outcome of a case. Hazel Genn has highlighted the importance of using specialist solicitors for personal injury claims in her research into how accident claims are settled, which we discuss in chapter 11 (8). She found that specialists were more likely to believe in aggressive negotiating tactics and tended to believe that proceedings should be issued early. Non-specialists tended to have a more conciliatory attitude to insurance companies and were often reluctant to issue proceedings unless negotiations had failed. This could lead to inadequate case preparation. Non-specialists found it more difficult to establish efficient case-preparation systems, and to keep up-to-date with changes in procedure.

It is often difficult for consumers to find specialist solicitors. Advertising may go some way towards increasing information about solicitors but it is not the whole answer. The publicity code specifically forbids solicitors from claiming to be a specialist or expert in a particular field. Although advertisements may list a firm's areas of concentration or experience this is no guarantee of competence or skill.

The *Solicitors' regional directory* published by the Law Society lists the categories of work undertaken by solicitors' firms. Although it gives some indication of the time individual solicitors spend on particular types of work, it does not provide any indication of their competence or skill. The information provided by solicitors is not vetted, entries may be inaccurate, and no sanctions are applied if they are misleading or erroneous. Furthermore, the directory is not generally available to members of the public.

Advice centres frequently refer clients to solicitors whom they know to be competent in particular areas of work. But most clients do not find solicitors through advice centres. In the Compensation Study only four out of 248 accident victims who consulted solicitors had been referred by an advice centre (1). Baldwin and Hill's survey of 124 green form scheme users found that 14 per cent had been referred by a citizens advice bureau (24). In both studies, most recommendations came from the victim's family, friends or neighbours, who may have limited experience of using solicitors, and may not have made a claim in the same field of law. In any event, advice centre staff have pointed out that it is difficult even for experienced advisers to find solicitors with the necessary expertise in certain areas (25).

Genn concludes that most personal injury plaintiffs have few means of discovering which solicitors genuinely specialise in personal injury work. She comments that:

> "Plaintiffs are a heterogeneous and inexperienced group of potential litigants. Defendants are a relatively homogeneous group and are experienced specialists themselves. When defendants instruct solicitors their choice is based on knowledge of expertise. They can pay for experts and choose, on the basis of their own knowledge or information from their networks, solicitors whom they believe to be specialist personal injury litigators. When plaintiffs instruct solicitors their choice is a matter of chance. Whether the solicitor taking on the claim is a specialist will similarly be a matter of chance unless it is a trade union case handled by a specialist union solicitor. This element of chance in plaintiffs' legal representation has the effect of reinforcing, rather than redressing, the structural imbalance between the parties to personal injury litigation" (8).

The case for and against specialisation schemes

Specialisation schemes are one solution to the problems of finding a solicitor who is skilled in a particular field of law. Under such schemes, lawyers who are certified by a professional body or who meet certain criteria may advertise their specialist status to attract clients. Specialisation schemes do not, in themselves, create specialists: lawyers are increasingly becoming specialists in response to the increasing complexity of the law and the demands of the market. But they allow claims to specialisms to be regulated by the profession and communicated to the public. This may encourage solicitors to acquire specialisms in order to market themselves.

Specialisation schemes have been pioneered in the United States of America. California led the way, and schemes are now well-established in Texas, New Mexico, and Florida. The Benson Commission called for specialisation schemes in England and Wales (10), and their call was echoed in the Civil Justice Review consultation paper on personal injury work (26). The Legal Aid Scrutiny Team suggested a scheme for all solicitors wishing to carry out legal aid work (27). This idea was pursued in the white paper on legal aid, which stated:

"The Government accepts that it is desirable in principle that solicitors doing legal aid work should have special skills in the area concerned, and is attracted by the idea that legal aid work should be done by panels of solicitors with specialist experience in each category. The Government will be discussing with the Law Society how such panels could be established and how their use could be enforced" (28).

The subject of specialisation is being debated within the solicitor's profession, and the issues have been outlined in a report of the Law Society's education and training committee published in July 1986 (29). In 1988 the Joint Committee on the Future of the Legal Profession (the Marre Committee) considered that specialisation was inevitable. They concluded "that recognition of post-qualification acquisition of specialist skills is in the public interest and that knowledge as to these qualifications ought to be made available to the public within the approved code of advertising accepted by the profession" (30).

Meanwhile a number of specialist panels have been established on an ad hoc basis. The Law Society vets solicitors wishing to take part in the duty solicitor scheme, and runs panels for those wishing to appear before mental health review tribunals or represent children in child care proceedings. Under the Insolvency Act 1986, the profession is required to license practitioners to undertake the restricted activities defined by the Act, which may not be performed by unlicensed lawyers (31).

Solicitors wishing to join the mental health review tribunal panel must attend an approved course and interview panel. They must either have experience of tribunals, or attend three tribunal hearings. The Law Society's panel of solicitors to act in child care cases requires solicitors to have not less than 18 months advocacy experience, attend a training course and satisfy the interview panel that they are suitable to be included. They must either have relevant experience of a contested case or attend at least one hearing. As of July 1988, there were 1,300 solicitors qualified for membership of the child care panel (32).

In both schemes, those choosing solicitors on behalf of others (such as hospital managers, guardians ad litem and magistrates court clerks) are strongly encouraged to use panel solicitors only, but the schemes are not exclusive. Mental patients and guardians ad litem may use non-panel solicitors if they wish.

The main advantages claimed for specialisation schemes are that they improve access to specialised legal services, by enabling consumers to identify lawyers with experience in specific fields, and that they increase competence among those providing such services. This, in turn, can lead to fewer delays, fewer complaints, and possibly reduced costs, because specialists will be able to deal with the matters more quickly and efficiently. Specialisation schemes may also encourage solicitors to expand into new areas of law, where legal services are lacking, such as landlord and tenant law or welfare benefits.

The most commonly voiced criticism of specialisation schemes is that they will lead to the demise of the general practitioner. At times the rhetoric of this objection contains more than a hint of nostalgia, with critics objecting more to de facto specialisation rather than its regulation through a recognised scheme. But there are real dangers if general solicitors are prevented from undertaking work in a particular area. Access to legal services is reduced in less populated areas which are unable to support specialists. Costs may rise, and it will become more difficult to simplify the law and procedure, because the new "specialists" have a vested interest in keeping their areas complex. Specialists can too easily lose peripheral vision, and fail to see the consequences of their advice on other legal aspects of the problem.

Most foreign proposals have stressed that non-specialists must continue to be free to provide their services within the speciality fields. This was the view of the Canadian Bar Foundation (33), the New South Wales Reform Commission (34), and all the American schemes with the exception of the Devitt Committee proposals for the admission of practitioners before federal courts. In this country the proposals of the Civil Justice Review and Legal Aid Scrutiny Team envisage that non-specialists will be prevented from undertaking work (26, 27). The Marre Committee, on the other hand, thought that exclusive schemes would be restrictive and monopolistic and could lead to an increase in prices (30).

It is also claimed that specialisation schemes can be misleading, or can use arbitrary criteria which discriminate against newly qualified lawyers, or lawyers without influential contacts. Great care is needed to ensure that this does not happen.

Specialisation schemes are expensive to run. Examinations, interviews, peer review and courses all cost money. The existing schemes are self-financing, but those who wish to become specialists may have to pay substantial sums. In California in 1985 the cost of taking the examination and gaining the certificate was $250, supplemented by annual and re-certification dues of $50 (35). In addition there is the cost of courses. It is unclear whether these costs are passed on to clients. Proponents of specialisation schemes claim that economies of scale and the absence of time spent looking up the law enable specialists to charge a lower overall amount for a case. Critics argue that specialists will use their additional qualifications as an excuse to put up their fees. At present there is no conclusive evidence to show either a rise or reduction in fees charged by specialists. Fears have also been expressed that specialists will have to pay higher insurance premiums because they will have to meet a higher standard of care. Such evidence as is available from the United States, however, suggests that to date insurance companies have taken no account of specialisation programmes in fixing premiums (35).

The levels of specialisation

It is important that if specialisation schemes are introduced, the level of skill required from practitioners is set at the right level.

High level certification schemes, such as those used in California and Texas, tend to involve a small number of broad subjects, such as family law or criminal law. The high standards mean that only a minority of the profession is eligible to join the scheme, and even among those who are eligible the high costs and examinations mean that only a small proportion of those eligible actually apply to become specialists (36).

New Mexico and Florida, on the other hand, adopted much lower level self-designation schemes, which used a much greater number of narrower specialisms (65 in the New Mexico plan and 24 in the Florida scheme). These schemes are much easier and cheaper to join. A greater proportion of lawyers are eligible and many more do, in fact, participate (37). This leads some commentators to observe that low-level schemes meet the access aim, but not the competence aim, while certification schemes with rigorous standards meet the competence aim but do little to improve access. There is clearly a need to find the right balance. Generally there has been a move towards the middle ground, whereby self-designation schemes have become more rigorous, while the Californian certification scheme has become more flexible. The 1980 model plan drawn up by the American Bar Association is a compromise, drawing elements from both low-level self-designation schemes and the more complex certification schemes (38).

Measuring competence

It is both difficult and vitally important to select the right criteria to measure competence. A working definition of competence produced by the American Law Institute and American Bar Association report on peer review has gained widespread acceptance in the United States (38):

> "Legal competence is measured by the extent to which an attorney (i) is specifically knowledgeable about the fields of law in which he or she practises, (ii) performs the techniques of such practice with skill, (iii) manages such practice efficiently, (iv) identifies issues beyond his or her competence relevant to the matter undertaken, bringing these to the client's attention, (v) properly prepares and carries through the matter undertaken and (vi) is intellectually, emotionally and physically capable."

But the consensus ends when it comes to deciding how competence should be assessed. Six main criteria have been used:

* years in practice

Most American schemes contain a provision restricting the programme to applicants who have spent a certain amount of time in practice—usually 5 years. The proposals put forward by the Royal Commission and, recently, by the Law Society's education and training committee also contain a "years in practice" requirement (10, 29). The rule has been justified on the grounds that "a practitioner ought to be able to show some general experience before claiming a speciality particularly so that he might be aware of dangers and difficulties outside his special area of practice" (29). But a "years in practice" rule is a poor indicator of general experience (39). A solicitor may have spent the first years working in a very narrow area, and need not necessarily have any general experience. It has been argued that a "years in practice" rule discriminates against the young, and indirectly against women and minority groups who are more likely to have qualified recently. The Californian scheme has now abandoned the requirement, in the absence of any evidence that it is an indication of competence. In our view, if it is thought necessary to require specialists to have acquired experience in other fields, this should be asked for directly.

* percentage of practice devoted to the speciality

This is also a common feature of specialisation plans, though its content has differed. The original New Mexico scheme required that lawyers spend 60 per cent of their time over the last five years in the specialised field of practice, while the Texan scheme requires 25 per cent of time over the last two years. The requirement measures concentration of practice rather than competence, however, and it is no longer used in "high level" schemes, such as the Californian plan or the scheme proposed for New South Wales in 1982.

* task performance

This has been a feature of the mental health review tribunal and child care panels in this country and is commonly used in other countries. Specialists are asked to produce evidence that they have undertaken certain required tasks, for example, that they have represented clients in a certain number of contested cases, or have drafted particular documents. Used flexibly, this indicator can work well, especially if it is linked to an assessment of the quality of performance. Used inflexibly it can discriminate against acknowledged experts, who supervise the work of others, who no longer undertake routine cases, or who settle most of their cases before going to court.

* course participation

Again this is a feature of the mental health review tribunal and child care panels and many American schemes. Applicants are required to attend educational courses in the specialist field for a certain number of hours before qualifying (15 is the norm). Some schemes also require recognised specialists to continue attending courses if they wish to be re-certified. Writing articles and books, passing a relevant diploma or giving instruction in recognised courses will frequently count towards the requirement. The requirement has proved relatively un-controversial. There is a widespread feeling that attendance at relevant courses can only improve the competence of practitioners. The main criticisms are the costs and that participants are rarely tested at the end of their courses. There is no guarantee that course participants are competent.

* examination

Examinations are commonplace in the medical field, but so far they have only been used in the Californian and Texan legal schemes. The American Bar Association model specialisation plan contains examinations as an option. Unlike other indicators, examinations attempt to measure substantive and procedural knowledge and, to some extent, skill in the application of this knowledge. But they have proved controversial. The Marre Committee was unable to reach agreement on whether examinations should be required (30). Critics object that examinations have a spurious objectivity: that they test ability to react under stress, and do little to test the skill and judgement involved in applying the law to life. It is also claimed that examinations favour recent graduates over older practitioners who are out of the habit of taking exams. In California the examinations have a high failure rate (between 25 and 30 per cent) and this discourages participation in the scheme. Examinations, however, are generally considered the best way of measuring competence on admission to the profession, and they are a more objective and direct guide than other requirements.

We would welcome experiments with "open book" and "take home" examinations, that try to measure practical skills rather than rote learning. In Texas, oral examinations were tried but were found to be both expensive and inherently subjective. This is also a problem with "searching interviews", such as those required by the duty solicitor scheme.

* peer review

This is a central feature of American schemes. Typically, applicants submit to the State Specialisation Board the names of a number of referees drawn from local lawyers and judges. The Board also consults a number of independent practitioners drawn from the applicant's locality. The danger here is that high profile lawyers, and those prominent in the "old boy network", will be favoured at the expense of lawyers who do not fit in with the established orthodoxy. Another problem is that while in some fields, such as court work, other lawyers may be familiar with an applicant's work, in other fields, such as tax planning, it is much more difficult to judge a colleague's work.

Until recently there has been no direct monitoring of an applicant's work, though this has been suggested in the new Californian plan, and it was recommended by both the English and Scottish Royal Commissions. Evaluation by clients has been suggested, but has not proved popular with the profession.

Our recommendations

In our view, well run specialisation schemes are in the interests of consumers because they improve access and raise standards. It is important that their introduction is carefully supervised and monitored, and much can be learnt from the American experience. We would like to see the Law Society set up pilot schemes on an experimental basis. Areas which we consider suitable for experimental schemes include personal injury, employment and matrimonial law.

We favour relatively high-level schemes, covering broad areas. We would not wish to see membership of the specialisation schemes depend on the number of years in practice or the percentage of time which the applicant devotes to the particular field of practice. Instead, the specialisation board should identify relevant experience, and apply "task performance" criteria. If possible, this should be combined with an inspection of the solicitor's work. For example, applicants could be asked to submit case files or documents which they have drafted. Applicants should also be required to attend recognised courses. We agree with the Law Society committee's comments that "a specialisation scheme must have some form of examination in order to command the confidence of the public and the profession" (29), and would prefer "open-book" examination to the traditional tests of memory. It is important that all the criteria are applied flexibly so as not to discourage clear experts. On the other hand we would not wish to see special exemptions for older established members of the profession who might be unwilling to take the examinations. In California, three out of four schemes gave special exemptions to such people (referred to as "grandparents"), as did one out of seven schemes in Texas. However, those specialist schemes in California and Texas which did not provide exemptions found that established practitioners were willing to take examinations. In our view, if the examinations are geared at measuring practical skills, there should be no particular problems with requiring established specialists to take part.

Specialisation schemes must be well publicised. The schemes are aimed primarily at members of the general public looking for a solicitor, and the public needs to know what a particular qualification or certificate means. The administrators of both the Californian and Texan schemes have acknowledged that insufficient institutional advertising of the schemes has been done in their states (35).

We disagree with the Civil Justice Review and the Legal Aid Scrutiny Team, who have both suggested "exclusive" schemes, in which only recognised specialists would be allowed to undertake certain categories of work (26, 27). There are three main dangers of exclusive schemes. First, general practices will be damaged, and it will be difficult for people in rural areas to gain access to any service. Secondly, exclusive schemes create new monopolies, which may cause costs to rise. Lastly, exclusive schemes usually set minimum rather than high standards of competence. If exclusive schemes try to raise standards and set high criteria, they may find that an inadequate number of practitioners participate and access to legal services could be seriously reduced. We have little experience in this country in running specialisation schemes and it would be wrong to introduce exclusive schemes before establishing a consensus about what competence in legal services is and how it can be measured.

Once a specialisation scheme is established, the legal aid scheme could permit accredited specialists in areas such as personal injury work to apply the "merits test". Solicitors, rather than the legal aid area office, would decide whether cases on which they are consulted stood sufficient chance of success and were of sufficient substance to merit legal aid. This would encourage solicitors to become members of the scheme and would reduce legal aid delays and administration costs.

References to chapter 5

1. Harris, D. and others, *Compensation and support for illness and injury*, Clarendon Press, Oxford Socio-legal Studies, 1984.
2. School for Advanced Urban Studies, University of Bristol, *Study of housing cases, final report to the Lord Chancellor's Department*, produced for the Civil Justice Review, Lord Chancellor's Department, 1987.
3. Research Surveys of Great Britain Limited, *Awareness, usage and attitudes towards the professional services and advice provided by solicitors*, February 1986.
4. Blacksell, M. and others, *Solicitors and access to legal services in rural areas; evidence from Devon and Cornwall*, Access to justice in rural Britain project, working paper 6, University of Exeter, 1986.
5. Law Society, *Solicitors' Practice Rules, 1987.*
6. Law Society, *Solicitors' Practice Rules, 1988.*
7. Law Society, *Solicitors' introduction and referral code, 1988.*
8. Genn, H., *Hard bargaining: out of court settlement in personal injury actions*, Clarendon Press, Oxford Socio-legal Studies, 1987.
9. Monopolies Commission, *A report on the general effect on the public interest of certain restrictive practices so far as they prevail in relation to the supply of professional services*, Cmnd 4463, HMSO, 1970. See also Monopolies and Mergers Commission, *Services of solicitors in England and Wales: a report on the supply of services in relation to restrictions on advertising*, HC 557, HMSO, 1976.
10. Royal Commission on Legal Services (Chairman: Sir Henry Benson), *Report*, Cmnd 7648, HMSO, 1979.

11. Law Society, *Solicitors' publicity code*, 1987.
12. *Bates & Van Steen v. State Bar of Arizona*, United States (1977), vol.433, p.350.
13. Macauley, S., *Lawyer advertising: "Yes, but..."*, DPRP working paper, Institute of Legal Studies, University of Wisconsin, Madison, WI.
14. A random poll of members of the American Bar Association published in 1984 found that only 13 per cent had tried advertising. See *American Bar Association Journal*, 1984, vol.70, pp.48-49. A study of Wyoming lawyers in 1982 found that 29 per cent had advertised of whom 41.5 per cent used a law directory and yellow pages. See Linenberger, P. and Murdock, G., "Legal service advertising: Wyoming attorney attitudes compared with Wyoming consumer attitudes", *Land and Water Law Review*, 1982, vol.xvii, no.1, p.209.
15. Fennell, E., "A wave of cheque books as the private men go public", *The Times*, 8 August 1987.
16. "Little response from advertising: brochures a success", *Solicitors Journal*, 5 June 1987, vol.131, no.23, p.760.
17. Taylor Nelson Media, "An analysis of solicitors' advertising", prepared for the National Consumer Council, October 1987.
18. Baldwin, J. and Hill, S., "Cut-price legal advice", *New Law Journal*, 20 May 1988, vol.138, no.6357, pp.344-345.
19. Schofield, C., "Accident legal advice services", *Legal Action*, August 1987, pp.8 and 23.
20. Genn, H., *Meeting legal needs?: an evaluation of a scheme for personal injury victims*, Centre for Socio-legal Studies, Oxford and Greater Manchester Legal Services Committee, 1982.
21. "ALAS leads to more claims", *The Law Magazine*, 31 March 1988, p.12.
22. Gibb, F., "BMA protests over lawyers' advertising to encourage claims", *The Times*, 18 April 1988.
23. This section draws on Paterson, A., "Specialisation and the legal profession", an unpublished paper commissioned by the National Consumer Council in 1986.
24. Baldwin, J. and Hill, S., *The operation of the green form scheme in England and Wales*, Lord Chancellor's Department, March 1988.
25. Beale, D. and Stow, B., *CAB and access to legal services in South Wales*, occasional paper 17, National Association of Citizens Advice Bureaux, April 1986.
26. Civil Justice Review, *Personal injuries litigation*, Civil Justice Review, 1986.

27. Lord Chancellor's Department, *Legal aid efficiency scrutiny*, June 1986.
28. *Legal aid in England and Wales: a new framework*, Cm 118, HMSO, March 1987.
29. Law Society, *Specialisation by solicitors*, a report of the education and training committee, July 1986.
30. Committee on the future of the legal profession (Chairman: Lady Marre), *A time for change*, presented to the General Council of the Bar and the Council of the Law Society, July 1988.
31. Insolvency Act 1986, sections 388-398.
32. "Note of The Law Society's Panel of Solicitors to Act in Child Care Cases" provided by the Law Society, July 1988.
33. Canadian Bar Foundation, *The unknown experts*, 1983, p.113.
34. New South Wales Law Reform Commission, *Third report on the legal profession*, 1982, chapters 2 and 5.
35. See Paterson, A., reference 23 above. This is based on interviews between our consultant and the scheme administrators.
36. In 1982, 1,350 out of 80,000 lawyers in California and 2,000 out of 27,000 lawyers in Texas had attempted the examinations. The failure rate was around 25-30 per cent. See Paterson, A., reference 23, above. Figures were derived from interviews between our consultant and the administrators of the California and Texas schemes.
37. Florida with a Bar about half the size of California has three times as many "designated" specialists as the latter has "certified" specialists. In New Mexico about one-third of the practising profession in 1982 "primarily limited their practice" to not more than three specialised areas. See Paterson, A., reference 23 above.
38. American Law Institute/American Bar Association, *A model peer law review system*, 1980.
39. Research evidence suggests that among doctors there is no correlation between years in practice and competence. See Peterson, O. and others, "An analytical study of North Carolina general practice 1953-54", *Journal of Medical Education*, 1956, vol.32, 1.

Chapter 6
Paying for lawyers

Mention lawyers, and most consumers think of the expense. There is little doubt that the problem of paying for lawyers is a significant factor in discouraging ordinary people from using the law. In the Compensation Study by the Oxford Centre for Socio-legal Studies, accident victims who had considered making a claim cited costs as one of the main reasons for not going ahead (1). The small survey of potential litigants in the housing study conducted for the Civil Justice Review also puts fear of costs as one of the most significant reasons for not taking court action (2).

In September 1988 we questioned 34 consumers who had complained to the Building Society Ombudsman about house surveys and valuations. Twenty complainants had received legal advice that they had a good or strong claim for negligence against their surveyor. Of these, eleven did not pursue their case, and all cited fear of legal costs as the reason for not taking the matter further (3).

The problem is not simply the level of charges. It is also the fear and uncertainty surrounding them. The costs of litigation are very difficult to predict or budget for in advance and are difficult to control as the case progresses. When the final bill arrives at the end of the case, it is difficult to understand.

In this chapter we look first at the current system—at the way in which solicitors' bills are drawn up and assessed, and how they may be challenged. We make recommendations for reforming the current system. We then look at alternative methods of paying for legal services, including standard fees, legal expenses insurance, contingent fees and mutual funds. We look at their advantages and disadvantages for the consumer, and at how far they can overcome the problems of access to justice.

How solicitors charge: the present system (4)

There are three major differences between the way solicitors charge and the fees of other professionals. Firstly, solicitors' bills are closely controlled by law. The way that solicitors may charge is governed by the Solicitors Act 1974, by high court rules (notably Order 62) and by considerable case law and customary rules. Secondly, solicitors' bills may be paid by a variety of different people—by clients paying their own solicitors, by the losing party in a case, or by the legal aid fund. The nature of the bill will depend on who is paying. Thirdly, separate procedures exist to challenge solicitors' bills. Dissatisfied clients in cases not involving litigation may apply to the Law Society for a "remuneration certificate", or alternatively, they may go to court and ask it to assess the amount of the bill. This process is known, somewhat confusingly, as "taxation" although it has nothing to do with tax.

The general principle is that solicitors' charges should be "fair and reasonable". Over the years, the question of how the reasonableness of costs should be assessed has developed into an extremely complex branch of law. Order 62 alone covers almost one hundred pages, and added to this are many hundreds of references to case law and precedence. Several legal text books—such as Butterworth's *Costs* and Cordery's *Law relating to solicitors* provide further clarification. These rules are not designed to be known or understood by the consumers footing the bill.

Often the rules will be too complex for lawyers to understand. Solicitors will consult specialist law cost draftsmen, described by a previous chief taxing master as "one of the most valuable, highest paid and most sought-after legal executives" (5). The procedure is expensive. Cost draftsmen working on their own account will generally charge between 5 and 8 per cent of the professional charge element of the bill. The "taxation procedure" will add another 5 per cent to the bill, and contested hearings can be considerably more expensive. The process is also very time consuming. A survey conducted for the Legal Aid Scrutiny Team found that for non-matrimonial county court legal aid bills, the average court procedure took 33 days, and the slowest case took 133 days (6).

Solicitors' bills of costs

Most solicitors charge by producing a bill of costs at the end of the case, showing the amount of work done. These bills come in two forms: gross sum bills and detailed bills.

Gross sum bills are the most common form of bill when solicitors are charging their own clients. In many ways they are similar to a plumber's invoice—for fixing your tap: £30 labour, £15 parts. A gross sum bill will state the work that has been done on a case, and will list "disbursements"—i.e. payments the solicitor has made to others, including court fees, barristers' fees, and fees for expert witnesses. In conveyancing cases disbursements will include land registry fees and stamp duty. The bill will state an amount to cover the work the solicitor has done. For many clients, a gross sum bill is sufficient, but if the bill is to be paid by someone else, such as the other party to the proceedings, or if the client challenges the bill, the solicitor must provide a more detailed one.

Detailed bills can be drawn up on two bases, depending on who is to pay. Both types of bill will look the same but the amounts will differ. If the bill is to be paid by the solicitor's own client, it will be drawn up on an "indemnity" basis. If it is to be paid by the other side or by the legal aid fund, it will be drawn up on a "standard" basis. The standard basis is relatively new—it came into effect in April 1986, when the main court rule, known as Order 62, was rewritten. Historically, the losing party was only made to pay those costs which were "essential to attain justice" (known as "party and party" costs). The standard basis is more generous and generally includes "such costs as have been reasonably incurred and are reasonable in amount" (7). The practical effect of the change is that there is less of a gap between the costs which a client will have to pay to his or her own solicitor, and the cost which will be refunded by the other side.

Like the gross sum bill, a detailed bill consists of "disbursements" (payments to third parties) and "professional charges" for work done by the solicitor. Calculating disbursements is relatively easy. In order to understand the "professional charges", however, one needs to understand two basic concepts—the "expense rate" and the "uplift".

★ the expense rate

This is the hourly rate at which solicitors charge. It is meant to cover the overheads of the practice and solicitors' salaries. The Law Society produces guidance known as *the expense of time* which includes a formula by which each firm of solicitors may calculate its own expense rate. Although the formula has no official status and is not legally binding (8), it is widely used. Basically, each firm calculates the costs of its accommodation, office equipment, clerical and junior staff. Added to this are salaries for legal executives and salaried solicitors and notional salaries for partners. The total sum is divided by the total number of hours which may be charged to clients. Different members of the firm will have different expense rates; that of the senior partner will be much higher than that of a junior legal executive. The expense rate for a firm with prestigious inner city offices and high staffing levels will be much greater than that for a small rural practice.

On an indemnity basis the solicitor is entitled to charge the actual expense rate. This will be calculated by each individual firm, either by applying *the expense of time* formula, by using another formula, or by comparing their expense rate to that of practices with similar overheads. On the standard basis, the court officers will use a rate which represents a "broad average" of expense rates in that area. For most ordinary types of business, the standard expense rate for that area will remain constant across a wide range of cases. If the case is very specialist, concerning commercial work for example, then the standard expense rate will be higher, based on a broad average of expense rates for commercial specialists.

The expense rate represents the hourly charge, and is multiplied by the hours spent on the case. Untimed letters and telephone calls are charged at one-tenth of the hourly expense rate.

★ the "uplift"

This is also called the "care and conduct" element. It is usually expressed as a percentage of the costs, and is added to the end of the bill as a lump sum. Whereas the expense rate is meant to cover the actual costs, the uplift is intended to provide the profit. It is effectively a responsibility allowance, paid to solicitors to reflect the complexity and difficulties of the case and the skill that was used. The uplift can vary from 15 per cent for simple cases to 150 per cent in complex or important ones.

Different uplifts may be applied to different parts of the same bill. Generally, bills split work between "standard items", "work done" and "travelling and waiting", and the uplift applied to each is different. Standard items are defined in the supreme court rules, and include the time a solicitor spends in court, or in conference with a barrister, or in issuing summonses or writs. Work done includes all the time the solicitors and legal executives spend on a case, except for the standard items. It will include such things as seeing the client, taking witness statements, speaking to expert witnesses, preparing documents for the court and for the barrister, inspecting documents and calculating damages. Travelling and waiting will be shown separately at the end of the bill. The rules of taxation state that time spent travelling and waiting, if reasonable and justified, should be paid for at the appropriate hourly rate, but it does not add to the responsibility of the conduct of the case. Thus it will not normally carry an uplift.

Information about charges

The Law Society's Council has issued written professional standards which describe "good practice" for informing clients about costs. The Law Society describes the standards as guidelines, and states that solicitors must use their own judgement in deciding whether or not to follow them. The standards state that on taking instructions solicitors should give clients the best information they can about the likely cost of the matter. They should state how much work is involved, and where possible give an estimate. The Law Society's guide, *The professional conduct of solicitors,* states that solicitors should take care not to bind themselves to an agreed fee unless this is their intention. If the actual charge varies substantially from the estimate, written reasons should be given. The solicitor should tell the client if the fee will be calculated on an hourly rate, but he or she need not disclose what the hourly rate is.

The standards state that privately paying clients should be told that they can put a limit on the costs which may be incurred without further reference to them. Whether or not such a limit is imposed, they should be told at least every six months the approximate amount of the costs to date. Unfortunately this standard does not apply to legally aided clients who may be subject to the statutory charge. The standards do not appear to be well-known in the profession.

Controls over charges

The controls placed on solicitors' charges depend on who is paying the bill and on whether the matter is "contentious" or "non-contentious". A "contentious" case is one which covers a dispute, such as personal injury, while conveyancing or drafting a will are "non-contentious". We look first at bills paid by the losing party, then at legal aid bills, and finally at bills paid by the solicitor's own client.

★ bills paid by the losing party

Where a case is heard by a court, the court will usually order that the winner's costs should be "taxed" and then paid by the loser. The winner's solicitor must lodge a bill with the court within three months of the end of the case. The bill is then scrutinised by a court official. In the county court this will generally be done by the registrar, whereas in the high court it will come before a "taxing master" or a senior court official. If the other side objects to the amount of the bill, a hearing takes place. Where the bill is not reduced by one-fifth or more, the costs of the taxation must be met from the party who has disputed the bill. If the bill is reduced by at least one-fifth, the solicitor pays the costs of taxation. The same procedure also takes place when cases are settled and the parties are unable to agree costs.

★ bills paid by the legal aid fund

Legal aid bills of more than £500 are also "taxed". The solicitor submits a bill to the court where the dispute took place, and the registrar or taxing master checks it and places a provisional figure on it. The solicitor may ask for a hearing, and may appeal against the taxation to a judge and two assessors. Since April 1986, the legally aided client also has a right to be heard at the taxation (9). This is an important right, because the legally aided client may end up footing the bill, either through contributions or through the statutory charge. Once the bill has been taxed, it is passed to the legal aid office for payment.

★ bills paid by clients

Under the Solicitors Act 1974, a consumer who receives a gross sum bill for a contentious case has the right to ask for a detailed bill within three months (10). The problem is that once the detailed bill has been presented, the gross costs bill has no effect. If the detailed bill is higher than the gross costs bill, then the client must pay the higher amount. Solicitors are not permitted to add the cost of drawing up the bill to the detailed bill, but must absorb these in the general overheads of the firm. However, the solicitor may have made a low estimate in producing the gross sum bill and detailed bills are frequently higher.

Bills for non-contentious business (i.e. business which does not involve disputes or court proceedings) can be challenged by asking the Law Society for a "certificate of remuneration". This has the advantage of being free and it does not involve the risk of an increase. The Law Society will call for the solicitor's file, and a special internal committee decides whether the charge was reasonable. They then issue a certificate stating the amount that they consider to be reasonable which may be the same as the solicitor's original bill or it may be less. It cannot be more. Clients who remain dissatisfied with the Law Society's decision may apply for the bill to be taxed.

In contentious business, the client who wishes to pursue the matter must apply for taxation. Where the bill is to be paid by a third party, the bill will usually be taxed in the court in which the matter was heard, but all disputes between solicitors and their clients must be heard in the high court before a "taxing master" (11).

Taxation is not a simple business. It is similar to other high court proceedings. The applicant must issue an originating summons and pay the appropriate fee. Where there is a dispute, the summons must be supported by an affidavit. Like other proceedings, taxations may involve practice directions, undertakings, payments into court and personal appearances in an adversarial manner before the taxing officer. Taxation proceedings may be as formal, complex and expensive as the original proceedings. The loser will end up meeting the winner's costs.

A further problem concerns time limits. Under section 70 of the Solicitors Act, the client has a right to taxation if it is applied for within one month of the detailed bill being delivered. This is a very short time for a client to consider a bill, seek advice about it and start proceedings. Clients who wish to apply for taxation between one and twelve months of receiving the detailed bill, must ask for permission from the court. Twelve months after the detailed bill is received the client loses the right to apply for taxation except in "special circumstances". Clients who have already paid their bills must also show that there are "special circumstances". Twelve months after the bill has been paid, the client loses the right to apply for taxation altogether (11).

Agreements about costs

In some cases, the usual rules about costs can be changed by agreement between solicitors and clients. Agreements about costs are controlled by the Solicitors Act 1974.

In "non-contentious" business (i.e. work which does not involve a dispute), all agreements to depart from the normal rules must be in writing and signed by the person who is to be bound by it. The Act states that the charges may be "by a gross sum, or by a commission or percentage, or by a salary, or otherwise". But if a client objects that the agreement is unfair or unreasonable, a court taxing officer may enquire into the facts of the matter and, if "it appears just to the court", the agreement can be set aside. The normal rules of taxation will then apply (12).

In "contentious" business (business which involves a dispute), a solicitor who wishes to exclude normal taxation rules must show that there is an agreement in writing, which complies with sections 59 to 63 of the Solicitors Act 1974. Again, the court may refuse to enforce the agreement if it considers that it is in any way unfair or unreasonable. The agreement may not provide for "contingent fees"—i.e. that payment will only be made in the event of the success of the action. Clients in contentious business, however, may rely on oral agreements, which fall outside the terms of the Solicitors Act 1974. A solicitor who agrees not to charge, or not to charge more than a certain amount, or only to charge out-of-pocket expenses, cannot require payment of the full bill (13).

It is difficult to say how common such agreements are. Our survey of solicitors' advertising shows that solicitors now routinely provide written quotations for conveyancing work, based either on a fixed sum, plus disbursements, or on a percentage of the house price. Agreements are often used in commercial work, where a firm may employ a solicitor on a retainer basis to carry out all their legal work. Fixed fees may also be used in simple disputes, such as motoring prosecutions, where a solicitor may agree to a fixed sum for a trial, for not more than two court appearances. But our survey also shows that written quotations are very rare in other disputes, such as divorce or personal injury work, where the uncertainties of litigation make it difficult to predict costs.

Problems with the current system

We have no reason to believe that solicitors make unreasonable charges. However, the present system has a number of faults. The first, and most serious one, is that clients are given very little idea of what the costs will be until the end of the case. This makes it difficult to know whether to pursue a case at all, or to make decisions about how the matter should be pursued. As we have seen, many people are deterred from bringing claims at all by the fear that on entering the solicitor's office they are signing a blank cheque. It also makes it very difficult to compare different firms of solicitors on the basis of value for money.

The problems apply to both privately paying clients and legally aided clients caught by the statutory charge. In a survey of divorced people in Bristol and Newport, 62 per cent of legally aided clients reported that their solicitors had never discussed costs with them at all. Typical comments included "you can never get any idea of costs from anybody" and "they cannot give you an estimate" (14).

Lack of information about costs hinders competition, because consumers cannot make the price sensitive choices which are characteristic of a competitive market. In their consultation paper on "general issues", the Civil Justice Review listed the main argument for and against price competition (15). On the plus side "open and fair competition is normally the appropriate mechanism for causing prices to find their right level, and such competition would enable fair prices to be fixed for litigation services". Competition would allow clients to obtain estimates of cost, and make judgements about value for money. Efficient practices would be given an incentive to keep prices down. On the other hand it is argued that in many cases it may be impractical or unwise to predict costs, and that competition may lead solicitors to lower standards of work or integrity. It is also argued that consumers are able to make adequate choices on the basis of reputation alone, or that small firms may be under-cut and their services lost.

The Civil Justice Review concluded that "competition, in an open market, of which advertising is a necessary feature, is a desirable means to maintain and improve standards of service. Meanwhile risks to the public should be dealt with by regulatory systems designed to control malpractice where it occurs" (16). They recommend that solicitors and barristers should be encouraged and expected to provide information to the public by stating rates per case or per hour and should be given free publicity about those rates in lawyers' referral lists.

We wholeheartedly agree that competition should be increased by giving consumers more information on which to make rational choices about using lawyers. In a non-competitive market, there is no mechanism to ensure that providers offer the mix of quality and price consumers want. Nor are resources necessarily used in the most efficient way. At present there is no incentive for efficient firms to reduce the time taken below what is generally regarded as "reasonable".

We do not agree with the argument that increased competition will drive all but the cheapest firms of solicitors out of business. As we have seen, many consumers are deterred from using legal services at all by their fear that legal costs are too high and outside their control. Greater competition is likely to expand the market for legal services.

Consumers are unlikely to choose firms on price alone. Price is simply one factor to be weighed against others, such as reputation, specialist skills and accessibility. Small local firms will be able to compete on accessibility even if they cannot compete on price. A cheaper service does not necessarily mean a lower quality service. The experience of mass market firms in the United States, which we discuss later in the chapter, shows that competitively priced services can do well on both objective and subjective measures of quality.

A final problem with the current system is the complexity, expense and delays involved in drafting a detailed bill and having it taxed by the courts. This alone can add substantially to the costs of legal proceedings. Disputes concerning solicitors' charges are handled entirely by lawyers. Consumers are at a serious disadvantage when conducting taxation proceedings in court against solicitors.

Our proposals for improving the existing system

In this section we assume that solicitors will continue to charge for work done by submitting a bill during or at the end of a case. Later we discuss alternative methods of charging.

Information

The first need is for more and better information for clients, both at the start of the case, as the case progresses, and when the final bill is delivered.

Much more needs to be done to advertise the written professional standards within the profession and outside it, and a stronger line should be taken in enforcing them. We recommend that the Law Society produces a simple leaflet explaining how solicitors charge, which the solicitor could enclose in the letter confirming arrangements with the client.

We endorse the Civil Justice Review's recommendation that lawyers should tell their clients their rate per hour (16). In our view, the written professional standards should be amended to require solicitors to declare at the initial interview the hourly charging rate of each solicitor or legal executive dealing with the case. This should then be confirmed in a letter to the client. The charging rate is not the only factor in the amount of the final bill: a specialist may have a higher rate, but take a much shorter time. But disclosing charging rates allows clients to know how much it costs to telephone their solicitor and it would be some help in making comparisons between different firms. This information should be provided for both privately paying clients and legally aided clients who may be subject to the statutory charge.

Bills would be simplified if the charging rate covered both the expense rate and the uplift. If the rate increases, either because the overheads increase during the course of the proceedings, or because the case becomes more complex, the solicitor should notify the client in writing before the increase takes effect.

We are concerned that some solicitors may not be aware of how the costs of a case are mounting as the case progresses. They may ignore costs until the bill is sent to an outside costs draftsman at the end of the case. This makes it almost impossible for either the client or solicitor to control costs. In our view, solicitors should set up internal procedures which keep track of costs as a matter of course. Solicitors should be required to provide their clients with accounts at regular intervals throughout the case, showing the costs incurred to date. The interval should be agreed between solicitor and client, but should not be more than every three months. Accounts showing costs to date should also be provided at the client's request.

Lastly, when delivering their final bill, solicitors should be required to provide the client with information about how the bill can be challenged.

Reforming taxation proceedings

We wish to see taxation proceedings radically simplified. The proceedings for challenging a bill should enable litigants to represent themselves. A consumer in difficulties over one solicitor's bill is unlikely to wish to go to another firm of solicitors to dispute it.

All disputes involving county court bills should be heard in the county court rather than the high court. The county court should also have power to hear cases about high court costs under a certain amount. We can see no reason why disputes about bills should be heard in a more formal forum than the original dispute.

The time limits for requesting taxation should be reformed. The Solicitors Act 1974 allows clients three months to ask for a detailed bill, but if they request taxation more than one month after the detailed bill is delivered, they need the permission of the court. One month is a very short time to read and understand the detailed bill, to seek advice, and to start court proceedings. The time limit should be extended to three months after the bill is delivered, or one month after the receipt of a remuneration certificate, whichever is the later.

The procedure for taxation should be simplified by allowing clients to complete an easily understood application form with the help of court staff. Objections to the bill should be listed on the form rather than in formal legal documents such as affidavits. The hearing before the registrar should be informal, with the registrar explaining the procedure and the rules to the client and asking questions. Normally, the decision of the registrar should be final, unless a point of public importance is at issue.

Lastly, the rules of taxation should be re-written in plain language. The name "taxation" is itself very confusing. When people are told that a bill may be "taxed", their first reaction is that a tax such as VAT or stamp duty will be added. In our view, it would be more informative to describe bills as "vetted by the court".

Standard fees

With standard fees the client agrees in advance to pay a set amount for a particular item of work. This may cover a whole case, or a stage of a case.

Standard fees are permitted, as "agreements" under the Solicitors Act 1974. But outside the field of conveyancing and some criminal work, they do not appear to be widely used. It is likely that they will become more popular in the future.

The Legal Aid Scrutiny Team recommended that in the legal aid scheme "wherever possible, payment should be on the basis of standard fees for particular types of case or stages of a case" (6). They considered that this would reduce the costs and delays of assessing bills, and provide better rewards to quick and efficient practitioners. The Team argued that standard fees would not be too radical a change. They have already been introduced for barristers in crown court cases and, in practice, registrars and taxing masters reduce bills when solicitors have charged more than is usual for a piece of work. Solicitors would retain the right to opt for taxation, and in particularly complex cases, they would be paid more than the standard fee.

The Team set a target for the introduction of standard fees in 75 per cent of cases in the subsequent two years (6). The government accepted that standard fees "should be introduced more widely" and stated that the "profession will be consulted about the details" (17).

Standard fees were also endorsed by the Civil Justice Review, particularly in debt and undefended divorce cases (16).

From the consumer point of view, there are advantages to standard fees, both for privately paying clients and for legally aided ones paying the statutory charge. Most importantly, they provide consumers with more information about how much a case is likely to cost, allowing them to make better choices about whether to pursue a matter and about which firm to use. Consumers also benefit from quicker, cheaper and easier procedures for drawing up bills. But there are dangers if standard fees are used inappropriately. They may offer an incentive to firms to cut corners and provide a poor service. In some types of litigation the work involved is very difficult to predict, and a standard fee may turn out to be set either too high or too low.

Standard fees are commonly used in the United States of America, and we look at their experience of fee schedules and mass market law firms to see whether standard fees have a potential to increase access to justice in this country.

Fee schedules

Standard fees enable organisations to publish fee schedules, showing how much it will cost to pursue different types of case. One such organisation is the Consumer Services Organization (CSO), a non-profit making body, set up by the Illinois Public Action Council. The Public Action Council is a federation of citizens' groups who lobby on behalf of consumers. CSO runs panels of law firms who meet their standards and have agreed to accept their standard fees. Consumers pay $30 a year to be members of the CSO and in return they can receive free legal advice from a firm on the panel, and can make a free will. If the problem cannot be solved by advice alone, the member can have the legal work performed at the rate advertised in the schedule, which represents a discount on normal fees. CSO will also investigate complaints against lawyers employed through their scheme (18).

Different fee schedules apply to different parts of the country. The following is an extract from the fee schedule for Northern New Jersey, effective from April 1987. It does not include "disbursements", such as court fees, paid on the consumer's behalf:

Estate planning

Simple will

Member *or* spouse	No charge
Member *and* spouse	No charge
With minor's trust	$100.00
All other estate planning	$90.00 per hr

Family law

Divorce or annulment

No issues	$475.00

Contested or issues to be resolved such as child support, alimony, property distribution or child custody	$775.00 (after 9 hrs. of time there will be a charge of $90.00 per hr.)

Visitation, support, domestic
violence, paternity, or other matters

Unrelated to a divorce	$350.00 (after 4 hrs. of time there will be a charge of $90.00 per hr.)
After a divorce	$500.00 (after 6 hrs. of time there will be a charge of $90.00 per hr.)
Child custody	$1,000.00 (after 12 hrs. of time there will be a charge of $90.00 per hr.)

If an answer is served, the case will be considered contested.

Tenant-landlord matters

Eviction & defense in eviction	$350.00 (after 4 hrs. of time there will be a charge of $90.00 per hr.)
Negotiation of residential lease	$90.00 per hr.
Non-business civil litigation	$90.00 per hr.

Estate matters

Probate	$500.00 (after 6 hrs. of time there will be a charge of $90.00 per hr.)

(Provided by Consumer Services Organization, Philadelphia.)

As can be seen, the fee schedule includes both standard fees and hourly rates. Standard fees do not cover the whole cost of contested actions but they do provide consumers with an idea of how much a case will cost.

Mass market law firms

Standard fees have been a crucial factor in the development of legal clinics and mass market law firms. Clinics have been described as "supermarket-type law firms" (19). They specialise in routine services, delivered in a standardised way, for flat fees. They advertise heavily in order to generate a large quantity of similar work. In recent years, the term "legal clinic" has become over-used, and many firms which refer to themselves as "clinics" differ little from traditional practices. The large chains, which do offer a radically different service, have adopted the description "mass market law firms".

One of the largest mass market firms is Hyatt Legal Services, which in 1984 had 127 branches in 20 different states. Its services are targeted at people in the lower and middle income brackets who do not usually use lawyers; about forty per cent of its clients are using lawyers' services for the first time. It aims to provide a limited range of routine services at affordable prices. It concentrates on simple divorces, adoption, wills, probate, bankruptcy, personal injury and traffic offences, and refuses to take on cases which involve intensive litigation. Cases are handled in a standardised way. When lawyers join Hyatt they spend two weeks working through the firm's training manuals, which give step by step guidance on each type of case. The firm makes heavy use of word processors to prepare forms, documents and wills. The fees are not the cheapest available but they aim to be competitive and affordable. In order to be cost-effective, Hyatt rely on a high throughput of cases, which they achieve by spending heavily on television advertising. Their adverts have been described as "dignified, although perhaps a little dull" (20). Their message is that Hyatt helps ordinary people with ordinary problems at affordable prices.

Hyatt has often been compared to fast food chains. Terence Purcell, Director of the Law Foundation of New South Wales, who studied the American system, comments that the analogy is appropriate because Hyatt "offers a limited menu, and, while not the cheapest around, the product is served efficiently, speedily and is of reasonable quality" (20).

Jacoby and Meyers, with 60 offices in 1984, operates on similar principles to Hyatt, although it offers a slightly larger range of services (20). A small research project published in 1979 looking at the experiences of Los Angeles divorcees shows that a standard routine service at competitive fixed fees does not necessarily involve a lowering of quality. The researchers used two measures of quality—an objective measure, based on the amount of child support awarded by the court, and a subjective measure, based on clients' assessment of the service offered. They found that, allowing for income differences, the legal clinic obtained significantly higher child support payments for wives than traditional practices. When they acted for husbands, their maintenance payments also tended to be lower, but the differences were not significant. The views of 22 people who used the clinic were compared with the responses of 52 users of traditional services. The clinic clients rated their lawyers as significantly better on such measures as "promptness in taking care of matters", "explaining matters fully", "interest and concern about your problem" and "paying attention to what you had to say" (21).

Our views

Our conclusion is that standard fees cannot be used in all forms of litigation but they can be applied to routine services, such as conveyancing, wills, probate and less complex divorces. Standard fees are an essential ingredient of mass market law firms, allowing standardised services at low cost. Such services are not everyone's choice, and they are not suitable in many cases. For some, however, they provide clear advantages, because they offer approachable, affordable services, and let consumers know what they will have to pay. They can make the law accessible to those who would not otherwise use a solicitor.

We support the government's proposals to introduce standard fees in legally aided cases. We wish to see consumers who may be subject to the statutory charge provided with details of what the fees are. We hope that the experience of standard fees in legal aid cases can be used for the benefit of paying clients.

Legal expenses insurance (22)

In legal expenses insurance schemes, the consumer pays an annual premium or membership fee. If a legal dispute covered by the scheme arises during the year, the legal costs involved in taking or defending proceedings are paid by the scheme. The scheme may also provide a free general advice service for members.

Legal expenses insurance is a relatively new idea in England and Wales. Until 1967, when the crime of "maintenance" was abolished, it was arguable that providing help with legal expenses was illegal (23). In recent years, however, the British market has been developing rapidly, and there are a range of schemes available.

Legal expenses insurance is much more developed in other European countries, most notably in Germany. It is also gaining ground in the United States. But the European and American traditions of legal expenses insurance are very different. In the USA, the development of "pre-paid legal services plans" has been motivated by a desire to make legal services available to people of limited means. In Europe, on the other hand, legal expenses insurance is based on purely commercial principles. Pfennigstorf, who carried out a comparative study of legal expenses insurance for the American Bar Foundation in 1977 comments that:

> "(In the USA) the larger social objective has had a profound impact on the development and design of legal service plans...many plans have been designed to provide the legal services that, according to research findings or informed estimates, the average citizen needs and that a prudent man would use, not only to take care of acute problems but also and even more important to provide services in the nature of 'preventive law'...

> "European legal expense insurers so far have not been subject to similar pressures and problems. Strict adherence to the principles of commercial insurance was early recognised as the key to economic success. There has never been a desire to provide coverage for all the legal services that a person might need. Rather, the emphasis has been, as in other lines of insurance, to protect the insureds from the financial consequences of uncontrollable and infrequent damaging events involving losses or expenses of a magnitude that cannot be absorbed in the average family or business budget. Moreover, coverages were designed for the middle class rather than the near-poor segment of the population." (24)

It is possible to identify two main types of legal expenses plan. Group plans, often organised on a co-operative basis by trade unions or motoring organisations, are prevalent in the USA, while individual plans sold by insurance companies are the typical European model. We look at how both types of plan are used, both in this country and overseas.

Group plans: the American experience

In the United States of America, group insurance plans began in 1971 and by 1984 were estimated to cover just under 10 million people (20). In some cases they are organised on non-profit making lines by affinity groups such as trade unions, or consumer groups. Alternatively, they may be sold commercially to members of such groups, or through employers. American tax concessions have made group plans an attractive part of remuneration packages, and the trade union organisation, AFL-CIO, has actively encouraged trade unions to include group plans in their collective bargains with employers.

Group schemes come in various forms. Some offer "open panels" of lawyers, where the client has a free choice of any practising lawyer; others provide "closed panels" in which the scheme operates through in-house lawyers or a small group of legal firms. In some schemes the entire group is enrolled, by making coverage an automatic benefit of group membership. In other schemes, legal cover is offered to members of the group and they decide whether they wish to pay an additional fee for it. The American experience is that plans based on automatic membership are much cheaper to operate, with 70 to 85 per cent of the premium being spent on providing legal services. This falls to between 50 and 60 per cent in voluntary enrolment plans, where marketing takes up a greater proportion of the cost (25). Automatic membership also involves less risk of "adverse selection", in which too many highly litigious people join the scheme.

The Law Foundation of New South Wales describe a number of different American group plans in their 1984 publication, *Innovations in legal service—new deals for consumers* (20). One of the smallest is the Green Bay Education Association Group Legal Service, covering 2,000 members, which has arranged with a local law firm to provide advice and consultation together with limited assistance with document drafting.

At the other end of the scale is MELS—Municipal Employees Legal Services—which in 1984 covered the 110,000 members of the union DC 37 and their families. All the members work for New York city council, many in low-paid service jobs, and the city corporation meets the costs of the scheme. The MELS scheme grew out of an initiative by social workers employed by the union, who recognised that union members often had legal problems which needed help. It differs from other group plans by providing legal services in the field of debt, eviction and welfare benefits, in addition to more traditional services such as wills, divorce and conveyancing. All services are provided by in-house lawyers, who work closely with social workers to resolve problems.

A third model is the Sheet Metal Workers International Trust for Legal Services in which the mass market firm, Hyatt Legal Services, contracts with the union to provide pre-paid services in family matters, wills, housing, debt collection and consumer law. In 1984 it covered 13,000 union members throughout the United States (20).

Group plans in England and Wales

The nearest equivalent to group plans in England and Wales are the legal services provided by trade unions. The TUC evidence to the Benson Commission, based on a 1976 survey of affiliated unions, showed that almost all unions provided some form of legal service to their members in the field of employment law and accidents at work. Few unions dealt with other matters, however, and only nine out of the fifty-five unions in the survey offered a general advice service for a nominal fee or no charge (26).

Most trade unions operate a "closed panel". This means that members who want the union to pay their legal costs must use the solicitors nominated by the union. Most unions have arrangements with one firm or a small number of firms, who handle all the union's cases on a regional or national basis. As a result, some of the solicitors' firms acting for trade unions are very large, with branch offices in all parts of the country. These firms are able to generate economies of scale and a high level of specialist expertise in such subjects as industrial accidents. This enables them to take on insurance companies' skilled solicitors on equal terms.

Other interest groups providing members with group legal expenses insurance include trade associations and motoring organisations. The Consumers' Association runs a scheme in which members who pay a premium (£20 in 1988) are entitled to free advice and assistance about consumer disputes from in-house lawyers; the scheme does not cover representation in court. Commercial initiatives in the field of legal expenses insurance have tended to concentrate on individual policies, but most companies now offer group schemes, targeted at employers and professional and trade associations.

Individual schemes: overseas experience

Individual plans first became common in Europe with the growth of leisure motoring between the wars. The first schemes began in France (27), but the most widespread coverage is in West Germany (28). At first most insurance schemes were limited to legal expenses in motoring accident claims. They were gradually extended to defending criminal motoring cases, and later other civil matters were added. Now around sixty per cent of German families have some form of legal expenses cover (29). Almost seventy per cent of claims concern motor accidents, and the remainder are largely employment and consumer matters (24). All the German schemes entitle the insured to use the lawyer of their choice. Insurers are not permitted to provide advice and assistance directly in pre-litigation negotiations.

Individual plans also exist in the United States. In particular, a number of Bar Associations attempted to establish legal services plans on behalf of the legal profession. These have not been a success. Terence Purcell comments:

> "Virtually all (the schemes) failed because the Bars lacked the necessary marketing expertise and were not looking at it from the consumer's, or marketplace, perspective. Another message which seems to emerge from this experience is that Bar Association identification with plans is counter-productive, as consumers are suspicious that it is simply a lawyers' ploy to expand business". (20)

Individual schemes in England and Wales

The first individual legal expenses insurance policies were launched in England and Wales in 1974. Since then the market has expanded and diversified, and includes family schemes and "add-on" policies attached to motoring and household policies. In 1982 the Law Society itself entered the field, by lending its name and approval to the Family Legal Expenses Insurance Scheme, which was backed by a consortium led by the Sun Alliance Insurance Company. Like the American Bar Association schemes, it appears not to have been a success and was abandoned in 1987 (30). The main providers are now DAS, IRPC, The Legal Protection Group, Hambro Legal Protection and Allianz.

The market is now worth around £35 million per year, and the insurance companies estimate between 3 and 4 million people have some kind of legal protection cover, even if only for motor-related uninsured loss recovery. The companies believe that the potential market is much greater (31).

The plans on offer come into three broad categories. Specialist plans cater mainly for business or for groups with special needs, such as people letting their homes. "Add-on" schemes can be taken out in addition to motoring or household insurance policies; they are cheap (often under £10 per annum) and cover narrow areas of law, such as uninsured loss recovery for motorists. Family plans are sold by themselves and cover wider areas of law. DAS Legal Protection Policy, for example, is relatively cheap (£30 in 1988) and covers initial advice plus employment, personal injury and consumer claims over £50. It also includes criminal defence cases, where the insured did not commit a deliberate act of violence or dishonesty. Disputes with builders (a common source of difficulty) are not included. The IRPC personal legal assistance plan is more expensive (£70 in 1988) but covers the above plus building disputes, all criminal cases, and disputes about the wills of parents and grandparents. Both plans have an upper limit of £25,000. It is very rare for plans to cover divorce.

Legal expenses schemes are usually sold through brokers, or direct by the insurers themselves. But a recent addition to the market, the Allianz Lawclub scheme, is marketed through solicitors. Lawclub covers consumer and personal injury disputes and is to be provided by the solicitor to the policy holder free of charge, as "a token of appreciation". Solicitors pay Allianz a minimum of £3.50, provided that they sign up at least 20 clients a month. If the policy holder wants more extensive cover, it is available through another Allianz plan, which the solicitor receives a commission for selling. The scheme has been promoted through the Law Society's *Gazette*, which has publicised the product in its editorial columns, and has accepted advertising from Allianz (32).

Telephone advice services

Several of the policies on sale in this country offer a 24-hour telephone advisory service free to policy holders. These services are run directly by the insurance companies, and provide initial advice on a wide range of enquiries. Some services also write simple letters on behalf of callers, or offer office consultations. The development of these services has been rapid, and The Legal Protection Group estimates that 7.5 million families now have access to one of these services (31). An analysis of calls received by Legal Benefits Ltd shows the use made of the service (31):

Problem	Percentage of calls
consumer	30%
accidents and injuries	23%
crime (including Road Traffic)	13%
hire-purchase and debt	7%
employment	7%
landlord and tenant	6%
matrimonial	5%
welfare benefits	3%
wills and probate	3%
miscellaneous	3%

Most American insurers also include free telephone advice as part of the plan. This is seen as an important marketing tool. A study of one of the major American commercial insurance schemes, Bankers, found that 92 per cent of all callers received advice only, 2 per cent received letters, follow-up telephone calls or a subsequent review of documents, and only 6 per cent were referred to an attorney for further representation (20). Some commentators have criticised insurance companies for overselling their advice lines. They state that most calls are dealt with quickly because they are not about legal matters, and that clients are led to think that they are getting a substantial benefit while in reality advice lines are devices for developing referrals to lawyers. On the other hand, Terence Purcell comments that:

> "There is agreement that initial fears of abuse of such schemes through over-usage or 'adverse selection' were unfounded...Second, it is not as difficult to quickly establish a professional rapport with the client over the phone as was foreshadowed. The traditional lawyers' concerns about the viability of such schemes appear to be groundless, and the schemes have in fact proved to be effective from a preventative point of view, as well as in removing many of the barriers which previously inhibited client contact with a lawyer." (20)

Conflicts of interest

In Germany, companies have not been permitted to offer both legal expenses insurance and other forms of insurance. It is felt that this leads to conflicts of interest where, for example, they finance accident victims to bring claims which they are liable to meet. These restrictions do not apply in the rest of Europe. In June 1987 the EEC approved a directive to harmonise the regulation of legal expenses insurance throughout Europe, to be implemented by 1990 (33). The Germans have agreed to abolish their regulations, and in return all other member states must adopt one of three possible solutions to prevent conflicts of interest. If they wish, member states can allow legal expense providers to choose which measure to adopt. The insurance companies must either:

(i)   ensure that no member of staff involved in managing legal expense claims or in providing legal advice carries out similar duties in respect of other forms of insurance;

(ii) establish separate legal identities for their legal expense subsidiaries;

(iii) allow policy holders to use a lawyer of their choice from the moment the right to claim arises.

In addition, policy holders must have a right to choose the lawyer who actually represents them in the court, tribunal or inquiry. They must also be able to choose their own lawyer where a conflict of interest arises.

The Marre Committee recommended that the government should require all legal expenses policies to comply with the third option, so that consumers must be given a free choice of solicitor from the start (34). They thought that no policy should require negotiations to be dealt with by the insurers' own staff. The Law Society considers that solicitors employed by legal expenses insurers should only deal with claims where the consumer gives specific consent and where the claim is less than the small claims limit. Under the 1988 *Solicitors' Practice Rules*, legal expenses insurance companies are only allowed to employ staff to deal with claims on this basis (35).

The effect of the directive will depend on how it is implemented and on how widely "legal expense insurance" is defined. It is not clear whether organisations, such as trade unions, which offer their members free legal services in return for an annual premium will be regarded as offering insurance schemes. Nor is it clear whether the Marre Committee wished to see trade unions continue to be able to select solicitors on clients' behalf, or whether they wished to see this practice banned.

The potential of group schemes

In our view, group schemes have the potential to reduce legal costs and increase access to justice. Large organisations are often at an advantage when buying legal services—because they buy in bulk they are able to find firms which are suited to their needs and specialise in the areas of most concern to them. Group schemes which operate through specially vetted solicitors are able to use the same bulk buying power on behalf of a number of individuals. Thus the schemes can benefit from economies of scale, obtain a more specialist service and exercise greater control over legal costs. Where the group represents the interests of its members, this can result in a cheaper and more finely-tuned service.

Trade unions who are considering extending the services they offer to members could consider increasing the scope of their legal service plans to cover other matters, such as debt counselling and housing advice. Tenants' groups, associations of leaseholders who are having problems with large landlords, community associations and credit unions could also benefit from group plans.

We wish to see the government and the legal profession encourage properly constituted group schemes, which are organised by affinity groups or which deal with specialist matters. We do not wish to see the UK government prohibit "closed panels" in the course of implementing the EEC directive, and we recommend that the government permits the insurer to choose which solution to adopt.

Another way in which group plans could be encouraged is to permit an overlap with legal aid. Legal aid is one of the few services in which private insurance disentitles consumers to state benefits. In the medical field, people with private insurance may still use the national health service. Yet under the legal aid regulations, a person who has legal expenses cover is likely to be refused legal aid for proceedings covered by insurance. Thus where a number of people in the group are eligible for legal aid, the existence of the scheme will deprive them of their entitlement, and this will substantially add to the costs of the scheme. In our view the Legal Aid Board should approve schemes which fill the gaps of legal aid, by paying contributions and meeting the statutory charge for example. This would enable tenants' and community groups, for example, to provide much cheaper group schemes.

The potential of advice lines

The advice lines run by legal expenses insurance schemes provide a useful service fairly cheaply. They increase awareness of legal rights, and overcome people's reluctance to take the first step towards pursuing them. They do not duplicate the services of an advice centre, because they deal with different sorts of problems from a different clientele. We are pleased that as from September 1988, the Law Society changed its practice rules to allow advice lines to employ solicitors to provide advice direct to members of the public (35).

It is important that consumers who receive bad advice are able to pursue complaints effectively. We wish to see the insurance companies develop guidelines on how advice given over the telephone is recorded, so that complaints can be investigated. Where advice is given or supervised by solicitors, consumers should be told that they may complain to the Solicitors Complaints Bureau. We also wish to see advice lines belong to the Insurance Ombudsman Scheme and consumers told about this.

The potential of individual schemes

Individual schemes provide a sensible way for relatively affluent families to meet legal costs arising out of unforeseen circumstances, such as accidents or dismissal. They remove the fear and uncertainty surrounding costs. Unlike the legal aid scheme, the consumer does not face high contributions or a statutory charge. "Open-panel" schemes provide a wide choice of solicitor, and approval is generally quicker than the issue of a legal aid certificate.

Nevertheless it should not be thought that legal expenses insurance offers an alternative to legal aid. Pfennigstorf comments that:

> "The most successful European insurers have started by offering well-defined coverages limited to controversies of a specified nature, notably automobile ownership, and have only slowly extended their scope to other, equally well-defined and limited legal matters. In contrast, universal coverages extending to legal matters and services of all sorts have been rarely tried and if tried have not been successful" (24).

He issues a warning against confusing business and social motives by trying to develop schemes which attempt to substitute for public programmes by redistributing "the high cost of justice among those who cannot afford it" (24).

Individual policies do not provide new types of legal service and do not in themselves achieve any savings in legal costs. Instead, marketing and administrative costs are added to the costs of solicitors. Figures provided by the insurance companies suggest that between 55 and 65 per cent of the premium is spent on claims (31). Insurance schemes do not help those too poor to use lawyers and they are not an appropriate way of funding services such as divorce which is under the control of the consumer.

Problems with legal expenses insurance

We wish to see an expansion of the legal expenses insurance market, but we consider that there is a need for regulation to prevent abuses and ensure that prospective policy holders have enough information to make choices. There are a number of problems with the way policies are designed and marketed, and it would be regrettable if these led to a loss of public confidence in legal expenses insurance.

The first problem is that consumers who are considering taking out a policy need a substantial amount of information in order to tell whether an insurance scheme offers good value for money and this is often not available in a comprehensible form. It is often difficult to compare one scheme with another because each is subject to different exceptions and the information is presented in different ways. In order to avoid this problem the German insurance companies agreed standard packages in 1969 and the federal supervising office discouraged deviations from the basic patterns (24). Standard packages do not exist in Britain.

Consumers also need to know whether help will be available under the legal aid scheme. Criticisms have been made of some of the promotional literature in this respect: for example, in 1983 the Advertising Standards Authority (ASA) upheld a complaint against the Sun Alliance Insurance Company. They had said of the legal aid scheme: "almost all wage earners can expect to make a contribution and if you earn above average income, you're unlikely to get any assistance at all". The ASA commented that this "did suggest that the proportion of the population which might benefit from legal aid was smaller than in fact appeared from official figures to be the case at present". The advertisers said they would take this into account in redrafting their brochure (36).

We are concerned that the insurance schemes' promotional literature and public relations campaigns may lead consumers to underestimate the coverage of the legal aid scheme. In chapter 3 we discussed who is eligible for legal aid, and the problems posed by the official figures. There is an urgent need for the Lord Chancellor's Department to produce accurate information on this subject.

The second problem is the application of "the merits test". It is clearly desirable that insurance contracts exclude frivolous and unmeritorious claims. But how is the decision to be made? Under the 1988 Allianz consumer and personal law plan, for example, cover is withdrawn if the appointed solicitor "reasonably refuses to continue acting for the Insured due to the Insured's conduct". The policy holder then becomes liable for the costs already incurred and any costs due to the opponent. The insurance company may "in their absolute discretion" allow a new solicitor to take over the case (37).

In practice disputes are rare but it is important that insurance companies develop fair procedures for deciding these issues. Under the German standard terms, whenever a policy holder disagrees with the insurer's opinion, the issue is referred to an attorney appointed by the policy holder, who prepares a written opinion. This is binding on both parties unless it "deviates substantially from the actual state of the facts or the law". The attorney's fee is borne by the insurer, regardless of the result (24). By contrast, several British terms are less favourable (38). According to the EEC directive, member states should ensure that there are appropriate arbitration procedures for sorting out disputes over legal expenses insurance. It states that these must be mentioned in the insurance contract (33). In Britain the main system for dealing with complaints against insurance companies is the Insurance Ombudsman Scheme, but this is voluntary, and, in 1988, of the companies offering legal expenses insurance only DAS were members of the scheme.

A third problem is that conflicts of interest are created when legal expenses insurance schemes are sold through solicitors. Consumers are entitled to look to their solicitor for independent advice about the legal aid scheme, the risks of litigation, and the advantages and disadvantages of the different schemes on the market. We are concerned that solicitors who have a quota of policies to sell each month, and stand to gain by selling some schemes but not others, will not be in a position to give independent advice.

Insurance companies providing legal expenses insurance are subject to the general supervision which the Department of Trade and Industry exercises over all companies transacting insurance business in the United Kingdom. The Department examines the proper incorporation, financial standing and business fitness of each company. It has power to make regulations about the form and contents of insurance advertisements and brochures. In practice, no such regulations have been made. The Department may also prosecute companies who induce people to enter into insurance contracts by making misleading statements or dishonestly concealing material facts (39).

We recommend that the main companies develop guidelines to ensure that information about coverage is presented in a standard and comprehensible form, and that all policies have fair procedures for dealing with disputes about cases. The Department of Trade and Industry should monitor progress in this field and be prepared to intervene by means of regulation if self-regulation does not appear to be sufficient.

The Law Society should ensure that solicitors give independent advice about the merits of different schemes. In 1982, the Law Society issued guidelines to solicitors about legal expenses insurance schemes but these are now seriously out of date and are not being enforced. The Law Society *Practice Rules 1988* require that the solicitor should account to the client for any commission received of more than £10, unless the solicitor discloses the commission to the client and gains consent to retain it. The rules do not cover commission of less than £10, but solicitors' general duty prevents them from retaining a "secret profit". We wish to see the Law Society state explicitly that solicitors should always account to clients for any commission received for selling legal expenses insurance.

Contingent fees (40)

Contingent fees (also called contingency fees) involve the lawyer assuming some of the risks of litigation. A contingent fee agreement can be defined as a contract for the provision of legal services in which the amount of the lawyer's fee is contingent in whole or in part upon the successful outcome of the case, either through settlement or litigation. Usually such agreements involve rewarding lawyers with higher fees than they would normally receive if they win, in return for running the risk of going without a fee if the case is lost.

Contingent fees are not permitted in England and Wales. Traditionally, they were prevented by the ancient crimes and torts of "maintenance", "champerty" and "barratry" (23, 41). When these offences were abolished in 1967, contingent fees continued to be banned on the grounds that they are contrary to the ethical rules of the profession (42) and because they are regarded as unenforceable contracts which are contrary to public policy (43).

Prohibitions on contingent fees are common throughout Europe, though there are partial exemptions in Spain and West Germany (44). Although they are generally permitted in Canada, they are not widely used (45). In Scotland, contingent fees are prohibited at common law, although there is an honourable tradition among Scottish lawyers of acting for the normal fee in the event of success, and nothing if the case is lost (46). Some English lawyers also adopt this practice, though its legality is uncertain.

The American experience

It is only in the United States of America that contingent fees have become widely used. This is partly because the Americans do not follow the "costs with the event" rule, in which the loser pays the winner's costs. Instead, the normal rule is that each side pays their own legal costs, whatever the outcome of the case (47). American damages are also much higher than in Britain. These features of the legal system, together with a relatively litigious population, and a "go-getting" legal profession, willing to take risks for profit, have combined to make contingent fees widespread throughout the USA.

In the USA, contingent fees are most frequently used in personal injury actions, though they are by no means confined to such cases. They are also used in professional negligence, product liability, debt collection, succession and breach of contract cases. Perhaps more surprisingly they are also found in tax-refund, employment discrimination, private anti-trust cases and in class actions. They are mainly used for representing plaintiffs, but some state courts have also permitted defendants to be represented on a contingent basis (48). In certain areas of law, however, the courts and ethical codes prohibit their use on public policy grounds. These are criminal cases, family cases, and in some states, legislative lobbying.

Contingent fees may be calculated as a percentage rate, as a fixed fee, or on an hourly basis. In practice, percentage rates are the most common. A typical contingent fee agreement in the United States may provide that the lawyer's reward will be 25 per cent of any settlement prior to a writ being issued, a third of any settlement or award made after a writ is issued, and forty per cent or more if either side appeals. For this, the expenses of the case (such as court dues, experts' reports and witness fees) are usually advanced by the lawyer. Until recently, professional ethical rules required that the client should remain ultimately liable for such expenses should the action be lost (49). This was rarely monitored, however, and some lawyers chose not to enforce the losing client's obligations. The new American Bar Association *Model rules of professional conduct* now permit such advances to be made on a contingent basis (50). The earlier *Code of professional responsibility* was ambiguous about whether lawyers could go further and advance the client's medical and living expenses. When the ethical rules were revised in 1981, American trial lawyers lobbied for permission to advance "reasonable and necessary medical and living expenses" to the clients on a contingent basis, but this was omitted from the final version of the model rules.

The rules permit clients to discharge their attorneys without cause at any stage up to the final award or settlement. After being discharged, the attorney is no longer entitled to a contingent fee, and should the client win, can only charge for services rendered. In most states, if the client subsequently abandons or loses the case, the discharged attorney under a contingent fee arrangement is not entitled to a fee (51).

Arguments in favour of contingent fees

The first, and strongest, argument in favour of contingent fees is that they permit poor clients who are unable to pay lawyers' fees to bring their cases to court. Judge Musmanno (described as America's nearest equivalent to Lord Denning) put it in the following terms:

"If it were not for contingent fees...the person who has, without fault on his part, been injured and who, because of his injury, is unable to work, and has a large family to support, and has no money to engage a lawyer, would be at the mercy of the person who disabled him, because being in a superior economic position, the injuring person could force on his victim, desperately in need of money to keep the candle of life burning in himself and his dependent ones, a wholly unconscionably meagre sum in settlement, or even refuse to pay him anything at all. Any society, and especially a democratic one, worthy of respect in the spectrum of civilization, should never tolerate such a victimization of the weak by the mighty" (52).

It is also argued that contingent fees allow risks to be spread more equitably. "One-shot" litigants, who engage in litigation very rarely, are in a poor position to bear the financial risks of going to court. The American system allows the risks to be shifted to the lawyer, who can spread the risks over many cases, and is therefore in a better position to bear them.

In addition, it is sometimes said that contingent fees give lawyers an incentive to win, and encourage them to act with zeal in the client's interest. They may be viewed as a "productivity bonus" for lawyers.

Lastly, contingent fees on a percentage basis are very easy for the client to understand and for the lawyer to account for. Complex billing arrangements are no longer needed.

Arguments against the American system

Contingent fees are frequently blamed for two ills which are said currently to beset the legal system in the United States: excessive awards and an explosion of litigation.

Critics point to a rise in the number of substantial jury awards in civil cases. In 1975, for example, there were 27 awards of over a million dollars, compared with 401 in 1984 (53). A survey in Illinois showed that the average damages award increased from $30,000 in 1966 to $82,000 in 1978 (54). This has led to sharp increases in insurance premiums, and some professionals are now "going bare", that is, practising without malpractice insurance. It is said that contingent fees are to blame for high awards because civil juries wish to ensure that the victim remains fully compensated after the contingent fee has been met. On the other hand, it should be remembered that most damages awards are for small amounts. In 1978, the majority of Illinois awards were for less than $10,000, and the high average was accounted for by a very small number of cases (54). There are many other reasons why civil juries may make an occasional large award. It may be to show public indignation against the wrongdoer or as a result of inadequate directions from the judge. It has not been proved that contingent fees are to blame.

The existence of a litigation explosion is the subject of heated debate in the United States (55). Even if there has been a substantial increase in litigation, it is by no means established that this is either undesirable or that contingent fees are responsible for it. Contingent fees have been used in the United States for over eighty years, and it is unlikely that they alone have brought about an increase in litigation in the last ten or twenty years. The objection usually made to "over-litigation" is not that people are taking legitimate complaints to court, but that people are indulging in frivolous cases, designed to obtain nuisance payments from insurance companies. It is very unlikely, however, that contingent fees are responsible for poor cases being brought to court. After all, lawyers will wish to minimise their risks, and it is sometimes argued that contingent fees act against those with doubtful cases because lawyers are only willing to take on cases with a strong chance of success (56).

Another argument against contingent fees is that they create a conflict of interest between the lawyer and the client. It is argued that lawyers will wish to avoid the heavy expense of preparing for trial and of the trial itself, when this will not add substantially to the award. They may encourage settlements which are not in the client's best interests. For example, a lawyer on a contingent fee of a third may decide that the true worth of the claim is $30,000, but this will require 100 hours of work to obtain. At an early stage, after just five hours work, the insurance company offers $5,000. The lawyer who successfully urges acceptance gains an hourly rate of over $300 per hour, compared with a rate of $100 if the case goes the full distance.

There have been two research studies to test whether this occurs in practice. The first, based on a non-random sample of 59 personal injury cases in New York, found some evidence to support the theory that contingent fee lawyers invest less time than hourly paid lawyers in a given case (57). The second, more recent, study had a considerably larger sample drawn from twelve courts around the United States (58). The authors found that in comparison with hourly paid lawyers, contingent fee lawyers invested 22 per cent less time in the cases involving sums of around $6,000. But they devoted more time than their hourly paid counterparts to cases worth over $10,000. There was no clear evidence that the difference in hours allocated made any systematic difference to the damages awarded. The authors state that the results are not easy to interpret, and the effects of fee arrangements on lawyers' behaviour are indirect rather than direct.

Our conclusion to these studies is that the case against contingent fees on the grounds of conflict of interest is not proven. All fee arrangements have their problems. There is no doubt that the British system where the victim bears the risk puts very heavy pressure on clients to settle. We do not consider that contingent fees would aggravate the situation.

The third argument against contingent fees is that lawyers may use their superior knowledge of the risks and costs involved to charge excessive fees. The client who has no other means of obtaining legal redress must accept the going rate. Certainly, at the turn of the century, lawyers in the USA routinely charged 50 per cent of the recovery as a contingent fee. Over the years this figure came to be seen as excessive and today's norm of one-third became established.

Controls can be placed on fees which are clearly excessive, but it is much more difficult to ensure that fees are fair in every case. In practice, American lawyers tend to charge very similar contingent rates. This means that it is difficult for clients to shop around. Although a third may be fair in some cases, it will be very high in other cases where damages are high and the risk of failure is low. These clients are effectively subsidising those with weaker cases.

It is also argued that contingent fees encourage lawyers to use unethical tactics in the way they conduct cases. The Royal Commission on Legal Services described these tactics as "the construction of evidence, the improper coaching of witnesses, the use of professionally partisan expert witnesses (especially medical witnesses), improper examination and cross-examination, groundless legal arguments designed to lead the courts into error..." (59).

This argument carried considerable weight with both the Benson and Hughes Commissions, but there is little hard evidence to support it. It appears to take an exceedingly pessimistic view of the ethical probity of the profession. Lawyers have a natural desire to win their cases, and we are not convinced that a different basis for charging will, by itself, transform an honest lawyer into a dishonest lawyer.

American controls on contingent fees

Many American states have taken action to control excessive fees. In recent years at least seventeen states have enacted laws limiting the size of contingent fees. In New York, lawyers must choose either to charge no more than a third of damages, or to limit their fees to a sliding scale. This allows fees of half the first $1,000 of damages, 40 per cent of the next $2,000, 35 per cent of the next $22,000 and 25 per cent of the remainder after disbursements have been deducted. Laws such as this succeed in controlling fees which are excessive, but create the problem that fee schedules may become minimums as well as maximums (48). Statutory ceilings have also been criticised for preventing lawyers taking on high-risk but meritorious claims, in the field of medical negligence (60).

The courts have a general supervisory power over attorneys as officers of the court and this includes the right to determine the propriety of fee arrangements. Since 1969 the ethical rules have insisted that attorneys' fees be "not clearly excessive", a phrase which has been reworded under the American Bar Association model rules to state that fees must be "reasonable" (61). The courts have the power to enforce compliance with the rules. This approach is not altogether satisfactory, however. Clients must be aware of their rights, and be prepared to follow one bad experience of lawyers by going to court again. The reported cases suggest that the courts' approach to these matters has been inconsistent and uncertain (48).

The American Bar Association model rules require that contingent fee arrangements must be explicit. They specify that the contract must be in writing and must:

> "state the method by which the fees are to be determined, including the percentage or percentages that shall accrue to the lawyer in the event of settlement, trial or appeal, litigation and other expenses to be deducted from the recovery, and whether such expenses are to be deducted before or after the contingent fee is calculated. Upon conclusion of a contingent fee matter, the lawyer shall provide the client with a written statement stating the outcome of the matter and, if there is a recovery, showing the remittance to the client and the method of its determination." (62)

The provision omits one crucial item. The fee arrangement should make it quite clear what the lawyer undertakes to do—whether the agreement extends to acting for the client on appeal, for instance, or enforcing the judgment. Some commentators have argued that the provision should go even further, and that lawyers should set out the amount of time they think the case will take, and the likely risks involved.

Some critics have argued that contingent fees should only be allowed on an hourly basis, in which winning clients would pay either a higher hourly fee for the work done, or a standard hourly fee plus a "risk premium" which may be a small percentage of the award, while the losing client would pay nothing (63). Hourly fees lead to more complex billing arrangements, but they reduce conflicts of interest and ensure that fees are more closely related to the amount of work actually done on the particular case. As yet no state has adopted this solution, and hourly contingent fees have been very little used.

Should contingent fees be allowed in England and Wales?

In recent years there has been increased interest in contingent fees. The Civil Justice Review recommended that the prohibition should be "open to re-examination" (16). The Marre Committee thought that "contingency fees should not be introduced at present but that they should form the subject of further research and discussion" (34).

The American experience has led us to the conclusion that the arguments against contingent fees are not insurmountable. We are not worried that contingent fees will lead either to excessive litigation or to excessive awards. In fact, the problem in this country is that awards are too low, and too many individuals are unable to seek redress. We do not think that solicitors will respond to contingent fees by abandoning their ethical standards. Safeguards can be enacted to prevent clearly excessive fees. Either maximum fees could be imposed by statute, or the law could require contingent fees to be approved by the courts, through the taxation procedure. The conflict of interest problem would be reduced if settlements made on a contingent basis needed the approval of the court registrar, or if fees were calculated on an hourly basis. We would also wish to see contingent fee arrangements made explicit and put in writing.

This does not mean, however, that contingent fees will solve problems of funding. If permitted, contingent fees are unlikely to become a common or very attractive method of charging in this country. One reason is the "costs follow the event" rule, by which the loser pays the winner's legal fees. This means that in most litigation over £500, including personal injury cases, losing involves the risk not only of paying one's own legal fees, but of having to pay the other side's fees as well. Although contingent fees could remove the former risk, they are unable to remove the latter, and there will continue to be considerable pressure on plaintiffs to settle for low sums, rather than take even a small risk of losing.

In cases where the "costs follow the event" rule does not apply, such as industrial tribunals and the small claims court, compensation awards are usually too small to leave much over to pay the contingent fee. The median industrial tribunal award in 1984, for example, was £1,345 (64) and this is intended to replace lost earnings. The legal aid statutory charge operates on a contingent basis, and illustrates the problems that are created when claimants are forced to use awards intended for one purpose (such as providing a home to live in) to pay legal fees. This is also a problem in personal injury cases. Compensation awards are much smaller than in the United States, and claimants have many other calls on their awards, such as meeting the costs of disability or replacing lost income. Little is left over for lawyers.

Although controls can be placed on contingent fees which are clearly excessive, this does not mean that contingent fees are an economical way of financing litigation. Lawyers are better placed than litigants to spread the risk but they cannot eliminate it, and profit-making enterprises expect to be paid for the risks which they assume. The low level of awards does not provide a very profitable market for speculative ventures by lawyers. In our view, mutual funds, operated on a non-profit making basis, are a more attractive solution to the problem of funding personal injury litigation. Tribunals and small claims courts should be sufficiently informal to allow most litigants to represent themselves, and those whose cases are especially complex, or have trouble speaking for themselves, should be given help through salaried services.

On the other hand, we would not rule out contingent fees in all cases. If it does not prove possible to introduce a mutual fund, we see advantages in permitting contingency fees on an experimental basis, to see whether they permit people to pursue cases which they would not otherwise bring to court. Advice centres may be able to meet some of the costs of tribunal representation from fees based on small percentages of awards.

Mutual funds

In recent years, two major proposals have been made to set up non-profit making funds to bear the risks of litigation. Unlike insurance schemes, it would not be necessary to take out cover in advance. Litigants would only approach the fund once they had a reason to make a claim. The first proposal, put forward by Justice, would work on a contingent basis, by taking a percentage from the award of successful litigants. The second scheme, proposed by the Law Society, would work on a fixed fee basis, with both winners and losers paying a fixed, non-returnable premium if they wished to be covered by the fund. We describe each scheme in turn.

Justice's proposal

Justice is an all-party group of lawyers concerned with the fair administration of justice. They first suggested a Contingency Legal Aid Fund (CLAF) in a report on motor accident cases in 1966. In 1978, at the time of the Royal Commission, interest in the scheme increased, and Justice put forward a more detailed proposal (65). The basic idea is that the fund would invite applications from prospective litigants who had reasonable claims which they were deterred from bringing through fear of costs. If the fund agreed to take on the case it would undertake to pay the litigant's costs in the event of failure, plus any costs awarded against him or her. If the litigant succeeded, the fund would receive the costs awarded from the other side, plus a percentage of any damages or property recovered in the proceedings. Eventually the fund would be self-financing.

The proposed fund would cover most contractual and negligence claims, including personal injury, in which the plaintiff was claiming substantial damages or property. It would also cover defamation actions. It would not cover matrimonial or family cases, or claims for injunctions where there was little prospect of a cash award. Small claims would also be excluded. Justice set the limit at the county court costs scale 3 threshold, which was then £500, and is now £3,000. It was hoped that the fund would also cover tribunal claims for more than this amount. At first, the fund would only help plaintiffs, unless the defendant was making a substantial counter-claim. In time, the fund could be extended to provide some cover to unsuccessful defendants.

It is unlikely that people eligible for full legal aid would use the CLAF. Those liable to pay contributions could choose between legal aid and the fund. If the fund were entirely self-financing, it would not impose an upper income limit. If public money were used, however, the very rich would be excluded, though the means test would not be rigorously enforced.

When deciding whether to take on a case the fund would apply the same merits test as applied by the legal aid authorities. Applicants would have to show that they had reasonable grounds for taking the action and that it was not unreasonable for them to be given support. All applicants would pay a non-returnable fee to cover the fund's administration costs. In 1978 this was set at £50. A committee would then decide whether applications should be granted. When cases were accepted, applicants would be told the level of the contingent fee, and would be free to choose and instruct solicitors in the normal way.

The fund would monitor the progress of the case. If it was found that an applicant had deliberately misled the fund, cover would be withdrawn, and the litigant would have to meet the full legal costs from the beginning. If the applicant had behaved honestly, but it became clear on further investigation that the case was very weak, the fund would offer the litigant a choice—either discontinue, and the fund would meet the costs to date, or proceed at your own risk. Similarly, the fund could withdraw cover if it considered that the applicant had unreasonably refused an offer of settlement. Litigants would then have to meet their own costs after the offer of settlement. The litigant who was proved right, and succeeded in obtaining a higher sum, would make a payment to the fund based on the amount of the offer, not on the sum obtained. Once litigants had accepted CLAF assistance, they would not be able to renounce it. They would continue to be liable to pay a percentage of their award to the fund.

CLAF would cover the cost of enforcing an award, and where the full award could not be recovered the fee would be calculated on the basis of the sum actually received. Where the litigant was successful and the other side appealed, the fund would cover the cost of the appeal. Litigants who were unsuccessful would have to make a separate application for assistance with the appeal, which would be decided on its merits.

Justice considered whether the amount of the fee would be set individually for each case, or whether standard fees would be applied to all cases. It was thought to be too complex to set individual rates. In most cases it would only be possible to judge the chances of success after the action had progressed, and it was thought that the fee should be certain from the start. Therefore, Justice proposed a standard fee, set in bands. Lower fees would be charged on settlements, and higher fees would be charged on high risk cases. It was suggested that initially, to err on the side of caution, the fee would be 20 per cent of the first £5,000, 15 per cent of the next £5,000 and 10 per cent of the rest. The fees would be halved for settlements reached before the trial had been prepared. In addition, the fund would receive full costs from the other side.

Justice proposed that the Law Society should run the fund and that the government should provide a loan to cover the fund's initial liabilities, to be repaid within a few years. If this did not prove possible, the government should guarantee the fund's liabilities so that money could be raised commercially. Setting up a Contingency Legal Aid Fund would need legislation, to permit it to use contingent fee contracts, but the legislation could be short and simple.

The main problem in implementing the Justice proposal is that it requires substantial start-up funds. Administrative costs and payments on account to lawyers will need to be made before the income is received. The government has not shown any interest in providing a loan. In October 1984, however, a scheme on very similar lines was established in Hong Kong for those whose means were too large for legal aid. It is restricted to major claims concerning death and personal injury. The government provided a loan of HK$1 million, with an interest free period. In 1987 contingent fees charged by the fund varied between 10 per cent and 12.5 per cent, with a reduction for settlements. The Director commented that it was too early to say whether the rates were viable, but there may be a need for minor increases (66).

The Law Society's proposal

The Law Society's contentious business committee put forward a proposal for a fixed costs legal services scheme in a discussion document published in July 1987 (67). The idea is currently being debated within the profession. The paper suggests that initially the scheme would be confined to negligence claims, but it could in time be extended to other forms of civil litigation where costs are awarded against the loser, such as contractual disputes, judicial review, and housing matters. It would not cover family matters. Unlike CLAF, it need not be limited to claims for money or property, but could include claims for injunctions. All assisted litigants, win or lose, would pay a non-returnable fixed fee to the fund, set at different rates for different types of litigation. In return, the fund would undertake to meet the costs of both sides if the assisted litigant lost. If the litigant won, the solicitor would be paid by the other side, and would not be able to charge the client any additional sums. The fund would be a supplement to legal aid. Those eligible for full legal aid would be unlikely to apply, while those liable to make contributions to the legal aid fund would have a choice of schemes.

The main advantage of the Law Society's proposal over CLAF is that money is paid "up front", before the case is started. The Law Society also proposed to keep administrative costs to a minimum, by permitting the vetting of cases in the initial stages to be carried out by the client's solicitor. They calculate that administrative costs can be held down to between £10 and £15 where proceedings are not started, and £30 to £50 where proceedings are started. Thus it may be possible to go ahead with the scheme without initial funding from the government. If the government refuses to underwrite the scheme, it may be possible for it to be underwritten by the insurance market.

The initial proposal is that the scheme would cover only negligence cases and would operate in two stages. The solicitor would offer the claimant a free interview in which the initial assessment would be made. If it appeared to the solicitor that the case was worth pursuing, the client would be offered the option, for a small fee (probably between £25 and £75), of being covered by the scheme up until the stage at which court proceedings would be needed. If the fee were paid, the fund would undertake to pay the solicitor's fees in the event of failure up to a maximum amount: the paper suggests a limit of between £750 and £1,000. Although the solicitor may have to ask for the fund's authorisation to incur large expenses, most cases would not be brought to the attention of the fund at this stage.

The second stage would arise when proceedings needed to be issued. The case would be submitted to the fund who would apply the legal aid merits test to decide whether there were reasonable grounds for taking the action. If the fund turned the case down, there would be an appeal to a committee of practising lawyers. If the case were accepted, the litigant would then have to pay a larger fee (between £350 and £550) to be covered until the end of the case. If the litigant were successful and the other side appealed, the scheme would cover the appeal. If they were unsuccessful and wished to appeal, the scheme would consider backing the appeal on the payment of a further fee.

Again, controls would be needed during the case. The fund would be notified of offers to settle, and could withdraw cover if the client behaved "unreasonably". The aggrieved client could appeal to the committee of lawyers.

The scheme would mainly be advertised by solicitors participating in it. It is expected to run in tandem with the Accident Legal Advice Service (or ALAS! scheme) described in chapter 5. Although the discussion paper suggests that the amount of the fees would be advertised on a national basis, the costs of publicity do not appear to have been included in the scheme.

The discussion paper suggests that the fund may produce some surplus investment income which could be used to cover the cost of a limited number of appeals before the immigration appeal tribunal and social security commissioners. The green form would cover the preparatory work and it is hoped that the representation itself would not be expensive.

Our views

There is clearly a need for a mutual fund of the type described in these two proposals, especially in the field of personal injury litigation. Mutual funds can reduce the fear of legal costs, which prevents a substantial number of accident victims from taking the first step to find out about their rights, and can encourage more people to claim. They can also ease the pressure to settle for very small amounts which the risk of costs places on victims. Unlike insurance companies, victims may be deterred by a very small risk of a large loss. The victim who is backed by the fund can take a more mathematical approach to whether or not to accept a settlement. We wish to see a form of mutual fund established.

From the consumer point of view, there are no clear reasons to prefer a fixed fee fund over a contingent fund or vice versa. The advantage of the Law Society's proposal, however, is that it does not require large start-up funds. We welcome the work done by the Law Society in developing the idea. If the scheme goes ahead, we wish to see lay representatives included on the national board and on the committees hearing appeals.

We are unable to say if the fund is financially viable. The legal aid figures are encouraging. They show that between eighty-five per cent and ninety-six per cent of personal injury cases are settled or decided in the plaintiff's favour (68). However, the Law Society will need to proceed cautiously. The Marre Committee thought that the proposals would not work in practice because solicitors whose clients have a good case would not advise them to join the scheme, while those with a poor chance would (34). The success rate of the scheme may also be lower than that of legal aid because where plaintiffs are legally aided, insurance companies know that they will not get their costs even if they win, and this puts pressure on them to settle poor cases. There is clearly a need for further experiment and research.

The scheme will only succeed if it is well publicised. The publicity should be directed at people who would not otherwise consult a solicitor for fear of costs. Although individual solicitors can advertise that they are members of the fixed costs scheme, there is also a need for advertising on a national basis to explain how the scheme works. It is important that an adequate allowance is made for publicity when the scheme is costed.

The most sensitive area of the scheme concerns settlements. The Compensation Study shows that the more offers the victim rejects, the higher the eventual settlement (69). However, the risks of receiving nothing also increase. The solicitor must explain clearly in the initial interview the circumstances which justify withdrawal of cover. We wish to see this explained in a leaflet about the scheme to be given to the client before the first payment is accepted.

It is important that costs are kept as low as possible. People who suffer serious injury rarely have money to spare and we do not think that disabled and injured people should be called on to subsidise other deprived groups. Thus we do not consider that the scheme should subsidise tribunal representation before the social security commissioners or the immigration appeal tribunal. If it is necessary to subsidise the costs of representation before these tribunals, the costs should be borne by the whole of society and not by one small and needy section of it. Any investment income generated by the scheme should be used to reduce the fixed fees charged by the scheme.

The scheme should start by covering personal injury cases only. We think it highly unlikely that it will prove viable to extend the scheme to other areas, where the chances of success are much lower.

The fund would not normally consider "high risk" cases. It would not be able to fund major drugs cases, such as the Opren case, for example, because the legal fees in the event of failure would be so high. Although it may be possible for some clients to buy extra cover for a higher premium, we do not consider that the fixed fee scheme offers a suitable means of funding contentious test cases and difficult multi-party litigation. We return to this subject in chapter 11, in considering the financing of multi-party cases.

References to chapter 6

1. Eleven per cent of respondents mentioned fear of legal expenses, compared with 19 per cent who mentioned the trouble and bother of claiming and 17 per cent who mentioned problems in providing evidence: see Harris, D. and others, *Compensation and support for illness and injury*, Clarendon Press, Oxford Socio-legal Studies, 1984.

2. School for Advanced Urban Studies, University of Bristol, *Study of housing cases, final report to the Lord Chancellor's Department*, produced for the Civil Justice Review, Lord Chancellor's Department, 1987.

3. National Consumer Council, "Complaints about negligent house surveys/valuations", November 1988.

4. This section is based on an unpublished background paper, Gardner, C., "Solicitors' charges" commissioned by the National Consumer Council in 1987.

5. Graham-Green, G.J., *Criminal costs and legal aid*, 3rd ed., Butterworths, 1973.

6. Lord Chancellor's Department, *Legal aid efficiency scrutiny*, June 1986.

7. See the *Report of the working party on the simplification of taxation* (Horne report), 1983.
8. See *R. v. Wilkinson* [*1980*] 1, Weekly Law Reports, 396, 1, All England Reports, 597.
9. Sir Jack I.H. Jacob, *The supreme court practice 1988*, Sweet and Maxwell, 1987, para.62/29/5.
10. Solicitors Act 1974, section 64.
11. Solicitors Act 1974, section 70.
12. Solicitors Act 1974, section 57.
13. See Horne, F.T., *Cordery's Law relating to Solicitors*, 8th ed., Butterworths, 1988, p.156.
14. Davis, G. and Bader, K., "Client costs: a failure to inform", *Legal Action*, February 1985, p.9.
15. Civil Justice Review, *General issues*, Lord Chancellor's Department, consultation paper no.6, 1987.
16. Civil Justice Review, *Report of the Review Body on Civil Justice*, Cm 394, HMSO, 1988.
17. *Legal aid in England and Wales: a new framework*, Cm 118, HMSO, March 1987.
18. See brochure of Consumer Services Organisation, the Legal Center, Philadelphia, Pennsylvania, 1987.
19. Auerbach, S., "The case for lawyers' advertising: it wins clients", *Washington Post*, 20 June 1978.
20. Purcell, T., *Innovations in legal services: new deals for consumers*, Law Foundation of New South Wales, Australia, 1984.
21. Muris, T.J. and McChesney, F.S., "Advertising and the price and quality of legal services: the case for legal clinics", *American Bar Foundation Research Journal*, 1979, p.179.
22. This section is based on an unpublished background paper, Hansen, O., "Legal expenses insurance", commissioned by the National Consumer Council in 1987.
23. Maintenance was defined by the Law Commission as "the giving of assistance or encouragement to one of the parties to an action by a person who has neither an interest in the action nor any other motive recognized by the law as justifying his interference", *Proposals for reform of the law relating to maintenance and champerty*, Law Commission memorandum no.7, 1986, para.3. It was also a crime under the Statute of Westminster 1275.
24. Pfennigstorf, W. and Kimball, S.L., ed., *Legal services plans: approaches to regulation*, American Bar Foundation, Chicago, 1977.
25. Levin, J., "Legal insurance?", *Legal Action*, August 1982, p.13.

26. Trades Union Congress, *Evidence of the TUC General Council to the Royal Commission on Legal Services*, 1976.

27. One of the first commercially successful schemes among the general public was the Défense Automobile et Sportive (DAS), a mutual insurance company founded in 1917 by members and officials of the Le Mans automobile club. It covered litigation arising from motoring and sports. Since then, a number of other unconnected companies have used the DAS initials. Pfennigstorf, W., see reference 24 above.

28. Pfennigstorf, W., see reference 24 above. Legal expenses insurance is also common in Austria, Switzerland, Belgium, France and the Netherlands.

29. Blankenburg, E., "Legal insurance litigation decisions and the rising caseload of the courts: a West German study", *Law and Society Review*, vol.16, 1981-82, no.4, p.601.

30. See *Law Society Gazette*, 18 September 1987, p.2416.

31. Letter from The Legal Protection Group Ltd., dated 16 March 1988.

32. See *Law Society Gazette*, 18 March 1987, p.792.

33. Directive of the Council of Europe on the co-ordination of laws, regulations and administrative provisions relating to legal expenses insurance, 22 June 1987, ref. (87/344/EEC).

34. Report of the Committee on the Future of the Legal Profession (Chairman: Lady Marre), *A time for change*, report to the General Council of the Bar and the Council of the Law Society, July 1988.

35. *Solicitors' Practice Rules 1988*, rule 4.

36. Advertising Standards Authority case reports 98 (29 June 1983); "Legal expenses insurance—complaints upheld", *LAG Bulletin*, July 1983, p.4.

37. Letter from Allianz Legal Protection dated 6 May 1988.

38. The specimen family legal protection policy put out by Hambro Legal Protection Ltd in 1986 states that the insured must meet the costs of an unfavourable solicitor's opinion; see Hambro Legal Protection Ltd, family legal protection master certificate of insurance, ref. FLP/REVI 2/86. The DAS legal protection policy states that differences shall be decided by counsel or a solicitor chosen jointly by the company and policy holder, and the costs shall be met by the party against whom the decision is made; see DAS Legal Expenses Insurance Company Ltd., specimen group legal protection policy (also available to individuals), DAS 576.

39. Insurance Companies Act 1982, sections 72-74 (see also Financial Services Act 1986, section 133).

40. This section is based on an unpublished background paper, Paterson, A., "Contingent fees", commissioned by the National Consumer Council in 1987.

41. Barratry was the "stirring up of litigation". Champerty involved agreements by persons to assist litigants in return for a share of the proceeds of the case; see *Proposals for the reform of the law relating to maintenance and champerty*, reference 23 above.

42. Law Society, *Solicitors' Practice Rules 1988*, rule 8; see also Solicitors Act 1974, section 59(2)(b).

43. See *Wallersteiner v. Moir no.2* [1975] 1, Queen's bench, 373; *Trendtex Trading Corporation v. Credit Suisse [1980]* 3, All England Reports, 721, and *Smith Kline and French Laboratories Ltd. v. Black, The Times*, 17 May 1982.

44. In West Germany percentage fees are invalid, but agreements providing for a fixed amount of costs or extra costs being payable in the event of success can be upheld in certain circumstances. See Schlesinger, R.B. *Comparative Law*, Foundation Press, Mineola, 1980, pp.659-60; and White, R., "Contingent fees: a supplement to legal aid", *Modern Law Review*, 1978, vol.41, pp.285 and 290.

45. In Canada the offences of maintenance and champerty were abolished in 1955 and this opened the way for contingent fees. Most provincial law societies chose not to amend their ethical rules to re-introduce a ban on such fees—see Arthur, A., "Public accountability and the legal profession" in Thomas, P.A., ed. *Law in the balance*, Martin Robertson, 1982, p.179; see also Wolfram, C., *Modern legal ethics*, West Publishing, St. Paul, 1986, p.527.

46. Paterson, A., "Paying for legal services", *Journal of the Law Society of Scotland*, 1979, vol.24, p.237; see also *X Insurance Company v. A and B* (1936) Scottish Cases p.225.

47. Statutory provisions allow for the recovery of the successful party's legal expenses in cases involving unfair trade practices, a violation of anti-trust laws, racial discrimination or civil rights law. Successful litigants can also recover their out-of-pocket expenses (as opposed to their legal expenses) in many actions.

48. Wolfram, C., *Modern legal ethics*, West Publishing, St. Paul, 1986.

49. See American Bar Association, *Code of professional responsibility*, draft rule 5-103 (B).

50. See American Bar Association, *Model rules of professional conduct*, model rule 1.18 (e).

51. *Fracasse v. Brent*, vol.100, California Reporter, 385.

52. *Richette v. Solomon*, vol.187, Atlantic Reporter, 2nd series, 910-919.

53. *US News and World Report*, "Sky-high damage suits", 27 January 1986, p.35.

54. Peterson, M.A. and Priest, G.L., "The civil jury: trends in trials and verdicts, Cook County, Illinois, 1960-79", Rand Corporation, Santa Monica, 1981.

55. See *US News and World Report*, "See you in court" 20 December 1982 and "Sky-high damage suits" 27 January 1986, in *American Bar Association Journal*, vol.37, February 1987; Galanter, M., "Reading the landscape of disputes: what we know about and don't know (and think we know) about our allegedly contentious and litigious society", Disputes Processing Research Program, working paper 1, Madison, Wisconsin, 1983.

56. The evidence suggests that the great majority of American plaintiffs receive some settlement in personal injury actions: see Franklin, M.A., Chanin, R.H. and Mark, I., "Accidents, money and the law" *Columbia Law Review*, 1961, vol.61, p.1; and Grady, J.F., "Some ethical questions about percentage fees", *Litigation*, 1976, vol.2, p.20. This can, however, be used to support both the arguments: that contingent fee lawyers bring nuisance lawsuits successfully, or that they are selective about the cases they bring.

57. Rosenthal, D., *Lawyer and client: who's in charge?* Russell Sage, New York, 1974.

58. Kritzer, H. and others, "The impact of fee arrangement on lawyer effort", *Law and Society Review*, vol.19, no.2, 1985, p.251.

59. Royal Commission on Legal Services (Chairman: Sir Henry Benson), *Final Report*, Cmnd 7648, HMSO, 1979.

60. See Mackinnon, F.B., "Contingent fees for legal services", American Bar Foundation, Chicago, 1964, p.182; and Slovenko, R., "Medical malpractice and the lawyer's contingent fee", *Journal of Psychiatry and Law*, 1984, vol.12, pp.587-611.

61. See American Bar Association, Code of professional conduct, draft rule 2-106; model rule 1.5 (a).

62. American Bar Association, model rule 1.5 (d).

63. See Schwartz, M.L. and Mitchell, D.J.B., "An economic analysis of the contingent fee in personal-injury litigation", *Stanford Law Review*, 1970, vol.22, p.1125; and Clermont,

K.M. and Currivan, J.D., "Improving on the contingent fee", *Cornell Law Review,* 1978, vol.63, p.529.

64. Central Office of Industrial Tribunals, *Industrial tribunals in England and Wales: fact sheet,* March 1988.
65. Justice, *CLAF: proposals for a contingency legal aid fund,* 1978.
66. A letter from Peter Moss, Hong Kong Director of legal aid, quoted in Law Society discussion document, see reference 67 below.
67. Law Society, contentious business committee, *Improving access to civil justice: the report of the Law Society's working party on the funding of litigation,* July 1987.
68. *Legal aid,* 37th annual reports of the Law Society and the Lord Chancellor's advisory committee, 1986-87, HC 233, HMSO, 1988.
69. Harris, D. and others, *Compensation and support for illness and injury,* Oxford Socio-legal Studies, Clarendon Press 1984.

Chapter 7
Complaints about lawyers

One of the questions the National Consumer Council asks in assessing any service is—can the consumer gain redress when things go wrong? We regard an accessible and effective complaints system as vital, not only in righting individual wrongs, but in maintaining a high standard of service to all consumers.

There is no doubt that complaining about professional services raises more difficulties than complaining about most goods or services commonly bought in the high street. This is demonstrated by the Office of Fair Trading survey of consumer dissatisfaction (1). The survey looked at complaints across a wide range of sectors. It found that consumers complaining about professional services were those least likely to report a satisfactory outcome to their complaint. Around eighty-five per cent of those taking action on a complaint about food or drink, footwear or clothing reported that they were satisfied with the outcome, but only nineteen per cent of those who complained about professional services were satisfied (1). The old adage that "customers are always right, even when they're wrong" is more applicable to the restaurant or the greengrocer than to the solicitor or doctor.

This is not necessarily the fault of the professions. To a considerable extent it is inherent in the nature of the professional-client relationship. As Whelan and Veljanovski point out:

> "the lawyer-client relationship is inherently one that involves an asymmetry in information—the lawyer is by definition in a superior position to evaluate the quality of and need for legal advice" (2).

The difficulties consumers have in evaluating services can result in poor service passing unnoticed, while good service which fails to procure the desired results provokes criticism. Consumers are usually reliant on other members of the profession to evaluate the service that has been provided and can feel confused and frustrated by procedures they do not fully understand.

It is therefore particularly important that the professions establish complaints systems which enjoy public confidence. There is no doubt that this is a difficult task. Complaints systems inevitably involve one professional assessing the service provided by another, but the system must be sufficiently independent to counteract the criticism that fellow professionals are "looking after their own". The system must be accessible, easy to understand, impartial, effective, and flexible in the range of sanctions that can be imposed.

Complaints against solicitors

Consumers who are dissatisfied with their solicitor may either bring an action for negligence before the courts, or make a complaint to the Law Society.

In order to bring actions for negligence, consumers must show that they have suffered loss as a result of their solicitors' inadequate care. Such an action usually involves finding a new solicitor and threatening or starting a case in the county or high court. It will be defended by the solicitor's insurers. Some consumers qualify for legal aid, while others will have to meet the costs themselves in the hope that they can be recouped if they win. Where solicitors have acted as advocates and the negligence is intimately connected with the conduct of the case in court, they are immune from court action against them. We examine this in more detail in the following section concerning complaints against barristers.

Alternatively, aggrieved clients can make a complaint through the profession's own complaints procedure.

History of the Law Society's complaints procedure

The Law Society has always claimed that the maintenance of professional standards and the investigation of misconduct is an important part of its function. According to the Benson Commission, an essential characteristic of a profession is that it is given "a measure of self-regulation so that it may require its members to observe higher standards than could be successfully imposed from without" (3).

Complaints investigation has proved to be a difficult and controversial task. Until 1986, complaints were dealt with by the professional purposes committee, whose task was to decide whether a solicitor had been guilty of "professional misconduct". Where this was proved the committee could rebuke the solicitor, intervene in the practice, impose conditions on the practising certificate or refer the matter to an independently constituted solicitors disciplinary tribunal. The tribunal could reprimand, fine, or suspend the solicitor or strike him or her from the roll. But they could not award compensation to the complainant. The procedure was monitored by the Lay Observer.

The definition of "professional misconduct" has long caused problems. It is said to include actions "which would reasonably be regarded as disgraceful or dishonourable by his professional brethren of good repute and competency" (4). The Law Society describes some of the practices which may be regarded as misconduct in the *Guide to the Professional Conduct of Solicitors* but this is not definitive. Misconduct includes dishonesty and serious and persistent breach of the solicitors' rules, and may include delay and failure to answer correspondence where these are sufficiently serious. How far incompetence may be regarded as misconduct is an open question.

During the early 1980s the work of the professional purposes committee was subject to considerable public criticism (5). It was felt that consumers were confused by the distinctions between negligence, misconduct and incompetence and that the sanctions available to the committee were too inflexible. People who had suffered a bad experience in going to law were often reluctant to sue their solicitors through the courts and were angry that the Law Society refused to investigate their cases. The procedure was also confusing, slow and inefficient.

Above all, there were doubts about solicitors investigating themselves, and concern about the conflict between the Law Society's roles in both furthering the interests of the profession and upholding the interests of consumers. The Glanville Davies affair, although untypical, became a *cause célèbre*. The Law Society rejected complaints against a member of the Law Society Council who was later found by the courts to be guilty of "gross and persistent misconduct". The Law Society's own committee of enquiry into the handling of the case concluded that:

"the failures were many and recurring... We have found administrative failures, mistakes, wrong decisions, errors of judgement, failures in communication, high-handedness and insensitivity on a scale which must have done great harm to The Law Society. The whole episode is a disgrace to The Law Society" (6).

The National Consumer Council's recommendations

In May 1984, some time after the scandal, the National Consumer Council conducted a poll to test public confidence in the solicitors' complaints system (5). Members of the public were asked who they thought should investigate complaints about the standard of service provided by solicitors. No replies were prompted, yet a third of people spontaneously said that it should be an independent person or body and not the Law Society. Only 15 per cent thought complaints should be investigated by solicitors or an organisation of solicitors. People were also asked who should be on a new body to investigate complaints—55 per cent thought it should be composed entirely or mainly of non-solicitors; 36 per cent thought there should be an equal number of solicitors and non-solicitors, and only 5 per cent thought there should be a majority of solicitors.

We concluded that there was a need for an independent body to investigate complaints (5). The Law Society looks after the interests of solicitors and regulates solicitors in the public interest. The research suggested that the public had lost confidence that it could exercise both roles at once. We stated that:

> "the new body for dealing with complaints against solicitors must be, and must be seen to be, independent of the solicitors' professional association. There is no other way to achieve credibility" (5).

Many different industries and professions have now established independent complaints procedures, including the medical professions, insurance industry, banking industry, licenced conveyancers and advertising industry. We recommended that the same principle should apply to solicitors and that a new legal council should be established under Act of Parliament, composed of a balance between solicitors and non-solicitors.

We recommended that the new council would not only investigate complaints but would also set standards for the profession. It should be required to publish and publicise an annual report describing its activities and highlighting areas of difficulty where solicitors—and the public—could learn from experience. An essential part of the council's task would be to report to the profession about how well clients' expectations were being met.

A system which handles such a large number of complaints is, inevitably, expensive to run. It needs to be adequately resourced and staffed. We recommended that the profession should pay for a system which would do so much to enhance its standing with its clients and the public at large. In reality, the costs would be passed on to consumers, but we believed that consumers would be more than willing to pay a very small increase in individual fees in order to have an effective complaints system in which they could have confidence.

The emphasis would be on an integrated and approachable system, with a single point of entry for complaints. It would be for the office rather than the complainant to draw distinctions between cases. The new system would have a wider and more flexible range of sanctions, including the power to award small damages of up to a limit of around £2,000, and the power to issue a certificate stating whether fees are fair and reasonable. Initially, the emphasis should be on local interviews and conciliation. Complaints would then progress to a more formal system, where decisions could either be reached on the basis of written submissions or after hearings. The parties would be told of the decisions and the reasons for them (5).

The Coopers and Lybrand report

The Law Society commissioned management consultants Coopers and Lybrand to examine the system of complaints handling. In 1985 Coopers and Lybrand published a consultation paper in which they also recommended establishing an independent organisation to investigate complaints. They stated:

> "the conflict of role, whether real or apparent, is becoming increasingly less acceptable to the public... Our conclusion... is firmly held—that complaints and discipline should be administered separately from the Law Society" (7).

The Coopers and Lybrand report provoked a mixed reaction from the profession. Among local law societies, about half supported and half opposed the proposal, but Law Society Council members were strongly against an independent body. In the end, the Law Society rejected the idea. Instead they voted for a new system in which the Law Society would keep overall responsibility for complaints, but in which there would be more lay involvement and a greater separation between the Law Society's various functions (8).

The Solicitors Complaints Bureau (SCB)

In September 1986 the Solicitors Complaints Bureau started work as part of the Law Society, but separated from it, with a different identity, address and management structure. In January 1987, the new complaints procedure began. A predominantly lay investigation committee was established to provide an independent element to the proceedings. At the same time new statutory powers were introduced which enabled the profession to investigate inadequate professional services, or "shoddy work", as well as misconduct, and could order solicitors to remit or repay fees to clients who have been given a poor service.

The number of complaints has been steadily increasing: from 11,817 in 1985 to 17,839 in 1987. In 1987, 3,987 complaints came from other solicitors, and 13,852 came from members of the public (9).

The new procedure is complex. The Bureau is responsible to two separate committees: the adjudication committee, with a majority of solicitors, and a predominantly lay investigation committee. The adjudication committee exercises the Law Society's statutory powers, and rebukes solicitors in minor cases. It refers important cases to the solicitors' disciplinary tribunal. The investigation committee oversees the procedures, monitors all complaints that go before the adjudication committee, and reviews complaints where the Bureau wishes to terminate the case but the complainant does not. The great majority of complaints, however, are handled by staff investigation officers and do not go before either committee. The role of the Lay Observer is unchanged. He continues to receive and investigate complaints about how the Law Society has handled cases.

We first attempt to explain how the SCB works and then evaluate how well it protects the interests of consumers.

What types of complaint does the SCB handle?

The Bureau will investigate two types of complaints: those where it is alleged that a solicitor is guilty of misconduct, and those where a solicitor has provided "inadequate professional services", generally referred to as "shoddy work".

Clients who consider that they have lost money through a solicitor's negligence may pursue a case in the civil courts. The Bureau keeps details of solicitors who are prepared to give free initial interviews of up to an hour to advise clients whether they have a good claim of negligence against previous solicitors. In some cases, where both the client and the solicitor agree, negligence claims can be submitted to a special arbitration scheme run by the Chartered Institute of Arbitrators. This scheme was established in March 1986 as an alternative to the courts and is entirely separate from the SCB. It is very rarely used. During its first year of operation it heard only six cases (10).

The Law Society runs a compensation fund to compensate clients who have lost money through a solicitor's dishonesty, financed by contributions from practising solicitors. Under the scheme, payments to clients are made at the discretion of the Council of the Law Society. The Council has delegated responsibility for making payments to the SCB's adjudication committee (9).

The SCB does not deal with disputes about bills, unless overcharging is so serious as to amount to misconduct. Consumers who think that they have been overcharged in cases which do not involve court proceedings can apply to another part of the Law Society, the "legal practice directorate", for a "remuneration certificate", which states whether the charges are fair. We describe this procedure in chapter 6. In cases involving court proceedings, clients must apply to the court to find out whether bills are reasonable.

Starting a complaint

The SCB operates from a central London address. It does not have any form of regional structure, though local law societies sometimes become involved in trying to resolve disputes. Complaints must usually be made in writing to the Bureau. Staff will deal with telephone queries but the emphasis is very much on written communications. It is rare for SCB staff to interview complainants, solicitors or witnesses.

People who appear to have particular difficulties in formulating complaints can be referred to solicitors on the interview panel, who will interview them and prepare a report to the SCB. Panellists are advised to see interviewees on neutral territory, such as a citizens advice bureau. They are discouraged from interviewing complainants at home because of the risk of violence. They are paid at legal aid committee rates and for their travelling expenses. In 1987 there were only 44 panellists for the whole country. The SCB is expanding the scheme and hopes eventually to have a national scheme with 150 solicitors on the panel.

Complaints are received at a central point in the Bureau. They are all logged into the computer and allocated to an investigation officer employed by the Bureau. Investigation officers have legal backgrounds but not all are solicitors. The investigation officer's first job is to decide whether the solicitor has a "case to answer". If so, the investigation officer will send a copy of the complaint to the solicitor and ask for his or her comments. The solicitor's reply will then be shown to the complainant, with the investigation officer's comments. The Bureau states that "the reply might be regarded as satisfactory by the bureau staff and the complainant and the matter ends there'' (9). However, investigation officers do not have the power formally to close investigations. Only the investigation committee can do that.

Shoddy work

Where the investigation officer considers that there is evidence of shoddy work, the Bureau will call for the solicitor's file. The file will then be read by two report writers, employed by the SCB, who are qualified solicitors or legal executives. The report writers prepare a report, based on a check list of twenty-seven questions drawn up by the Bureau. Questions include ''was it a field of law with which the solicitor was familiar?'': ''were progress reports given to the client?'' and ''did the solicitor explain why instructions were not carried out?'' (11). The report is sent to the solicitor, but not to the complainant.

Where the report writers recommend action against the solicitor, the solicitor may appeal to a ''peer review panel'' of practising lawyers who ensure that the decision is based on current legal practice. The SCB comments that this is rare, and that ''the majority of solicitors who have been placed in this position are indeed happy to agree with the Bureau's staff that the work was not up to the standard by which they wish their firm to be known'' (9). The Bureau thinks that the peer review panel does not work well and they are considering abolishing it (12).

Where the solicitor agrees or the panel upholds the recommendation of the report writers, the matter is passed to the adjudication committee to take action. In 1987 the Bureau received 815 complaints classified as shoddy work. They have recorded the outcome of 191 cases. The claim was upheld in 67 cases, rejected in 76 cases and 48 cases were found to involve misconduct rather than shoddy work. Costs were reduced by more than £250 in only nine cases (9).

The adjudication committee

The adjudication committee exercises the Law Society's statutory powers. At least half its members must be members of the Law Society's Council. In all, the adjudication committee has 18 members, of which nine are members of the Law Society Council, three are solicitors who are not on the Council and six are lay people (9).

Where the investigation officer considers that a complaint is justified, he or she will submit it to the adjudication committee. Until recently, the committee did not give reasons for its decisions, but the policy has now changed (9). In serious cases of misconduct, the committee will refer the matter to the independent solicitors disciplinary tribunal. They may also refuse a practising certificate or impose conditions, such as requiring the solicitor to attend a training course. In less serious cases, the committee can administer a "deprecation of conduct", a "rebuke", a "severe rebuke" or a "chairman's rebuke". They can also invite a solicitor to take action or provide an explanation, under threat of disciplinary proceedings.

In cases of shoddy work the adjudication committee may order the solicitor to reduce the bill, rectify the mistake or take other necessary action (13). It is unclear whether this includes the power to order the solicitor to pay the costs of another solicitor rectifying the mistake (10). The committee cannot order the solicitor to pay compensation to the client. Clients seeking compensation must make a negligence claim, either through the courts or through the arbitration scheme.

In 1987 the adjudication committee dealt with 1,377 complaints and found that action was not necessary in 143 (9).

The investigation committee

The investigation committee has 11 members: seven, including the chairperson, are lay people, appointed by the senior appeal court judge, the Master of the Rolls; two are members of the Law Society Council and two are non-Council solicitors. According to the Law Society's president, their function is to "oversee the complaints procedure generally in addition to looking at individual cases" (14). The committee is not officially part of the Law Society, and cannot exercise any of the Law Society's statutory powers.

Much of the investigation committee's time is spent in scrutinising all the cases going before the adjudication committee. It also reviews all cases which the investigation officer wishes to end but the complainant does not. In 1987 it reviewed 556 such cases (9). Only the committee can officially end a case but they have no power to take any particular action. Where they are unhappy about ending an investigation, they may make suggestions to the Bureau for further action. The file is read by two members of the committee, who give reasons to the complainant for their decision. They will also review cases which are passed to the Lay Observer (10).

The investigation committee's members are unpaid, and the scrutiny of individual cases is extremely time-consuming. Pressure of work has led the Bureau to consider expanding the committee and paying members (12). The committee is trying hard to make time to carry out its more general "overseeing" role, but this is difficult, given the number of individual cases to review. The committee may make formal recommendations to staff for improving procedures. So far, it has recommended that the committees should give reasons for their decisions, and that the Bureau should publish an annual report. The committee's chairman, Jean Horsham, has stated that their next area for survey will be "cases where the Bureau has concluded investigations to the apparent satisfaction of complainants. Some 90 per cent of all cases dealt with by the Bureau fall into this category. As soon as time permits, the Committee will examine the standard of service given in such cases" (9).

Investigation accountants

The Bureau also employes investigation accountants, whose job is to ensure that a solicitor's accounts are in order. Where the SCB receives serious complaints of mismanagement or dishonesty, an investigation accountant can be asked to make an inspection without informing the solicitor of the allegations.

Interventions

In the most serious cases, where the public is at risk, the SCB has the right to "intervene" in a solicitor's practice. The adjudication committee appoints an agent who takes control of the client account and files, returns money and papers to clients as quickly as possible, and advises them to find new solicitors. In 1987 there were 39 interventions, mostly as a result of dishonesty or serious breaches of the account rules. The SCB may also intervene where a solicitor is sent to prison, declared bankrupt, struck off the register or incapacitated by illness (9).

The solicitors disciplinary tribunal

The disciplinary tribunal was established under the Solicitors Act 1974 and is independent of the Law Society and the Solicitors Complaints Bureau. Its members are appointed by the Master of the Rolls. Complaints are heard by three members: two must be practising solicitors and one must be a lay person who is neither a solicitor nor a barrister. The tribunal may impose a number of sanctions on solicitors, including striking them off the roll, suspending them from practice, and imposing a fine of not more than

£3,000. Decisions are public and are regularly reported in the Law Society's *Gazette*. In 1986-87, the tribunal made 160 orders against solicitors and 22 against solicitors' clerks. This is an increase from 88 cases against solicitors and 18 cases against clerks in the previous year (14).

The Lay Observer

The Lay Observer predates the Bureau and the investigation committee but his role continues unchanged. He is appointed by the Lord Chancellor. Members of the public who consider that the SCB has not handled their complaint properly may write to the Lay Observer at the Royal Courts of Justice. The Observer will not investigate the complaint directly but he will investigate the way the SCB has investigated the complaint and make a report. In 1987, 456 new complainants contacted the Lay Observer and he accepted 249 as being within his remit, an increase of 10 per cent on the previous year. He reported on 174 cases, in six of which he recommended that the Law Society took further action. In a further 40, he was critical of shortcomings in the handling of complaints, but considered that these did not affect the substance of the decision or prejudice the interest of the complainant. The main shortcomings were delay, lost papers, incomplete files, insufficient explanations for decisions and insufficient initial analysis of the complaint (10).

The Lay Observer has drawn attention to the fact that complainants receive reports up to a year after the SCB has finished its investigation. Part of the problem is that before sending a file to the Lay Observer, the SCB submits the case to the investigation committee. This means that three to five months can pass between the Lay Observer asking for a file and receiving it (10).

Feedback to the profession

Complainants are not typical customers. Most customers will be satisfied with the service they receive. Of those who are not satisfied, only a minority will make a formal complaint. Nevertheless, a complaints system is an important source of information to any business or profession about how its service can be improved. It highlights issues which cause the greatest problems. The SCB is aware of the need to report to the profession about what can go wrong by participating in training courses, organising seminars and publishing articles in the professional press (12). Unfortunately this represents only a small part of the Bureau's work, to be fitted in around the main task of handling complaints as and when resources permit.

Advantages of the new complaints scheme

There is no doubt that the Solicitors Complaints Bureau provides many welcome improvements. The "shoddy work" powers significantly extend the redress which can be provided. The power to call for the solicitor's file enables more investigation to be carried forward.

Previously, the professional purposes department was responsible both for dealing with complaints from the public and advising solicitors on matters of professional conduct, including how to deal with complaints. We agree with the Lay Observer that separating complaints handling from pastoral care to solicitors is a welcome organisational improvement (15). In 1987 the Lay Observer also commented on the improvements in accommodation, staff morale and recruitment (15). In 1988 he considered that complaints were still being handled better, but he said that there were signs that "Bureau staff are again coming under increasing pressure because of the sharp increase in the number of complaints to be dealt with and the difficulties of recruiting and retaining experienced staff" (10).

The investigation committee provides a lay element in the proceedings and ensures greater openness. We welcome its recommendation that both committees should give reasons for their decisions and that the Bureau should publish an annual report (9).

The interview panel provides personal contact on a regional basis and we very much welcome the decision to expand the panel. We are also pleased that the Bureau is experimenting with conciliation by telephone in cases where the client is more concerned to persuade the solicitor to get the work done rather than to change solicitors. This is a welcome break with a system that had previously relied almost entirely on the exchange of letters (9).

Problems with the procedure

Despite the improvements, a number of difficulties remain.

1. Negligence, misconduct and shoddy work

The Bureau continues to make a distinction between misconduct and shoddy work, which it can investigate, and negligence where clients must pursue civil remedies in the courts. The Bureau refers cases of alleged negligence to solicitors on the "negligence panel", who give the complainant a free interview to advise on whether it is worth pursuing the matter.

In the past the Law Society refused to investigate complaints of misconduct where a question of negligence was also involved, on the grounds that it could not investigate misconduct until the negligence action had been decided. In January 1987, the court of appeal found that the Law Society's approach was too sweeping. The Master of the Rolls, Sir John Donaldson, remarked that "it cannot be right merely because there is a claim of negligence to refuse to investigate a matter of misconduct. It is only if there is a risk that the investigation of misconduct will in some way muddy the waters of justice in the context of the negligence claim that the Solicitors Complaints Bureau should... refrain to investigate" (16). This echoes the views of the Benson Commission (3) and the Lay Observer (15).

Nevertheless the Bureau continues to define both misconduct and shoddy work in such a way as specifically to exclude negligence. They define misconduct as follows:

> "Broadly professional misconduct is wilful behaviour by a solicitor which may involve disregarding certain rules of conduct or may be of a type that could bring the profession into disrepute in dealings with a client. It may also now include incompetence falling short of negligence." (9)

The definition given by the SCB includes minor incompetence and serious malpractice, but excludes a middle category of negligence. We do not think that this is right. In our view, conduct which is below the standard a consumer has the right to expect may be misconduct, even if it is also negligent.

Shoddy work, or "inadequate professional services", are "services provided by a solicitor for a client which were, in any respect, not of the quality that could reasonably have been expected" (9). This appears to include negligence, but the Bureau states that it "will not in the first instance at least, treat as shoddy work any complaint where there is potential for the recovery of substantial damages. That must remain for the Courts" (9).

The Bureau states that it is difficult to explain these distinctions to the public (9). Around 3,000 complaints of negligence or inadequate services which are not regarded as "shoddy work" are received each year. Clients may be confused and suspicious when they are told that the Bureau does not have jurisdiction. The Law Society is aware of these problems and has set up a working party to consider professional negligence (12).

Telling consumers to pursue their remedies through the courts is not a satisfactory solution to their problems. Those who have already had a bad experience of the law may be reluctant to become involved with new solicitors and a new court action, especially if they will be faced with a large bill if they lose. It is widely felt that lay people are at a disadvantage in pursuing lawyers through the courts. We wish to see the Solicitors Complaints Bureau act as a cheaper and easier alternative to the courts.

In our view, the SCB should investigate complaints that solicitors have provided inadequate professional services which have resulted in loss to their clients. Legislation should be introduced to give the SCB the power to award small amounts of compensation, up to a limit of £2,000. It should also make clear that the SCB may order solicitors to pay the costs of rectifying their mistakes.

2. Lack of written standards

Clients often find it difficult to recognise inadequate work because there is very little clear guidance on what a solicitor is meant to do. This problem was recognised by the Benson Commission which recommended that the profession should produce written professional standards as an authoritative indication of what good practice requires. They considered that serious or repeated failure to comply with written standards should be treated as a breach of professional discipline (3).

Since the Benson Commission, the profession has produced written standards on responsibility for the client's case, communication with the client (which we discuss in chapter 8) and information on costs (discussed in chapter 6). The Civil Justice Review considered that this was a useful first step. They stated that the next step should be "the adoption of specific standards relating to the conduct, from start to finish, of the principal types of litigation" (17).

We support the Civil Justice Review's recommendation. Written professional standards would provide useful information for clients wishing to evaluate the service their solicitor had provided, and would be an important guide to the SCB in ensuring consistent decisions. The standards should be incorporated within solicitors' training courses and be well publicised within the profession.

3. The cases which do not go to the committees

Another worry is the high attrition rate among complainants. Out of almost 18,000 cases received by the Bureau in 1987 only about 2,000 complaints were formally concluded—around 1,400 reached the adjudication committee and 600 were terminated by the investigation committee (9).

The Bureau does not provide details of what happens to the others. Some are rejected at the first hurdle when the investigation officer decides that there is no case to answer. Others end because the client is apparently satisfied with the solicitor's reply. A case may also end where the investigation officer explains to the complainant that they intend to take no further action and the complainant makes no objection. In our view it would be wrong to regard cases where the complainant is silent as successfully concluded conciliation. Complainants may remain silent because they are satisfied with the way the complaint has been handled, or equally, they may be very dissatisfied and think that pursuing a complaint through the Bureau is a waste of time and effort.

We agree with the investigation committee that the matter needs further research. We recommend that the Bureau should commission independent researchers to conduct a study.

4. The procedure is too centralised

A system designed to deal with a large number of relatively low-level complaints needs to be more local and approachable. Initially, the emphasis should be on talking to complainants, explaining procedures and negotiating with solicitors rather than on formal written communication. For this there needs to be a regional presence, rather than a single London-based office.

The Law Society has recognised this need. Their 1986-87 annual report states: "it is widely accepted that the only sensible way of dealing with so many of the complaints received from members of the public which involve no significant issue of professional misconduct should be at a local level on a conciliation basis" (14).

The Bureau's response has been to expand the interview panel. This is an important first step, but in order to provide a form of conciliation the role of the panel will have to be changed. At present, complainants are only referred to the interview panel if they are unable to put a complaint into writing or explain it clearly on the telephone. The panellist's role is confined to reporting to the Bureau. The Bureau is considering a pilot scheme in which panellists attempt to conciliate (12).

5. The role of the investigation committee

During its first year, the investigation committee has been

overwhelmed by the task of monitoring all cases going before the adjudication committee. This is a considerable duplication of effort. It has had very little time to examine the procedures used to investigate the great majority of cases which do not go to the committee.

A number of matters to be tackled by the committee have been raised by the Lay Observer, concerning the way that correspondence is followed up and files are kept and cross-referenced (10, 15). We would like to see the committee issue guidelines to staff about how files should be kept.

6. Remuneration certificates

One of the criticisms we made of the previous system was the confusing number of different schemes (5). We are pleased that misconduct cases and shoddy work cases now have a single point of entry and that the SCB, rather than the consumer, now decides which is which. Complaints handling could be further integrated by making the SCB, rather than the legal practices directorate, responsible for remuneration certificates. Consumers should not have to distinguish between overcharging which is unreasonable, overcharging which involves misconduct and overcharging for inadequate services. Consumers dissatisfied about bills already use the SCB for complaints: in 1987 the Bureau received 1,213 complaints about excessive charges (9). They should be able to make a single complaint to a single organisation.

Conclusions

There is no doubt that the Solicitors Complaints Bureau faces a very difficult task. It has to reassure a highly sceptical public that it is taking a firm line on poor quality work. It has to maintain the confidence of solicitors, who pay its bills and ultimately control its future. It has grown from a system designed to handle a small number of very serious complaints about "disgraceful or dishonourable" conduct to a large organisation dealing with many thousands of complaints about incompetence, delay, and failure to communicate. These matters are rarely trivial to the consumer concerned but most solicitors would not regard them as disgraceful or dishonourable. The director of the Bureau can be forgiven for thinking that he is in a "no win" situation (18).

Over the years new elements have been added to the procedure in response to different criticisms. The result is an extremely complex procedure which is difficult for ordinary consumers to understand. The Lay Observer has spoken of the "growing difficulty of explaining to the public how different categories of complaints will be handled" (15).

We are concerned that under the present structure, the majority of complaints fade away. We would prefer to see a single decision-making structure rather than two. At present, one committee can decide to take action but not to discontinue the case; the other committee can discontinue a case but cannot take action. This inevitably leads to duplication. Busy investigation committee members spend considerable time monitoring adjudication committee decisions. There is a risk that important cases will fall between two stools. The investigation officer may not feel sufficiently certain to put the matter before the adjudication committee, but may be equally reluctant to recommend that the investigation committee discontinues all further work. The public are unlikely to be reassured if investigations are seen to be dragging on for years.

In our view, there is a need to examine the fundamental structure, rather than simply add a new panel, or committee, or appeal mechanism in response to a particular problem. The existing structure is over complex. People do not understand how their complaints will be processed and the majority of complaints fall between the two committees. Public concern about conflict between the Law Society's multiple roles will continue and we doubt whether it will be assuaged by the introduction of a lay investigation committee. If the Law Society fails to improve the procedure so as to satisfy public opinion that it is both independent and efficient, the Lord Chancellor should take the initiative by drawing up legislation to establish an independent legal council. Our 1985 report, *In dispute with the solicitor*, sets out how we see an independent legal council operating (5).

Complaints against barristers (19)

The subject of complaints against barristers has not attracted the same public attention as complaints against solicitors. There are far fewer barristers (less than 6,000 barristers compared with 39,000 solicitors) (20), consumers are less likely to use them, and the relationship is more remote.

Nevertheless, complaints about the standard of service provided by barristers do arise. The Benson Commission stated:

"There has... been justified criticism of the way barristers handle briefs. They are not always read promptly and even when delivered in good time, some receive detailed attention only a day or two before the hearing. Again, if there is a clash of engagements and a brief is returned, there may be insufficient time for adequate preparation or a pre-trial conference if one is required" (3).

A serious problem is that barristers may be double-booked, and hence unavailable on the day of the trial. They return the brief, often sending a last minute substitute. A 1985 study of barristers carrying out legal aid work found that the level of returned briefs was very high. London chambers specialising in criminal work returned 53 per cent of briefs delivered to them and provincial chambers returned 25 per cent (21).

The system by which young barristers are trained relies on learning by doing. Many of the barristers appearing in run-of-the-mill London magistrates courts will be young and inexperienced. In 1979 the legal correspondent of *The Times* attended a number of such cases to assess the quality of service. He reported:

"I was appalled. It was not just that so many young barristers seemed incapable of forming a grammatically correct English sentence... Much more distressing was the poor, sometimes inexcusable, standard of presentation of the lay client's case. I was present on two occasions when counsel managed to forget the crime with which his client had been charged. I saw more than one example of counsel clearly being unaware of the leading relevant case or the relevant piece of legislation. Mistakes about the detail and circumstances of the crime and, in pleas of mitigation, about the defendant's age, occupation and personal circumstances were commonplace" (22).

In the last two years there have been a number of improvements in the way in which young barristers are trained and supervised. On the other hand, members of the Bar have expressed concern that rates of legal aid may lead to a situation where only the incompetent or inexperienced are available to do the work (23).

Barristers, like everyone else, make mistakes. In a very few cases, barristers may be negligent, in that they fall short of the standard of skill and care which the client has the right to expect. One problem is that in an adversarial system the consequence of mistakes can be serious. The advocate will have a wide discretion in deciding how the case is to be presented and the judge will usually listen to the evidence and arguments put forward, rather than enquiring into the truth of the matter. The point was put clearly by Lord Justice Roskill in his evidence to the Benson Commission which is quoted, with approval, in the note of dissent to the Marre report:

"No-one without judicial experience can perhaps fully appreciate how much a judge relies upon the advocates before him in arriving at what he believes to be the correct decision. Bad advocacy may lead to the right points being missed, the right questions not being asked, and therefore the right answer not being given by the judge" (24).

There are two possible ways of pursuing a complaint against a barrister—through the civil court for negligence, or through the Bar's own disciplinary machinery for professional misconduct or breach of professional standards. We look at each in turn.

Negligence actions against barristers

In law, barristers are not regarded as having contracts with their clients. Thus they cannot sue for their fees and cannot be sued for breach of contract, even if they were to take their fees and fail to carry out the work. Until recently, it was thought that barristers were also immune from being sued for negligence actions. In 1967, in the case of *Rondel v Worsley*, the House of Lords found that barristers were wholly immune from being sued for negligence in connection with their work (25). They also suggested that solicitors who acted as advocates in the county court or magistrates courts may be similarly protected.

In 1978 the House of Lords reconsidered the matter, in the case of *Saif Ali v Sidney Mitchell and Co* (26). They decided that barristers could be sued for negligent advisory work but not if the negligence was closely connected with the conduct of a case in court. Thus barristers may be sued if they negligently advise on non-contentious matters such as drafting wills or trust deeds, or if they negligently advise clients to sue the wrong party. But they may not be sued if they fail to put a defence before the court, or fail to call an important witness. The case confirmed that solicitor-advocates enjoy the same immunity.

The position is similar in New Zealand. Indeed, the *Saif Ali* case specifically approved the New Zealand case law on the subject (27). But advocates are not immune from negligence actions in other common law jurisdictions. In Victoria, Australia, the immunity was abolished when the professions were fused by statute in 1958 (28). In Canada, the Ontario high court ruled in 1979 that a client could proceed with an action against an advocate (29). She claimed that judgement had wrongly been awarded against her when her counsel failed to appear and sent an inexperienced replacement. The court noted that courts in the United States of America have also refused to hold an advocate immune in respect of the conduct of cases in court.

In England and Wales, cases in which barristers have been liable for negligence are very rare. Since the *Saif Ali* case there have been no reported cases in which damages have been awarded against a barrister for negligence. Between 1971 and 1979, four claims were settled, for a total sum of £35,000 (3). It is not known how many cases have been settled since 1979.

From 1 April 1988 all barristers who practise must be insured with the Bar Mutual Indemnity Fund Limited against claims for professional negligence (30). The cover must provide for up to £250,000 per claim. Initially, premiums were set on a sliding scale, from 0.3 per cent of gross fee income (up to a maximum of £390) for barristers specialising in criminal work, to 0.7 per cent of gross fee income (up to a maximum of £910) for barristers specialising in civil work (31). It is envisaged that the scope for negligence actions outside the area of immunity is much less in criminal work, which is heavily court based, than in civil work.

Professional discipline

As with solicitors, barristers' professional bodies impose standards of discipline on the profession.

At present complaints of professional misconduct or breach of proper professional standards are handled by a sub-committee of the General Council of the Bar (or Bar Council), known as the professional conduct committee. Standing orders state that the committee may be composed of up to 14 members of the Bar Council, up to 18 barristers who may or may not be members of the Council and up to 6 lay representatives. The committee meets every two weeks and two of the lay members are invited to attend each meeting.

"Professional misconduct" covers dishonesty, a serious failure to observe the ethics, etiquette and rules of the profession, and a "serious failure to be competent in all professional activities". Less serious complaints fall under the heading of "breach of proper professional standards" (32).

Unlike the Solicitors Complaints Bureau, most of the work of investigating complaints falls on committee members rather than on paid staff. The procedure starts with either a telephone call or a letter to the secretary of the committee, who will send the complainant a form to fill in. The secretary then writes to the barrister and contacts material witnesses, such as the solicitor who instructed the barrister against whom the complaint is made. The file is then passed to a committee member who writes a note for the committee recommending how the matter should proceed. The committee can dismiss the complaint, take no action or deal with it informally. In order to dismiss the complaint, they need the agreement of both lay representatives. Alternatively they may refer the case to either the "summary procedure" or to the disciplinary tribunal (33).

The summary procedure is used where the complaint is less serious, and there is no apparent dispute of fact. The barrister concerned is given notice of a hearing before a special committee of the professional conduct committee. An informal hearing is held at which the barrister may appear in person or be represented. If the complaint is found proved, the barrister may be directed to attend upon the chairman to be "admonished" or "advised as to his future conduct". Admonitions may be published (33).

Serious complaints or complaints in which there is a material dispute of fact are referred to the disciplinary tribunal, which is a committee of the Inns' Council. Each tribunal consists of a judge, one lay person and three practising barristers. The professional conduct committee acts as prosecutor. In the case of professional misconduct, the tribunal may reprimand, suspend or disbar barristers before them, or compel them to repay or forego fees. Where a complaint of breach of proper professional standards is proved, the tribunal has the same powers as the committee operating the summary procedure. A barrister may appeal to the Visitors of the Inns of Court, where the case will be heard by at least three judges of the high court, nominated by the Lord Chief Justice (34).

The procedure is currently being reviewed by the profession and changes are being introduced. A summary tribunal will replace the summary procedure and the distinction between misconduct and breach of professional standards will be abolished. Instead all breaches of professional standards will be regarded as misconduct. The Lord Chancellor has been asked to appoint a panel of twelve lay people who will be asked to participate, two at a time, in the professional conduct committee, summary tribunal and disciplinary tribunal (35).

The Bar Council estimates that about eighty per cent of complaints come from members of the public, of which fifteen per cent come from serving prisoners. The rest come from judges, other barristers, solicitors and magistrates. In 1986, 209 complaints were received, of which 115 were dismissed, 34 were withdrawn or resulted in no action, 9 were dealt with informally, 10 were dealt with summarily and 19 were referred to the disciplinary tribunal. The remaining 22 are still outstanding. During the same year, the disciplinary tribunal held 7 hearings—four barristers were suspended, two were reprimanded, and one was admonished (36). Although the disciplinary tribunal has the power to order barristers to repay or forego fees, the figures since 1985 do not record any such orders.

An assessment of the procedures

Negligence actions

As a starting point, we expect barristers to be treated in the same way as other suppliers of services who hold themselves out as possessing particular skills and knowledge. However, the Benson Commission accepted that barristers and solicitor-advocates should be given immunity from actions for negligence in respect of advocacy work and pre-trial work closely connected with the trial. They gave the following reasons:

> "It is pointed out that a barrister has a duty to the court, which may conflict with his duty to the client; that he must take his client as he finds him and runs the risk of acting for a litigious client likely to start vexatious or harassing proceedings if dissatisfied; that the action for negligence would require re-trial of the proceedings and might be used as a device to side-step the regular machinery of appeals and re-open a civil or criminal case, perhaps after several years had passed; and that, in order to avoid the risk of misconceived claims, a barrister might call all available witnesses and take every point, however unnecessary, thus greatly extending the duration and cost of proceedings." (3)

The Marre Committee commented that they had nothing to add to this and recommended that no change be made in the present rule (24). We do not believe that these arguments are of sufficient force and gravity to outweigh the hardship to consumers who may fall victim to an advocate's negligence.

In the court of appeal in *Rondel v Worsley*, Lord Denning stated that a barrister should be immune as a matter of public policy "to prevent him being harassed by vexatious actions such as this present one now before us". He declared that:

> "It is a fearsome thing for a barrister to have an action brought against him, to have his reputation besmirched by a charge of negligence" (37).

This is not a convincing argument. All professional people dislike negligence actions and this is no reason to treat barristers differently from surveyors, accountants or doctors. In some ways barristers are in a stronger position than other professionals, because they are familiar with the law and with court procedures and can more easily resist unjustified claims. A more sophisticated version of the argument was put forward by Lord Wilberforce, who stated that:

> "a barrister owes a duty to the court as well as to his client and should not be inhibited, through fear of an action by his client from performing it..." (26).

It is true that an advocate owes a duty to the court as well as to his or her client, but it can never be negligent to put the duty to the court first. Barristers who have acted correctly will have a full defence to actions of negligence. We do not think that barristers will be so worried by the fear of unjustified claims of negligence that they will act in a dishonourable way.

It is true that advocates are not alone in being immune from negligence actions arising out of the conduct of trials. Witnesses, judges and jurors enjoy similar immunities. We can see strong arguments that lay people involved in court proceedings, such as jurors or witnesses, who act in good faith, should be given some protection against actions for negligence. Courts are already very frightening places for lay people, and we would not wish to add to people's fears. Paid advocates, however, hold themselves out as having special skills and knowledge, and the public are entitled to expect that people claiming such skills will exercise reasonable care. By the same token, there is a case for re-examining the immunity given to paid expert witnesses who mislead the court by providing seriously incompetent evidence.

The main argument against allowing claims against advocates is that it would lead people to question court verdicts. It is argued that there is a strong public interest in the finality of court verdicts; permitting a negligence action would allow a retrial in another guise and, if a client won, the court verdict would be called into question. However, the public interest in the finality of court verdicts has to be balanced against the public interest in getting the result right. As Michael Zander has stated:

> "it is true that negligence actions might permit convicted men to re-open their convictions, but if they have been convicted owing to the negligence of their lawyers this may not be unreasonable" (38).

In the case of *R v Irwin*, the court of appeal accepted the strength of this argument (39). The defendant's barrister failed to consult his client about his decision not to call two alibi witnesses. The defendant was convicted, and appealed. The court quashed the conviction on the grounds that the barrister's failure to consult his client was a material irregularity which made the conviction unsafe.

We wish to see the immunity abolished. We do not believe that this will lead to a flood of cases. There are strong disincentives to bringing actions for negligence in terms of cost, worry and time, and these are likely to apply more strongly when the opponent is a barrister. The onus will be on the lay client to prove that the barrister performed services in a manner which professional colleagues would recognise as negligent.

We consider that in criminal cases and cases which cannot be put right by money, such as those involving the welfare of children, clear cut gross negligence by a party's own lawyer should provide a potential ground of appeal. This should be in addition to any claim for compensation. Negligence would not mean that a retrial should automatically be allowed, but there would be the possibility of a retrial where it was shown that the advocate was negligent, and this affected the outcome of the case.

In other civil cases, the negligence of the advocate would not affect the outcome of the trial. The remedy would be damages only. In some cases, damages would seek to recompense people for the additional costs incurred as a result of the barrister's negligence. In other cases, money would compensate for loss of the chance of winning.

In some cases, the negligence may not have affected the outcome of the case but may have caused unnecessary delay and costs. Under the present costs rules, where undue costs have been incurred by poor quality representation, the court can penalise solicitors, by refusing to allow their claim for costs, or making an order that they should pay the other side's costs out of their own pockets (40). No similar provision exists against barristers. We wish to see the rules of court changed to allow a court, where it considers it appropriate, to make an order of costs against a barrister or to vary or disallow a barrister's fees.

Professional disciplinary sanctions

The disciplinary procedure has an important deterrent effect in reducing the incidence of shoddy work, dishonesty or other misconduct, and in recent years, there have been welcome moves to improve the procedure.

However, it remains the case that the professional complaints procedure is concerned with disciplining barristers rather than with providing consumers with redress. There is no power to award compensation to clients; only the disciplinary tribunal can order barristers to repay or forego fees and it does not appear to have used this power in the last three years. Although barristers can be admonished or advised as to future conduct, there is no formal method of compelling them to apologise to the client. Consumers who make complaints are informed of their progress and outcome but are not regarded as having any right to take part in the proceedings. They are not invited to be present or represented at the committee or tribunal hearing, nor do they have the right to see any relevant documents or transcripts.

In our view, the professional complaints procedure should provide consumers with redress. We wish to see the professional complaints procedure have the power to award compensation against barristers, whether or not such a right exists before the courts. In our view, complainants should be shown relevant documents and invited to hearings.

Despite the recommendation of the Benson Commission in 1979, the Bar had not produced any written standards by 1988. The Civil Justice Review comments "it is understood that a committee of the Bar Council has the matter under consideration. It is difficult to see what justification there could be for further delay in this crucial area of self-regulation" (17). We wish to see standards providing advice to clients on the service they may expect.

There are current proposals that all breaches of the code of conduct should fall under the category of professional misconduct (35). In our view, the procedure should provide redress against behaviour which falls short of the standard consumers have a right to expect of the profession. The term "inadequate professional services" would be easier for clients to understand than "misconduct". We wish to see the written standards enforced in the same way as the code of conduct.

There is a perceived lack of independence in the fact that complaints against barristers are dealt with by barristers and by judges who have been barristers. This can lead to a lack of public confidence in the procedure.

In our view, if an independent council to investigate complaints against solicitors is established, it should also deal with complaints against barristers. This would provide much needed simplicity, as well as independence, because it would be up to the council rather than the consumer to decide whether the solicitor or the barrister was to blame. The council would include a more substantial lay element and would have a wider range of sanctions, from explanation and apology to suspension and disbarment. It would be able to award compensation and order the repayment of fees.

References to chapter 7

1. Office of Fair Trading, *Consumer dissatisfaction: a report on surveys undertaken for the Office of Fair Trading*, February 1986.
2. Whelan C.J., and Veljanovski C.G., "Professional negligence and the quality of legal services—an economic perspective" *Modern Law Review*, November 1983, p.700.
3. Royal Commission on Legal Services (Chairman: Sir Henry Benson) *Final report*, Cmnd 7648, HMSO, 1979.
4. Horne F.T., *Cordery's Law Relating to Solicitors*, 8th Ed., Butterworths, 1988.
5. National Consumer Council, *In dispute with the solicitor: consumers and the professions: a review of complaints procedures*, Spring 1985.
6. The Law Society, *Report of the Law Society's committee of enquiry into the Law Society's treatment of the complaints of Mr L.A. Parsons against Mr G. Davies and Mr C. Malim* ("the Ely Committee"), 1984, para. 43.
7. Coopers and Lybrand, Review of the Law Society's affairs, phase 1, report 1, *The regulatory functions*, exposure draft 1985.
8. Coopers and Lybrand, Review of the Law Society, phase 1, report 4, *Complaints handling and discipline*, final report, January 1986.
9. Solicitors Complaints Bureau, *First Annual Report*, 1988.
10. *Thirteenth Annual Report of the Lay Observer 1987*, HC 626, HMSO, July 1988.
11. "The Solicitors Complaints Bureau" *Legal Action*, July 1987, p.6.
12. Letter from Peter Thompson, director of the Solicitors Complaints Bureau, dated 17 October 1988.
13. Solicitors Act 1974 section 44A, added by the Administration of Justice Act 1985, section 1.
14. The Law Society, *Annual Report of the Council 1986-1987*.
15. *Twelfth Annual Report of the Lay Observer 1986*, HC 26, HMSO, July 1987.
16. *Lipman Bray (a firm) v. Hillhouse and Jacob* [1987] New Law Journal Report, 20 February 1987, p.171.
17. Civil Justice Review, *Report of the Review Body on Civil Justice*, Cm 394, HMSO, 1988.

18. See *Solicitors' Journal*, 6 March 1987, p.293.

19. For a fuller discussion of this subject see National Consumer Council, *Barristers and their clients: consumer redress*, a review of complaints procedures and the immunity from negligence (forthcoming). This is based on a commissioned background paper by Tim Kerr.

20. Figures produced by the General Council of the Bar show that in 1987 there were 5,642 practising barristers in England and Wales. This compares with 38,839 principal and assistant solicitors in private practice: see the Law Society, *Annual statistical report 1987*.

21. Coopers and Lybrand, *Study of remuneration of barristers carrying out criminal legal aid*, the Senate of the Inns of Court and the Bar, September 1985.

22. *New Law Journal*, 15 November 1979, p.1117.

23. *Guardian*, 28 March 1988, p.2.

24. Committee on the Future of the Legal Profession (Chairman: Lady Marre), *A time for change*, report presented to the General Council of the Bar and the Council of the Law Society, July 1988.

25. *Rondel v. Worsley* [1969] 1 Appeal Cases, p.191.

26. *Saif Ali v. Sidney Mitchell and Co and others* [1980] Appeal Cases, p.198.

27. *Rees v. Sinclair* [1974] 1 New Zealand Law Reports, p.180.

28. Legal Professions Act 1958, section 10.

29. *Demarco v. Ungaro* [1979] 95 DLR 3d, p.385.

30. *Code of conduct for the Bar of England and Wales*, third edition, January 1985, para. 28A.

31. Bar Mutual Indemnity Fund Limited, proposed rating schedule, February 1988.

32. *Code of conduct for the Bar of England and Wales*, third edition, January 1985, paras. 6, 7 and 8.

33. *Code of conduct for the Bar of England and Wales*, third edition, as amended in October 1987, annex 1.

34. *Code of conduct for the Bar of England and Wales*, third edition, as amended in October 1987, annex 2.

35. Correspondence with the professional standards committee of the Bar Council, September 1988.

36. *Counsel*, September 1987.

37. *Rondel v. Worsley* [1966] 3 Weekly Law Reports, p.950 [court of appeal].

38. Zander M., *Legal services for the community*, Temple Smith, 1978, p.135.
39. *R. v. Irwin* [1987] 2 All England Reports, p.1085.
40. Order 62 rule 11.

Chapter 8
The structure and training of the legal profession

Advocacy is a highly restricted activity. Although litigants are entitled to address the court in their own case, if they wish someone else to do so on their behalf, they are usually obliged to use a recognised practitioner.

Generally, in the House of Lords, court of appeal and high court, only barristers can appear. Solicitors have limited rights to appear in some of the less important proceedings. These include high court matters which are held "in chambers" (in the judge's room rather than full court), proceedings in the criminal division of the court of appeal before a single judge "in chambers", and applications to the House of Lords for leave to appeal. Exceptions in favour of solicitors are also made in certain high court bankruptcy proceedings. Since May 1986, solicitors can appear in matters which are "formal and unopposed". In the case of *Abse v. Smith* a solicitor was allowed to read out a statement of the terms of settlement in a libel case for the first time (1).

Barristers also have a near monopoly in the crown court. Solicitors' firms who act for clients in magistrates court trials may appear in the crown court if the matter goes to appeal, or if the client is committed to the crown court for sentence. There are a few areas in the country, namely Lincoln, Caernarvon, Barnstaple, Bodmin and Doncaster, where solicitors have traditionally been permitted to appear in criminal cases. Although the crown court is now a national institution rather than a local court, the Lord Chancellor's Department continues to make special rules allowing solicitors to take on certain work in these areas.

Both solicitors and barristers can appear in the county court. Judges and registrars sometimes permit non-lawyers to appear before them, at their discretion.

In the magistrates court, barristers and solicitors may appear and custom permits a number of other people to address the court, including police officers and local government officials. Some statutes give specific authorisation for other enforcement officers, such as wages inspectors, to bring cases. The magistrates also have a discretion to permit non-lawyers to appear.

Otherwise, the role of lay people is restricted to being a "McKenzie person"—named after a court of appeal case, *McKenzie v. McKenzie* (2), which stated that lay friends or relatives could accompany litigants to court "to take notes, quietly make suggestions and give advice". But McKenzie people are not allowed to address the court (3).

Tribunals are much less restrictive about allowing people to act as advocates. In most tribunals the parties are allowed to choose anyone to represent them, including advice workers, trade union officials, friends or relatives. This also applies in the higher tribunals, such as the employment appeal tribunal, which is equivalent in status to the high court.

The debate between solicitors and barristers

These restrictions have been the subject of considerable controversy between solicitors and barristers. The Law Society argues that solicitors should be able to appear in all courts and in the crown court in particular, while the Bar Council believes that barristers' monopoly should remain. In 1979 the Benson Commission concluded that barristers' existing monopolies should continue (4). But the debate continues. It is a matter about which "both branches of the profession feel deeply" (5).

In April 1986, both organisations set up a committee consisting of six practising barristers, six practising solicitors, six independent members and an independent chairman, Lady Marre. They were asked to examine the structure, education and practices of the professions. The committee reported in July 1988 (5) and considered that there should be no change in the restrictions on advocates in the high court and court of appeal. As far as the crown court was concerned they failed to come to an agreement. The majority recommended that solicitors who have proved their competence to a new Rights of Audience Advisory Board should be allowed to represent clients in the crown court. The barrister members, and one independent member, argued that the Benson Commission was correct to recommend no change in the present arrangements.

The consumer interest

This report is concerned with civil law, so we have not considered who should appear in the crown court. But we have considered whether there is a case for relaxing the restrictions on advocacy in the civil courts.

The consumer interest is to ensure that those who do not wish to represent themselves have a genuine and informed choice of competent advocates and pay no more than is necessary. As we discussed in chapter 7, consumers also need redress when something goes wrong.

In chapters 10, 12 and 13 we discuss cases which can be handled by lay advisers. It is clear, however, that in many types of cases including most personal injury claims, consumers need qualified legal advice and assistance. Consumers should be sure that the lawyers they consult have adequate training and are subject to professional discipline. On the other hand, restrictions should be kept to a minimum. Our starting point is that legal services should be responsive to consumer demands and should be allowed to develop in a competitive market.

The adversarial system

The most powerful argument against removing restrictions on advocacy is that this is incompatible with an adversarial system of justice. The Benson Commission commented that:

> "In our jurisdiction, judges have no professional staff to assist them and legal argument is presented orally. Since the judge in most cases delivers judgement either immediately the evidence and argument are concluded or very shortly thereafter, he relies on the advocates who appear before him to bring out the facts of the case, to test the evidence and argue the law fully, referring to all relevant authorities, whether they advance their clients' cases or not" (4).

The Commission argued that advocates are there not only to help the litigant but to help the judge as well. The legal system was therefore entitled to impose restrictions to control the quality of advocacy, even if these ran counter to the express wishes of the litigant. In other words, the "interests of justice" could outweigh the interest of the consumer.

There are very close connections between judges and barristers in the higher courts. All high court judges and the majority of circuit judges are experienced barristers and judges and barristers often meet socially. A limited number of barristers appear before a small number of judges. As a result, they are familiar with each other's ways and share a common outlook. One witness described the relationship between the judge and barrister-advocates as "a three-legged stool" in which "three experts" have "all been trained in the same tradition and in the same pattern" (4). The Benson Commission thought that this close relationship between barristers and judges made trials quicker and more efficient.

We accept that the character of our courts would change if new representatives appeared in great numbers. But this would not necessarily be a bad thing because we see disadvantages in an "adversarial" system, in which judges rely on advocates to put facts and arguments before the court.

The first is that many litigants simply cannot afford advocates. In housing and debt cases the great majority of lay defendants either fail to attend hearings, or appear unrepresented. The Civil Justice Review commented that:

> "In debt, housing and small claims institutional and commercial plaintiffs and defendants are frequently represented by solicitors... In the same types of case, individual plaintiffs and defendants are not often represented by solicitors... In a system of procedure and adjudication which is constructed on the adversary principle it must appear to be a matter of concern that the great mass of business amounting to some 2 million cases a year is in fact conducted on a basis of inequality between the parties. Where a litigant is not legally represented the court cannot assume that the litigant will know what to do and how to get on and do it. Moreover this unequal basis almost certainly deters some from seeking to pursue their just claims" (6).

The second problem is that the more "specialist" the advocate, the greater the barriers between the consumer and the judicial process. Judges and advocates may talk a language and go through procedures which only they understand. Where both barristers and solicitors are used, the lay client is kept at two steps removed from the proceedings. This contributes to the widespread belief that litigation is a remote and mysterious process. Even if justice is done it is not seen to be done unless the litigant understands what has happened and why.

We are not suggesting that the adversarial system should disappear overnight. But the recommendations we make in chapters 9 to 13 are designed as cautious steps towards less remote, more investigative justice.

We agree with the Civil Justice Review that in small claims, debt, and minor housing cases in the county court, registrars should be trained to elicit the facts for themselves, find out the law and apply it to the circumstances before them (7). People should, as far as possible, be encouraged to bring cases for themselves, helped by clearer forms and rules, more advice from court staff, simpler language in court, and more explanations from the registrar. As in tribunals, those who are unable to represent themselves should have the right to be represented by an advice worker or friend of their choice. Registrars should only be allowed to refuse representatives who are corrupt or uncontrollable, and if they decide to do so, they should give reasons for their decisions.

We accept that in most personal injury cases and in larger claims, most people will continue to need qualified legal representation. Nevertheless, more cases should be dealt with in the county court; there should be less reliance on oral argument; obscure legal jargon should be cut down; and the court should take firmer control of the progress of cases. The Civil Justice Review proposals to move cases from the high court to the county court, described in chapter 9, will mean that many more litigants will be able to choose whether to be represented by a solicitor or a barrister. Solicitors will be able to appear in the great majority of cases involving less than £25,000, and in many cases worth between £25,000 and £50,000 (7).

In the longer term, if these changes work well, there is a case for allowing solicitors to represent clients in the high court and appeal courts. We would not wish to see a small elite high court remain immune from the changes in the rest of the court system.

Restrictions on advocacy: the Bar's arguments

There are a number of other arguments put forward by the Bar and accepted by the Benson Commission for not allowing solicitors to represent clients in the higher courts. They are set out in the note of dissent to the Marre Committee (5).

First, it is argued that advocacy involves special skills and techniques and that correspondingly greater demands are made on those skills in the higher courts. It is suggested that barristers are specialist advocates, and that because they appear in court more often, they do it better. Of course, not every barrister is a more experienced advocate than every solicitor. A newly-qualified barrister will not have the experience of a solicitor who has spent the last ten years in the county court and magistrates court. But broadly speaking, most barristers will tend to spend more of their time appearing in court than most solicitors.

In our view, it does not always follow that because someone does something often they do it well. We see no reason why solicitors cannot become competent advocates, given adequate training and supervision. There are some skills which solicitors are more likely to possess than barristers. These include familiarity with the case and the ability to communicate with clients.

It is suggested that barristers make better advocates because they can concentrate on preparing a case without the distraction of a busy practice. But we see no reason why solicitors' practices could not provide their staff or partners with a quiet room to prepare difficult cases.

It is often argued that barristers are better advocates than solicitors because they are less involved in the client's case. The advice they provide is more objective and detached. Detachment cuts both ways. It can be an asset and consumers who wish to have someone approach their cases afresh should be able to use a barrister. It also has a negative side, leading to a superficial understanding of the case, and a lack of interest in the client's problems.

The Benson Commission argued that only large solicitors' firms would be able to offer an advocacy service. Small firms who relied on barristers would not be able to compete with large firms offering full representation and this could lead to monopolies in local areas. The Benson Commission considered that this was particularly likely to occur in criminal work if solicitors were able to represent clients in the crown court. Geographical access could also be reduced if firms were more concentrated. Fears were expressed that the number of barristers might decline, and firms which relied on barristers would not be able to offer their clients such a wide choice of advocates (4).

This argument ignores the fact that firms able to offer a full in-house representation service will only have a competitive edge over those relying on barristers if they offer their consumers an improved service. If they can offer an improved service, they should be allowed to do so. Large firms can open branch offices, and will have every incentive to do so in areas where the local service is poor, perhaps as a result of a local monopoly. If the public still wishes to use barristers, they will continue to be available.

Both solicitors and barristers argue that they are cheaper. Barristers say that their overheads are lower and therefore a day of their time in court costs less. Solicitors say that because barristers must be accompanied by someone from the solicitor's firm, the present system leads to wasteful double-manning. They argue that delays would be reduced if only one person were involved, and the confusion involved in passing pieces of paper from one professional to another would be eliminated. Clients would be able to meet their advocate before the hearing without travelling long distances to barristers.

It is very difficult to quantify the effect that reducing restrictions on advocacy would have on costs. The Benson Commission asked the high court taxing masters to make comparative estimates of costs for a sample of cases on the basis of both a two-branch and one-branch profession. The taxing masters memorandum suggested estimated savings for a one-branch profession varying from five per cent to thirty-one per cent (8). The Benson Commission commented that the taxing masters had made a number of assumptions about the conduct of litigation in a fused profession which, they warned, "were speculative, and about which both the Senate and the Law Society expressed strong reservations. In the light of the views expressed, we consider that no firm conclusion could be drawn from this exercise" (4).

We do not think that increased competition between solicitors and barristers will raise prices. It is possible that barristers' lower overheads will give them the competitive edge, but these benefits are more likely to be realised if consumers can ask for costs estimates from both barristers and solicitors, and make an informed choice between them. In some cases, two lawyers will continue to be used. In others, two lawyers are not necessary and double manning can be reduced.

The Benson Commission commented that the indirect purpose of the present restrictions was "to prevent the fusion and blurring of the two categories of practitioner" (4). It is argued that if solicitors could compete, barristers' practices would no longer be financially viable. Barristers would turn into solicitors, the Bar would no longer exist as a separate institution, and its learning, independence and traditions would be lost.

We do not believe that the advantages which solicitors can offer over barristers are so great or clear cut that barristers will cease to exist. There will continue to be a market for the services of barristers, and barristers will continue to serve it. It should be said, however, that even if it were shown that the advantages which solicitors could offer were so significant that no informed consumer would ever use a barrister again, we would not find this a convincing reason for supporting the Bar's monopoly.

If the monopoly is removed, inexperienced barristers may find it more difficult to get work. Few clients would choose to be one of the first cases on which a trainee barrister makes mistakes. If this happens, there is an argument for revising the training regulations to allow more young people to gain experience in a solicitors' office, where levels of supervision are likely to be higher, before becoming barristers.

Lastly, the Bar argues that permitting solicitors to appear in court would reduce choice. Instead of solicitors making an informed choice of barristers on the client's behalf, clients would be referred to a member of the solicitor's firm, who may not necessarily be the best advocate (5). We consider that there is a real danger that some firms of solicitors may not allow clients to choose barristers. Safeguards need to be provided. Written standards should specify that solicitors must instruct a barrister if they are asked to do so and payment is made. Solicitors who refuse to do so should be found guilty of professional misconduct.

Our conclusions

Our examination of the argument leads us to the conclusion that the balance of advantage is in favour of allowing solicitors to represent clients in the civil courts. The Civil Justice Review recommendation that more cases are dealt with in the county court will have the effect of allowing solicitors to appear in a much wider range of cases. These changes should be monitored and reviewed. If it is clear that there are experienced and competent solicitor-advocates representing clients in substantial county court cases, the restrictions on solicitors appearing in the high court and appeal court should be relaxed.

It is important that if advocates are incompetent, they should be liable to be sued, as we discussed in chapter 7. Lifting the restrictions on advocacy gives added impetus to the arguments for removing advocates' immunity from negligence, and we are very disappointed that the Marre Committee recommended no change in the status quo (5).

Solicitors' firms which offer full representation services should be allowed to advertise the fact, so that consumers can decide which practices to use. They should also be prepared to give written estimates for how much representation will cost, both for paying customers, and those likely to be subject to the legal aid statutory charge. Solicitors should be subject to a professional rule stating that where a client expresses a wish to be represented by a barrister and is prepared to pay the appropriate fee, this should always be respected.

Restrictions on forms of practice

Both branches of the legal profession are bound by a number of rules about how a practice may be organised which restrict the form of organisation and the employment of other professionals. Greater competition in the conveyancing market, coupled with government policy towards deregulation, has led to an extensive review of these rules throughout Britain. There has been heated debate among lawyers on whether solicitors should be allowed to form mixed practices with other professionals. These are often referred to as multi-disciplinary partnerships.

We examine the arguments for permitting new forms of solicitors' practices, and consider whether barristers should be able to form partnerships.

The current rules governing solicitors' practices

Solicitors must practise either as sole practitioners or in partnership with other solicitors. Non-solicitors may not be partners in a solicitors' firm (9). Until recently solicitors were prevented from forming limited companies. This is changing. In June 1988 the Law Society proposed rules which would allow companies managed and controlled by solicitors to provide legal services, provided that all directors and shareholders were solicitors (10). These will be introduced once section 9 of the Administration of Justice Act 1985, which gives the Law Society powers in this area, has been brought into effect.

Generally, solicitors who are employed by non-solicitors may give assistance to their employers but not to members of the public. Rule 4 of the *Solicitors' Practice Rules 1987* stated:

> "A solicitor who is an employee of a non-solicitor employer shall not as part of his employment do professional work for any person other than the employer".

In 1988 the rule was amended to allow a number of limited exceptions in favour of solicitors employed by trade unions and other associations, insurance companies, legal advice lines, local government, law and advice centres and solicitors providing conveyancing to fellow employees in compulsory moves (11). Previously, employed solicitors were expected to obtain waivers from the Law Society to carry out these activities.

The history of the debate

The restrictions on forms of business among professionals first received critical public scrutiny in 1970, when the Monopolies

Commission considered the restrictions imposed by a number of different professional organisations (12). They noted that it was traditionally argued that mixed practices would "unfairly" attract business, create local monopolies, reduce the choice of professional people open to the client and expose practitioners to conflicts of interest. However, they did not consider these arguments were sufficiently strong to prevent mixed practices. They thought that when consumers needed to consult more than one professional at once—in property transactions, for example—mixed practices could provide an easier channel of communication and more comprehensive and integrated advice. They saw no reason why conflicts of interest would be more likely to occur in a mixed practice than in a practice consisting of only one profession. They pointed out that professional partners would continue to be bound by their own professional standards, and would take care to ensure that their standards were not compromised by another profession.

In 1979, the Benson Commission upheld the current restrictions on mixed practices between solicitors and other professionals (4). They thought that there was no demand among solicitors, estate agents or accountants for mixed practices; that mixed practices might not be any cheaper; that there were practical difficulties in forming a code of conduct to apply to mixed practices; and that such practices would tend to refer clients within the practice rather than to the person best suited to solve their problems.

In 1980 the Scottish Hughes Commission took a more liberal view and recommended that mixed practices with other professionals should be allowed (13). They thought that even if there was little demand for them, this was not a reason for preventing their development altogether. They considered that the details of which practice rules applied to mixed practices could be resolved by the various professional organisations, and that the risk of restricting the client's choice of professional adviser would be small. They pointed to the advantages of cross-fertilisation between disciplines, and easier access to professional services.

In 1986 the Director General of Fair Trading prepared a report which considered the restrictions that professional bodies placed on the kind of organisation through which their members could offer their services (14). The Director General considered that since 1979 interest in mixed practices had increased. He felt that such practices could lead to cost-savings and efficiency gains, though the argument had not been tested. He thought that the current rules formed an unnecessary impediment to the formation of practices which had potential benefits, and that the government should consider legislation to remove the statutory restrictions. The government should then seek discussions with the Law Society with a view to altering the practice rules, without the need for a reference to the Monopolies Commission.

The Law Society discussion paper, *Multi-disciplinary partnerships and allied topics*, published in April 1987, outlines both sides of the argument (15). It states that there is a need to preserve "the solicitor's traditional role as an independent and impartial adviser of integrity enjoying a unique position as an officer of the court, who is readily accessible to the public". Independence is defined as "the ability of a solicitor to give fearless advice to his client and to act fearlessly in the client's interest, subject only to the solicitor's duty to the court". The discussion document states that "independence is said to be weakened if in serving the public he is in the employ of a non-solicitor, or his practice is owned wholly or in part by a non-solicitor". It is argued that permitting mixed practices with other professionals may lead to confusion because members of the same firm would be subject to different sets of professional practice rules, and this would reduce the control which solicitors and the Law Society exercise over the way legal services are provided. It may favour large practices at the expense of smaller ones, and hence reduce the number of solicitors' firms available to the public.

On the other hand, the discussion paper states that mixed practices could enable solicitors to respond to a more competitive environment, by offering a broader range of services and specialising according to clients' needs. Overheads could be shared, it would be easier for such practices to run intensive training programmes, and economies of scale could be developed.

In November 1987, the Scottish Home and Health Department published a discussion paper, *The practice of the solicitors' profession in Scotland*, which looked at a number of issues including mixed practices (16). It summarised the arguments set out in the 1986 report of the Director General of Fair Trading (14) and concluded that the weight of the argument is in favour of permitting mixed practices of solicitors and other professionals. The Secretary of State's initial view was that the legislation should be amended to allow the Law Society of Scotland to make practice rules permitting specific combinations of professions in multi-discliplinary practices, subject to appropriate safeguards for clients. The Law Society of Scotland's response was one of wholehearted opposition. It considered that high quality professional services were incompatible with "fierce client-driven, Government encouraged, price competition" (17).

The Marre Committee, set up by the Law Society and General Council of the Bar to examine the structure and practices of the profession, reported in July 1988 (5). They distinguished between "multi-disciplinary practices", in which different professions joined together to offer services which were not governed by any one disciplinary code, and "multi-capacity practices" where the services of different professionals are offered under the disciplinary code of one professional body. They thought that the public interest was best safeguarded by effective self-regulation and that mixed practices might undermine self-regulation. Members of different professions would not share the same training and culture and would therefore have different attitudes towards professional rules. Consumers might be confused about where to complain if services were inadequate.

They thought that mixed practices should be initially confined to multi-capacity practices and that the title "solicitor" should only be used by firms where control rests firmly with solicitors and all the other partners accept all the disciplinary rules of solicitors. They felt that the question of multi-disciplinary practices and mixed titles would need much fuller consideration and discussion with other professional bodies and concluded that any action on the matter should await the Law Society's examination of the issues.

Our views

Consumers' demands for legal services are becoming more sophisticated and demand for new services is growing. Restrictions inhibit consumer choice and tend to prevent the development of new services. They may also cause delays, duplication and extra costs, because consumers are prevented from obtaining the services they require in one place. In our view, restrictions on forms of practice should only be permitted if they are clearly needed to protect the consumer.

Changes which allow solicitors to offer a more sophisticated service to their clients may favour larger, better capitalised and more experimental firms. Fears have been expressed that if mixed practices are allowed, small rural firms will disappear, and access to the law will be diminished. However, large firms will only gain a competitive edge if they provide a better service for consumers. We do not think that firms which could provide a better service should be prevented from doing so simply because this might drive firms which provide a worse service out of business.

Consumers should have a choice between a large practice, able to offer a number of different professional services under one roof, and a smaller, local, more personal firm. In our view, both types of practice will gain by the need to prove their worth in a competitive market. In any case, we do not think that large firms will necessarily ignore the needs of rural areas which can be served by branch offices, surgeries or mobile vans. A mixed practice of, say, accountants and solicitors, may be able to survive in small towns which could not support two separate practices.

We do not believe that solicitors will lose their integrity by associating with other professions. The Marre Committee talks of the "advantages of a common culture" among professions (5). We also see advantages in cross-fertilisation between different disciplines.

We agree with the Marre Committee that there are dangers. Consumers must know what they are getting, and how to complain when things go wrong. We support their proposal that firms calling themselves solicitors should be confined initially to firms which are controlled by solicitors. They should be subject to solicitors' accounts, insurance and compensation rules and the solicitors' complaints procedures.

We consider that there are a number of ways in which consumers could benefit from a relaxation of the rules on business structure. We look at each of these in turn and examine ways in which consumers could be protected.

★ "one stop" house-transfer

If consumers choose, they should be able to obtain a mortgage, a survey, help with selling a house and conveyancing services in one place. With "one stop" services, there are fewer people to contact, failures in communication become less likely and it is easier to budget for one bill rather than several.

In 1988 the Law Society took a small step in this direction by permitting arrangements for "package deals", in which consumers pay one price to an estate agent or other business, and the other business pays the solicitor. But solicitors may not agree with lenders, developers or sellers' agents to offer conveyancing packages to purchasers or borrowers (18).

We would go further and support the introduction of the provisions in the Building Societies Act 1986 to allow building societies to provide conveyancing services. In our view they should be permitted to act for their own customers, and employ solicitors to provide the service. We consider that the Law Society's fears of conflicts of interest have been exaggerated. Most house buyers do not go to a solicitor for advice about a loan (19) and standard mortgage terms from large organisations are almost never re-negotiated (20). Solicitors frequently act for both the purchaser and purchaser's building society, and it is accepted that this is a useful way of saving costs and duplication.

It is possible that building societies will seek to exploit their market position, and we wish to see a number of safeguards to protect the consumer. No mortgage offer should require a borrower to use a particular conveyancing service, and all the different parts of a house-purchase package should be costed separately so that consumers can make price comparisons. Where building societies are prepared to add their own conveyancing fees to the mortgage, they should also be willing to increase the mortgage to cover independent conveyancing fees. Building societies, like solicitors, should be compelled to carry professional indemnity insurance and disclose the commissions they receive. They should account for them to their clients unless they are specifically authorised to retain them. Employed solicitors should be under a specific duty to advise clients of potential conflicts of interest and where an actual conflict arises, they must advise the client to seek independent advice. We also wish to see a duty placed on the Director General of Fair Trading to monitor the conveyancing market to identify anti-competitive behaviour.

Consumers who do not wish to use their building society's conveyancing service should be free to go elsewhere. Solicitors in private practice are able to offer a service which is independent of the mortgage lender and can use this as a marketing point.

Conveyancing packages should not just be available from mortgage lenders. Solicitors should be free to offer estate agency and surveying services, subject to the same safeguards. Indeed, it appears from our survey of solicitors' advertisements that many solicitors have already acknowledged the demand for "packages" and are offering surveys, mortgage broking, and property selling in addition to conveyancing (21). Solicitors should be able to employ surveyors and other professionals, provided that they remain subject to their own disciplinary rules and are insured in the event of negligence. We do not see any reasons why other professionals should not be allowed to become partners or share in the profits.

It is important, however, that consumers know what they are getting. We agree with the Marre Committee that if a practice is called "solicitors" it should have a majority of solicitor partners, should be controlled by solicitors and should be bound by solicitors' account rules and insurance and compensation arrangements. Complaints about charging, clients' money, disclosure of commissions, the way the practice is run or the legal services provided should be investigated by the Solicitors Complaints Bureau (or independent legal council).

We wish to preserve the restriction that solicitors or licensed conveyancers should not be permitted to act for both the buyer and seller of a house or flat. This does give rise to clear conflicts of interest. The practice is permitted in Scotland, and the Lay Observer for Scotland, who monitors complaints against solicitors, has drawn attention to the large number of problems that occur as a result (22). The same considerations apply to mixed practices offering estate agency as part of the conveyancing package: they should not act for the purchaser and as agents for the seller.

The *Solicitors' Practice Rules 1988* allow a number of exceptions to the general rule preventing solicitors from acting for both buyers and sellers, provided that "no conflict of interest appears" (23). Thus a solicitor can act for both parties when they are related to each other, when the price paid for the property is under £5,000, where there are no other solicitors in the vicinity, or when both parties are established clients. When an exception arises, we wish to see the solicitor write to both buyer and seller, explaining the potential conflict, describing why the normal rule does not apply, and asking the parties to consent in writing.

★ mixed practices with accountants

Mixed practices of accountants and solicitors could save duplication, delay and extra costs in fields such as tax planning. Chartered and certified accountants are also subject to detailed professional rules and are proud of the high standards of their profession. We have no reason to think that solicitors' conduct would deteriorate because they associated with accountants.

We are highly sceptical about the arguments put forward in the Law Society discussion document that mixed partnerships would be more likely to seek to maximise profits at the expense of the client. The profit motive already applies to a solicitor's practice, and we have no reason to think that accountants as a group behave less ethically than solicitors.

The same safeguards are needed. All the elements of a package should be separately costed and authorised, so that consumers are free to go elsewhere for part of the service. Firms which call themselves solicitors should have a majority of solicitors, and should be bound by solicitors' accounts, disciplinary and compensation rules. The partnership should disclose the commissions it receives, and should account for them to their clients unless they are specifically authorised to retain them.

★ management expertise

In order to succeed in an increasingly competitive environment, solicitors' practices require a high level of management expertise. These are very different skills from those which make a good lawyer, and legal skills and management skills are not necessarily combined. There may be benefits if solicitors are able to take into partnership non-lawyers who are skilled in running an efficient practice. The Law Society would need to ensure that partners met acceptable standards of probity. Again, solicitors should continue to form the majority of partners and the partnership should abide by the Law Society's rules.

Management and marketing expertise is particularly important to mass market law firms offering standard services at low cost, which we describe in chapter 6. We consider that such firms do offer advantages to consumers who wish to use a standard service, and their development would be encouraged by such a move.

We look forward to changes by the Law Society to the practice rules. Amendments may be needed to the Solicitors Act 1974 and we hope that the government will make parliamentary time available.

There will be problems where different professional rules clash, but we do not consider that these are insoluble. We recommend that the Office of Fair Trading convenes a liaison committee between consumer representatives, the Law Society and professional bodies representing accountants and surveyors to discuss how their various professional rules apply to mixed practices. As a general principle, those rules which give the highest degree of consumer protection should be given priority.

Barristers' partnerships

According to the Bar's professional rules, barristers may only practise as individuals, not in partnerships or companies (24). In practice, barristers join together in chambers to share the expenses of clerks, clerical support, accommodation and books. But they are not permitted to share profits.

It is argued that barristers offer their knowledge and skill to the public as individuals, and partnerships would reduce a barrister's individualism and detachment. Members of the same chambers often appear against each other, representing different sides of the same case, and this would not be possible if barristers belonged to the same partnership. It is argued that partnerships would therefore reduce the availability of barristers in provincial centres and in specialist practices.

Since the beginning of the century there has been a minority of barristers who favour partnerships (25). Partnerships may find it easier to train and supervise new barristers, and they could provide trainees with a salary. Partnerships may also provide barristers with an income which is more secure and more evenly spread over a working life. It is possible that this would attract new entrants from more varied social backgrounds who do not have private means to fall back on in the first few years.

But these arguments have been rejected by the profession as a whole. Both the English and Scottish Royal Commissions thought that the arguments in favour of barristers' partnerships did not outweigh the need to preserve a barrister's individual responsibility to the court and the client (4,13). The Marre Committee considered that partnerships would fundamentally change the nature of the Bar. They thought that the matter should be kept under review but recommended no change at the present time (5).

The rules against partnerships at the Bar do not appear to offer significant protection to consumers, and we are not convinced that they need to be continued. Permitting partnerships will not make partnerships compulsory. Specialist and provincial chambers in which members regularly appear against each other would remain free to practise in the traditional way. Consumers would benefit from greater competition and variety if partnerships were able to recruit new entrants from more varied backgrounds.

Lawyers' training

The training given to lawyers is being reviewed by both branches of the legal profession. The Marre Committee discussed the main educational issues and recommended a new Joint Legal Education Council to consider, as a high priority, a common system of vocational training (4).

We have not tried to consider all the issues involved in lawyers' training examined by the Marre Committee. Instead we outline the present arrangements, and discuss the low emphasis given to social welfare law, and the need to train lawyers to write in plain English and communicate effectively.

Solicitors' training—the current rules

The Law Society regulates the education and training solicitors must undergo, before and after qualification.

Candidates must first enrol as students. To do so, they must be 18 or over, have a good knowledge of English and be suitable people to become solicitors.

They must then pass the "academic stage". Around three-quarters of students are law graduates, who are exempted from this stage (26). The next largest category are graduates in other subjects, who must take the common professional examination after a year's full time study in a polytechnic. Qualified legal executives and justices clerks' assistants who are over 25 may take the common professional examination without a full-time course, and may be exempted from some subjects if they have already passed an examination of equivalent standard. The rules discourage school leavers from becoming solicitors without taking a degree. Those who wish to become solicitors in this way take a separate qualification, the solicitor's first examination, after a year's full time polytechnic course and two years part time study and apprenticeship (27).

The academic stage is followed by "vocational training". For most students this involves a full time course of study, passing the "final examinations" and undergoing an apprenticeship which solicitors call "articles of clerkship". Most vocational courses take a year, and are held either at a branch of the Law Society's College of Law or at a designated polytechnic.

The papers for the final examination are as follows:

Head A: The solicitor's practice accounts   2 hours

Head B: The solicitor and the business client
1. Business organisations and insolvency   3 hours
2. Consumer protection and employment law   2 hours

Head C: The solicitor and the private client
1. Conveyancing (divided into two parts of 2 hours each, the marks of which shall be aggregated)   4 hours
2. Wills, probate and administration   3 hours
3. Family law   2 hours

Head D: Litigation
Litigation (divided into two parts of 2 hours each, covering respectively Civil Procedure and Criminal Procedure, the marks of which shall be aggregated)   4 hours

Source: the Law Society, *The final examination rules 1987.*

Articles have been a compulsory part of a solicitor's training since the early eighteenth century. The basic idea remains the same—the prospective articled clerk enters into an agreement with a qualified and experienced solicitor or "principal", who agrees to provide training. Today the Law Society requires that the clerk should be paid a minimum salary, should be trained in a number of areas of law and should keep records of the training received. Graduates must complete two years articles, which are usually served immediately after the finals course.

Since August 1985 the rules have required that a solicitor's training should continue after qualification. New solicitors must now complete a course of continuing education during the three years following admission. This includes compulsory courses in office management, communication skills and professional conduct, and a wide range of optional subjects. The optional subjects include areas where legal expertise has been lacking, such as child care, industrial tribunal procedure and social security law. Legal aid, civil advocacy and many commercial subjects such as insolvency and EEC competition law are also included.

Barristers' training

The Bar is now largely a graduate profession, and applicants who graduated after 1983 are expected to have a first or second class honours degree. Graduates in subjects other than law must pass the academic stage. Until 1988, the Bar required prospective barristers to take a separate academic course, the Diploma of Law, at the City University or Polytechnic of Central London. It has now been agreed with the Law Society that non-law graduates should sit the same academic examination, whether they wish to become solicitors or barristers (5).

The second, or vocational stage, involves attending a year's course at the Inns of Court School of Law in London, which is run by the Council for Legal Education. This leads to the Bar finals examination. Practising barristers are required to take papers in common and criminal law, equity, civil and criminal procedure, and two other papers. The choice includes family law, landlord and tenant, sale of goods and credit, and labour and social security law, as well as commercial subjects such as international trade. In addition, student barristers have to undergo "practical exercises" which include mock trials and drafting. Courses are also held on subjects such as accounts, auditing and company law.

The rules require all prospective barristers to eat at least twenty-four dinners in their chosen Inn. This provides training in the social side of a barrister's life. It is designed to foster a close-knit profession whose members trust each other (28).

The last stage is an apprenticeship or "pupillage" with another barrister of at least five years' experience. During the second six months, pupils are allowed to accept briefs from solicitors, provided they work under their pupil-master's supervision. Pupils are rarely paid, although there are increasing numbers of scholarships available.

The General Council of the Bar is worried that they may not be attracting the best candidates. In June 1987 they announced a number of reforms, including many new scholarships, a greater emphasis on practical skills, learning how to communicate with clients, and some post-entry training classes (29).

Lawyers are not permitted to be both solicitors and barristers, but special rules allow people to transfer from one branch of the profession to another. The Marre Committee recommended that some of the formalities of transfer should be reduced (5).

Training in social welfare law

In chapter 4 we identified the failure of legal aid to provide a service in areas of welfare law such as social security and debt, and in other areas involving citizens' rights, such as employment and immigration. Part of the problem lies in the low level of training solicitors are given in these areas.

The introduction of compulsory continuing education courses for solicitors is a welcome improvement. The optional courses now cover hitherto neglected subjects such as legal aid and social security law. But we are concerned that in the solicitor's final examinations "social welfare law" is seen as a marginal issue. Consumer protection and employment law are taught in the section on the solicitor and the business client; landlord and tenant law is seen as a minor part of the conveyancing examination, and welfare benefits make only a brief appearance as part of family law. Enforcement is seen from the creditor's viewpoint rather than the debtor's. Conveyancing plays a central part in a solicitor's training. The conveyancing paper is four hours long, equivalent to the litigation paper which covers both civil and criminal procedure.

The Bar examination, however, treats social welfare law more seriously, with optional courses on landlord and tenant, sale of goods and credit, and labour and social security law.

The serious difficulty with the solicitors' vocational course is that all elements are compulsory. As the scope of work dealt with by solicitors increases, it becomes more and more difficult to fit in all the necessary material. The Marre Committee stated that they were impressed with the force of the argument that the course should cover a smaller core of essential material, with options available for those who wished to practise in different areas of law (5). This is broadly the format of the barristers' course.

We recommend that optional subjects should be available and these should include courses for those wishing to concentrate on advising individual clients outside the traditional spheres of conveyancing, matrimonial and criminal work.

Communication skills

There is a general agreement that solicitors often have difficulties communicating with clients. The Solicitors Complaints Bureau has noted that "poor communications seems to be at the root of the majority of the complaints" (30). The Lay Observer comments:

> "With the growth for example of house-purchase, divorce and associated maintenance and custody matters, claims for industrial and other injuries and so on, many more people are now using solicitors, often for the first time. Legal matters are unfamiliar to them and legal language and jargon largely incomprehensible. Even where a solicitor thinks he has explained matters he may in fact without realising it have lapsed into using technical language which his client does not follow. And some, daunted by professionals, may be afraid to ask for an explanation or do not find it easy to put their enquiries coherently. And some solicitors might even feel that time taken to communicate with clients and tell them what is happening is time taken from more productive work. I do not see any easy short term answer. But greater awareness of the problem and greater emphasis on communication in the training of solicitors might help" (31).

This echoes the finding of the Benson Commission in 1979;

> "We consider that more should be done to emphasise the importance of gaining the client's confidence and establishing a sound professional relationship with him. This should be stressed at every stage of a lawyer's professional training. It may not be possible to learn how to do it entirely from books or theoretical teaching but the basic principles can and should be taught to students. To establish good communications with another person is a professional skill which must be, and is, learnt by many others besides lawyers" (4).

There is no doubt that it is difficult for solicitors to communicate well. In interviewing clients, solicitors must separate the relevant from a great deal which is irrelevant. They may have to diffuse aggression, draw out reticent or frightened people and calm those who are distressed, while explaining complex laws to people with no legal knowledge. The cases brought to our attention by citizens advice bureaux and divorce court welfare officers have highlighted that solicitors commonly fail to:

★ tell clients everything they need to know;
★ explain costs adequately;
★ explain why they cannot help;
★ appreciate how easily a client can be initimidated, forgetting that the client may never have employed a solicitor before;
★ understand just how obscure legal language can be;
★ confirm the decision made in an interview and keep their client informed;
★ use clear, simple language in written or oral communications (32).

The Law Society's written professional standards set out the basic principles. Clients should be told in simple language at the start of the case what issues are raised, how they should be dealt with and the name and status of the person dealing with the case. They should be kept informed of progress and the reasons for any serious delay. At the end, the solicitor should write confirming that the matter is over, and summarising any continuing consequences (33). We are concerned that these guidelines do not appear to be well known within the profession. It is important that they are taught to students.

We agree with the Benson Commission that the importance of good communication should be stressed at an early stage. It is much easier to teach good habits than to undo bad ones. With this in mind, we have examined the solicitors' final examination course to see how they approach oral and written communication skills.

Oral skills

We are heartened that a number of those who teach the course are interested in communication skills, and that some attempt is being made to introduce them into basic training. But they do this within a course designed to cram the maximum amount of information into the shortest possible time.

There appears to be no incentive for students taking the final examination course to be interested or skilled in interviewing clients. Teaching staff who are aware of the importance of oral communication fit it in as best they can. They do this without themselves being trained for the task (32).

Oral communication will not be taken seriously unless it is included in the marking system. We would suggest that in carrying out its review the Law Society gives consideration to practical exercises designed to ensure that trainee solicitors can provide clear explanations of the law and procedures involved in simple problems.

Drafting in plain English

The National Consumer Council set out the basic principles of drafting legal documents in plain English in *Plain English for lawyers*, published in 1984 (34). We accept that legal documents need to be precise and may often have to use terms which have specific legal meanings. But long sentences, unnecessary words such as "the said" or "hereinafter", and obscure words and phrases can often be avoided. We took a sample of course materials used in the final examination course and asked the Plain English Campaign to comment on them (32). We found that some of the examples of leases, contracts and partnership deeds given to students were appalling.

This is an example of a single sentence from the draft form of service contract, given to students with the notes on individual employment law. It contains 102 words, has no punctuation and reads:

> "If the Employee shall be incapable of attending to the Employee's duties by reason of injuries sustained wholly or partly as a result of the actionable negligence nuisance or breach of any statutory duty on the part of any third party all payments made to the Employee by the Company under this Clause shall to the extent that compensation is recoverable from that third party constitute loans by the Company to the Employee which shall be repaid when and to the extent that the Employee recovers compensation for loss of earnings from that third party by action or otherwise."

In the whole document, the Plain English Campaign counted only eight full stops and three of these were errors.

Lawyers sometimes argue that it does not matter if leases and contracts are incomprehensible to lay people because solicitors are available to explain them. But consumers should not have to go back to solicitors every time they need to find out their terms of employment or their obligations under a lease. If people are expected to sign documents, it is right that they should be able to read and check them. Very long sentences lead even careful writers into grammatical errors. They are also very difficult to type, and there is a serious danger that if they are mistyped, errors will not be spotted.

It may be that many of the worst documents included on the course are given as examples of bad practice. It is true that students will be faced with badly written documents during their professional lives, and it is a useful exercise to take a poorly written document and turn it into plain English. But it is regrettable that students are given so few examples of good practice. We wish to see students given both good and bad examples of documents. The Plain English Campaign has provided examples of what can be done.

This is a paragraph taken from a draft lease:

"To paint with two coats at least of good oil paint of suitable colours in a proper and workmanlike manner in the year One thousand nine hundred and sixty-seven and afterwards in every third year of the term and also during the last year thereof howsoever determined all the outside wood metal stucco and cement work of the demised premises and any additions thereto and other external parts usually painted".

The Plain English Campaign suggests that this could read:

"Using at least two coats of good oil paint of suitable colours, the tenant will paint in a proper and workmanlike way:

all the outside wood, metal, stucco and cement work; any additions and other outside parts usually painted.

Painting will take place first in 1967, then in every third year afterwards and finally in the last year of the tenancy regardless of how the tenancy ends."

This is the first sentence of a document given to students with the notes on conveyancing. It is to be sent to HM Land Registry, but is intended for lay people buying and selling houses to sign:

"In consideration of fifty-five thousand pounds (£55,000) the receipt of which is hereby acknowledged, we Elizabeth Corrigan and Ian Nicholas Corrigan both of Birch House Nether Crumpton Beresfordshire (hereinafter called "the Vendors") as trustees hereby transfer to Frederick Green and Hazel Anne Green both of 18 Rectory Close, Oldwich, Beresfordshire (hereinafter called "the Purchasers") the land comprised in a conveyance dated the 2nd August 1976 and made between James William Evans (1) and Elizabeth Corrigan and Gillian Mary Corrigan (2) known as Birch House Nether Crumpton aforesaid subject to the restrictive covenants conditions and stipulations referred to in the said conveyance''.

A possible plain English alternative is to start by defining:

"The Vendors

Elizabeth Corrigan and Ian Nicholas Corrigan both of Birch House, Nether Crumpton, Beresfordshire.

The Purchasers

Frederick Green and Hazel Anne Green both of 18 Rectory Close, Oldwich, Beresfordshire.

The Land to be transferred

The Land comprised in a conveyance dated 2 August 1976 and made between James William Evans (1) and Elizabeth Corrigan and Gillian Mary Corrigan (2). The Land is known as Birch House, Nether Crumpton''.

It is then possible to use sentences of sensible length as follows:

"The Vendors acknowledge receiving fifty five thousand pounds (£55,000). In return for this money, the Vendors as trustees transfer the Land to the Purchasers, subject to the restrictive covenants, conditions and stipulations referred to in the conveyance of 2 August 1976.''

We recommend that the Law Society reviews all the materials used on the final examination course, to ensure that students are given good examples of legal drafting. Students should be examined on their ability to draft legal documents in plain English.

Solicitors will also be encouraged to use plain English in documents if they are provided with examples of good drafting. The publishers of legal precedents should review their books to see if they are clearly and plainly written.

Writing to clients

In general, the Plain English Campaign found that the examples of solicitors' letters given in the course notes were clear, well written and had human warmth. Students were not offered letters beginning "I refer to yours of even date" or "Thank you for your letter of the 10th instant" (32).

The following is an example of a well-written letter used on the course. It is personal, the solicitor refers to himself as "I" and signs it with both his forename and surname. It uses relatively short sentences, active rather than passive verbs and a normal English vocabulary:

"Dear Mr and Mrs Carter

Your Son's Accident

I have had an opportunity of studying the Police Report on your son's accident and have interviewed the lady who witnessed the accident. I feel that your son has a strong case and I have written to both drivers stating that they are responsible for the accident and that we are looking to them for damages.

I have received replies from the insurers of both drivers. Both insurers deny that their insured was negligent and in effect blame the other driver, although the insurers of the driver of the blue Cortina also suggests that John was partly to blame because he was wobbling about on his bicycle.

The evidence I have indicates that John was not at fault. However there will obviously be no immediate settlement and it is now necessary to apply for legal aid, so that we can proceed further with the claim. I understand that Andrew Davis was convicted of driving without due care and attention as a result of the accident, and this will assist our case against him.

I should be grateful if Mr Carter would telephone my secretary to arrange a mutually convenient time to come in and sign the legal aid application form."

However, the Campaign did find that some examples of solicitors' letters to the police and the courts were more formal and legalistic.

It is important that students are aware that they will be examined on their ability to write plain and cordial letters to clients. Examiners should mark down letters which are difficult to understand, verbose or pompous, even if they are technically correct.

Our conclusion is that good communication should be seen as an essential part of vocational training, rather than as a desirable extra to be fitted in when circumstances permit.

References to chapter 8

1. *Abse and others v. Smith and others* [1986] 1 Queen's bench p.536.
2. *McKenzie v. McKenzie* [1970] 3 Weekly Law Reports p.472.
3. *Mercy v. Person unknown* [1974] Current Law Yearbook p.3003.

4. Royal Commission on legal services; *Final report* (Chairman: Sir Henry Benson), Cmnd 7648, HMSO, 1979.
5. The committee on the future of the legal profession (Chairman: Lady Marre), *A time for change*, report to the committee of the General Council for the Bar and the Council of the Law Society, July 1988.
6. Civil Justice Review, *General issues*, consultation paper no.6, Lord Chancellor's Department, 1987.
7. Civil Justice Review, *Report of the Review Body on Civil Justice*, Cm 394, HMSO, 1988.
8. Taxing master, *Evidence of the taxing masters to the Royal Commission on Legal Services*, EV 884.
9. *Solicitors' Practice Rules 1987*, rule 7; see also Solicitors Act 1974.
10. *Solicitors' Incorporated Practice Rules 1988*.
11. *Solicitors' Practice Rules 1988*, rule 4.
12. Monopolies Commission, *A report on the general effect on the public interest of certain restrictive practices so far as they prevail in relation to the supply of professional services*, Cmnd 4463, HMSO, 1970.
13. *Royal Commission on Legal Services in Scotland* (Chairman: Lord Hughes), Cmnd 7846, HMSO, 1980.
14. Office of Fair Trading, *Restrictions on the kinds of organisation through which members of professions may offer their services*, a report by the Director General of Fair Trading, August 1986.
15. Law Society, *Multi-disciplinary partnerships and allied topics*, April 1987.
16. The Scottish Home and Health Department, *The practice of the solicitors' profession in Scotland*, November 1987.
17. The Law Society of Scotland, *Response by the Council of the Law Society of Scotland to the Scottish Home and Health Department discussion paper in respect of the sharing of fees or profits with non-solicitors (mixed discipline practices)*, July 1987.
18. *Solicitors' Introduction and Referral Code 1988*.
19. A survey by Marplan for the Consumers' Association of 422 *Which?* readers showed that 11 per cent of house buyers sought advice from their solicitor about a mortgage and 28 per cent recieved some advice. See Consumers' Association briefing on the Administration of Justice Bill, House of Commons committee stage, 1985.
20. The similarity of mortgage documents has led to calls for standardisation: *Royal Commission on legal services* see reference 4, annex 21.1, para.14. See also Law Commission, *Land mortgages*, working paper 99, HMSO, 1986, p.150.

21. Taylor Nelson Media Ltd, "An analysis of solicitors' advertising", prepared for the National Consumer Council, October 1987.

22. *Ninth Annual Report of the Scottish Lay Observer 1985*, para.44, HC 303, HMSO, 1986; *Tenth Annual Report of the Scottish Lay Observer 1986*, para.14, HMSO 1987.

23. *Solicitors' Practice Rules 1987*, rule 6(2).

24. The Bar of England and Wales, *Code of Conduct*, 1985, para.28.

25. See Office of Fair Trading Report, reference 14 above, p.43.

26. The Law Society, *Annual Report of the Council and accounts 1986-87*, p.11.

27. The Law Society, *The education and training of entrants to the solicitors' profession*, 1987.

28. General Council of the Bar, *A career at the Bar*, 1987.

29. General Council of the Bar, "Eight point training and improvement programme for the Bar", press release, 25 June 1987.

30. Solicitors Complaints Bureau, *First Annual Report*, 1988.

31. *Twelfth Annual Report of the Lay Observer 1986*, HC 26, HMSO, July 1987.

32. Church, E., "Plain language, communication skills and the training of solicitors: a review", a paper commissioned by the National Consumer Council, June 1988.

33. The Law Society, *The Professional Conduct of Solicitors*, appendix C/41.

34. National Consumer Council, *Plain English for lawyers*, 1984.

Chapter 9
The courts: their organisation and facilities

There are two main civil courts in which cases start—the county court and the high court. In addition, the magistrates courts hear some civil cases, and there are over 50 different tribunals to sort out various disputes between individuals, and between individuals and the state. Tribunals are particularly important in the fields of social security, employment, immigration, housing, tax and rates. This chapter describes the county and high courts and the judges who work in them, and gives a brief outline of the civil work of magistrates and tribunals. We then consider how the structure of the civil courts should be reformed in the light of the proposals of the Civil Justice Review.

In subsequent chapters we look at the reform of court procedures in four specific areas: small claims, personal injury, housing and debt.

County courts

County courts were set up in 1846 as more accessible, cheaper and quicker alternatives to the high court for small disputes. There are now 267 county courts in England and Wales. They deal with the great majority of civil claims, accounting for three-quarters of all judicial time spent on civil business (1).

County courts can only hear relatively minor disputes. For most disputes in contract or negligence the county court can award no more than £5,000. They may award more when cases are transferred down from the high court. They may also hear disputes under the Consumer Credit Act up to £15,000, probate and trust cases involving not more than £30,000, and possession cases where the rateable value of the land is not more than £1,000 (2). Divorce actions may be heard in the 174 county courts which are designated "divorce courts" (1). In addition, specific statutes give the county court jurisdiction to hear a variety of different matters, such as sex discrimination in schools. There are powers to transfer cases to the high court when an important question of fact or law is likely to arise, or where one party is likely to be entitled to an amount exceeding the county court limit (3).

In practice, the bulk of county court work involves debt, in various forms. In 1987 2.4 million cases were started in the county court. Of these, around 1.52 million were claims for payment for goods sold or work done. A further 403,000 claims involved credit agreements and 155,000 were for miscellaneous debts, including rent arrears and income tax. By comparison, only 30,000 claims were for personal injury, 18,000 were classified as "breach of contract" and 5,000 were classified as "nuisance, trespass, fraud, malicious prosecution, assault and conspiracy" (1).

The other substantial parts of county court business are housing possession actions (167,000 cases in 1987) and divorce (177,000 cases). There were a further 41,000 applications involving housing, mostly concerned with business tenancies, and 10,000 applications involving the adoption or guardianship of children. Around 10,000 applications were for bankruptcy or the winding up of companies (1).

The vast majority of cases do not involve a court hearing. In all, only 69,000 judgements were given after a trial or arbitration. Most cases are for small amounts—almost two-thirds were for less than £500 (1). It appears that county courts handle a large amount of routine, administrative business involving relatively small amounts of money, mainly on behalf of businesses, lenders and landlords. The contested trial is the exception rather than the rule.

The county court is staffed by two tiers of judges. Full trials are usually heard by circuit judges, who also hear criminal cases in the crown court. Pre-trial applications and small claims arbitrations are heard by the lower level of judge, called registrars. Registrars may also hear full trials involving less than £1,000. In recent years, registrars have become increasingly important in the work of the county court. The expansion of the small claims procedure means that registrars now hear more contested cases than circuit judges. In 1987 registrars heard 45,600 arbitrations and 8,500 full trials, compared with a total of 15,000 cases heard by circuit judges (1). They also hear almost three-quarters of housing possession cases (4).

In chapter 10 we examine the small claims procedure, established in 1973 to provide an informal forum for people to use without lawyers. Today, it deals with disputes of £500 or less. Cases are heard by registrars in private, and the strict rules of evidence do not apply (5). Small claims arbitrations are now more common than full trials.

Appeals from the county court are heard by the court of appeal and may proceed from the court of appeal to the House of Lords. Generally, appeals involving amounts of money of less than half the county court limit require the leave of either the county court or court of appeal and there is a very limited right of appeal from small claims proceedings (6). Appeals from the county court are rare: in 1987 only 330 county court appeals were set down for hearing in the court of appeal (1).

The high court

The high court is the more formal of the two courts. It may hear all cases, irrespective of the amount claimed. Work tends to be concentrated in London, where 45 per cent of all business is started in the Royal Courts of Justice (1). Elsewhere, cases may be started in one of 134 high court registries, which are based alongside county courts. Trials are limited to London and 26 provincial trial centres (7).

The high court is also staffed by two tiers of judges: high court judges hear full trials, and high court masters hear pre-trial applications. Rather confusingly, masters are called registrars in the family court and in district registries. In practice, county court registrars act as high court registrars in the provinces. All high court judges are based in London and spend some of the year touring the provinces to hear cases—a relic of medieval times when kings would send their judges around the country. In order to match cases to judges, deputy judges may be appointed on a temporary, part-time basis, and circuit judges and registrars can be asked to sit in the high court. These provisions are often used: in 1987 only half of all high court sitting days were taken by high court judges (1).

A costs sanction is imposed to discourage plaintiffs from using the high court for small cases. A plaintiff who is awarded less than £3,000 is usually entitled to costs on the county court scale only and plaintiffs who receive less than £600 are not entitled to any legal costs (8). Lesser cases may also be "transferred down" to the county court on the grounds that the amount at issue appeared to be less than £5,000, or that the case appeared to raise no important issues. But neither of these procedures succeeds in keeping small disputes out of the high court. Of the money claims started in the Queen's bench division of the high court, half are for £3,000 or less and two-thirds are for £5,000 or less (1). The figures for 1987 produced by the Civil Justice Review show that 38 per cent of all high court personal injury trials in which damages were awarded were within the county court limit (7).

The high court is divided into three divisions, which partly reflect historical differences, and partly differences in work and working style. Judges work for one division only but may be transferred with their consent. The largest and most significant division is the Queen's bench division, which is headed by the Lord Chief Justice and has 51 other high court judges. It deals with contract and negligence claims and contains within it three specialist courts—the commercial court, the admiralty court (dealing mainly with shipping claims) and the official referees court (dealing mainly with building and construction cases) (1). The divisional court of the Queen's bench division hears cases for judicial review of administrative decisions by central and local government, as well as hearing appeals on points of law from magistrates courts. Usually high court judges sit alone, but in the divisional court two or three judges sit together.

Like the county court, most Queen's bench division business is concerned with debt enforcement. In 1987, out of 229,000 cases started, 133,000 were claims for payment for goods sold or work done; 19,000 involved credit agreements, and 21,000 were for miscellaneous debts. The great majority of these cases are disposed of without a hearing. As far as the judges are concerned, most of their time is taken up with personal injury work. In 1987, 32,600 personal injury claims were made, 11,000 were set down for trial and 1,400 reached a hearing. Personal injury cases account for around three-quarters of all cases set down for trial in the Queen's bench division (1).

The family division consists of the president of the division and 15 other high court judges, and deals with divorce, wardship and other children's cases, as well as uncontested probate (1). The chancery division is the smallest of the three divisions: it is headed by the Vice-Chancellor and has 12 other high court judges. It deals with property and land cases, trusts, wills, partnerships, company matters and patents. Only the Royal Courts of Justice in London and 8 provincial centres handle chancery work. Around 23,000 cases a year are started in the chancery division, of which 1,600 are set down for trial, and 1,000 reach a hearing (1).

Unlike the county court, the high court observes vacations. The court is officially closed for a long vacation of two months during the summer and for a further four weeks, spread between three short vacations, during the rest of the year. It is increasingly common for some judges to sit during the vacations to deal with urgent business in return for compensatory leave at other times of the year (7).

Appeals from the high court are heard by the court of appeal, and may proceed to the House of Lords. In 1987, 389 appeals from the high court were set down for hearing before the civil division of the court of appeal. The number of cases reaching the House of Lords is very small. In 1987 the House of Lords heard 57 appeals from the civil division of the court of appeal, and one from the divisional court of the Queen's bench (1).

Court administration

The administration of the courts is the responsibility of the Lord Chancellor's Department. The principle is that judicial salaries are paid out of general taxation, and other court costs, including staff and buildings, are paid for by court users out of court fees. In 1985-6, non-judicial costs amounted to £125.5 million and court fees raised £126 million, giving the court service a small profit which is paid to the exchequer. The judicial salaries budget was £23.5 million (9).

The court administration is now unified. Six circuit administrators are responsible for the efficient dispatch of all the county court, high court and crown court business in their regions. They have direct responsibility for court staff, accommodation and finance and may arrange temporary sittings by deputy registrars. The allocation of permanent judges, however, is a matter of negotiation between administrators and judges. A consultation paper published by the Civil Justice Review suggested that administrators have the greatest influence in the allocation of circuit judges and registrars, but that the allocation of high court judges is decided by the Lord Chief Justice. The paper comments that "there are likely from time to time to be tensions and even conflicts as to the priorities which administrators and judges would wish to see adopted" (9).

Procedural rules

The way that business is dealt with in the civil courts is governed by procedural rules, drawn up by committees of lawyers. The county court rules are set out in a volume of around 2,000 pages called *The County Court Practice*, otherwise known as the green book (10). The rules themselves take up 291 pages. Where the situation is not covered by an appropriate rule, the high court rules apply. The equivalent for the high court and court of appeal is the white book of around six thousand pages in 2 volumes (11).

The high court and court of appeal rules are decided by a committee of judges, barristers and solicitors, presided over by the Lord

Chancellor. Another committee of lawyers is responsible for the county court rules. Draft rules are prepared by the Lord Chancellor's Department, and, in the cases of the county court, need the approval of the Lord Chancellor to take effect. The Supreme Court Procedure Committee acts in an advisory capacity, looking at middle-range reforms in the procedural rules affecting the high court and court of appeal. Again, it consists entirely of judges, barristers and solicitors, and does not have any representatives of court-users (7).

Judges

In Britain, judging is seen as the culmination of a successful career as a lawyer, rather than as a career in its own right. Traditionally, only barristers could be judges. Even today, judges in the high court must be barristers of at least ten years standing (12). Circuit judges must either be barristers of at least ten years standing, or solicitors of at least ten years standing who have also served at least three years as a recorder (a part-time judge in the crown court) (13). During the passage of the Supreme Courts Act 1981 it was suggested that solicitors who were experienced circuit judges should be eligible for promotion to high court judge. But this argument was resisted by the government, on the grounds that experience as an advocate in the high court was more important than experience as a judge (14).

In practice, most circuit judges are barristers. In 1985 Lord Gifford estimated that less than ten per cent of circuit judges were solicitors (15). County court registrars, on the other hand, must be solicitors of at least seven years standing (16). High court masters may be either solicitors or barristers of at least 10 years standing (17).

Candidates do not apply to become circuit or high court judges, and there is no open selection procedure. Instead, candidates are selected by the Lord Chancellor on the advice of senior barristers and judges. Surveys have shown that judges tend to be elderly (with an average age of over 60), male (less than five per cent are women) and predominantly from upper or upper middle-class backgrounds (most went to public school and either Oxford or Cambridge University) (18).

As of October 1987, high court judges are paid £65,000, circuit judges are paid £43,500 and registrars and masters are paid £33,500 (19). The courts sit for five hours a day, and judges do some work in private, reading papers and law reports, and preparing judgements. The high court vacations mean that the maximum number of working days for a high court judge is 190 per year. Circuit judges and registrars, on the other hand, have a target of 210 sitting days per year

(9). A day's hearing before a high court judge is therefore substantially more expensive for the taxpayer than a day's hearing in the county court. The Civil Justice Review *General issues* paper estimated that in 1987 a day before a high court judge cost the state £910, a day before a circuit judge cost £510, and a day before a registrar cost £350 (9).

In the past, judges received no training for their work. In 1979, the Judicial Studies Board was established to provide study programmes, but at first its work was confined to criminal trials and sentencing. Its role was extended to cover civil and family work in October 1985. So far it has concentrated on training for part-time deputy registrars. All new deputy registrars now attend a three-day induction course and sit-in with an experienced registrar for a period of time. The Board also organises regional one-day seminars for serving deputy registrars. No training in civil matters is provided for circuit judges or full-time registrars, although this is being considered by the Board (20).

Magistrates courts

The magistrates court is primarily a criminal court. Nearly all criminal cases start there and most are tried there. Serious matters are committed to the crown court for trial by jury. Magistrates courts do, however, deal with a limited amount of civil business, mainly in the field of family and matrimonial disputes, and care proceedings concerning children. Their other main areas of civil work are enforcing payment of rates and income tax, and licensing pubs and betting shops. They also deal with a number of other matters including disputes about deposits and charges for electricity, gas and water.

Magistrates are predominantly lay people who carry out their work on a part-time basis. They are advised about legal matters by their legally trained clerk. There are a few full time stipendiary magistrates who are barristers or solicitors and sit alone (21).

Tribunals

Tribunals have a long history, dating back to the end of the 18th century. They have developed considerably in the last fifty years, as part of the machinery of the welfare state and the regulation of the economy and employment (22). The number of tribunals and their case loads have continued to increase as it becomes accepted that citizens have rights against the state and against each other. Recent additions have been in the field of vaccine damage, data protection and investor protection (23). According to the Council on Tribunals, the number of cases dealt with by tribunals has for several years been "some six times the number of contested civil cases disposed of at trial before the high court and county courts together". Tribunals hear well over a quarter of a million cases annually and, if one includes cases which are withdrawn or settled, the figure is over one million (24).

It is not always clear why some matters have been given to the courts to decide, while in other areas special tribunals have been established. The Council on Tribunals has commented: "certain basic guidelines can be detected, but the choice is influenced by the interplay of various factors—the nature of the decisions, accidents of history, departmental preferences and political considerations—rather than by the application of a set of coherent principles" (22). A number of advantages have been claimed for tribunals, including specialist knowledge, a non-legal approach, informality, freedom from technicality, speed and cheapness. Few tribunals charge fees and therefore tend to be cheaper than courts for litigants, but more expensive for tax-payers (25).

There are now over fifty separate tribunals. Those with the largest workloads are listed in table 9.1.

Table 9.1: tribunals with the largest workloads in Great Britain (GB) and England (E) and Wales (W).

Tribunal	No. of cases heard in 1986
social security appeals tribunal	90,440 [GB]
local valuation courts	48,335 [E&W]
rent assessment committees	15,346 [E&W] (*)
industrial tribunals	11,532 [E&W]
medical appeal tribunals	10,410 [E&W]
general commissioners of income tax	7,689 [E&W] (**)
educational appeal committees	9,100 [E] (***)
immigration adjudicators	6,664 [GB]

(*)   includes cases withdrawn and settled

(**)   estimate of contentious cases

(***)   1985 figure for admission appeals

Source: Council on Tribunals, *Annual Report 1986/87.*

There are also a number of important tribunals which hear appeals from tribunals of first instance. These include the employment appeal tribunal which hears appeals from industrial tribunals, the immigration appeal tribunal, hearing appeals from immigration adjudicators, and social security commissioners hearing appeals from social security tribunals.

In 1957 the Franks Committee outlined three basic principles—openness, fairness and impartiality—and made a number of recommendations to improve tribunals. These included: developing statutory rules of procedure; improving the qualifications and methods of appointment of chairmen and members; the right to be represented; the giving of reasoned decisions; and further rights of appeal (26). In 1958 the Council on Tribunals was established to advise the government on the constitution and working of tribunals. This has led to a general trend towards greater formality in tribunals, with more legally qualified chairmen, better training, more complex rule of procedures, and more case reports. The Council on Tribunals described the trend towards formality as follows:

"The process started with reforms following the Franks Report which, in general, made tribunals more like courts. It had to be demonstrated that tribunals were not adjuncts of government departments and that in their decision-making they followed a judicial process. Since then the trend towards judicialisation has gathered momentum with the result that tribunals are becoming more formal, expensive and procedurally complex. Consequently they tend to become more difficult for an ordinary citizen to comprehend and cope with on his own." (22)

Reforming the courts

There is general agreement that the civil courts should be reformed. In February 1985, the then Lord Chancellor, Lord Hailsham, initiated the process by setting up the Civil Justice Review. A team of civil servants within the Lord Chancellor's Department were advised by a committee of ten people. The committee was unusual in that lawyers were a small minority. The committee was chaired by Sir Maurice Hodgson, chairman of British Home Stores, and included a former legal officer of the National Consumer Council. Their terms of reference were:

"to improve the machinery of civil justice in England and Wales by means of reforms in jurisdiction, procedure and court administration and in particular to reduce delay, cost and complexity" (7).

They conducted five factual studies about different areas of court business: personal injuries, small claims, debt, housing and commercial cases. They did not look at family work. They issued consultation papers about the various subject areas, followed by a consultation paper about general issues. The final report was published in June 1988 (7).

In this section we discuss the Review's main recommendations which affect the court structure as a whole. In chapters 10 to 13 we look at specific types of court business.

Generalist courts or specialist tribunals?

In chapter 1 we identify a number of areas of concern to individuals, currently dealt with by the ordinary civil courts, including personal injury, consumer complaints, debt, and housing cases. The first question is whether these issues should continue to be dealt with by the courts, or whether disputes should be heard by specialist tribunals?

In *Justice out of reach*, the Consumer Council considered whether a consumer tribunal should be established to hear small consumer claims (27). They thought that tribunals had obvious attractions in terms of accessibility and informality. Most were not bound by rules of evidence, people were not usually legally represented and the chairmen questioned the parties to find out the facts. Hearings were in less imposing surroundings, tribunals often included experts, and members would often go and inspect the subject matter of the dispute. But they concluded that there was an insuperable difficulty in defining the area of law which a consumer tribunal would cover. Consumer claims involve a large number of common law and statutory provisions, and they did not wish to see the tribunal dogged by problems over its jurisdiction. They thought that consumer claims should remain in the county court, but that much could be borrowed from tribunal procedure.

In recent years, a number of organisations have called for specialist housing courts or tribunals (28). They argue that specialist housing forums would bring all housing matters together (including rent assessment, possession and repairs), would have specialist knowledge of housing issues, and would be more accessible and informal than the courts.

In 1985 the General Consumer Council for Northern Ireland argued against separate consumer and housing tribunals. Instead they wished to see the development of a new system for dealing with all minor claims which affected individuals, rather than a series of partial exceptions to "normal" court procedures (29). They stated:

"Although there is much to be said from the consumer's point of view for the Consumer Tribunal, it represents a further element of 'forum fragmentation', for the logic on which it is based justifies separate housing, employment, consumer and various other specialised procedures. This appears to us to be in principle the wrong approach. Instead of a number of discrete procedures, each with its own particular 'forms of action', a unified minor civil adjudication system seems to be a more promising, if necessarily longer term goal.'' (29)

We agree with the General Consumer Council's approach. Rather than look for partial remedies in particular work areas, we would prefer a general reform of the civil courts to make them more accessible to individuals. There are two main problems in setting up specialist tribunals. First, there is a good geographical network of local county courts, and it would be very costly to replicate this with new buildings. The money would be better spent on improvements within the county court.

Secondly, the greater the number of forums, the more overlap, gaps and jurisdictional disputes there will be. Although there are advantages in dealing with rent assessment and possession together, a housing tribunal would move the boundaries rather than bring all disputes under one roof. Possession actions are usually a form of debt collection, and we wish to see all an individual's debt problems looked at together in one place. Problems would be caused if debtors faced an administration order hearing in the court and a possession action hearing in a tribunal.

In our view, the longer term approach is to tackle the problems of formality and inaccessibility within the civil courts themselves rather than remove specific areas from their jurisdictions.

This was also the conclusion of the Civil Justice Review. They decided against proposing a separate housing court. Instead, housing should be seen as an important and identifiable body of work within the county court, to which improved procedures should be applied.

In deciding against specialist courts, we have not examined the arguments for or against a family court which involves different issues from the areas of law we are discussing.

Transferring work to the county court

A major criticism of the present court structure is that too many cases are dealt with in the high court. Cases take longer in the high court, they cost more, the locations are less accessible, and the procedure is more formal and intimidating. The £5,000 county court limit is much too low, yet many high court writs are issued for amounts under

£5,000. Half of all money claims started in the Queen's bench division are for less than £3,000 and two-thirds are for less than £5,000 (1). Although the high court has power to transfer insubstantial cases to the county court before trial, this has only a limited effect. In 1987 a third of general list Queen's bench trials in which money was awarded resulted in awards of £5,000 or less (7).

The Civil Justice Review recommends that far fewer cases should be handled in the high court. It states that the "leading objective" of the Review is that cases should be handled at the lowest appropriate level. It comments:

> "It appears that the present system encourages a tendency among some litigants and their lawyers to make unnecessary claims on the higher court. Even though the county court disposes of cases faster, offers earlier trials and makes better overall use of its resources, there is constant pressure upwards. This may reflect a genuine belief in the superiority of the high court, established habits or expectations as to remuneration. Financial limits, costs sanctions and transfer systems have not so far proved to be effective in dealing with this propensity, whatever its motive." (7)

A high court writ is an intimidating document which is difficult to defend without professional assistance. We are concerned that the high court may be used for its coercive effect, in the hope that recipients will be sufficiently frightened to pay up rather than argue. Although litigants should respect the authority of the court, they should not be deterred by fear of legal costs from putting forward a legitimate defence.

The clearest solution is to amalgamate the high court and county courts into a single unified civil court. As the general issues consultation paper points out, the present two-court system is inflexible. It is difficult to make rational allocations of judges, accommodation, staff and finance between the different parts of the system. As a result, some courts have much longer delays than others. The itineraries of high court judges are fixed largely by reference to past arrangements rather than to current needs (9). In a unified court, the allocation of resources would be much more flexible. All cases would start in the same way. There would continue to be three levels of judges (equivalent to high court judge, circuit court judge and registrar) and cases would be allocated to the appropriate level of judge for a hearing. Higher level judges would be based in regional centres, rather than concentrated in London.

Integrating the high court and county court is not a new idea. It was first recommended by the Judicature Commissioners in 1872 (7). In

1966 the Beeching Commission came to a similar conclusion as regards criminal business (30). They recommended that the distinction between assizes court and quarter sessions should be abolished and replaced by a single crown court which would allocate cases to one of three levels of judges. They raised the question of whether the civil courts should also be integrated but were unable to pursue the subject within the time available.

A unified court is supported by solicitors and advice centres, but opposed by barristers and high court judges (7). Barristers fear that solicitors would have greater rights of audience in a unified court and high court judges fear that administrators may have more power over how the court operates. They argue that high court judges will have less standing and independence in a new court.

In the event the Civil Justice Review stopped short of recommending a unified civil court. They argued that a unified court would require major legislation, lengthy implementation and unknown costs and would run into substantial opposition from high court judges and barristers. They considered that the present two court structure has some advantages for handling specialised cases, such as judicial review, commercial and admiralty work, building construction and patent cases (7).

Instead they recommended a series of measures for dealing with more cases at county court level and for integrating county courts between districts. The main proposals are:

★ the county court upper limit should be abolished;

★ public law and specialist cases would continue to be heard in the high court only. Plaintiffs would be free to start all other cases in the county court. Cases of "importance, complexity or substance" could be transferred from the county court to the high court on the order of a high court master or district registrar;

★ the Lord Chancellor and leading high court judges would issue a practice direction on what amounts to "substance", justifying a high court trial. Initially this should be set at £25,000, with a flexible band between £25,000 and £50,000 in which cases could be heard in either the high court or county court;

★ all personal injury cases would have to start in the county court;

★ the review did not decide whether all debt cases should start in the county court. This depends on the progress the Lord Chancellor's Department makes in establishing a central computerised county court claims registry (31);

★ for the moment plaintiffs would be free to choose either the high court or the county court for debt cases and any other non-personal injury cases, irrespective of the sum involved. But cases would only be listed for high court trial if a high court master or district registrar considered this justified on the grounds of substance (i.e. over £25,000), importance or complexity;

★ in most cases, plaintiffs would be free to start county court cases in any county court of their choice. Only housing possession cases and money claims for £5,000 or less would have to be started in the defendant's local court, or in the court for the area in which the transaction took place;

★ housing possession actions, small claims and short hearings would continue to be heard in local county courts. But full county court trials would be heard in a limited number of county court trial centres;

★ a single procedural code and costs regime would apply both to the high court and county court: lower costs would apply to county court cases below £3,000;

★ the small claims jurisdiction would be raised to £1,000, and registrars would be able to hear full county court trials involving £5,000 or less. Thus in general, registrars would hear all claims under £1,000; claims between £1,000 and £5,000 would be heard by either registrars or circuit judges; circuit judges would hear all claims between £5,000 and £25,000; claims between £25,000 and £50,000 would be heard either by circuit judges or high court judges; and high court judges would hear all claims over £50,000. There would be special arrangements for important or complex cases involving small sums.

The Review Team stated:

"In the event that selective measures did not prove adequately effective, further steps need not be ruled out. The programme for these measures should provide for evaluation of their effectiveness by a fixed date and by reference to specified criteria, including the volume of work removed from the high court and current waiting periods for trial" (7).

We very much support the objective of the review that cases should be heard at the lowest appropriate level of the court system. Lower courts tend to be simpler, quicker, cheaper and less intimidating for the user. The recommendations are undoubtedly a step in the right direction.

Nevertheless, we are disappointed that the Review did not recommend a unified court. This would have meant that the court, rather than the parties, would decide the level at which cases should be heard. The Review's recommendations permit plaintiffs' solicitors to start minor non-personal injury cases in the high court. Given the long-standing habit of lawyers to favour the high court irrespective of delay and costs to litigants, it will be difficult to keep cases under £25,000 out of the high court. A unified court would not have needed complex arrangements for transfer between courts, and there would have been greater flexibility in allocating resources where delays were greatest.

We fully support the recommendation that the implementation plan should specify a date for reviewing the success of the changes and the criteria by which their effectiveness should be judged. If the high court continues to deal with large numbers of minor cases, or if the transfer arrangements cause problems, the establishment of a single civil court should be reconsidered.

The proposals involve substantially more work for the county court. There is a danger that unless adequate resources are made available for county court staff and judges, the main effect of the proposals will be to transfer high court delays to the county court. Many county courts are already short staffed. A survey of local law societies in April 1988 found increasing complaints of administrative delay in many county courts: summonses regularly took over ten days to be issued and some inner London county courts took 35 days (32).

We do not wish to see the reforms implemented if resources are not available to make them work. The Review does not recommend any increase in the number of circuit judges, on the grounds that circuit judges will no longer be needed to deputise for judges in the high court and registrars will be handling more work under £5,000. They do recommend a new level of senior circuit judge to take responsibility for heavier civil work, and at least 10 new registrars to take the transferred work. Further registrars will be needed for the other reforms discussed in chapters 10 to 13, such as increased court control, housing actions and the reformed administration order. The Review has not costed the number of new county court staff which will be needed.

The cost of registrars comes from general taxation but court staff are paid for by court fees. Unfortunately, the Treasury does not regard an increase in court staff, paid for by court fees, as self-financing. Although the court service makes a profit (32), court staff remain subject to rigorous expenditure and staffing controls. There is a strong case for reviewing the accounting procedure so that an increased volume of business (and hence an increased fee income) automatically provides resources to be spent on the court system.

Registrars have the greatest experience in dealing with unrepresented litigants and we agree that their role should be strengthened. Many litigants are puzzled by the term "registrar" and we agree that they should be referred to as judges. We favour the term "district judge".

The Review states that trial centres will lead to a more efficient service. At present, circuit judges visit small courts for a number of days a week or month. This can work well when judges complete their business that day, but if cases do not finish as expected, long delays occur as litigants wait for judges to return to the court. The trial centres would offer continuous trials.

It is important that sufficient trial centres are provided and centres have adequate space and facilities to cope with the increased use. Administrators should be aware that litigants will often have to travel many miles. The centres should be near to public transport. They must be adequately signposted, should make provision for car parking and provide refreshments. We recommend that when litigants and witnesses are notified of trial dates they should be sent maps of the centre.

We wish to see all consumer debt claims start in the county court. We discuss this in more detail in chapter 13.

In chapter 11 we discuss the particular problems of personal injury claims where a large number of individuals are claiming against a single defendant. The new system will need to make special arrangements for dealing centrally with multi-party claims.

Investigative justice

The British system of justice is adversarial: the onus is on the parties to present their cases, with judges playing a passive role, evaluating the evidence put before them. The Civil Justice Review recognises that this causes injustice when unrepresented individuals are opposed by experienced organisations:

> "many small claims, debt and housing cases are in effect conducted on the basis of inequality between the parties: that is to say that unrepresented individuals are frequently opposed by corporate or municipal litigants whose representatives are either legally qualified or experienced in handling litigation. Meanwhile unrepresented litigants are unlikely to know what to do or to get on and do it" (7).

The Review recommends that cases in which individual litigants are not often represented should be conducted on an interventionist basis. This means that registrars ask questions to establish the relevant facts and explain legal terms and procedures to litigants. The onus is on registrars to find out the law and to apply it to the facts.

This is a key recommendation and one we very much support. As we discuss in chapter 10, many registrars already use an interventionist approach in small claims, but others are unhappy about taking an active part in the proceedings. The Review wished to see the approach extended to housing and debt cases.

The difficulty is that experience as a lawyer is little training for dealing with such cases on an investigative basis. Before their appointment as judges, lawyers will never see cases in which neither party is represented. Investigative justice requires greater judicial skill because judges must find out the facts and the law for themselves, rather than relying on the lawyers appearing before them. Skill in judging can no longer be regarded as something lawyers acquire before appointment: it is a new skill to be learnt. A move towards interventionist justice requires a new approach to training judges, which we discuss below.

Judicial training

The Review recommends that there should be a substantial expansion of judicial training in civil business, to be set up by the Judicial Studies Board. In particular, judges and registrars should receive specific and systematic training in housing work, to include social security, local authority management practices and relevant legislation. The Board should also prepare manuals on civil adjudication.

But the Review introduced a note of caution: they stated that "judicial training on a large scale is expensive to mount. It also takes judges away from courts, creating either new delays or a demand for deputy judges with the attendant expense." (7). They recommend that pilot schemes should be carefully evaluated before being taken further.

We agree that there should be a new approach to judicial training. The present Judicial Studies Board exists on a shoe-string budget. It relies largely on the efforts of members of the Board, nearly all of whom have full-time posts elsewhere, ten of them as judges. It is serviced by a secretariat of five people and draws on the services of a part-time study consultant in criminal law. The Board has commented that although a few members have extensive teaching experience it does not have the continuous professional services of any teacher or of any expert in the techniques of adult education. They state:

"Thus far, the efforts of the members and those others who have been willing to give up their time to help have proved sufficient. It has, however, become quite clear to us that this will no longer do...the shape which was given to the Board when the new mandate was conferred shows very clearly that the studies are to remain firmly in the hands of the professional and lay judiciary, as they have always been in the past. We regard this as axiomatic. So also is the immediate involvement of the judiciary in the teaching process. At the same time we have come to see it as undeniable that some aspects of our activities must be professionalised" (20).

We recommend that the Judicial Studies Board should be restructured and provided with its own teaching staff. The development of pilot courses for registrars and circuit judges should be treated as a priority.

Court facilities

For most people a visit to court is a stressful experience which can be made worse if the court building is difficult to find or if there is nowhere to sit down or get a cup of tea or coffee.

The Review recommends that "the programme of improvements to facilities in court buildings, providing for better waiting areas and interview arrangements, refreshments and information to the public, should be maintained as a matter of priority" (7).

We agree. Some improvements, such as full access for disabled users, need to wait for new buildings. But many of the most important improvements require thought rather than money. Two surveys of court facilities show what can be done.

In 1984 a pilot survey produced jointly by the National Federation of Consumer Groups and the National Consumer Council looked at facilities provided in 10 county courts in England and Wales (33). Most court buildings were centrally located and accessible by public transport, but eight of the courts were not well sign-posted, and three were not clearly identified. In two courts, a newcomer to the court would not know where to go, because there was neither an enquiry desk nor a person on duty. Although two courts had excellent cafes, most had no refreshment facilities at all.

The county courts in the survey generally allowed children to attend but provided few facilities. By contrast, several magistrates courts took a more positive attitude. One organised a nursery in a near-by hall, and another advertised a creche in a local church.

In 1988, the Welsh Consumer Council conducted a survey of 8 county courts in Wales (34). They found that most buildings were clean, but looked dingy. Bargoed was in the worst state of repair: the registrar sat with a bucket behind him to catch the rain.

None of the courts were adequately signposted, and one in five court-users reported some difficulties in finding the court offices. Problems were compounded by the fact that court offices were usually separate from the court rooms. Often users knew the court rooms, which were in imposing public buildings, but did not realise that the offices would be more difficult to find. There is a need for court buildings to be signposted, and clearly identified from the outside. Some courts provide location maps, and these should be general practice. Ideally, there should be a reception point at the door, so that users can ask directions. Alternatively, clear signs should be provided within the building.

Half of the users expressed dissatisfaction with the lack of privacy at the court counter. Ideally, soundproof cubicles should be provided, and where this is not possible, a sign could be displayed offering a private room to discuss personal or money matters.

Waiting rooms generally had adequate seating, but tended to be featureless, and were more likely to heighten rather than alleviate anxiety. Pictures and information posters could liven up blank walls and magazines could be provided. Only county courts which shared sites with criminal courts had refreshment facilities. Public telephones were provided in some court houses, but not in court offices where users attended appointments with registrars. Even the oldest courts could provide a drinks machine and an adequate number of pay phones on a self-financing basis.

Many county courts in Wales have replaced ushers with an intercom system, in which the registrar announces the next case over a loud-speaker. The survey concluded that ushers were worth the extra cost. Ushers provided a human face, knew when people had left the room briefly, and could postpone cases which were not ready. Sometimes intercom messages were unclear, and could not be heard from the corridor, interview room or toilet. This led to considerable anxiety, as people were worried that if they missed their case, judgement could be given in their absence.

Leaflets about the court procedure were available but were often not displayed. Litigants were expected to ask for them but most did not know that they were available. In our view, a full range of up-to-date literature, including legal aid leaflets should be clearly displayed and freely available. Posters should give information about legal aid, local advice centres and solicitors.

The Welsh Consumer Council identified a need for a new short leaflet explaining what the county court does, for those coming into contact with it for the first time. This should have a locally produced insert sheet, with a location map and details of facilities available.

Only one court made provision for wheelchair access. Staff were generally willing to assist people with disabilities—staff at three courts said they would make home visits—but facilities left much to be desired. New courts must take the needs of people with disabilities into account. Meanwhile, bells should be provided at ground level and court staff should be trained to assist users. Courts should publicise the availability or absence of facilities, and should ask litigants to inform them of special needs.

There are three main ways of listing appointments: "blocklisting" all cases together, once or twice a day; listing cases in batches (often every quarter or half hour); or giving individually timed appointments. The survey found that blocklisting was the least satisfactory and often led to waits of up to two-and-a-half hours for a fifteen minute hearing. Individual appointments, on the other hand, could lead to judicial time being wasted if litigants failed to appear. Batch listing appeared to work well—waiting times for registrars' appointments averaged 20 minutes, and rarely exceeded 45 minutes (34). In our view, blocklisting should be abandoned for appointments and hearings before registrars.

We wish to see most small claims, debt and housing hearings held in informal rooms, rather than in imposing courts. Court rooms designed to intimidate the user should, where possible, be avoided.

Lay involvement in the courts

It is often difficult for practitioners, staff and judges to see the courts from the point of view of the ordinary person. They may not notice how strange the procedures and language seem to those unused to them.

Since 1971, there has been a power to set up advisory committees in county courts. In 1984 we reported that this was not widely known and that committees were few and far between (33). In 1988 the Welsh Consumer Council found that there were no advisory committees in Wales, although about half of the chief clerks asked thought that they were potentially useful (34).

The Review suggests that consultative arrangements should be revived. They state that solicitors and barristers will also have their own views on the changes in court structure and procedure and that "Presiding Judges, should, with Circuit Administrators, take steps to see that there are opportunities for practitioners' views to be heard at circuit and local level" (7).

Consultative committees should be broadly based, and should include representatives from advice centres and consumer groups. Outsiders can recommend ways in which the facilities of the court can be improved and how more advice and information can be made available. We wish to see the committees sufficiently independent to set their own agendas and lobby for improvements.

At present, no lay people are involved in formulating the procedural rules and this is reflected in the language used. All too often words are used which have no meaning outside the court. This language finds its way into court forms and into the vocabulary of lawyers, judges and court staff, to the confusion of litigants. We recommend that the membership of the committees involved in drawing up procedural rules should be expanded to include representatives of court-users, and lay people with a good knowledge of writing in plain English.

In the following chapters we examine the Civil Justice Review's proposals for reforming court procedures in the fields of small claims, personal injury, housing and debt work.

References to chapter 9

1. Lord Chancellor's Department, *Judicial statistics: Annual Report 1987*, Cm 428, HMSO, 1988.
2. County Courts Act 1984, section 15, County Court Jurisdiction Order 1981 (SI 1981 No.1123).
3. County Courts Act 1984, sections 41-42.
4. School for Advanced Urban Studies, University of Bristol, *Study of housing cases: final report to the Lord Chancellor's Department*, produced for the Civil Justice Review, Lord Chancellor's Department, 1987.
5. County Court Rules 1981, Order 19.
6. County Courts Act 1984, section 77(2).
7. Civil Justice Review, *Report of the Review Body on Civil Justice*, Cm 394, HMSO, 1988.
8. County Courts Act 1984, sections 19 and 20.
9. Civil Justice Review, *General issues*, consultation paper no.6, Lord Chancellor's Department, 1987.
10. Gregory, R.C.L., His Honour D.E. Peck and Myers, A.M., *The county court practice 1988*, Butterworths, 1988.
11. Sir Jack I.H. Jacobs, *The supreme court practice 1988*, Sweet and Maxwell, 1987.
12. Supreme Court Act 1981, section 10(3).
13. Courts Act 1971, section 16.

14. "Solicitors-puisne judges", *New Law Journal*, 12 March 1981, p.273.
15. Gifford, A., *Where's the justice?*, Penguin, 1986.
16. County Courts Act 1984, section 9.
17. Supreme Court Act 1981, section 88, schedule 2.
18. See Gifford, A., above, and "Judges on trial", *Labour Research*, January 1987, vol.76, no.1, p.9.
19. Review Body on Top Salaries (Chairman: Lord Plowden), *Tenth report on top salaries*, Cm 128, HMSO, 1987.
20. Judicial Studies Board, *Report for 1983-1987*, HMSO, 1988.
21. Under the Justices of the Peace Act 1979, sections 13 and 31, there may be up to 60 full-time stipendiary magistrates in London and up to 40 in the provinces.
22. Council on Tribunals, *The functions of the Council on Tribunals: Special Report by the Council*, Cmnd 7805, HMSO, 1980.
23. Council on Tribunals, *Annual Report for 1984/5*, HC 54, HMSO, 1985.
24. Council on Tribunals, *Annual Report for 1985/6*, HC 42, HMSO, 1986.
25. Council on Tribunals, *Annual Report for 1986/7*, HC 234, HMSO, 1988.
26. Committee on Administrative Tribunals and Enquiries (Chairman: Sir Oliver Franks), *Report*, Cmnd 218, HMSO, July 1987.
27. Consumer Council, *Justice out of reach: a case for small claims courts*, HMSO, 1970.
28. These include the Royal Institution of Chartered Surveyors and the Association of Metropolitan Authorities; the *Report of the Review Body on Civil Justice*, reference 19 above, p.134.
29. Greer, D.S. and Mulvaney, A., *A description and evaluation of the small claims procedure in Northern Ireland*, General Consumer Council for Northern Ireland, 1985.
30. Royal Commission on Assizes and Quarter Sessions (Chairman: Lord Beeching) *Report*, Cmnd 4153, HMSO, 1969.
31. Lord Chancellor's Department, *Computerisation of county court procedure in debt cases: the claims registry*, consultation paper, July 1987.
32. Law Society, *County court delays*, civil litigation committee, 1988.
33. National Federation of Consumer Groups/National Consumer Council, *Court facilities in England and Wales: a consumer survey*, November 1984.
34. Welsh Consumer Council, *Courting the consumer*, October 1988.

Chapter 10
Faulty goods and services:
small claims in the county court

Almost every consumer will have a problem with a faulty purchase at some time. According to a large-scale survey commissioned by the Office of Fair Trading in 1984, 42 per cent of the adult population reported some cause for dissatisfaction with goods and services over the previous 12 months. In the United Kingdom as a whole, around

Table 10.1: number of complaints in UK where the average price of goods or services is over £100

Type of good or service	Average cost of item or service	No. of complaints	Percentage of people who took action about complaints	Percentage of people with successful outcome after 1st action
	(£)	(000s)		
Goods				
furniture and floor-coverings	324.1	1,263	85%	47%
household appliances	113.7	3,403	80%	64%
motor vehicles and accessories	2,258.0	1,831	87%	57%
Services				
building work	1,104.0	3,090	87%	22%
repairs and service (motor vehicles)	137.5	1,627	83%	46%
holidays	307.2	945	80%	18%
Total complaints		12,159		

Source: Office of Fair Trading, *Consumer dissatisfaction: a report on surveys undertaken by the Office of Fair Trading,* 1986.

18 million people will have almost 30 million consumer complaints every year (1).

Many complaints are about small purchases, but the survey showed six categories of complaints where the average price of the purchase was over £100. These are furniture, household appliances, cars, car servicing, building and holidays. Between them, these categories accounted for around 12 million complaints.

Over eighty per cent of consumers with complaints about high value goods and services took the matter up. By far the commonest course of action was to contact the supplier. A small number contacted the manufacturer and a few went to outside bodies such as an advice centre, trade organisation or trading standards department. People with complaints about services were particularly unlikely to report a satisfactory outcome to their initial complaint: the satisfaction rate was only 18 per cent for holidays, and 22 per cent for building work.

One message of the survey was that persistence generally pays. People who refused to accept an initial rebuff and took further action were more likely to receive satisfaction. Table 10.2 shows the proportion of people who went on to take further action after being dissatisfied with the result of their first action. In most cases they persisted in their approach to the retailer or manufacturer, often writing to the head office, or speaking to the manager. Again, this tended to be more successful with goods than with services. The second column in table 10.2 shows how taking further action raised the overall level of satisfaction. In the case of furniture and motor vehicles there was a significant improvement. With building repairs and holidays, further action made much less difference. In all, only 26 per cent of complainants taking some form of action about building repairs obtained redress which they regarded as satisfactory.

The last column gives an estimate of the number of residual problems in the UK. This is the number of complaints about high value goods in which consumers took some action but failed to obtain a satisfactory result. The overall figure of 4.5 million in the UK (equivalent to around 4 million in England and Wales) is remarkably high. A substantial proportion of the complaints are about building work. This appears to account for a large number of claims on legal expenses insurance, and consequently several legal expenses insurance policies now exclude building work disputes (2).

The survey demonstrates that there is a large potential demand for an accessible, cheap, and easy procedure for resolving consumer disputes. We are not suggesting that such a procedure should deal with four million cases a year. But if it were to work effectively it would encourage traders to resolve problems more quickly and sympathetically.

Table 10.2: proportion of people who went on to take further action after being dissatisfied with results of first action

	Percentage of people dissatisfied after first action who took second action	Percentage of complainants taking action who eventually had a satisfactory outcome to the complaint	Residual problems among people who took some action (000s)
Goods			
furniture, and floor-coverings	35%	65%	376
household appliances	22%	71%	789
motor vehicles and accessories	27%	67%	558
Services			
building work	33%	26%	1,989
repairs and service (motor vehicles)	19%	51%	662
holidays	22%	20%	151
Total			4,525

Source: Office of Fair Trading, *Consumer dissatisfaction: a report on surveys undertaken by the Office of Fair Trading,* 1986.

What sort of complaints are there?

In the case of goods, the OFT survey can be supplemented by research we carried out for the Law Commission in 1982-83, published in *Buying problems* (3). We looked in greater detail at 646 problems about unsatisfactory goods brought to citizens advice bureaux and consumer advice centres during the survey period. Complaints about food and drink were excluded from the survey, but shoes, clothes, furniture, electrical goods and, to a lesser extent, cars featured prominently.

All but six per cent of consumers in the survey had already contacted the supplier but had been dissatisfied with their response. Ninety per cent of the goods were bought new. A quarter led to problems immediately and 90 per cent went wrong within 15 months.

Half the sample described the goods they had bought as not fit for their intended purpose. Others complained that their purchases were scratched, dented or faulty in appearance. Twenty per cent of goods did not work at all and this increased to 45 per cent for electrical goods. One in ten purchasers thought the goods were dangerous.

One of the clearest messages from the survey was that consumers wanted what they had originally sought. If they had tried to buy a washing machine, they continued to want a washing machine that worked or their money back so they could go elsewhere. They did not want endless repairs, rudeness, or to be fobbed off with "shop policy". Most people were not experienced complainers. More than half had made no other complaints in the previous three years.

Advice workers thought that the majority of complainants were entitled to a remedy. They said that 60 per cent were definitely entitled, over a quarter may be entitled, and only one in ten consumers were definitely not entitled to a remedy. Consumer law, however, is far from certain, and this can only be treated as the opinion of the adviser.

Failure to go to court

Very few people in the OFT survey used the county court to resolve their dispute. In fact, less than 2 per cent of those taking some form of further action threatened court action (4). Even fewer people actually take their case to court.

Why do people use the courts so rarely to resolve consumer disputes? The answers are complex, and differ from person to person. Research into the small claims experiment in Dundee points out that there will always be some disputes which do not lend themselves to a legal solution, and that people do not base their decision to raise or defend legal action solely on factors related to court procedures (5).

But the way the courts are perceived is one significant factor. Part of the problem is that consumers do not know their rights and do not know about the court. In 1978, the Welsh Consumer Council looked at consumer awareness of legal redress in Wales and the results were published in *Simple justice* (6). Respondents were given five hypothetical problems and asked how they would handle them. These included buying faulty shoes or a faulty vacuum cleaner, and having a car damaged by a service garage. Generally consumers answered that they would take the matter up with the shop, but if the shop denied responsibility, a substantial minority of consumers were unsure about standing their ground. People were over-impressed by the importance of guarantee cards and thought that no redress at all was available for faulty second-hand goods.

Respondents in the Welsh survey were asked what matters they thought were dealt with by the county court. The answers are given in table 10.3.

Table 10.3: matters respondents thought were dealt with by county courts*

unpaid bills	65%
evictions	60%
shoplifting offences	55%
divorce	54%
parking fines	34%
contaminated food	22%
complaints about faulty goods	19%
permission to build a garage	13%
don't know	12%

Base: 491 respondents

*More than one answer possible
Source: NCC/WCC *Simple justice,* 1979.

Most people thought, rightly, that the county court dealt with unpaid bills, evictions and divorce. But only 19 per cent thought that the county court was a place to sort out complaints about faulty goods. More than twice as many people thought, quite wrongly, that the county court dealt with shoplifting.

Even when people know that they can go to court, they are reluctant to use it. Consumers were asked what would worry them about going to court. Forty-five per cent mentioned the cost; a third said they would be worried about the whole atmosphere; a quarter mentioned the formalities; and a quarter mentioned the possible disappointment of losing. Twenty-seven per cent said they were worried about their name getting into the paper. For these people 'going to court' is seen as a personal disgrace.

In *Simple justice* (6) we asked advice agencies and trading standards departments to rate the small claims procedure in the county court according to various criteria. Those questioned rated the county court lowest for having an approachable public image and said that in their experience people were often frightened of using the courts.

In the *Buying problems* survey, advice workers thought that in theory most complainants did have a remedy, but they were much less optimistic that people would actually get the redress to which they were entitled (3). Advisers thought that only a third of clients were "certain" or "very likely" to get what they were entitled to. One in four were thought "fairly likely" and one in seven people were thought "unlikely" to get their entitlement. Advisers were asked why people wouldn't obtain their rights. The reasons given included the expense, complexity and delay of court action, and difficulties in getting proof. Advisers often thought that callers lacked the necessary skills or would be intimidated by the court, while the other party was likely to fight the case strongly (3).

The small claims procedure

In 1970, the then Consumer Council proposed a solution to these problems. It recommended that:

> "the registrar of each county court should be charged with running an informal court for small claims, as a branch of the county court, designed for individuals to have their claims adjudicated without legal representation. Practising solicitors or professional people with experience in arbitration might help to man the court. The court's judgements would be enforceable by county court machinery" (7).

In October 1973 the arbitration scheme, commonly known as the small claims procedure, was introduced into the county courts. Under this scheme any claim for not more than £75 (now raised to £500) could be referred to arbitration by a county court registrar. Practice directions from the Lord Chancellor indicated that the strict rules of evidence would not apply and registrars would be free to adopt their own method of procedure. The hearing would be as informal as possible and held in private.

The small claims system in England and Wales exists within the ordinary court structure. There is no separate "small claims division", but only a modification of the normal rules. The basis of the small claims provision is set out in order 19 of the County Court Rules 1981 (8). This provides for defended claims of not more than £500 to be referred to arbitration before the registrar or, in exceptional circumstances, by a circuit judge or outside arbitrator. It states that the reference to arbitration may be rescinded if difficult questions of law or fact are involved, if there is an allegation of fraud, or if the parties agree.

The terms of reference are set out in rule 5, sub-section 2. These provide for an appointment before the registrar for "the preliminary consideration of the dispute and ways of resolving it, unless the size or nature of the claim or other circumstances make such a course undesirable or unnecessary". During the preliminary hearing, the registrar fixes a date and gives directions for the hearing. The rules state that the hearing "shall be informal and the strict rules of evidence shall not apply" (8). The arbitrator may adopt "any method of procedure which he may consider to be convenient and to afford a fair and equal opportunity to each party to present his case" (8). Although the rules provide for the registrar to call on an expert report, this must be paid for by the parties to the proceedings.

The courts have tended to interpret these provisions narrowly. In the case of *Chilton v. Saga Holidays* (9) the registrar prevented a represented party from cross-examining an unrepresented party but insisted that all questions were put through him. The court of appeal found that this was not permitted. Even in small claims proceedings each party had the right to cross-examine witnesses. In practice, this helps represented litigants because individuals find it difficult to frame questions rather than make statements.

Legal representation is permitted but is discouraged by the rule on costs. The winning party can only recoup very limited legal costs from the other side. The fixed legal costs of issuing the summons and enforcing the award may be recouped, but the costs of legal advice or representation may not, unless they have been incurred through the unreasonable conduct of the other side (8).

Does the small claims procedure work?

The small claims procedure is intended to allow ordinary people to seek legal remedies to claims which, although significant, do not justify the expense of a lawyer. In our view it should provide a system which is:

★ accessible—both geographically and in the image it presents to the public;
★ simple to use and understand;
★ informal enough to allow individuals to present their own case;
★ cheap—both for the user and the state;
★ quick and effective in the settlement of disputes;
★ just.

Fifteen years experience and a number of research studies have thrown some light on how well the procedure meets these aims. In

1979 we reviewed the operation of the procedure, and produced a report, *Simple justice*, jointly with the Welsh Consumer Council (6). In 1986 the system was examined by the Civil Justice Review (10).

There are many advantages to the small claims procedure. It is much quicker, cheaper and simpler than that for personal injury cases over £500. Litigants generally believe the procedure to be fair and say that they would use it again (10). The booklet, *Small claims in the county court* (11), is very useful in telling people how to go about suing. Research for the Civil Justice Review found that two-thirds of plaintiffs had seen the booklet and four out of five had found it useful (10). Similar booklets could be produced for other areas of law.

On the other hand, there are a number of problems. The greatest disappointment is that cases are rarely brought by consumers. The great majority of plaintiffs are businesses and institutions although it is difficult to be precise about the numbers. Research carried out by the Civil Justice Review was deliberately biased towards small plaintiffs and therefore over-estimated the number of individual plaintiffs. It would seem, however, that no more than a third of cases are brought by individuals. On the other hand, over half the defendants are individuals. The research found that only 13 per cent of claims are about faulty goods or services (again this is likely to be an over-estimate) (10). It appears that less than 12,500 disputes about faulty goods and services are referred to arbitration each year (12). This is a low figure in relation to the use made of the small claims court and to the number of unresolved disputes. By comparison, in 1987, the Solicitors Complaints Bureau received almost 14,000 complaints from consumers (13), and local authorities and advice centres received over 600,000 consumer complaints (14). Much more needs to be done to publicise the procedure and improve the image of the county court. The small claims limit of £500 is too low. Many of the problems described in table 10.1 are outside the small claims limit, and this discourages people from threatening to go to court.

The Civil Justice Review research found considerable variation between registrars. At one end of the spectrum, registrars who adopt an informal, "investigative" approach begin by asking both parties to explain their stories, hear witnesses, and move quickly to the points they identify as significant. At the other end of the spectrum, more formal registrars who consider the proceedings to be essentially adversarial expect plaintiffs to establish their own case according to the rules of evidence, and give the defence an opportunity to cross-examine. The registrar intervenes only if important points are neglected. This can cause difficulties for people unused to the law. Just under a half of litigants complained that the registrar had not helped them to put their case (10). The variations also make the procedure more confusing because litigants are not sure what to expect.

Although the Lord Chancellor's Department has tried to improve the main summons and reply forms, many of the other small claims forms which tell people when to attend hearings and how to prepare their cases are produced by local courts. These are often poorly laid out and reproduced, and use legal jargon. Examples include:

> "the parties do give discovery of documents by list under Order 14 rule 1 limited to special damages within 28 days with inspection within 7 days thereafter";

> "the costs of the action up to and including the entry of judgement shall be in the discretion of the arbitrator to be exercised in the same manner as the discretion of the Court under the provisions of the County Court Rules" (10).

Important information about how long the hearing will last, what papers should be brought and who should attend is often left out.

Well over half of litigants had attended court on two or more occasions. This clearly causes difficulties for people in work. Over half of those taking time off work had lost pay. A majority of people had attended a preliminary hearing, where the registrar had tried to sort the matter out and give advice about the hearing. Most people thought it had not helped but had added to the time and trouble of the proceedings. Generally, the more formally minded registrars held preliminary hearings while informal registrars did without, except in complicated cases (10).

Almost two-thirds of cases took more than three months and almost a half took more than five months. The longest cases took two years (10). Obviously, the procedure is not as quick as it should be.

Despite attempts to discourage legal representation, around a third of plaintiffs used lawyers to issue the summons and over a quarter were represented at the hearing. Large organisations were much more likely to be legally represented than individuals. A quarter of unrepresented litigants who had met a represented opponent commented that it made their case more difficult to prove (10).

Lastly, consumers often found that getting a judgement was easier than getting payment. Individuals often did not realise that it was up to them to enforce the debt and they were given little advice about how to set about it (6). We examine this further in chapter 13.

Lessons from other countries

England and Wales are not alone in recognising a need for more informal court procedures in small disputes. During the 1970s, many other common law jurisdictions brought in new procedures to help individuals fight their claims without lawyers. Different procedures were established in the different states of America, Canada and Australia; an experimental small claims tribunal was set up in New Zealand; and in 1978 the Northern Irish county courts were given the power to hear claims under £300 by arbitration (15). In Scotland an experimental scheme was established in Dundee from 1979 to 1982 (5).

There are a number of questions which concern all small claims procedures, and we discuss the various answers which have been provided, before making our own recommendations for reform.

Should businesses be allowed to use the small claims procedure?

In *Justice out of reach* (7) the Consumer Council recommended that only individuals should be allowed to start small claims. Companies, partnerships, associations and assignees of debts would be excluded:

> "the purpose would be to prevent the courts becoming widely used by firms for debt collecting and its approach thus becoming more geared to businesses than to individuals. . . Business representatives are usually easier for the court officers and judges to deal with than are individual litigants: they speak the same language, and are generally more articulate and less emotionally involved in the dispute. If company representatives—particularly representatives of the same companies—become a familiar part of the scene, there would be a danger that individuals would become the 'odd' parties, the ones to be dealt with on sufferance, with the implication that they were wasting the court's time" (7).

They recommended that individuals sued by firms in the county court should have the opportunity to transfer their case to the small claims court.

The Consumer Council were influenced by the experience of the small claims procedure in New York, which prevents claims from being brought by businesses. A number of other American states prevent professional debt collectors from using small claims procedures, including Texas and California. But several states, such as Connecticut and Washington DC, permit business and debt claims. The Australian states of New South Wales, Victoria, Queensland and

Western Australia have set up special tribunals which are restricted to consumer plaintiffs. But South Australia, Northern Territory and the Australian Capital Territory have adapted existing court procedures which may be used for business debts. Business claims are allowed in all the small claims procedures in Canada, with the exception of Quebec. Business plaintiffs are also permitted in Northern Ireland and in the New Zealand small claims tribunal. In New Zealand, however, claims are limited to "disputes" and the tribunal may not be used for simple debt collection (15).

The great majority of jurisdictions which permit business plaintiffs are used to a much greater extent by businesses than by consumers. As we have seen, in England and Wales less than a third of small claims are brought by individuals (10). Similar or lower figures emerge from studies in Canada, America, and Northern Ireland (15, 16).

The New Zealand small claims tribunal is an exception to this general rule. Although businesses are permitted to bring cases, a small initial study has suggested that around two-thirds of plaintiffs are individuals (15). The small claims tribunal was set up specifically to help individual consumers. It relies on mediation; decisions are made on the substantive merits of the case, rather than the strict application of law; the great majority of arbitrators are non-lawyers; legal representation is not permitted; and the registrar and officials are under a duty to assist the public to make claims. These factors lead to a high proportion of consumer claims.

On the other hand, the fact that small claims procedures are used more by businesses than by consumers does not necessarily mean that business debts will 'crowd out' consumer claims. An American study by the National Center for State Courts found that although the proportion of consumer claims fell when businesses were permitted to use the procedure, the absolute number of consumer claims did not (17). The researchers looked at 15 courts in 14 different states, including two courts in New York. In seven states, there were no restrictions on business claimants; in six states, debt collection agencies were not allowed to use the procedure; and in New York there was a ban on all corporate claimants. They concluded that there was no relationship between the number of individual claimants per 1,000 of the population and whether debt collection agencies or businesses were permitted to use the court. They found that the great majority of defendants in debt cases were individuals and that defendants found it easier to defend their cases in the small claims jurisdiction (17).

The General Consumer Council's study of small claims in Northern Ireland reached a similar conclusion:

"we have found little concrete evidence to suggest that individual applicants suffer as a result of the decision to permit claims by businesses and other organisations. The system appears to be able to cope with the large number of applications involved and still enable most consumer claims and other claims by individuals to be dealt with within a reasonable period. Indeed, were it not for the volume of claims made by businesses, it could well be that an economically minded government would consider a special procedure unwarranted for the number of occasions to which resort was had to it. In principle also we believe that a procedure designed to encourage use by individuals as applicants should also be available for use by individuals as respondents" (16).

Defendants who have refused to pay because goods or services are faulty raise the same issues as plaintiffs. There are advantages in allowing these cases to come within the small claims procedure without the extra complication of defendants having to ask for a transfer. In *Simple justice* (6) we concluded that the small claims procedure should include disputed debts, whether claims were brought by businesses or individuals, because individuals who are being sued by companies are more likely to submit a defence if it is clear from the start that the case will be heard by arbitration. An additional procedure for applying for a case to be transferred to arbitration might prevent individuals submitting a defence. The American study confirms us in the belief that the small claims procedure should be open to all types of plaintiffs.

It should be remembered, however, that the county court was established as a businessman's court. Large institutional plaintiffs dominate the proceedings. The Welsh survey for *Simple justice* (6) found that people associated the county court with unpaid bills, eviction and divorce, rather than with complaints about faulty goods. Special efforts need to be made to publicise the small claims procedure as a way in which consumers can sort out their problems, and staff and judges must ensure that the individual is not regarded as the "odd one out".

Should lawyers be banned?

In 1970 the Consumer Council argued strongly that lawyers should be banned in the small claims court:

"Obviously, we have not adopted the view that lawyers should be excluded without searching consideration. The principle that a man should be entitled to have a lawyer to speak for him at a judicial hearing is one deserving of great respect. But one must remember that this is principle and not practice: in practice, because of the expense, the majority of individuals would not have lawyers even if they were permitted to do so. And if it gradually became customary for lawyers to appear in the small claims court, then people would feel that they could not proceed without a lawyer, as is the case in the county courts now. We should then be back where we are now, without justice for small claims...Another consideration is the effect that the presence of lawyers would tend to have on the atmosphere of the court...When lawyers appear regularly, courts tend to become more formal, more forbidding, slower and altogether less geared to the individual. Procedural rules grow up" (7).

Lawyers have been banned in a few jurisdictions. Eight American states have prevented lawyers from appearing in small claims, as have Quebec and New Zealand. In New South Wales and South Australia lawyers can only appear with the agreement of the parties and if the tribunals are satisfied that this will not lead to an unfair advantage. Banning lawyers has tended to meet with fierce opposition from the legal profession. In Quebec, the profession argued unsuccessfully that denying the right to legal representation was unconstitutional. Judges in Quebec also opposed the idea, arguing that lawyers make their job easier by marshalling facts and arguments and sifting out hopeless cases (15).

The danger is that when lawyers are present judges will play a much more passive role, deciding on the evidence presented, rather than asking questions and seeking the facts. The Consumer Council commented that in American small claims courts which permitted lawyers, judges found it more difficult to conduct a case informally:

"this informal procedure goes against the grain of trained trial lawyers, and the judge himself did not always seem confident enough, in the presence of other lawyers, to dispense with the procedures in which he too had been trained. As a result, when there were lawyers on both sides, the trial tended to proceed by the traditional method of examination and cross-examination" (7).

The National Center for State Courts study of 15 American courts found that representation made little difference to the plaintiff's chance of winning. Both represented and unrepresented litigants won in over eighty per cent of cases, and were awarded over eighty per cent of the original claim (17). The Civil Justice Review research in England and Wales also found that there was no significant difference between the success rate of represented plaintiffs (70 per cent) and the overall success rate of 67 per cent (10). On the other hand, the American study did find a significant difference between the success of represented and unrepresented defendants. When individual defendants faced a corporate plaintiff they received little assistance from the court and possible defences could be overlooked (17).

One of the principal conditions of a small claims procedure is that legal representation should not be necessary. It is a fault of the present system that lawyers appear too often. The Civil Justice Review figures show that one side or the other has some form of representation in just under half of all cases. They found that the plaintiff alone was represented in 27 per cent of cases—in 23 per cent by an outside lawyer, and in four per cent by an in-house solicitor. The defendant alone was represented in 12 per cent of cases and both sides were represented in 9 per cent of cases (10). This high level of representation increases the formality and adversarial nature of the proceedings and may discourage individual, unrepresented litigants. Twenty-eight per cent of unrepresented litigants who had met a represented opponent thought that this made their case much harder to prove (10).

The debate is between those who wish to improve the proceedings so that the need for legal representation disappears, and those who wish to impose an outright ban on lawyers. In *Simple justice* (6) we found these two approaches difficult to reconcile. On the one hand, banning lawyers is a restriction on individual freedom and choice. It may also limit the chances of individual defendants getting justice. On the other hand, progress towards informality is very slow when lawyers are so often involved. In 1979, we concluded that, on balance, representation should not be permitted in the great majority of cases heard by arbitration. Exceptions should be made when difficult questions of law or fact were involved, when the registrar certified that it was in the interests of justice, or where both parties agreed (6).

In 1987, in response to the Civil Justice Review, we reconsidered the matter (18). Since 1979 there has been an expansion in both the number and expertise of lay representatives; they have proved their ability to increase access to justice, and to represent inarticulate and disadvantaged litigants. Money advisers have been effective in ensuring that those pursued for debts who have legitimate defences are able to put their case to the court. At present, provision is not anywhere near adequate to meet the demand, and we wish to see an expansion of lay representation through advice and law centres. Registrars have a discretion to permit lay representatives, but many do not permit them to appear. We are concerned that in the interviews carried out for the Civil Justice Review, none of the registrars said they would normally allow non-legally qualified representatives to present cases on behalf of litigants (10). There is a strong case for reducing the discretion of registrars to decide which representatives should be permitted. It would be illogical to allow lay representatives but to ban those with legal training.

We concluded that although the procedure should aim to make representation unnecessary, litigants should have the right to be accompanied or represented by the person of their choice. Legal costs should not be allowed. A similar conclusion was reached by the Civil Justice Review (19) which states that there should be a clear presumption in favour of allowing a litigant to be accompanied by anyone he likes at the hearing. It argues that registrars should retain a discretion to restrict the involvement of corrupt or unruly representatives, but that they should give reasons for doing so.

It is very important that the presence of a representative does not change the nature of the proceedings. Arbitrators should still conduct cases in the same order and insist that all questions to witnesses are put through them, whether or not the parties are represented.

What role should the judge play?

In England and Wales, court proceedings are traditionally adversarial: the parties are responsible for presenting the facts and the law to the judge, who makes a decision on the basis of what is said in court. In a system designed for individuals to use without lawyers this is no longer possible. The judge or arbitrator must play a much more active and investigative role, by asking questions to elicit the facts, and finding out which laws to apply to the facts.

Where key information is not before the court, the arbitrator should take steps to obtain it. The American National Center for State Courts study found that those judges who take their investigative role seriously, postpone cases to allow the parties to bring more evidence to court and visit evidence that cannot be moved. They also telephone impartial witnesses to ask questions in the presence of the parties (17). The General Consumer Council's report on small claims in Northern Ireland gives an example of how the telephone can be used:

> "An expert report had been obtained in connection with a suede coat which the respondent dry cleaner was alleged to have

negligently damaged, while cleaning. The report was unfavourable to the respondent and he challenged its findings. The Registrar adjourned the case briefly to allow the respondent to obtain a document and he himself took the opportunity to telephone the laboratory which had prepared the report. The additional information he obtained satisfied him that the respondent had indeed been negligent.'' (16).

Many registrars have found difficulties in adapting to a more investigative style. The research for the Civil Justice Review included 29 interviews with registrars and found wide variations between them. Those who were happiest with the investigative approach would invite one party and then the other to tell their story, hear any witnesses and then move quickly to asking the questions that they thought necessary. They would not try to prevent litigants from giving hearsay evidence and would not encourage formal cross-examination. At the other end of the scale were registrars who tried to follow the traditional pattern of adversarial proceedings. They would hold preliminary hearings at which they would outline the legal and factual points to be proved, and they would expect the parties to produce the necessary evidence with the minimum intervention. They would invite the other side to cross-examine witnesses before asking their own questions (10).

All the registrars said that when one side was represented they would intervene much less, though they would try to assist the unrepresented party. Unrepresented parties did not always agree. Over half of those able to recall their feelings said that the registrar had not helped them to present their case (10).

The investigative role is a new one for judges in England and Wales, and it is hardly surprising that they have found it difficult to adapt to. This does not appear to be unusual. Canadian judges have also reported misgivings about departures from traditional adversarial proceedings. In New South Wales, Queensland and New Zealand policy makers have ensured a break with the traditional adversarial approach by appointing lay arbitrators. In the experimental New Zealand scheme, non-lawyers outnumber lawyers by thirteen to two (15). On the other hand, these jurisdictions require that cases be decided according to the ''substantial merits of case'' rather than according to the strict application of legal rules. In jurisdictions which require the arbitrator to know and apply the law it is much more difficult to ask lay people to arbitrate.

We are very pleased that the Civil Justice Review unequivocally supports registrars playing an interventionist role. They state that registrars should dispense with formal rules of evidence and procedure, assume control of questioning parties and their witnesses, and explain any necessary legal terms (19).

We agree with the Review that training has a crucial role in promoting this approach. It should not be assumed that lawyers already know how to conduct small claims. Their only experience of court proceedings will be when at least one party is represented. Investigative hearings require greater judicial skill, because registrars must put litigants at ease, explain complex legal rules clearly, and prevent litigants from wandering from the point without appearing biased. They must also know or find out the law for themselves. We look forward to the establishment of pilot training schemes for all registrars, not just new recruits, based on discussion and practical exercises. We agree with the Review's suggestion that training should be accompanied by a manual giving guidance about the proceedings. This should be open to the public but not have an official status.

How far should court staff help litigants?

In *Justice out of reach*, the Consumer Council foresaw a major role for court staff. It was envisaged that a court officer would interpret a plaintiff's story, write out the claim and advise about what evidence to bring. A senior court officer would be available to help in sorting out the issues in complex cases (7).

In practice, court staff do not go this far to help claimants. They advise on court procedures, but are not allowed to give advice on the law or the merits of the case. This contrasts with the Australian small claims tribunals where court staff are placed under a positive duty to assist in the completion of forms. In Victoria, claimants do not have to provide a full legal description of the business, because a member of staff spends a considerable part of the week searching company office records. In New Zealand, tribunal staff must assist the public in completing forms, lodging claims, applying for a re-hearing or appeal, and enforcing orders. This inevitably involves giving guidance on the law. One commentator has described this task as "critical to the success of the tribunals" (15).

The National Center for State Courts survey in America found that advice was more readily available for plaintiffs than for defendants. They recommended that trained staff should be attached to the court to advise litigants on whether they had a good case or defence. Plaintiffs and defendants should both be provided with a telephone number to ring for advice (17).

The Civil Justice Review researchers concluded that court staff dealing with the public were patient and sympathetic and had a good understanding of the practicalities of the system. But two factors reduced their ability to provide help. First, only the larger courts allocated specific staff to counter duty so that relatively junior staff were sometimes called on to deal with the public. Secondly, there was a danger that instructions not to offer legal advice would be followed too rigidly. This could be interpreted as deliberate unhelpfulness, particularly as staff sometimes lacked detailed knowledge of other sources of advice. Most litigants found court staff friendly and helpful but a quarter were less complimentary. Of these, a third suggested that court staff did not give enough advice and a third implied a lack of courtesy (10).

The Review concluded that staff should be trained to give direct assistance to members of the public on the remedies open to them in relation to a particular claim, on the procedure for pursuing those remedies and on the precise manner in which court forms should be completed. We very much agree (10). In our view, the attitude of court staff is crucial to the approachability of the small claims court.

In Birmingham county court, which is one of the largest in the country, a special small claims section has been established with six staff to assist litigants in person. This has provided better training for staff, and has been welcomed by advice agencies and judges. It is especially useful in giving advice about enforcing judgements. Out of the warrants issued, 65 per cent have been paid, compared with only 50 per cent for the court overall (20).

We wish to see a small claims division with a much clearer identity within the court. Wherever possible, it should have its own specially trained staff assigned to it. Individual plaintiffs have particular difficulties getting advice about how to enforce a court judgement, and advice about enforcement should be given as a matter of course.

Should judges try to conciliate?

The Consumer Council recommended that the registrar's first aim should be to achieve an amicable settlement between the parties (7). This proposal was implemented half-heartedly. The rules allow for the registrar to hold a preliminary hearing for the "consideration of the dispute and ways of resolving it" (8)—a provision which has been interpreted in a variety of different ways. In *Simple justice* we found that the hearing could be an invaluable step, encouraging parties to settle before arbitration, helping litigants to prepare their case and giving litigants an idea of what to expect in court. Alternatively, it could be an unnecessary formality, requiring the parties to appear twice in court instead of once. We recommended that the preliminary hearing should be retained but that its purpose should be clarified in an arbitration code. We recommended that the Lord Chancellor's Department should hold discussions with registrars, court staff and advice agencies to look at ways in which it could be improved (6).

Since 1979, little progress has been made. The Civil Justice Review research found that those registrars most committed to an investigative approach usually dispensed with the preliminary hearing. Where a hearing had been held, the possibility of a settlement had been raised in under a third of cases, and only 12 per cent resulted in a settlement. Fifty-nine per cent of litigants who had attended a preliminary hearing said that it had not helped (10). Instead, it had added to the length of the case and to the number of court appearances. This proved expensive for those who had to take time off work.

It is clear that attempts to make conciliation an integral part of small claims proceedings in England and Wales have failed. Should the preliminary hearing be abandoned, or should conciliation be taken more seriously? The advantages claimed for conciliation are that it is better for the parties, and for society, if litigants leave the court in an amicable frame of mind, and that arrangements based on consent are more likely to be complied with. It may also be cheaper than a full hearing. But there are also dangers associated with conciliation. The weaker and more insecure party is the one most likely to give way to the pressure to settle—and this is likely to be the consumer. An emphasis on settlement could weaken the effect of consumer protection legislation if consumers settle for less than their full rights. A high settlement rate may either reflect litigant satisfaction or the perceived difficulties of continuing with the case. It may also be difficult for judges to change their role from conciliator to arbitrator in the middle of the case. In reaching a decision, judges may be more influenced by how reasonable a party has been in reaching a compromise that in the legal merits of the case.

In New Zealand, policy makers have not been deterred by the pitfalls of conciliation. The Act establishing the tribunal states clearly that "the primary function of a tribunal is to attempt to bring the parties to a dispute to an agreed settlement" (21). Each hearing starts with an attempt at conciliation. Referees reach a decision on the substantial merits of the case, rather than on the strict application of the law. Referees are chosen for their conciliation skills, and lawyers are in a minority (15).

In our view, the dangers of conciliation and the disadvantages in terms of delays and costs outweigh the advantages. We do not think that county court registrars are appropriate conciliators, nor that conciliation can be usefully combined with decisions on the law. We consider that the first aim of the small claims procedure in England and Wales should be to provide a simple, cheap and quick way of reaching a decision on the law. It is clear that preliminary hearings interfere with this aim and add to the length, cost and complexity of the procedure.

We agree with the Civil Justice Review that small claims should normally be disposed of at a single substantive hearing (19). Pre-trial reviews should be confined to housing and personal injury cases, and to cases which are important or complex or involve a large number of witnesses or documents. Staff should scrutinise the papers, and where issues are unclear they should try to contact the parties by telephone or letter.

Where and when should hearings take place?

The Consumer Council recommended that litigants should have the option of a hearing outside working hours (7). This was also the conclusion of the National Center for State Courts in the USA (17) who found that evening sittings were strongly favoured by litigants. Evening trials take place in New York and the system appears to work well. Judges and courts staff are quite favourable to evening work because they receive a day off in lieu. Evening hearings also take place in New South Wales (15). We strongly support the Civil Justice Review recommendation that evening hearings should be held on an experimental basis (19).

At present, small claims arbitrations are held in private. The arguments for and against private hearings are finely balanced. Some litigants may not like spectators, while others may welcome publicity for their grievance. The Welsh survey found some evidence that litigants were deterred by fear of publicity (6). On the other hand, potential litigants may welcome the chance to see a hearing before facing their own "ordeal".

On balance, we agree with the Civil Justice Review that hearings should be in private. But we do not wish to see this interpreted too rigidly. If the parties agree, interested members of the public should be allowed to sit in on hearings, so they can see for themselves how the procedure works.

Arbitrations should not be held in large echoing court rooms where the sense of informality will be lost. Wherever possible, smaller offices or retiring rooms should be made available.

Should expert reports be available?

In Northern Ireland, the registrar may consult an expert or call for an expert report at no cost to the parties. The cost is met out of public funds. However, this provision is not often used and in six years only 33 expert reports have been called for. Happily, its use is increasing and over half the requests have been since the beginning of 1984. Almost all the reports have been about faulty goods and services— most involved clothing, footwear, furniture or carpets. It is clear that such reports can provide a very useful service but there is concern about the costs. The average cost has risen from £29 in 1979 to £48 in 1985. Most reports are obtained from the government's industrial science division, but independent laboratories may provide a cheaper service (16).

We wish to see a similar provision introduced in England and Wales. We recommend that the Institute of Trading Standards Administration compiles and exchanges information about local and national facilities, so that courts are aware of how reports can be obtained most cheaply.

How can people be told about the procedure?

The small claims procedure can only resolve people's problems if they know about it. There is a clear need to promote the county court as a place where ordinary people can go to sort out consumer and other disputes.

In the Dundee small claims experiment, widespread publicity was seen as an integral part of the scheme. The most successful way of providing general information was found to be posters in local buses. Other useful publicity was given in press and radio items and in a display in the shopping centre and libraries. Posters and leaflets in advice centres were less successful because they only reached people who already thought they might have a remedy (5).

We wish to see the Lord Chancellor's Department take steps to promote the small claims procedure as a place to resolve consumer disputes.

The future of small claims

We very much welcome the Civil Justice Review's study of small claims. The time has come for a major reform of the procedure along the lines recommended by the Review.

A system of justice which meets the needs of unrepresented litigants is a radical step, needing major departures from traditional court practices and a new attitude from court staff and judges. Over the last 15 years, England and Wales have gained considerable experience of how a small claims procedure can work, and there are many examples of good practice. It is now time to build on good practice to ensure a nationally consistent procedure, which is simple, cheap, quick and fair, and can be used by ordinary people without lawyers.

The main changes which need to be introduced are:

1. Improving the identity of the small claims procedure

In *Simple justice* (6) we found that individual litigants often did not know the difference between the county court, the small claims court, or arbitration. We agree with the Civil Justice Review that rules, forms and signs within county courts should specifically refer to "small claims" and "the small claims court". An entry should be placed under "small claims court" in the telephone directory.

We recommend that the Lord Chancellor's Department takes steps to publicise the small claims court as a place for resolving consumer disputes.

2. More advice from court staff

We are very pleased that the Review has recommended that court staff should be trained to advise litigants on the procedure and to give help completing forms. Where possible, small claims should have their own staff, trained to help individuals enforce small claims decisions.

3. A separate arbitration code

We agree with the Review's recommendation that the small claims procedure should have its own short code, written in simple English. It should be self-contained, and other county court rules should not apply. Small claims litigants should not have to deal with lawyers brandishing copies of the green book.

4. Court forms

The Review recommends that the Lord Chancellor's Department should produce well designed forms written in plain English for use throughout the country. These should be piloted before being introduced. The explanatory small claims booklet should also be updated and simplified. We agree.

We wish to see standard claim forms covering the most common consumer disputes, together with leaflets on how to complete them. There should also be a short leaflet on how to prepare for the hearing sent to litigants with the notice of hearing.

5. Serving the claim

It is often difficult for consumers to find the address of the registered office of the company they are suing. We consider that consumers bringing claims for faulty products or services obtained from a shop should be able to serve the claim on the shop rather than on the company's registered office. In order that corporate defendants are not inconvenienced, the time for filing a defence could be extended from 14 to 21 days in such cases.

6. Dispensing with the preliminary hearing

We agree with the Review that a preliminary hearing should only be held in a limited number of cases. Normally, court staff would look through the claim form and defence and clarify matters by telephone or post. Court staff will then set a date and send a notice to the litigants, enclosing advice on preparing for trial. The notice should include a phone number and contact name so that litigants can contact staff if they are unsure about the procedure or need to ask for another date.

7. Legal jargon in court documents

We wish to discourage lawyers from writing documents in legalese, especially in small claims proceedings. Where claims or defences have been written by lawyers in language which is incomprehensible to lay people, the court should have the power to return their documents and ask that they be re-written.

8. Conduct of hearings

We agree with the Review's recommendation that the arbitration code should provide the outline of how hearings should be conducted. Registrars should try to set the parties at ease, explain the procedure and law, and take the initiative in finding the facts. They should explain why they have reached their decisions. The object is to make lawyers unnecessary. The way in which hearings are conducted should not change when lawyers are present.

We are pleased that the Review has recommended that witnesses should not be cross-examined directly by lawyers and that questions should be asked through the registrar. The ruling in *Chilton v. Saga Holidays* (9) needs to be reversed.

9. Training for registrars

We agree with the Review's proposals for improving training for registrars in conducting small claims. The training could include videos of hearings, discussion, and practical exercises, and should be supplemented by a manual on the conduct of hearings. We wish to see the manual made public but it should not have any official status. Registrars will also need regular updates on the substantive law.

10. The time and place of hearings

We endorse the Civil Justice Review's recommendation that evening courts should be established on an experimental basis. Hearings should be in small informal rooms, and need not always be on court premises. Hearings should be in private, but, if litigants agree, interested onlookers should be allowed to sit in.

11. Expert evidence

The court should have the power to ask for expert reports out of public funds, as in Northern Ireland. We would like to see the Institute of Trading Standards Administration provide the courts with details of where test reports can be obtained at reasonable cost.

12. Expenses

We agree with the Review that the arbitration code should spell out the standard approach to travel expenses and lost earnings. The registrar should ask the successful party about these as a matter of course at the end of the hearing, and should award them against the loser. Other expenses, such as expert reports, should be a matter of discretion.

13. Advice and representation

The greater use of small claims proceedings will increase rather than diminish the need for free, independent advice from an advice centre. People thinking of using the small claims court should be able to seek advice about the merits of their case and the procedure. In a few cases, which involve complex points or where individuals have particular difficulties expressing themselves, litigants will need to be accompanied to the hearing.

We agree with the Review's proposal that litigants should be able to be accompanied by the representatives of their choice. Representatives should only be excluded if they are unruly, and registrars should give reasons for excluding anyone.

The rule that legal costs may only be awarded in exceptional circumstances should continue. Lawyers should not be necessary and the risk of having to pay high legal costs would deter people from using the court.

14. Link officers

The Review recommends that courts should appoint a link officer, from whom advice agencies can obtain information and guidance about court proceedings. The link officer should ensure that litigants are aware of sources of advice and that forms and leaflets about the small claims scheme are prominently displayed in the locality.

15. Increasing the small claims limit

In 1979 we recommended that the small claims limit should cover the purchase price of most major consumer durables, with the exception of new cars, and we urged that it be increased to £500 (7). We endorse the Review's recommendation that the limit should now be raised to £1,000. This would also cover minor personal injury claims, including pavement trips.

There may be a case for a further increase in the limit if the changes we have recommended prove effective. But we do not wish to restrict the availability of legal aid for claims over £1,000 until it is shown that consumers can use the procedure comfortably without lawyers.

16. Appeals

Simple justice need not necessarily be rough justice. As the small claims limit is increased and the system grows in importance, we recommend that rights of appeal should be extended.

References to chapter 10

1. Office of Fair Trading, *Consumer dissatisfaction: a report on surveys undertaken by the Office of Fair Trading*, February 1986.
2. For example, DAS legal protection policy 1988.
3. National Consumer Council, *Buying problems: consumers, unsatisfactory goods and the law*, July 1984.
4. This is based on results of the 1985 survey provided by the Office of Fair Trading.
5. Connor A. and Doig B., *A research based evaluation of the Dundee small claims experiment*, Central Research Unit, Scottish Office, 1983.
6. National Consumer Council/Welsh Consumer Council, *Simple justice: a consumer view of small claims procedures in England and Wales*, 1979.
7. Consumer Council, *Justice out of reach: a case for small claims courts*, HMSO, 1970.
8. *County Court Rules 1981*, order 19, part I.
9. *Chilton v. Saga Holidays* [1986] 1 All England Reports p.841.
10. Touche Ross Management Consultants, *Study of the small claims procedure*, produced for the Civil Justice Review, Lord Chancellor's Department, 1986.
11. Birks M., *Small claims in the county court: how to sue and defend actions without a solicitor* (form ex 50), Lord Chancellor's Department, revised November 1984.
12. The 1987 judicial statistics suggest that 62 per cent of claims started were for less than £5,000. In 1987 there were 2,163,488 default actions, and the Civil Justice Review survey of debt proceedings suggest that 7 per cent of claims were defended. This gives a figure of 93,895 cases referred to arbitration (of which only 45,841 reached an arbitration hearing). If 13% related to small claims were complaints about goods and services, this gives a figure of 12,206 such claims using the procedure.
13. Solicitors Complaints Bureau, *First Annual Report*, 1988.
14. Office of Fair Trading, *Annual Report of the Director General of Fair Trading 1987*, HC 544, HMSO, 1988.
15. Whelan C.J., ed., *Small claims courts—a comparative study*, Clarendon Press (forthcoming).
16. Greer D.S. and Mulvaney A., *A description and evaluation of the small claims procedure in Northern Ireland*, General Consumer Council for Northern Ireland, October 1985.
17. Weller S., Ruhnka J.C., and Martin J.A., *Small claims courts: a national examination*, National Center for State Courts (Williamsburg, Va), 1978.

18. National Consumer Council, "Small claims in the county court in England and Wales: a response from the National Consumer Council to the Civil Justice Review", February 1987.

19. Civil Justice Review, *Report of the Review Body on Civil Justice*, Cm 394, HMSO, June 1988.

20. Appleby G., "Small claims in Birmingham county court" *Civil Justice Quarterly*, 1984, p.203.

21. New Zealand, Small Claims Tribunals Act 1976, section 15(1).

Chapter 11
Compensation for personal injuries

Accidents and the law

Accidents are common, though it is difficult to say how common. Each government department keeps partial statistics, in its own way, about the injuries that most concern them. It is probable that each year well over three and a half million people will require medical treatment having suffered some sort of injury through accidents at home, at work, in school or on the roads or pavements (1). In 1976 the Pearson Commission estimated that around three million people in the United Kingdom were sufficiently seriously injured to have their normal activities interrupted for at least four days (2). This would suggest around 2.6 million serious accidents in England and Wales per year.

In law, where the accident was caused through someone else's fault, the victim has a right to claim compensation. This is largely based on judge-made law and is known as the law of negligence. For example, claims can be brought against an employer who fails to maintain safe systems of work, against a dangerous driver, against manufacturers or shops which supply dangerous products, or against local authorities which fail to maintain safe pavements. Where employees make mistakes in the course of their work, the employer is held liable for their errors. Naturally, it is only worth bringing a claim when the person who caused an accident is able to pay—either because they have large resources or because they are insured. In practice, over 90 per cent of successful claims are met by insurance companies (2).

The amount of money payable is governed by complex legal rules which attempt to meet individual circumstances. The aim is to put the victims, so far as money can do so, back into the position they would have been in had the accident not occurred. Payments can be made for loss of wages, for loss of future earning prospects, for the expenses of disability and as compensation for pain, suffering and loss of amenity. Where victims are held to be "contributorily negligent"— that is, to have contributed to causing the accident—their compensation is reduced.

In theory, the amounts payable can be very large. In July 1987 the high court awarded a record £1,032,000 to a gifted student who was permanently brain-damaged by medical negligence and would require twenty-four hour nursing care for the rest of his life (3). In another case, a sixteen year old girl who had lost the use of all four limbs was awarded £323,050 (4). On a more mundane level, a woman who broke her wrist, finds housework difficult and cannot carry heavy bags was awarded £4,000 (5). A badly broken leg, which caused permanent injury, making it impossible for the victim to run and difficult for him to walk over rough ground, was valued at £7,500, plus £2,500 for loss of earnings and £1,441 for special damages (6). In practice, injured people settle for much smaller amounts. We discuss the reasons for this later in the chapter.

It is impossible to say what proportion of the people injured each year have a potential negligence claim. In a survey carried out for the Pearson Commission, two-thirds of those injured thought that someone else had caused their injury, either in whole or in part (2). Commonsense views of blame, however, may not equate with legal liability.

The initiative for making a negligence claim comes from the accident victim. If no claim is made, no payment is due. The state does not consider that it has any responsibility to inform people of their rights to claim—only to provide courts to decide the cases that are brought. In practice, publicity about how to make a claim is limited, although the Law Society has taken a useful initiative in launching the accident leaflet scheme (discussed in chapter 5).

Who claims?

Between 1976 and 1977, the Oxford Centre for Socio-legal Studies carried out a large-scale study of accident victims, known as the Compensation Study (7). They interviewed just over 1,000 people who had suffered injuries which stopped them from carrying out their normal activities for over two weeks in the past five years. As people were selected from the general population, rather than through legal or medical records, the survey provides valuable information about people who didn't claim, as well as those who did.

The survey found that almost three-quarters of injured people did not even think of making a claim. Among the quarter who did consider it, only about half took any further steps. Thus around 85 per cent of victims did not take the first steps towards making a claim. They therefore received nothing from the legal system. Those who thought about claiming but who didn't proceed were asked why not. Their answers are given in Table 11.1.

Table 11.1: reasons for not claiming given by those who had considered the possibility of claiming compensation (damages)

Reasons for not claiming	No.	Percentage
trouble or bother: no "claims-consciousness"	31	19%
problems in providing evidence	29	17%
fear of legal expenses	18	11%
accident due to own fault	17	10%
ignorance or confusion	16	10%
injuries not serious enough	13	8%
fear of affecting continuing relationship	9	5%
legal and insurance issues	9	5%
no income loss	8	5%
severity of injury not realised	8	5%
satisfied with Industrial Injury Benefit	4	2%
no one at fault	3	2%
Total	165	100%

Source; Harris and others, *Compensation and support for illness and injury,* Clarendon Press, 1984.

Some people did not realise that the initiative lay with them and thought that an insurance payment would come through automatically. One person commented, "the police came to see me and I thought I should hear from the bus company, but never did". A few people thought that money would be paid after they had made a claim for social security benefits.

One of the main reasons given for not making a claim was that victims felt the strain of a legal claim would be too much, especially when they were ill. One said, "I felt so poorly after the accident I couldn't face doing anything". Another commented, "I just wanted to forget about it. All I wanted was to get better". People were reluctant to get involved in legal wrangles: "I did not wish to mix in such things"; "I don't think you should have to go through all the rigmarole".

A few victims did not want to jeopardise their relationship with their employer by making a claim. Some thought they might lose their jobs and others did not want to be seen to be ungrateful to a good employer. One person said, "(I was) grateful that the firm employed me at my age of 62 and I didn't want to cause them any bother".

Fear of costs and problems in collecting evidence were frequently mentioned. These worries were sufficient to deter people from taking the first step to get legal advice.

Those who thought that their injuries were insufficiently serious to justify a claim had not necessarily suffered trivial problems. Everyone had been injured for two weeks or more. "I was too thankful to be well and alive and walking around" was a typical attitude. A few people did not realise at the time how serious the injuries would be and had therefore not reported the accident.

Some people blamed themselves for the accident and gave this as a reason for not claiming. Only a few (2 per cent) said they had not claimed because no-one was at fault.

The study was also able to compare those people who did not claim with those who did. In fact, making a claim was not directly related to blaming someone else for the accident. Of those who did blame someone else, over forty per cent took no steps to claim compensation. On the other hand, 21 per cent of those who did claim did not blame anyone else.

Nor were those who claimed necessarily those with the most severe injuries. The elderly were among those least likely to claim, but often suffered the most severe effects. For an old person, a "minor" accident such as tripping over an uneven paving stone can signal the end of independent life. Among younger people, those most severely injured were more likely to claim, but, even so, fewer than one-fifth of severely injured people actually did so.

The greatest single factor in whether or not people claim is the type of accident they have. One in three road accident victims made a claim, as did one in four of those injured at work. But only one in fifty of those injured elsewhere claimed compensation. The study showed that people in the workforce are more likely to consider claiming than the young, the old, or those looking after a home. Trade union members were much more likely to claim, not only for work accidents but generally.

The factor most likely to lead people to claim is being advised to do so by someone else. Ninety per cent of those who claimed compensation had discussed the matter with someone else. Just under three-quarters report that the idea first came from someone else. Trade union officials play a particularly important role in encouraging people to claim, but doctors, motoring organisations (such as the AA or RAC), employers, workmates, friends and relatives all play a vital part. The more the victim is in contact with such people, the more likely he or she is to make a claim (7).

Pedestrian accidents

Although the Compensation Study was carried out ten years ago, little appears to have changed. In February 1986, the National Consumer Council carried out a survey of pedestrians injured on the roads and the pavements, as part of a review of the pedestrian environment (8). Among people injured on the roads, around twenty per cent made a claim.

We found that pavement accidents were a serious problem: an estimated 450,000 adults in the United Kingdom require medical treatment for pavement falls each year. But pedestrians who fall as a result of cracked, damaged or obstructed pavements are even less likely to claim than road victims. Between 87 and 97 per cent of people who had experienced a pavement accident had not claimed. The reasons for not claiming are given in Table 11.2.

Table 11.2: reasons given for not claiming compensation after a pavement accident

	Tripped/fell on damaged pavement	Slipped on wet leaves/ice/snow etc.	Walked into obstruction
No. of people injured	135	181	56
Reason for not claiming			
accident not serious enough	59%	60%	47%
didn't know could claim	13%	10%	7%
too much effort/trouble to make claim	12%	4%	6%
accident was own fault	3%	6%	5%
other	4%	3%	5%
don't know/can't remember	11%	19%	30%

Source: National Consumer Council, *What's wrong with walking*, HMSO, 1987.

Again, ignorance of the right to claim and unwillingness to incur the trouble and difficulty of claiming are important factors. Seventy-five people who had considered claiming told us of their experiences: they complained of delay, uncertain laws and unhelpful—and at times positively misleading—attitudes from the local authority and their insurers (8).

Settling the case

Those who do claim damages are generally successful in obtaining some compensation. In the Compensation Study, 80 per cent of those claiming obtained some money, nearly always as a result of an out-of-court settlement. Only five people (2 per cent of those claiming) had their cases heard and decided by a court (7). The Pearson Commission estimated that 86 per cent of claims were settled without a writ or summons being issued—ie before the first step had been taken to bring the matter before the court (2).

The main problem is that the settlements which victims receive are very low. Half of all claimants in the Compensation Study received under £500, and three-quarters received under £1,000. Even from 1973 to 1977, when the settlements were made, these sums were remarkably low. The authors comment

> "these findings show that in practice the damages system produces relatively low sums of money, which can seldom achieve the goal of the system, viz to put the plaintiff, so far as money can do so, back into the position he would have been in had the accident not occurred... The full amount which a court would be likely to award, if 'full' liability were established against the defendant, is heavily discounted in an out-of-court settlement" (7).

Research by Hazel Genn supplements the Compensation Study by shedding light on the process by which settlements are reached between injured plaintiffs and insurance companies. She carried out formal in-depth interviews with 30 solicitors, 20 barristers and 12 insurance companies involved in the bargaining process, and analysed the results of 131 questionnaires sent to solicitors' offices (9).

It is clear from her work that claiming compensation is a highly adversarial activity. Insurance companies owe their primary obligation towards their policy holders and strive to keep costs to a minimum. They do not offer a "fair" amount but the least that they think the plaintiff will accept. Where the plaintiff is legally represented, insurance companies feel that it is legitimate to take advantage of any weaknesses in the way the case has been prepared.

There are a number of difficulties facing accident victims which persuade them to settle for very low amounts. These include: problems in finding skilled advice, lack of evidence, uncertainty, fear of legal costs, and delay. We look at each in turn.

Finding skilled legal advice

The Compensation Study found that eight per cent of those recovering money had not used a solicitor but had written directly to the insurance company (7). They tended to receive quick offers of settlement, but the amounts were very small, often well below the amount at which a solicitor would advise acceptance. For example, a man off work for six weeks accepted £75; another, off work for 30 weeks and suffering permanent injuries which meant he had to change jobs, was offered and accepted £600. A woman who tripped over a paving stone and broke her arm and wrist received an "immediate" offer of £200. Victims who proceed without legal advice tend to think that the amount they are offered represents "what the claim is worth", and will therefore accept it, however low the amount.

Good legal advice is clearly vital in obtaining a favourable settlement. The Compensation Study described the main feature of the relationship between the solicitor and the client as "the client's almost complete dependence on the solicitor's knowledge and advice and on his combativeness" (7). Solicitors differ markedly in their experience and expertise of personal injury litigation. A study of solicitors in Devon and Cornwall found very few who did no accident work, but for a third of solicitors it represented a very small proportion of their work (10). At the other end of the scale, many trade union lawyers specialise in personal injury litigation and may do nothing else.

The choice of solicitor is crucial but claimants have very little information on which to base their choice. Advertising of any sort is a new idea for this generation of lawyers, and solicitors are not allowed to advertise that they specialise in one area of work (see chapter 5). Most people rely on a recommendation, either from a trade union, or from family or friends. People may have very little to go on in making such recommendations—they may have used the solicitor for conveyancing or a will, but not for personal injury work. Genn concludes that a plaintiff's choice of solicitor is largely a matter of chance, and this reinforces the imbalance between accident victim and insurance company (9).

Genn cites a number of pitfalls open to the inexperienced or unskilled solicitor in personal injury work. It is difficult for non-specialists to keep up to date with court procedure, and this may make them fearful of going to court. Non-specialist solicitors tend to delay issuing court proceedings while negotiations are continuing, in the hope that a settlement can be reached without the need to go to court. The danger with this approach is that they may delay collecting evidence on the grounds that court proceedings are unlikely. Defendants may gain the impression that the claim is not being seriously pursued and make a low offer or none at all. Once negotiations have broken down, it may be too late to prepare an adequate case for court. It may be simpler to advise the claimant to accept a low amount in the knowledge that this advice is unlikely to be challenged (9).

Lack of evidence

Genn shows that plaintiffs and defendants have very different approaches to collecting evidence. Employers must usually inform the insurance company of accidents at work, and the insurance company may send a representative to the site while the victim is still in hospital. The representative can interview witnesses, take measurements and photographs, and assess the need for an expert's report. Where needed, a report can be undertaken quickly and the cost met by the insurance company. Plaintiffs' solicitors on the other hand are generally office-bound. Most solicitors do not consider it their job to visit the site or take photographs. If a site report is needed they may use an engineer, but engineers' reports are expensive, and this is a deterrent. Plaintiffs' cases tend to rely heavily on the plaintiff's evidence. But the injured person will rarely be in the best position to observe and recall exactly what happened (9).

Uncertainty

Claiming personal injury compensation is fraught with uncertainty. It is very difficult to predict whether a claimant will be able to prove that the defendant was at fault, whether the medical evidence will be accepted, whether damages will be reduced because a claimant is found to be "contributorily negligent" and how much a judge would award for future loss of earnings, loss of amenity and pain and suffering. Each factor is used to reduce the amount of full liability.

Nearly all settlements are for "lump sums". The Compensation Study could find only one case where damages were paid in instalments, and that was against an uninsured defendant (7). This has clear advantages for the insurance company, who can close the files, and it is thought to give the victim greater choice about how the money is spent. But it does introduce a significant element of guesswork into the calculations. It is very difficult to say how a condition will develop in the future—whether a head injury will lead to epilepsy or when osteo-arthritis may develop in a joint for example.

Doctors are asked to make prognoses, putting a percentage chance on whether a further complication will develop. But doctors disagree, and victims cannot be sure which prognosis will be accepted. Where serious complications do develop, the victim is likely to be substantially under-compensated.

Since 1969 there have been various changes to court procedures to stop claimants having to wait for full prognoses before receiving their first payment. Where it is clear that the defendant is liable for the accident, the plaintiff can ask for an interim payment before the full trial. In July 1985, section 32A of the Supreme Court Act 1981 came into force which allows the high court to award damages on a provisional basis. If the claimant's condition later deteriorates, he or she can return to court to ask for more. But interim payments are rare, and it is unlikely that provisional damages will benefit any but the tiny minority of cases coming to trial. It will have no effect on settlements, which will still be made on a "one-off" lump sum basis, and full medical prognoses will still be needed to negotiate settlements.

The doctrine of "contributory negligence" also has a significant effect on the level of settlements. Solicitors in the Compensation Study reported that it was raised in about half the cases, and used to discount the level of the award (7).

Genn comments that "decisions as to whether to accept an offer, abandon a claim, or push on to trial are therefore taken in a context of risk and uncertainty which pervades personal injury litigation; and this context creates the conditions in which almost any strategy or decision can be justified" (9).

Fear of costs

The Compensation Study showed that both knowledge and use of the legal aid scheme are very low. Less than half the people who had consulted a solicitor had heard of legal aid, and out of 51 solicitors replying to the questionnaire, only six reported that legal aid certificates had been obtained. The victim's costs were nearly all met by the defendant's insurance company as part of the final settlement (7).

Nevertheless, worry about costs has a profound effect on claims. First, people are deterred from consulting a solicitor at all. Secondly, non-legally aided claimants who reject the insurance company's offer and subsequently abandon or lose the case will be faced with a large bill from their own solicitor and possibly from the defendant's solicitor. The 1985 research for the Civil Justice Review found that for cases where court proceedings were started, the average plaintiff's costs ranged from £6,800 in the high court in London to £1,500 in the county court. Defendants' costs were less in the county court but of an equivalent amount in the high court (11). The risk of losing sums of this sort weighs particularly heavily with accident victims who are generally without spare resources and who encounter the system only once in their lives. Faced with a good chance of receiving a further £10,000, but a real risk of losing £5,000, claimants may well decide that they simply cannot afford to take the risk of losing.

Where a claimant persists in a claim, the defendant's insurers have the option of making a "payment into court". Claimants who refuse to settle the case by accepting the payment-in, but who are subsequently awarded nothing extra from the court, may have to meet both their own and their opponent's costs from the date the payment is made (12). It is often impossible to be sure how much a court will award, and the decision whether or not to accept the payment-in appears to be more of a gamble than a rational decision.

Delay

Claiming damages is a lengthy business. The Compensation Study found the average time between the accident occurring and the claimant receiving payment was 19 months. Half the cases took more than 16 months to settle (7). Research conducted for the Civil Justice Review in 1985 found that for cases that go before the courts the delays can be much longer. For cases started in the high court, the average time between the accident and settlement was between five and six years. Even the smaller county court cases took between two and a half and three years (11). As the Civil Justice Review comments:

> "delay causes continuing personal stress, anxiety and financial hardship to ordinary people and their families. It may induce economically weaker parties to accept unfair settlements" (13).

Most accident victims have returned to work before the payment arrives (7) and the compensation does nothing to help with the immediate financial effects of the injury. Accident victims may well have incurred debts which will not wait five years to be paid.

Delay causes great anxiety. It saps the will of claimants to continue to fight their cases and makes them more prepared to accept low offers. At its most extreme, it may cause people to abandon their claims. The Compensation Study found that out of 262 people who began claims, 80 people later abandoned them. A fifth of those interviewed cited delay, the bother of the case and problems with their solicitors as reasons for not proceeding. Comments included, "I just gave up because I waited 12 months and nothing came of it"; "It's nearly three years...I've just given up hope"; and "it took so long I lost interest" (7).

Delay also adds considerably to the difficulties of proving a case. Within the years following an accident, witnesses may forget and physical evidence disappears. Several claimants abandoned their cases because evidence was no longer available. One commented, "after three and a half years it was too late to get [statements]" (7).

When do delays occur?

The study conducted for the Civil Justice Review identified five stages in personal injury cases at which delays may occur (11):

★ from the incident to the victim first seeking the advice of a solicitor;

★ from the solicitor first being consulted to starting court proceedings by issuing a writ in the high court or a summons in the county court;

★ from the issue of the writ or summons to the next stage in the proceedings which involves giving the defendant a copy of the court document together with a statement of the plaintiff's case (known as the "statement of claim" in the high court, or "particulars of claim" in the county court);

★ from the "statement of claim" to the stage when both sides are ready for the trial, and the case is "set down" for trial in the court lists;

★ from "setting down" to the trial or settlement.

The Civil Justice Review research data should be treated with caution because some of the samples are very small. But the study does provide an indication of the time taken to complete each stage of the process.

Although some claimants delay a very long time before seeking advice, most see a solicitor quite soon after the accident. Two-thirds of all claimants for whom information was available consulted a solicitor within three months (11).

More serious delays occurred between advice being sought and the start of proceedings. The average time taken was a year, with half of all solicitors taking ten months or more. Except in exceptional circumstances, an action for personal injury compensation must be started within three years of the victim being aware of injury (14). The

Civil Justice Review research found that there were two peak times for starting a case. Most solicitors would issue proceedings around a year after the incident, but others would wait until the three years time limit was approaching. In 13 per cent of cases, solicitors waited until the very last minute before starting proceedings (11).

In legally aided cases, solicitors must wait for a legal aid certificate before they can incur any expenses on the case over the green form limit. This imposes delays in starting negotiations as well as going to court. In 1986-87 it took an average of 67 days to issue a non-contributory certificate, and 124 days to issue a contributory certificate, though some areas were much slower (15). The Civil Justice Review research found that these delays were included in the general delay in starting court proceedings and did not add to it. However, any moves to reduce the general delay will need to tackle delays caused by the legal aid system.

In the high court the most serious delays identified by the study occurred between the writ being issued and the claimant's solicitor taking the next step of serving it on the defendant's insurers' solicitors with a statement of the plaintiff's claim. The time it takes to serve the statement of claim averaged just over two years in the high court in London, and 15 months in provincial district registries (11). In the county court, particulars of claim must be provided when the summons is first applied for, but the summons does not have to be served on the defendant until twelve months after it is issued (16). The study found that the average time taken to serve a county court summons was six months (11).

After the statement of claim has been served, the insurance company's lawyers submit a defence, setting out their side of the case. Solicitors may then ask for greater details of the other side's case by making requests for "further and better particulars". Lawyers will also exchange documents and copies of experts' reports. The rules of court allow for many other procedural niceties. Either side can be asked to "admit facts". If they refuse, they may be made to pay the cost of proving those facts that they deny. There may be a pre-trial hearing to decide what evidence should be disclosed, and either side may be asked questions, known as "interrogatories". Defendants can be asked to make interim payments. In the county court, the parties are asked to attend a pre-trial review before the registrar to check on the progress of a case. Where both sides agree, this can be carried out by letter.

The study found that few of the more complex procedures were used. The most commonly used procedure was the "request for further and better particulars". Where this was made, it could add five to six months to county court cases, around three months to high court proceedings in London, and between five and ten months to district registry cases. Even where no request for further and better particulars is served, there are commonly delays between issuing the writ and setting down for trial of over a year in the county court, 20 months in district registries and two years in the high court (11).

For those cases which proceed to high court trial, there are long delays in waiting for a court date after the parties have indicated that they are ready and the case has been "set down" for trial. In February 1987 the Civil Justice Review reported that the Queen's bench division of the high court in London, was taking 20 months to provide a trial date (17). Since then urgent steps have been taken to reduce the delays and by June 1988 fixed dates could be offered within 10 months. In district registries waiting times vary between three months and 11 months. On the other hand, all county courts can offer a trial within 10 weeks, and most offer dates within 8 weeks (13).

Why the delay?

Although research evidence can highlight when delays occur, the reasons for delay are much less clear. It would appear that one set of delays feeds off another: the court waiting times remove any sense of urgency from plaintiffs' solicitors and insurance companies take advantage of plaintiffs' solicitors' delays.

The impetus for action must come from the plaintiff's solicitor. Genn comments that "he must operate an efficient diary system and be in a position to know when the defendant, or indeed his own expert, is procrastinating and take rapid action. In other words he must have a well-ordered system of file maintenance and in practice this may be difficult to accomplish." (9). Even with an efficient diary system it may be difficult to apply pressure without issuing court proceedings. There are many ways a defendant can stall: delaying answering letters; responding by requests for more information; raising complex points of law and procedure; or failing to provide documents.

In the Civil Justice Review research, 71 out of 288 plaintiffs' solicitors cited the defendants as a cause of delay, claiming that they had failed to comply with the rules of court, failed to provide information, or failed to respond to letters. Comments included: "there seems to be little enthusiasm by defendants to settle cases early"; "the biggest delay is undoubtedly caused by the insurance companies. Inefficiency pays for them and in our opinion the only way to counteract this would be to have substantial rates of interest..." (11). Seventy-two solicitors said that they had spent time waiting for medical reports, and this had taken an average of 15 weeks. A further 54 solicitors commented that they had waited for the plaintiff's medical condition to stabilise before negotiating a lump sum settlement, and this added an average of almost two years to the case (11).

In some ways delays are not in the defendants' interests, because they are often associated with high costs, which usually fall on insurance companies. But in other ways, insurance companies benefit from delays, because plaintiffs become more prepared to settle for low sums, and find it harder to prove their cases.

Abandoning the claim

The reasons given by the 20 per cent of claimants in the Compensation Study who abandoned their claims are similar to those given by people who considered claiming but decided not to (7). This suggests that the fears expressed by victims who did not claim may have some foundation. A quarter were advised that they had no claim, either because the accident was their own fault, or no-one's fault, or because of some other legal difficulty. Others cited problems over obtaining evidence, fear of legal costs, a firm denial by the defendants, problems with solicitors, delay, the bother and trouble of claiming, and the fear of affecting a continuing relationship.

It is clear that large numbers of injured individuals do not receive the compensation they are entitled to. They are unaware of their right to claim, or deterred from claiming by fear of the costs, delay, trouble and unpleasantness of legal proceedings. When they do claim, victims find themselves engaged in a difficult, long-winded and potentially expensive battle with an insurance company. How they fare depends more on their stamina and resources, and on the skills of their lawyers, than on the intrinsic merits of their case. Although the legal system purports to give high levels of compensation, most victims will settle for small amounts that do little to cover the cost of their disabilities.

Reforming the procedure

It is easy to highlight the problems of claiming compensation for personal injury. Recommending improvements is more difficult. In previous chapters we have suggested ways in which more people could be encouraged to make a claim: these included better publicity about legal aid (chapter 4) and specialisation schemes to make it easier for people to find suitable solicitors (chapter 5). The accident leaflet scheme is an important step in the right direction (see chapter 5). We have also examined alternative methods of paying for legal proceedings, which reduce the risk for consumers if they lose (chapter 6). In chapter 7 we discussed the recommendation of both the Benson Commission and the Civil Justice Review that the professions should produce written professional standards, to act as an authoritative indication of good practice. These would be particularly useful in the personal injury field, as a means of raising professional standards.

Some small personal injury claims, involving claims under £1,000, could be dealt with without lawyers in the small claims procedure (chapter 10). But these cases will be rare. The results of the Compensation Study suggest that most people who try to handle compensation claims for themselves will be induced to settle for very small sums (7).

In this section we look at ways in which improvements can be made in court procedure to reduce the delays and uncertainties of litigation. In our view the procedure should aim to:

★ establish the facts on which the decision depends with the minimum of delay;

★ encourage fair settlements as soon as the facts are established;

★ if no settlement is reached, identify the issues in dispute and bring the matter to trial as soon as possible.

We wish to encourage the early collection and disclosure of evidence. This may have the effect of increasing overall costs by front-loading cases and preventing investigations from being postponed pending settlements. Nevertheless we agree with the Review that it is a price worth paying for the speedier resolution of cases and more informed settlements. We support the Review Team's recommendations for a tighter timetable, more court control, and a more open exchange of information between the parties (13).

However, we are not optimistic that the reforms will produce a system in which accident victims are provided with fair compensation at the time they need it, without undue worry and costs. Many of the problems we have outlined are an inevitable consequence of a system which demands that injured individuals prove fault against insurance companies experienced in resisting claims. For this reason, we are very pleased that the Review has raised the issue of no-fault schemes. We return to this at the end of the chapter.

We wish to see the following changes:

1. All cases to start in the county court

In chapter 9, we discussed the Review's recommendation that all personal injury cases should start in the county court and that only cases involving matters of "importance, complexity or substance" should be transferred to the high court. This would ensure that a greater number of cases are dealt with by the county court. We support the proposal on the grounds that the county court is generally quicker, cheaper and less complex than the high court.

2. Time limits

At present, proceedings must be started within three years of the injury or the victim runs the risk of losing the right to claim. We are pleased that the Review does not propose a reduction in the limitation period. In practice, most claimants go to see a solicitor within a few months. Where claimants do delay, it is often because they are unaware of their rights, or do not realise the long-term consequences of their injuries. The main effect of reducing the limitation period would be to prevent people from making claims.

On the other hand, once solicitors have been consulted they should be expected to start proceedings within a reasonable time. This should be contained in written professional standards.

At present, solicitors may wait twelve months between issuing a writ or summons and serving it on the defendant. The Civil Justice Review recommends reducing this period to four months. We agree that twelve months is too long, and the period should be reduced. In our view, two months would be an adequate time. A statement of the plaintiff's claim should be provided with the writ.

3. A court controlled timetable

The Civil Justice Review recommends that the parties should no longer be free to take as long as they wish to bring a case to trial. Instead, a case should be set down for trial within nine months of the defendant giving notice of an intention to defend. The parties would be reminded of the setting down date three months beforehand. Where a case was not set down within the prescribed period, the plaintiff's solicitors would be sent a reminder and would be invited to fill in a standard report on the state of a case. If no reply was received within 14 days, a second reminder would be sent. Where there was no satisfactory explanation for the delay, the registrar would arrange a hearing. The registrar could not only demand an explanation but could order the case to be struck out unless certain steps were complied with, or could set the case down for trial. In particularly complex cases, a special timetable could be agreed at an early stage in the case (13).

We agree that in ordinary well-run cases the investigation should be completed and the issues clarified within nine months. If the matter is not ready to go to trial, good reasons should be given. It is important that the client should also be sent a notice at the time of the second reminder explaining what has happened.

We are concerned that solicitors will only comply with the timetable if delays can also be reduced after the matter has been set down for trial. In order to instil a sense of urgency into litigants and their lawyers, a trial date needs to be provided within a few months of the case being set down.

4. Exchange of witness statements

At present, the parties to litigation are allowed to keep part of their cases secret. Each side must provide the other with a statement setting out the matters alleged (known as "pleadings") but the parties do not have to disclose the evidence which supports their allegations.

The Civil Justice Review recommends a more open exchange of information. They propose that it should not be possible, without special leave, to call a witness whose statement has not been served on the other side. They suggest that both sides should exchange witness statements simultaneously within 10 weeks of "close of pleadings" (which occurs fourteen days after pleadings have been exchanged).

The Review argues that this would lead to earlier, better informed settlements, improve pre-trial preparation, and shorten trials by helping to identify issues. The arguments against disclosure are that the plaintiff's solicitor will need to incur the costs of interviewing witnesses and preparing statements at an earlier stage. It is suggested that solicitors will send statements to counsel for drafting, leading to added formality and complexity.

We support the proposal to exchange witness statements. We wish to see solicitors gather evidence at an earlier stage, and we believe that it will benefit plaintiffs to see the defendant's evidence before reaching a settlement. The additional costs of an early investigation would be justified if they led to settlements which more accurately reflected the merits of the case rather than the bargaining tactics of the parties. A secondary consideration is that it would benefit the few cases which come to trial because the parties would have a clearer idea of the issues in dispute, would spend less time preparing irrelevant points, and would be less likely to be surprised by unexpected evidence at the trial.

5. *Making accident reports available*

The Review found that it was often difficult for plaintiffs' solicitors to get hold of police reports of accidents. Where the police were considering a prosecution, or a prosecution was in progress, they would refuse to disclose the report. The Review recommended that the Home Office should ensure that the police release accident reports notwithstanding a pending or potential prosecution (13). We agree. The factory inspectorate should also ensure that reports are released at the earliest opportunity.

6. *The payment-in rule*

The payment-in rule is intended to encourage settlements by making plaintiffs who refuse reasonable offers pay for the cost of the case. At any time after proceedings have started, a defendant may make a formal offer of compromise by paying a sum of money to the court intended to satisfy the claim. The plaintiff then has three weeks in which to accept or reject the payment. Where the plaintiff accepts, the case is ended. Where the plaintiff rejects the offer, the case proceeds to full trial. The judge is not told about the offer. If the plaintiff wins, but recovers less than the amount of the "payment-in", the normal rule that the winner recovers the costs of the action from the other side is changed. Non-legally aided plaintiffs must bear both the defendant's costs and their own costs incurred after the date of the payment-in (12). Legally aided plaintiffs are protected against paying the other side's costs, but they will have to pay their own legal costs out of their compensation through the "statutory charge" (described in chapter 3).

Where a defendant makes a payment-in, an injured person can be left with a very difficult choice. It is usually very difficult for either the plaintiff or his or her legal adviser to know how much a court will award. There are too many uncertainties. The final award may be reduced as a result of contributory negligence, medical evidence may not be accepted, or the judge may make a low estimate of loss of earnings or the pain and suffering involved in the accident.

Thus the choice is often between accepting an offer which appears to be considerably less than the court would award, and going ahead in the knowledge that there is a small chance that the court may award less, and the victim will be faced with a large legal bill to be met out of the compensation money. The decision all too often appears to be a gamble. One problem is that an accident victim who meets the system only once cannot take a decision in the same way as an insurance company which minimises its risk over a large number of cases.

We are disappointed that the Review recommends no change to the payment-in rule. In our view it puts unacceptable pressures on plaintiffs to accept low offers. In 1968 the Winn Committee on personal injury cases concluded that payment-in was a blunt instrument which could cause injustice. They proposed that costs should be awarded separately for proving liability and proving quantum, and that defendants should state whether their offers related to liability or quantum or both (18). Their proposals were not implemented. In 1979 the Cantley Committee pointed out that plaintiffs could be asked to respond to offers without seeing the defendants' documents or being able to make an accurate assessment of the strength of their cases (19).

In our view, the payment-in rules should differentiate between plaintiffs who unreasonably refuse offers to settle, and those cases in which opinions about what is a reasonable offer may genuinely differ. In our response to the consultation papers, the National Consumer Council recommended that a payment-in should not make the successful party liable for the other side's costs unless the judge is satisfied that the winner behaved unreasonably in refusing it (20). The problem with this approach is that it adds a new uncertainty to the existing uncertainties. Judges will differ in what they consider to be unreasonable refusals. We have reconsidered the matter, and would prefer a more objective test. The payment-in rule should only apply when the amount of the award is considerably less than the amount of the payment-in. The plaintiff and the plaintiff's advisers should be allowed a margin of error. We would recommend that the plaintiff should only be liable for the defendant's costs where the payment-in exceeds the eventual award by 25 per cent or more. If a quarter of the sum awarded was less than £500, the plaintiff should be allowed a £500 margin of error.

Some will argue that our proposal is unfair to defendants. We disagree. It is the defendant who, by causing the accident, has precipitated the plaintiff into court proceedings. Therefore it is right that the defendant's insurer should have to pay for the vagaries of judicial decisions by making settlement offers which are somewhat above the anticipated average award for the case in question. The resulting relatively small increase in insurance premiums will be a small price to pay for a fairer deal for accident victims.

We agree with the Cantley Committee that plaintiffs should not have to decide whether to accept a payment-in until they have been able to assess the strength of the defendant's case. The deadline for acceptance should not expire until three weeks after the plaintiff has had the opportunity to see the defendant's documents and witness statements.

7. Reducing court delays

Long periods spent waiting for court hearings affect not only the small minority of cases going to trial. They also set the pace at which cases proceed. As the Civil Justice Review Team point out: "as the prospect of trial approaches, preparation becomes more intensive and the likelihood of settlement increases. Conversely, if the trial is seen as an event remote in time, preparation slackens and the prospect of settlement recedes" (17). In our view, the success of other measures to reduce delays depends on a reduction of high court waiting times after cases are set down for trial.

In the county court, circuit administrations are set targets, which provide a measure of the efficiency of the court system. In 1985/6 a standard was set for a hearing before a registrar within 6 weeks, and a hearing before a judge within 8 weeks. Different circuits were asked to achieve these standards in a different proportion of courts. Most courts succeeded in meeting their targets. Unfortunately, the target system does not apply to the high court. The consultation paper on general issues considered that it should (17). We agree. We do not wish to see litigants waiting for more than twelve weeks in any part of the court system. In our view the Lord Chancellor's Department should publish its targets, together with management information on how far the targets have been met.

The onus is on the Department to ensure that county courts are provided with sufficient staff, judges and accommodation to provide speedy trials. The new single entry system must not transfer the existing high court delays to the county court.

8. Shorter trials

The Civil Justice Review makes a number of proposals to reduce the length of trials. The parties would be under a firm obligation to organise and summarise case papers to assist the judge; judges would always read case papers before hearing evidence; witnesses would not repeat the uncontroversial parts of their statements; and barristers would no longer be expected to read out case papers. Statements which are relied on in court but not read out would be open to the press and public for a limited time after the trial.

The Review suggests an experimental scheme for major cases in which lawyers attend a hearing with the trial judge three to four weeks before the trial (13). This would determine the "trial agenda", or facts and points of law to be decided and documents and witnesses to be called. The hearing would replace the pre-trial review (in the county court) and summons for directions (in the high court) which are thought to come too early to be of much use.

We agree that the present system places too great an emphasis on oral evidence and argument, and would support proposals to shorten trials, provided that evidence referred to but not read out in court is made available to the public.

Multi-party personal injury claims: Opren and after (21)

So far we have looked at personal injury litigation from the point of view of the single claimant. But what happens if many people are injured in the same accident, or by the same defective product or drug?

The problems of personal injury claims in which a large number of plaintiffs are pursuing similar claims have recently been brought to public attention by the Opren litigation, in which around 1,500 plaintiffs issued proceedings for compensation claiming that they had been injured by an anti-arthritis drug called Opren. They alleged a variety of different symptoms including photosensitivity and liver failure, with different users finding different symptoms. The plaintiffs were a diverse and scattered group of mainly elderly and sick people. Two-thirds of the group qualified for legal aid, and a third were excluded, often on the grounds that they had too much capital. The defendants included a multi-national drug company, Eli-Lilly, and the government which was accused of negligence in the way it had licensed the drug.

The plaintiffs were faced with many of the problems common to all personal injury claimants, including low legal aid eligibility limits, difficulties in collecting evidence, delay, and low levels of settlement. They also ran into several additional problems, which are unique to multi-party claims. We describe the Opren case in some detail because it was the first time in which multi-party litigation was made the subject of special costs rules. Several previous claims had been underwritten by trade unions.

Each claimant issued an individual writ in the high court, but it soon became clear to the court that it would be unmanageable to deal with 1,500 different claims. A high court judge, Mr Justice Hirst, grouped all the cases together. There were many pre-trial matters to decide, and for reasons of convenience, summonses on these matters were issued in the name of one legally aided plaintiff, but it was understood that the hearings were designed to benefit the group or part of the group.

The first problem is that there is no explicit power in the high court rules to deal with cases in this way. The "representative action" provided for under order 15 rule 12 is generally thought not to apply to claims for damages (22). The scheme went ahead on the grounds that it was voluntary, in that both the plaintiffs and the defendants agreed that it was a sensible and convenient method of streamlining litigation. This left open the question of what would have happened if one of the parties had threatened to withdraw their agreement to the scheme after the judge made an interlocutory decision with which they disagreed.

More serious was the problem of costs. What would happen if the plaintiffs lost one of the interlocutory hearings and the judge did not award the costs of the application in their favour? On the face of it, the individual named plaintiff would have to repay any of his costs which were not recovered from the defendant through a legal aid statutory charge on any compensation he might receive at the end of the day. Such costs would have been large, and threatened to wipe out any compensation he could reasonably expect to get.

As the case progressed the costs problem became more acute. The claimants selected a number of "lead" cases which would illustrate the key issues in the trial. The outcome of the lead cases would have determined the outcome for other plaintiffs. The claimants decided to select lead plaintiffs who were legally aided, so that the costs would be paid out of the legal aid fund if they were unsuccessful, and so that they would not be ordered to pay the costs of the successful defendants. The defendants argued that this was unfair, on the grounds that the 500 or so claimants who were not eligible for legal aid would be given a free ride on the backs of those who did qualify.

In the spring of 1987, the government, as defendants in the action, took out an interlocutory summons to obtain guidance from the court on how the costs of the case should be shared between the various plaintiffs. Mr Justice Hirst decided that the only proper order was that any costs to be borne by the plaintiffs would be borne equally. Thus in the event of the litigation being unsuccessful, each litigant would be liable for 1/1,500 of the total bills for both plaintiffs and defendants. Those with legal aid would be given protection against having to pay these sums. Those without legal aid had no such protection (23).

The judge acknowledged that this was rough justice, since a large amount of the costs might be expended on an issue which affected only a small proportion of the plaintiffs. Thus, if 100 claimants alleged that the drug had caused a particular side-effect and the court found that it did not, the costs of making the allegation would be borne by all the claimants, including those who had not made it. Even those who were legally aided would be liable to pay the costs out of their compensation by way of the statutory charge. The plaintiffs appealed to the court of appeal, which upheld the costs-sharing order made by Mr Justice Hirst (24).

The costs of the action were very high indeed (an estimate of £6 million has been made) and if the case had proceeded to trial the costs would have been higher still. The non-legally aided plaintiffs were generally elderly people who had some savings put by. Very few could have afforded to take the risk that they might lose and end up paying large sums to the defendants. They would have had to withdraw had it not been for the help of a millionaire, Mr Godfrey Bradman, who stepped in to underwrite their claims. Faced with the prospect of interminable and vastly expensive litigation the parties came to an agreement, and most of the plaintiffs accepted a scheme of settlement in February 1988.

Even if the costs had not been so great, the costs-sharing order set up serious conflicts of interest among members of the group. Claimants with relatively straightforward claims would have had every interest in excluding those with less straightforward claims, which would increase both the costs and the fear of losing. It would also be extremely difficult for individual paying plaintiffs to know the risks they were running. In order to assess the risks one must be aware of all aspects of the complex litigation—the numbers of people in the scheme, the costs of all parts of the litigation, and the chances of success on each individual issue. It is difficult to see how each individual could be kept informed of the costs risk.

A further difficulty lies in regulations 33 and 34 of the Legal Aid (General) Regulations 1980. These state that the means of all the plaintiffs in the group should be taken into account in determining the legal aid application of a representative plaintiff. Up until now the regulations have been interpreted narrowly. In the product liability claims concerning thalidomide, primodos and whooping cough vaccine, the "lead" cases chosen to illustrate essential common points were selected from those who qualified for legal aid without a contribution. The legal aid authorities did not raise any question about the means of others who would benefit from the decisions. The regulations were regarded as applying only to truly representative actions, rather than to lead cases where a number of people each claimed compensation for themselves individually. Since Opren, the application of regulations 33 and 34 will need to be re-examined.

The Opren case reflects little credit on the English legal system. The present state of the law is highly unsatisfactory. It effectively deprives non-legally aided clients from being able to participate in expensive "test" litigation. There is an urgent need for reform. At the time of writing (1988) there are three more collective actions ready to be started, from the veterans of UK nuclear bomb tests, from those addicted to benzodiazepines (tranquillisers), and from those who are HIV positive as a result of blood products. All these cases will be affected by the problems raised in the Opren litigation.

Class actions

One suggestion for reform which has been canvassed widely is the "class action". During the hearing in the court of appeal, the Master of the Rolls commented:

> "The concept of the 'class action' is as yet unknown to the English courts. In some jurisdictions, notably in the United States, where large numbers of plaintiffs are making related claims against the same defendants, there are special procedures laid down enabling all the claims to be disposed of in a single action. Clearly this is something which should be looked at by the appropriate authorities with a view to seeing whether it has anything to offer and, if so, introducing the necessary procedural rules." (24)

The Master of the Rolls' call has recently been repeated by the Civil Justice Review. They have invited the Lord Chancellor to institute a separate study by one of the law reform agencies "of the case for extending the availability of representative or class actions, or establishing other procedures, to be available in cases where there are large numbers of litigants whose claims or defences have a common basis." They state that the study should extend to the funding of such cases (13).

The distinguishing characteristic of the American "class action" is that claims can proceed on an "opt out" basis. In an "opt out" claim, a writ is issued on behalf of all the members of the class, whether or not they have been identified. All members of the class are automatically part of the action unless they "opt out", by writing to the court. The court will direct that the plaintiffs give notice to other members of the class, although it is not always possible to give individual notice. Thus class actions can result in people being parties to an action without knowing it. If the claim is successful, the court can award a global sum of money for all members of the class. The onus is then on the trustees to seek out the members of the class, and distribute compensation to them. Where members of the class cannot be identified, the court may make directions about how undistributed sums are spent. In the USA undistributed damages may be used for funding organisations to work for the good of the class in the future.

We agree that the question of class actions needs to be studied. Class actions can provide consumers with easier access to the law in a wide variety of different areas. They are particularly effective where an anti-competitive practice may have disadvantaged a large number of consumers by a relatively small amount each. They may also benefit housing consumers, where a whole estate of houses or flats suffers from the same structural flaws. We hope that the Australian Law Commission's report on the subject will give added impetus to the debate.

On the other hand, we do not think that it is necessary to introduce a full "opt out" procedure to deal with claims of personal injury. More immediate and less sweeping changes can be introduced to the high court rules and legal aid scheme to deal with the most pressing problems. In our view, personal injury claimants should receive personal compensation—the injuries are too serious for global payments to be made to representative bodies. Personal injury claims also involve considering individual issues relating to causation and the extent of the injuries separately for each claimant. A full "opt out" class action is not necessarily the most suitable way of resolving disputes about personal injuries.

A new "representative action"

The problems raised by the Opren case are too urgent to await the outcome of a lengthy study into class actions. In our view, much less sweeping or controversial changes could be introduced without delay.

We wish to see the informal system of lead actions which was applied in the Opren case formalised in new rules of court. This would reduce the scope for dispute, achieve greater certainty, and maximise savings of time and cost. We wish to see a new court order drafted, possibly as an amendment and amplification of order 15, rule 12 of the rules of the supreme court, which deals with the representative action.

The type of procedure we are looking for is one in which individual claimants are encouraged to come forward. Where there are, or are likely to be, numerous claims dealing with the same issues, the court should be given the power to certify that individual claims may be grouped together. The judge would need to be satisfied that this would lead to substantial savings of time and costs, and that the claims of all the plaintiffs could be represented by one or more lead actions.

At the initial hearing the judge would give directions about who should and who should not be members of the group, and what form of notice, if any, potential members should be given. The judge would also give directions about how the case should be pleaded and about the documents to be listed and inspected (known as "discovery"). Where inspecting documents would involve very substantial labour and technical expertise it would happen only once, in a specimen lead case, but could be used for the benefit of other members of the group.

Plaintiffs who wished to benefit from the group case would need to come forward and issue writs, but the pleadings on individual cases would be very short. Individual pleading would simply refer to the group case and give individual details.

After discovery, there would need to be another hearing in which the judge would outline the common issues and questions to be decided, and would select lead actions for trial which illustrated the main common points.

The next stage would be the trial of the common questions. These would be framed so as to provide the maximum guidance for all plaintiffs but would not resolve questions of individual liability.

If the common questions were resolved in the plaintiff's favour, questions of individual causation and damage could be resolved by settlement or trial. It may be possible for the court to appoint an arbitrator to hear such cases.

It is not clear whether group claims will be affected by the Civil Justice Review's proposal that personal injury claims must start in the county court. We consider it appropriate for group claims to start in the high court.

Legal aid for group claims

Changes in procedure must go hand in hand with amendments to the legal aid scheme, to solve the problems of financing such actions.

During the passage of the Legal Aid Bill through the House of Lords, the problems of the Opren litigation were raised and discussed. The Law Society put forward an amendment which would allow for non-means tested legal aid, exempt from both contributions and the statutory charge, in group actions which had been certified by the court. The amendment put forward by the National Consumer Council was more limited in scope. We suggested that non-means tested legal aid should be available to rebut the development risk defence which may be raised by manufacturers in product liability cases. The development risk defence will only be argued successfully in a very small number of cases but, by raising it, manuafcturers can significantly add to the costs and complexity of the litigation and may thus deter plaintiffs from proceeding with their claims.

The Lord Chancellor saw some merits in these proposals, but was unable to accept amendments which could have uncontrolled and far-reaching consequences for the legal aid scheme. Later in the Bill's passage he introduced his own amendments, to enable the Legal Aid Board to make contracts with a firm or a number of firms of solicitors to undertake certain types of litigation, specified in regulations. Where such contracts are used, legally aided litigants would only be allowed to use the firms specified in the contract, and the Board would have the power to alter the legal aid means test (25).

These provisions are very wide ranging and it is unclear how they will be used. Detailed provisions are not found in the Act, but are left to regulation. A measure of the Lord Chancellor's thinking appears in his speech on the third reading. He stated that his amendment would allow a whole group of plaintiffs involved in common claims against a defendant to use the same solicitors. The statutory charge in respect of work undertaken for the whole group of plaintiffs would fall proportionately on each plaintiff and its effect would be diminished (26).

The effect of these proposals will depend on how they are interpreted by the Legal Aid Board. There are some advantages if the Legal Aid Board is able to insist that multi-party cases are co-ordinated by firms who have the resources to deal with complex and technical generic issues. But we would not wish the Board to insist that these lawyers act directly for all members of the group. Individual claimants will need lawyers who are near to them, who are able to take instructions, and who are able to give advice and reassurance on an individual basis. Local firms should liaise with central specialist solicitors.

The Legal Aid Board will need to ascertain the experience, skill, and resources of particular firms of solicitors. This is a sensitive task, and one for which the legal aid authorities have no experience. There are a number of difficulties. The Board will be looking for experienced firms, but how are new firms to gain experience, unless they are given contracts? How will the Board balance the need to provide good services against a desire to limit costs? These and other questions will need considerable thought and public discussion.

If ordinary people who are injured by defective products are to be allowed to challenge the government and corporate manufacturers, the legal aid means test will need to be relaxed in multi-party claims. We recommend that where litigants can show that they are involved in multi-party claims certified by the court, that there is a reasonable possibility of success, and that without legal aid they would be unable to start or maintain court action, the upper income and capital limits should be waived. We recommend that a limit should be placed on the amount litigants may be asked to pay, whether through capital or income contributions, or through the statutory charge, so that litigants are aware of the full extent of their liabilities. In our view, no litigant should be asked to pay more than £1,000 in total.

A long-term solution

These proposals will go some way to reducing the delay and risk involved in personal injury cases. But very serious problems will remain. Accident victims are unlikely to receive payment when they most need it, in coping with the after-effects of the accident. The emphasis will continue to be on lump-sum payments, with the result that victims will continue to have to wait for medical prognoses. The onus will remain on victims to fight their claims, and those without knowledge and stamina will continue to be disadvantaged. The system will remain extremely expensive. In 1978 the Pearson Commission estimated that for every £1 given to injured people, a further 85 pence was spent on administration and legal fees (2). This high cost is ultimately borne by society at large.

Broadly speaking, the current system has two main objectives. The first objective is to provide money to those in need as a result of injuries sustained in accidents. The second concerns the wrongdoer: society wishes that those who cause accidents should be made to pay for the consequences of their actions. The concept of "paying for the consequences" is a complex one but would appear to involve four elements: first that there should be a public investigation of the accident, secondly, that, if appropriate, there should be an allocation of blame; thirdly, that following the allocation of blame there should be some form of appropriate penalty; and lastly, that steps should be taken to see that the accident does not happen again.

The present system does not succeed in meeting either objective. Most victims get nothing. Such money as is paid out is given at the wrong time, after a difficult battle, and at exorbitant cost. Personal injury litigation does not provide an efficient mechanism for investigating accidents or allocating blame. The initiative is left to the victim who may be poorly equipped emotionally or financially to carry out an investigation. Blame is rarely allocated because the great majority of cases are settled, often on an "ex gratia" basis, without admission of liability. The greater the wrong committed, the more likely that the insurance company will settle early, before a full investigation. In some cases, the existence of litigation may stop those involved from admitting their errors or apologising for what has happened (27).

It is over ten years since the Pearson Commission reported on possible alternatives to personal injury litigation. No action has been taken on that report. The Civil Justice Review raises once again the need to reform our system of compensating injured and disabled people. They state that the Lord Chancellor should consider, in consultation with the insurance industry, the feasibility of a no-fault scheme, restricted to less serious road accidents and financed by private insurance (13).

We agree that the issue of no-fault schemes should be returned to the political agenda. The type of scheme which should be introduced is outside the ambit of this report but it is an issue which needs to be examined further. We hope that forthcoming research from the Office of Population, Census and Surveys will shed light on the financial needs of injured people.

References to chapter 11

1. This includes 2,804,800 million home accidents, in which people were treated by general practitioners or in hospital (see the Home Accident Surveillance System, *Ninth annual report—data*, Department of Trade and Industry, 1985); 450,000 pavement accidents, see National Consumer Council *What's wrong with walking*, HMSO, 1987; and 228,000 accidents on the road, see *Road accidents Great Britain, the casualty report 1986* (This figure is for accidents on the road, rather than injured people. Accidents were classified as fatal, serious or slight: a fatal accident is one in which at least one person is killed; a serious accident is one in which at least one person is detained in hospital as an in-patient; and a slight accident is one in which one person is slightly injured). Some 21,000 accidents occurred at work, see *Health and Safety Commission report 1985/6*. This figure includes injuries to employees, the self-employed and visitors to the premises.

2. Royal Commission on Civil Liability and Compensation for Personal Injury (Chairman: Lord Pearson), *Report*, Cmnd 7054, HMSO, 1978.
3. *Aboul-Hosn v. Grant, Crawford and Nouri, The Independent*, 11 July 1987.
4. *Housecroft v. Burnett* [1986] 1 All England Reports p.332, CA.
5. *Brown v. North West Gas*, 27.4.88, Halsburys Laws, August 1988, para. N1555e.
6. *Wakeman v. Bournemouth District Council*, 14.2.86 Current Law Yearbook 1986, para. 1041.
7. Harris D. and others, *Compensation and support for illness and injury*, Oxford Socio-legal Studies, Clarendon Press, 1984.
8. National Consumer Council, *What's wrong with walking: a consumer review of the pedestrian environment*, HMSO, 1987.
9. Genn. H., *Hard bargaining: out of court settlement in personal injury actions*, Oxford Socio-legal Studies, Clarendon Press, 1987.
10. Blacksell, M. Economides, K. and Watkins, C., *Solicitors and access to legal services in rural areas: evidence from Devon and Cornwall*, Access to Justice in Rural Britain Project, University of Exeter, working paper 6, 1986.
11. Inbucon Management Consultants, *Study of personal injury litigation*, conducted for the Civil Justice Review, Lord Chancellor's Department, November 1985.
12. *Rules of the Supreme Court 1981*, Order 22.
13. Civil Justice Review, *Report of the Review Body on Civil Justice*, Cm 394, HMSO, June 1988.
14. Limitation Act 1939, section 2(A); Limitation Act 1975, section 1.
15. *Legal aid*, 37th annual reports of the Law Society and the Lord Chancellor's advisory committee, 1986-87, HC 233, HMSO, 1988.
16. County Court Rules 1981, order 7, rule 20.
17. Civil Justice Review, *General issues*, consultation paper no.6, Lord Chancellor's Department, 1987.
18. Committee on Personal Injuries Litigation (Chairman: Lord Justice Winn), *Report*, Cmnd 3691, HMSO, July 1968.
19. Personal injuries litigation procedure working party, *Report*, Cmnd 7476, HMSO, March 1979.
20. National Consumer Council, "General issues—response to the sixth consultation paper of the Civil Justice Review", July 1987.
21. For further discussion see, "Group actions: learning from Opren", National Consumer Council, based on a background paper by Mildred, M.

22. *Market and Co. Ltd v. Knight Steamship Co. Ltd* [1910] 2 Kings bench p.1021.
23. *Davies v. Eli Lilly and Co. and others, The Independent,* 10 December 1987.
24. *Davies v. Eli Lilly and Co. and others* [1987] 1 Weekly Law Reports [1987], p.1136, CA.
25. Legal Aid Act 1988, sections 4(5), 15(5), 15(6), 16(10).
26. *Hansard* 29 February 1988, col. 20-22.
27. Respondents to our survey on pedestrian accidents frequently complained that local authorities to whom accidents had been reported did not apologise, see *What's wrong with walking,* above, p.57.

Chapter 12
Housing cases: possession and repairs

Possession actions

In residential possession cases, landlords and lenders seek the right to evict people from their homes. The majority of cases are started by local authorities and building societies against individuals and their families, usually because the rent or mortgage has not been paid.

In 1986, 153,870 possession actions on residential premises were started in the English and Welsh county courts (1). Around forty-six per cent were brought by mortgage lenders and 38 per cent were brought by local authorities and housing associations. The remainder were brought by a mixture of private landlords and public employers (such as the Ministry of Defence) against service tenants, or were taken against trespassers (1). Three-quarters of cases involved unpaid rent or mortgage payments (2). A feature of the last few years has been a substantial increase in cases of mortgage arrears (3).

In practice around a third of cases result in an outright order of possession, requiring the occupiers to leave their homes within a specified period. In another third, the court makes a suspended order, stating that the occupier will be evicted unless they pay a specified amount off the arrears each week or month. The remaining cases are withdrawn, adjourned or dismissed, or result in a money judgement only (2).

Most defendants to housing possession cases "can't pay" rather than "won't pay", though the reasons why people get into trouble are often complex. In 1985 we examined the problem of mortgage arrears. Our report, *Behind with the mortgage*, identified marital breakdown and unemployment as key factors which caused arrears, together with increased "budget stretch" as new buyers committed a greater proportion of their available income to house purchase (4).

A study by the Department of the Environment found that local authority tenants with rent arrears tend to be families with children, on low incomes (5). Large families and single-parent families are particularly prone to get into difficulties, as are those out of work. The study found that extravagance was a factor in only a small minority of cases. Tenants in arrears tend to plan their budget in much the same way as other families, but their budgets are tighter and they have more problems keeping to their plans. For these people, budgets are more easily upset by a large bill or drop in income. Rent arrears are rarely the only money problem. Three-quarters of those in arrears said that they had difficulties meeting other bills and two-thirds were behind with at least one other debt (5).

The study found that tenants in arrears tended not to get the social security benefits they were entitled to. In fact, 47 per cent of tenants in arrears who qualified for help with housing costs failed to receive their full entitlement, compared with 32 per cent of the control sample of other tenants (5). A study of local authority possession actions against tenants, carried out by Jenny Watts between 1983 and 1984, found that in a quarter of cases coming before the courts there was evidence of past or existing problems with welfare benefits or maintenance payments (6).

In 1987 we drew attention to the small but growing number of people taking out consumer loans secured on their homes (7). Failure to repay the loan can result in a possession action, and sometimes eviction. Press advertisements stress that secured loans can be used as a way of rescheduling debts. Unfortunately, many advertisements are misleading about the costs of the credit and the consequences of default. The interest rates, expressed in terms of annual percentage rates of charge (APR), can be very high. We surveyed 114 people who had problems repaying such loans. Most were supporting families on low incomes and had already had money problems when the loan was taken out. The APRs they were paying varied between 11 per cent to 44 per cent and some borrowers had paid large brokers' fees (in one case a fee of £800 for a loan of £2,000) (7).

What the court must decide

Depriving a family of their home is a serious business. In theory the law provides protection.

All cases must go before a registrar or judge. In local authority rent arrears cases, the court may make an order for possession if it is satisfied that it is "reasonable" to do so, and it may not suspend possession on terms which would cause "exceptional hardship" or "would otherwise be unreasonable" (8). In order to decide whether possession is reasonable, the court needs to look at tenants' financial circumstances to see why the arrears occurred and what they can afford to pay. It is important to check that tenants are receiving the benefits due to them. The courts should also ensure that the landlord has kept the property in good repair: if the landlord has neglected repairs and hence caused damage to the tenant's health or property, the tenant may counter-claim for damages.

The legal protection for the existing tenants of private landlords and housing associations are the same (9). Under the Housing Act 1988, future tenants will be offered "assured tenancies". In assured tenancies, courts must give possession where tenants are three months or more in arrears. Where tenants are less than three months in arrears, the court may only grant possession where this is reasonable (10).

In mortgage possession cases, the court may postpone or suspend a possession order to give the borrower time to pay off the arrears. The court must be satisfied that the arrears will all be paid within a reasonable time (11). There are provisions under the Consumer Credit Act 1974 to reduce interest rates where the charge for credit is extortionate (12). Some loans, including those under £15,000 which are not for house building or purchase, are "regulated" agreements under the Consumer Credit Act 1974. Here the court has more extensive powers to suspend possession or reschedule the original payments (13).

Unfortunately, court proceedings can all too often become a formality. Debtors are rarely involved. They do not attend or write to the court and important decisions are taken without the necessary information.

Activity before the hearing

It is often felt by those involved in possession proceedings that landlords and lenders make extensive efforts to sort matters out before starting court proceedings, and that the cases where possession is sought are those where no other alternatives are available. In truth, however, the effort put into sorting out arrears is variable, and may be inadequate.

Research for the Civil Justice Review found that a third of banks and building societies and a fifth of local authorities did not enquire about the defendant's circumstances before the hearing (2). The Department of the Environment recommends that local authorities should "make intensive checks of entitlement to rebates and other welfare benefits before taking the case to court" (5). However, three-quarters of local authorities did not follow this advice (2).

In *Behind with the mortgage* we commented that lenders do not always approach borrowers in a way that encourages contact. Standard letters do not always invite borrowers to come into the office, and in some cases they do not give a contact name and telephone number. Home visits are the exception rather than the rule (4).

Another problem is that lenders can over-estimate the amount of contact which precedes court cases. It is one thing to have a policy to make personal contact with defaulters, but quite another to achieve a hundred-per-cent success. We found one large building society where senior management believed that they operated a watertight rule that all borrowers had to be visited before court action could be taken. They were under the impression that before the hearing every alternative had been explored, and therefore they always sought outright possession. In reality it was not always possible to visit borrowers, and arrangements to pay off the debt had not always been considered (4).

Arrears tend to be associated with some personal crisis such as redundancy or divorce and as a result defendants can be depressed and lethargic, or highly anxious and confused. They may adopt an "ostrich" approach, leaving letters unopened. The lender's or landlord's task in establishing contact is often difficult. It is important that the court looks afresh at whether loss of the home is the only answer, without assuming that alternatives have been investigated before the case comes to court.

Excessive settlements

Local authorities often make arrangements with their tenants before the hearing to pay off rent arrears at so much a week. The court is then invited to make a suspended order, threatening eviction if the payments are not met. Particular problems arise where tenants agree to excessive payments, which they have no realistic chance of meeting.

The Department of the Environment study commented that local authority staff in contact with tenants were quite junior and were given little formal training. They may not appreciate the complexity of the family's budget, or other debt problems faced by the family (5). Meanwhile, tenants were often desperate to save their homes, and would agree to make unrealistic payments because they felt that the alternative was losing it.

According to the Civil Justice Review research, local authorities often tell tenants that they need not bother to turn up to court on the grounds that an "agreement" has been reached (2). Thus the court does not have the chance to hear about tenants' circumstances, and will convert the excessive settlement into a court order. When the tenant later defaults, the local authority may evict without returning to court.

The Civil Justice Review research supports the contention that suspended possession orders are set too high. At the time of the research, DHSS guidelines stated that families on supplementary benefit should not pay more than £1.50 per week towards rent arrears. Yet despite the fact that 21 per cent of families were on supplementary benefit, no orders in the sample were for less than £2 per week. Only 14 per cent of orders were for less than £3 per week (2).

The summons and form of reply

In mortgage cases the court case will begin with a "summons for possession". The borrower receives a summons specifying the time and date of the hearing, together with "particulars of claim", and a "form of reply" to complete and return to the court. The particulars of claim set out the lender's case and include the date of the mortgage, the amount of the advance, the instalments and the arrears. It also includes technical information (such as whether a Class F Land Charge has been registered) which will be couched in legal terms with references to statutes (4).

The form of reply gives space for the borrower to dispute the claim, but most of the questions are of a general nature and do not give any clear indication of the information required. Small print suggests that advice can be obtained from the court office or citizens advice bureau and that borrowers who wish to dispute the claim may be entitled to legal aid. The documents are sent without advice on completing the form or on what issues the court will decide (4).

The procedure against tenants is similar. The tenant receives a summons giving the time and date of the hearing, together with particulars of claim and a form of reply. Defendants are asked whether they intend to defend the claim and their grounds for doing so, and whether they admit or deny the accompanying monetary claim. However, the form does not contain space for the defendant to give details of their income or outgoings, or to make an offer about how much they can pay. The papers do not state that the court can only make an order for possession if it is reasonable to do so; nor do they suggest the possibility of a counter-claim for poor repair. The Civil Justice Review found that when forms were returned they rarely contained any useful information (2).

The hearing

Most defendants do not attend the hearing. According to the Civil Justice Review research, around three-quarters of local authority tenants, half of private tenants and two-fifths of mortgage borrowers fail to go to court (2).

One of the most common reasons given for not attending court was that tenants had been told by their landlords that this was unnecessary. Other reasons for not appearing included, I "did not think it important to go", the "court was too far away", I "was ill" or I was "not able to spare the time" (2). The forms sent out to tenants and borrowers do not do enough to stress the importance of attending court.

In the absence of the defendant, or any information about the defendant, the hearing becomes a formality. 1986 research into local authority possession cases found that most possession hearings took between one and two minutes (14). A judge has described the work as "purely administrative, somebody independent of the local authority to rubber stamp the document" (6).

Representation

Only eight per cent of defendants are represented at the hearing (2). This is despite guidance issued by the Law Society that legal aid should be granted in cases where possession is threatened but where it might not be reasonable to make an order (15).

Research suggests that where defendants do appear or are represented, they are more likely to receive a favourable outcome. Where no-one was in court for the defendant, outright possession orders were made in 49 per cent of cases, compared with 39 per cent where the defendant was present but not represented, and 29 per cent where the defendant was represented (2).

The Lord Chancellor's advisory committee has examined a number of schemes run by advice and law centres and lay advocacy to provide representation for defendants (16). They concluded that there is a real need for assistance, but in many areas the need is not being met. Where schemes do exist, the committee was struck by the "almost universally unsatisfactory nature of their funding arrangements".

Costs

The plaintiff's costs are usually added to the defendant's arrears at the end of the hearing. In mortgage cases the amount is rarely specified by the court, but for tenants the court specifies a sum. The Civil Justice Review research found that the average specified award was for £90 (2). This appears excessive in "bulk issue" cases where the landlord has a large number of cases to deal with on the same morning, and the individual hearing takes less than 5 minutes.

Housing the homeless

Homeless families with children, elderly people and those who are especially vulnerable have rights to be housed by the local authority, provided they are not "intentionally" homeless (17). A Shelter survey into how local authorities interpret their duties following mortgage arrears found that families are more likely to be accepted as unintentionally homeless if they wait for a possession order to be made through the courts than if they clear the arrears by a voluntary sale (18).

We are concerned that local authorities' interpretation of the legislation may unnecessarily increase the number of cases before the courts. There are many advantages to families if they are able to arrange "voluntary" sales. They save the costs of possession and sale, secure a better price and the experience may be less traumatic for the family.

What reforms are needed?

The Civil Justice Review concluded that "there should be reforms in procedure and forms to provide the court with fuller evidence on the basis of the claim and the circumstances of the defendant". Meanwhile, a reformed "rent action" procedure should be available to landlords who are seeking rent arrears rather than possession of the property. The rent action would operate as a default procedure so that the matter would not normally come before the court unless the defendant disputed the amount owed or issued a counter-claim (19).

We endorse the Civil Justice Review's proposals. In our view, the courts must take decisions on the basis of more information. Inevitably, this means that they will take longer to decide cases and will need more resources to cope with their work. However, we are conscious of the need to keep expenditure to a minimum. For this reason we are anxious to encourage social landlords to bring fewer cases to court, and to encourage voluntary sales for mortgage arrears by new guidance on housing the homeless under part III of the 1985 Housing Act. Cost rules could encourage plaintiffs to use the cheaper and simpler rent action where possession is not likely to be granted.

We look in more detail at the reforms that are needed:

1. Plaintiffs should provide details of the defendant's circumstances

The Review states that "plaintiffs are best placed to provide a history of the letting or mortgage, details of the calculation and handling of the arrears and of efforts made to recover them including previous legal action" (19). They recommend that local authorities, housing associations and mortgage companies such as banks and building societies should provide details of the defendant's circumstances, including details of entitlement and receipt of state benefits. Where landlords and lenders are unable to supply this information, they should indicate to the court the efforts made to obtain it.

We agree. The proposal has two advantages: the court would be provided with more information; and it would encourage local authorities and housing associations to follow Department of Environment guidance by checking benefit entitlement before starting court action (5).

The Lord Chancellor's Department should provide forms for different types of landlords to send to the court. Local authorities should give detailed accounts of housing benefit receipt and entitlement, while housing associations, banks and building societies should use simplified versions of the form.

The form would be copied to the defendant, and would contain space for the defendant to amend or add to the information.

2. Landlords should state whether the property is in good repair

Rent arrears and disrepair should be considered together. Plaintiffs should include a statement in the particulars of claim that the property is in good repair, and defendants should be asked if they agree. Where it is clear that landlords are in breach of their repairing obligation, the court should take this into account in deciding whether it is reasonable to make an order, and should consider awarding compensation.

3. The summons and form of reply should be redesigned and tested

The Review proposes that the possession summons should give directions on completing the form of reply to the court and should stress the importance of attending the hearing. It should be accompanied by a list of local advice centres.

The Review also states that "the present Form of Reply which accompanies the summons should be redrafted to ensure that it enables defendants to provide detailed and relevant information about their personal circumstances and those surrounding the history of the arrears, an offer of repayment in respect of the arrears, or enter a defence or counterclaim. . . The defendant should have the opportunity to comment on the information supplied by the plaintiff, add to it and disclose any mitigating circumstances''.

We agree that both the summons and form of reply should be redesigned. We would like to see different versions piloted before a new national form is introduced.

4. Plaintiffs should not tell defendants that they need not attend court

The court is under a duty to ensure that repayment terms under suspended orders do not cause excessive hardship. Plaintiffs should not ask for agreements to be rubber-stamped in the defendant's absence. Court rules should state that a plaintiff who tells a defendant not to appear is in contempt of court, and it is a matter which the court can take into account in deciding whether to make an order.

5. The courts should scrutinise costs orders more carefully

The plaintiff's costs are usually added to the defendant's arrears bill at the end of the hearing, and increase a family's difficulties in paying off the arrears. The Civil Justice Review consultation paper on housing cases argued that the costs awarded to large landlords may be excessive: ''many possession summons are issued by large landlords who regularly book numerous applications at the same time. It is reasonable to assume that such landlords will have standardised their procedure and that their costs for one block application will therefore be considerably less than the cost of issuing the same number of summonses singly'' (20). We agree. We wish to see the Lord Chancellor's Department set limits for ''bulk-issue'' possession costs, which should only be exceeded in exceptional circumstances.

We also agree with the Review Team that in mortgage possession actions costs should not be added to the bill the defendants must pay without an amount being specified.

6. Unnecessary possession proceedings should be discouraged

In their consultation paper, the Review Team argued that the less serious cases should be removed from the possession list, so that the court could give greater consideration to cases where eviction was threatened (20). The final report recommends a reformed ''rent action'' procedure in which the plaintiff could issue a form of default action for rent arrears (19).

In the proposed rent action, the plaintiff would serve the defendant with a summons, which would include a history of the arrears, an indication of whether the defendant is receiving housing benefit, and a statement of the rate of repayment sought. Where the defendant did not reply within 14 days, judgement would be entered without a court hearing. The defendant would be reminded to continue to pay the current rent as well as an amount off the arrears. Where the defendant contested the claim, or issued a counter-claim, the matter would be heard as a small claim, whatever the amount involved. If the defendant offered a smaller amount, the registrar would make an order based on the information in the papers. In difficult cases the registrar could ask the parties to a hearing.

We agree with these proposals. We wish to see plaintiffs provided with an incentive to use rent actions rather than more expensive possession proceedings. Where possession proceedings are brought but the court makes a money judgement only, no costs should be awarded to the plaintiff. Instead, the plaintiff should meet the defendant's expenses in attending court.

7. Transferring business to registrars

Most mortgage cases are heard in chambers by registrars. But courts differ in whether cases involving tenancies should be heard by registrars or judges. The Civil Justice Review research found, for example, that in Willesden all non-mortgage possession cases were heard by judges, while in Warwick none were (2). We wish to see courts make the most efficient use of their judges' and registrars' time, and in some courts this will involve registrars playing a greater role in possession actions. Both judges and registrars will need training (see below).

In principle, cases should be held in public, so that decisions are open to public scrutiny. But wherever possible, they should be held in relatively small rooms, so as to be less daunting to the defendant.

8. More training

At present, new registrars are given half a day's training in housing matters. We agree with the Review Team that this should be increased: the Judicial Studies Board should provide judges and registrars with systematic training in housing work, including training in social security and local authority management practices. We would also like to see registrars trained to recognise and deal with extortionate credit bargains.

Possession cases form an extremely important part of the county court's work and there is a clear need for better training. In *Behind with the mortgage* we drew attention to inconsistencies between registrars in dealing with mortgage cases (4). The Legal Aid advisory committee has even suggested that some courts are ignorant of their obligations under what is now part IV of the Housing Act 1985 (21). Our report on secured loans drew attention to the need for registrars and judges to scrutinise potentially extortionate credit bargains before granting possession (7). The housing benefits scheme is constantly changing, and judges and registrars need to be kept up to date. We would hope that the training sessions would be a chance for judges and registrars to talk to each other about their local practices, to discuss the issues and to learn from one another.

9. Representation and advice

In theory, only qualified lawyers are allowed to represent the parties in possession cases. In fact, lay people do represent both plaintiffs and defendants. The research study found that out of 78 plaintiffs' representatives, 50 were solicitors or barristers, 18 were legal executives and 10 worked for firms of solicitors but had no legal qualifications (2). Staff from advice centres and volunteers trained by the Lay Advocacy Service represent defendants in some areas.

We agree with the Review that lay representation should be allowed. Although guidance from the Legal Aid Fund states that legal aid should be provided whenever it may not be reasonable to make a possession order, the research found that only 8 per cent of defendants were represented (2). Permitting and encouraging lay representation would increase the number of represented tenants. Lay representation has advantages over representation by private solicitors acting under the legal aid scheme. A lay service which was available within the county court would be more accessible; lay people skilled in welfare rights and debt counselling would be able to offer a more comprehensive service; and a lay service which dealt with many cases on a single possession day would be cheaper and more efficient than legal aid on a case by case basis.

As we discussed in chapter 4, there is an urgent need to encourage and develop assistance and representation for possession action defendants within the court. The Legal Aid Board should work with regional legal services committees to encourage the growth of such schemes on a regional and local basis.

10. New guidance on housing the homeless

We are concerned that local authorities' interpretations of the homelessness legislation may unnecessarily increase the number of cases coming before the courts. We wish to see local authorities given clear guidance that families who are unlikely to be able to save their homes should not be forced to wait for a possession order to be made against them. This would encourage voluntary sales and reduce the number of cases coming to court.

Other housing cases

Possession cases brought by landlords and lenders form the bulk of housing cases heard by the county court. But parliament has given tenants a number of rights against landlords, including the right to get repairs done, to challenge unreasonable service charges, and to buy council houses. Where a dispute arises about these matters, the onus is on the tenant to start an action in the county court.

Despite widespread problems about repairs, very few cases are brought. Below, we look at the nature of the problems, and some of the reasons why tenants are so reluctant to go to court.

Repairs problems

In 1980 the National Consumer Council carried out a survey of consumers' concerns in which we interviewed 2,000 adults to find out the problems they encountered in their everyday lives (22). The survey revealed widespread dissatisfaction with the way repairs were carried out by both public and private landlords. A third of council tenants said that they suffered from damp or condensation, a third said that they needed repairs which were not carried out, and a third complained about the time repairs took. Among private tenants, the problems were worse; over half complained of damp, and two-fifths said they needed repairs which had not been carried out. A recent survey confirmed that council tenants attach considerable importance to getting repairs done (23). Ninety-one per cent of local authority tenants rated "having repairs done promptly and effectively" as very important. It was considered to be more important than low rents or other tenants' rights.

Many repairs problems are serious. The 1981 *English house conditions survey* found that 60 per cent of privately rented homes and 30 per cent of local authority homes required repairs of over £1,000. Almost 400,000 tenanted homes required repairs of over £7,000, and

437,000 tenanted homes were regarded as "unfit" (24). In *Cracking up* (1982) we listed the most common serious faults in council housing: rising damp; water penetration; severe condensation; defective windows, cladding and brick work; dry rot; wall subsidence; and dangerous concrete panels and beams (25).

Repairs are also a problem for leaseholders. In 1985, the Committee of Inquiry on the Management of Privately Owned Blocks of Flats (the Nugee Committee) published its report (26). They found evidence of widespread problems: excessive delay in responding to requests for maintenance and repairs, difficulties in getting landlords to carry out their obligations, lack of information for lessees, and dissatisfaction with the level of service charges and the quality of the service provided.

The law on repairs

The law imposes a variety of obligations on landlords to keep their properties in good repair. Where a house or flat is let to a tenant, the Landlord and Tenant Act 1985 section 11 (previously Housing Act 1961 section 32) requires the landlord to keep the structure and exterior in good repair. The landlord must also ensure that the plumbing, wiring and heating is in working order. If not, the tenant can go to court to compel the landlord to carry out the repairs, and to pay compensation for any damage done to the tenant's health and property. A tenancy agreement may give tenants more rights to get repairs done, but it cannot take away rights under section 11.

Where the premises are prejudicial to health, the tenant has additional protection under the Public Health Acts. The local authority's environmental health officers can take proceedings before the magistrates court to require a private landlord to prevent a health risk. But where the local council itself is the landlord, environmental health officers cannot act and tenants must take court proceedings by themselves (27).

For leaseholders with leases of seven years or over, the landlord's repairing obligations are set out in the lease. Under the Landlord and Tenant Act 1985, the costs of repairs must be no more than is reasonable, and should only form part of the charge if the work is carried out to a reasonable standard (28).

In our report *Cracking up* we were critical of these provisions (25). The scope of section 11 is far from clear. Where the problem is caused by a design defect in the building, the law requires landlords to repair damage caused by the defect but not to remedy the defect itself. The protection granted by environmental health officers is lost where the council is causing the problem. Nevertheless, in theory, many consumers who have difficulties getting repairs done do have legal remedies available to them.

Going to court

In practice very few tenants or leaseholders go to court to get repairs done. The Civil Justice Review considered a long list of housing actions other than possession hearings which could be dealt with by the courts. This included not only repairs cases and problems with leases but also the right to buy, other rights under the "tenant's charter", mobile homes, homelessness, and other issues under the Rent Acts. The Review estimated that all these problems between them accounted for not more than 1,500 county court cases a year (20).

These figures are tiny compared with the scale of the problem. We do not know why people are so reluctant to go to court, but lack of information and advice, fear of harassment, and fear of the time, trouble and costs of court proceedings are likely to be factors.

Naturally, before consumers can consider court action, they must be aware of their rights. Before 1980 only a minority of councils gave their tenants a summary of their rights to repairs. Since 1980, the situation has improved for public tenants. Councils are under a legal obligation to provide their tenants with information which explains "in simple terms" the effect of these express terms of the tenancy and of the right to repairs under section 11 (29). In 1982-3, the Housing Research Group at City University analysed the information provided by 173 local authorities (30). Most did give information, but the Research Group found that 129 authorities used formal language. Only seven authorities mentioned the right to compensation if the landlord failed to carry out repairs and seven local authorities failed to give a clear account of their obligations under section 11. There is no obligation to provide information about what to do when things go wrong or where to seek independent advice. As we saw in chapter 2, skilled housing advice may be hard to find.

Private tenants are unlikely to have access to detailed information about their rights. Many will not be sure if they are protected from eviction, and may therefore be reluctant to argue with their landlords.

Even when people consider going to court, they are unlikely to decide to go ahead. The Nugee Committee looking into leasehold problems found that 60 per cent of flat owners who considered taking court action decided not to. Sometimes the parties were able to reach a settlement, but many residents' associations said that they were reluctant to go to court because of the time, costs and worry involved.

Other problems included difficulties in getting agreement among residents over what to do and, in a few cases, fear of harassment (26).

The Civil Justice Review looked at the cases of 65 people who had sought advice about housing problems but had decided not to go to court (2). The interviewees had shown considerable desperation, and had contacted a large number of different people and organisations in an attempt to sort out their problems, including councillors, members of parliament, environmental health officers, social services, and tenants' organisations. Unfortunately, the study was too small to draw any firm conclusions, but it did suggest that fear of costs was a significant factor in deterring people from going to court. Knowledge about legal aid was very low—two-fifths of the sample had not heard of it.

The proposed housing action

The Civil Justice Review recognised the problem that tenants often forego their rights rather than use the county court. They recommended the introduction of a "housing action", which would operate as a small claims procedure for housing matters such as service charges, repairs, the right to buy, leasehold enfranchisement, and mobile homes. There would be no fixed monetary limit, but the registrar would have discretion to decide which cases were suitable for the new action.

The tenant would start the action using a standard form, giving a brief outline of the complaint and an indication of the remedy sought. The court would then set a date for the preliminary hearing and serve the papers on the landlord.

At the preliminary hearing the registrar would identify the issues in dispute, decide whether the case should be heard by arbitration or full trial, and give directions about how the cases should be prepared. Litigants who were unhappy with the registrar's decision on how the case should be heard would have the right to appeal to a judge.

The most novel aspect of the proposal is that the registrar would be able to appoint a surveyor, valuer or other suitable expert to act as an assessor, to be paid for out of public funds. The assessor's role would be to provide advice to the registrar—either by providing a written report available to the court and the parties, or by sitting with the registrar during the hearing. This is an important improvement on the proposal set out in the consultation paper, which stated that "although registrars might have access to assistance on technical matters, such as valuation, either by way of assessors or court-appointed experts, this is an expense which would fall on the parties" (20).

Arbitrations would be carried out in much the same way as small claims hearings. They would be informal, with the registrar playing an investigative role, eliciting information from the parties. Legal representation would be permitted but discouraged. Legal costs would not be awarded against the loser and full legal aid would no longer be granted. Green form advice would be available and lay representatives would be permitted to present cases.

The registrar would have the power to grant injunctions and order specific performance as well as award damages.

The Review drew attention to the diversity and complexity of the substantive law, but they recommended that the new procedure should be established independently of any revision of housing law (19).

The proposals are in line with the recommendations of the Nugee Committee for a new, informal small claims-type procedure for dealing with housing disputes within the county court. The Committee stressed that independent experts should be available to the court, paid for out of public funds. However, unlike the Review, the Committee recommended that legal aid should continue to be available (26).

Our views

A few local authorities have already established informal arbitration procedures for tenants' disputes. One example is the independent Southwark arbitration unit, funded by the local authority. It was established in 1983 under the tenancy agreement between the local authority and its 60,000 tenants, to deal with all tenancy disputes affecting council tenants (31).

The unit receives around 70 applications per month, mostly about repair problems. Tenants are given help in filling in a form by the unit staff, who give advice about the tenancy agreement and the procedure. If the case is not settled, the unit must arrange a hearing within 30 days before a tribunal. The tribunal consists of a councillor, a representative of a tenants' organisation and an independent chairperson. The chairpeople are all volunteers who live or work in Southwark and who are trained for the job. Where necessary, the unit will commission and pay for independent surveys. Representation is permitted, but rare. The atmosphere is designed to encourage tenants to speak for themselves. In 1986 the tribunal made 271 decisions, which are legally binding on council and tenants (31).

The number of cases coming before the unit demonstrates the potential demand for an accessible forum for tenancy disputes. The unit has several advantages over the county court. The rules are clearly spelt out in the tenancy agreement and a copy is given to all tenants. The unit staff are active in providing advice and help. The procedure is free to applicants and there is no risk of costs if the tenant loses. The procedure is quick and informal, and the tribunal will take an "investigative" approach to the problem. The tribunal will be aware of local housing conditions and policies, and will be familiar with the tenancy agreement. Expert reports are available, free of charge. The council is committed to co-operating with the unit, so that tenants need not fear retaliation for using the procedure. The main difficulty concerns the orders made which tend to be in vague terms, and may lead to further disagreements (32).

There are several lessons to be learnt from the success of the Southwark scheme: the law must be simple and easily understood; tenants need information about the scheme; staff should be active in giving advice; and arbitrators need an understanding of repairs problems and access to expert evidence.

The Review is right to identify a need for a cheaper, simpler procedure in which consumers can resolve disputes about repairs and service charges without using lawyers.

Nevertheless, a new informal "housing action" is not an easy or cheap option. It will need substantial changes not only in the existing procedures of the court but in the attitudes of those who work in them. At present, county courts have little experience of dealing with repairs problems, even with the help of lawyers. The small claims experience shows how difficult it is to create procedures which are genuinely available to unrepresented litigants. Over half of small claims cases still involve lawyers. We are therefore cautious about withdrawing legal aid, before the new procedures have been proved to work.

In our view, housing actions should be established on an experimental basis, along the lines of the Dundee small claims experiment, which was monitored for three years by the Scottish Office's central research unit (33).

The new action must be well publicised. In the Dundee experiment, posters on local buses proved to be effective. Local authorities should also provide their tenants with information about the housing action procedure and how to seek advice about it. The Lord Chancellor's Department should produce a guide to the procedure, along the lines of their booklet, *Small claims in the county court*, which is distributed free to litigants.

Court staff will need special training to give advice about the procedure and help people complete the forms. They will also need some basic understanding of the substantive law.

We agree with the Nugee Committee that it is very important that the court has access to independent expert reports about the state of the property and the need for repairs (26). In most cases, this will be the nub of the case. We are very pleased that the Review has recommended that expert assessors should be paid for out of public funds. We would not wish to see the housing action go ahead without access to expert evidence.

Registrars will need to be trained in housing matters, so that they know what questions to ask and can decide disputes without the help of lawyers appearing before them. The training must include not only the law but a practical understanding of repairs problems.

We wish to see the Legal Aid Board actively involved in monitoring the experimental housing action, and the implications it has for advice centres. Legal aid should be retained for claims over the small claims limit until the housing action has been shown to be accessible to unrepresented litigants.

We wish to see the reforms in court procedure go hand in hand with a review and simplification of the substantive law relating to repairs and service charges. The Law Commission has recognised the need for simplification in this area (34) and we recommend that the Commission should as a matter of priority prepare a repair code which covers the most common disrepair difficulties.

References to chapter 12

1. Department of the Environment, Scottish Development Department and Welsh Office, *Housing and construction statistics 1976-1986*, HMSO, 1987, table 11.10.
2. School for Advanced Urban Studies, University of Bristol, *Study of housing cases: final report to the Lord Chancellor's Department* produced for the Civil Justice Review, Lord Chancellor's Department, 1987.
3. The figure for mortgage possessions had increased from 39,460 in 1982 to 71,526 in 1986 (see *Housing and construction statistics*, reference 1 above, 1972-82 and 1976-86).
4. National Consumer Council, *Behind with the mortgage, lenders, borrowers and home loan debt: a consumer view*, Summer 1985.
5. Duncan, S. and Kirby K., *Preventing rent arrears*, Department of the Environment, HMSO, 1983.

6. Watts J., "Local authority possession proceedings", *Legal Action*, February 1987, p. 7.

7. National Consumer Council, *Security risks: personal loans secured on homes*, Autumn 1987.

8. Housing Act 1985, sections 84 and 85.

9. Housing assocation tenants are covered by the Housing Act 1985 above. For private tenants the relevant provision is Rent Act 1977 section 98.

10. Housing Act 1988 section 7 and schedule 2, grounds 8 and 10.

11. Administration of Justice Act 1970, section 36.

12. Consumer Credit Act 1974, sections 137-140.

13. Consumer Credit Act 1974, sections 129 and 135.

14. Burrows L., *Rent arrears and the courts*, a report by the Lay Advocacy Service, 1986.

15. The Law Society, *Legal aid handbook 1986*, HMSO, 1986.

16. Lord Chancellor's Department *35th legal aid annual reports* [1984-85], HC 156, HMSO, January 1986.

17. see Housing Act 1985, part III.

18. Matthews, R., "Mortgage arrears—report on local authority survey", Shelter, 1984 (unpublished—but quoted in *Behind with the mortgage*, see reference 4 above).

19. Civil Justice Review, *Report of the review body on civil justice*, Cm.394, HMSO, 1988.

20. Civil Justice Review, *Housing cases*, consultation paper no.5, Lord Chancellor's Department, January 1987.

21. Lord Chancellor's Department, *34th legal aid annual reports* [1983-84], HC 151, HMSO, January 1985.

22. National Consumer Council, *An introduction to the findings of the consumer concerns survey*, August 1981.

23. Gallup Omnibus Report, "Council tenants", research conducted on behalf of the National Consumer Council between 30 March and 12 April 1988.

24. Department of the Environment, *English house conditions survey 1981*, HMSO 1982 and 1983.

25. National Consumer Council, *Cracking up—Building faults in council homes: proposals for a new deal*, 1982.

26. Department of the Environment, *Report of the Committee of Inquiry on the Management of Privately Owned Blocks of Flats* (the Nugee Committee), 1985.

27. *R v Cardiff City Council ex parte Cross*, *Journal of Planning and Environmental Law* 1981 p.748.

28. Landlord and Tenant Act 1985, section 19.

29. Housing Act 1985, section 104.
30. Kay A. and others, *The 1980 tenants' rights in practice: a study of the implementation of the 1980 Housing Act rights by local authorities 1980-83*, Housing Research Group, The City University, 1986.
31. Correspondence dated 2 April 1987 with Southwark Arbitration Unit.
32. See the Legal Action Group's report on their conference on the Civil Justice Review held on July 4th 1988.
33. Connor, A. and Doig, B., *A research based evaluation of the Dundee small claims experiment*, Scottish Office, Central Research Unit, January 1983.
34. Law Commission, *Landlord and tenant: reform of the law* consultation document no.162, Cm.145, HMSO, 1987.

Chapter 13
Debt

As we saw in chapter 9, the majority of county court and high court business is concerned with collecting debts. In 1987, 2.16 million default summonses were issued in the county court (1). All but a handful of these are issued by institutional plaintiffs and the great majority are brought against individuals (2). Most summonses are for relatively small amounts: two-thirds are for less than £500 (1).

The last five years have seen an explosion in the amount of credit granted (3), accompanied by a slower but steady rise in the number of consumer debt claims coming before the courts (4). The Scottish Consumer Council's survey of debt advice in Scotland identified three broad types of debt problems (5):

★ debts caused by a reduction in income—often brought about by unemployment, illness or divorce. Families who have become accustomed to a stable income may find themselves trying to maintain living standards that are only tenable if the problems prove short-lived. They experience the most acute problems paying household bills and often borrow money at high interest rates;

★ debts caused by long-term poverty. Typically, these are fuel or housing debts arising after several years on state benefits or very low wages. Families may also have borrowed to buy an essential item such as a cooker or furniture;

★ debts of relatively affluent families who have been seduced by the consumer credit market offering apparently easy credit terms. Families may commit their income very fully, or in some cases, over-commit themselves and a slight change in circumstances can precipitate an immediate financial crisis. The report states that these debts are "highly visible in the folklore of debt" because of their rapid rise over very recent years and because "some can be truly spectacular in their scale and enormously complicated and time consuming to solve" (5). However, this kind of debt still appears to constitute a minority of the total debt problems presented.

These are only broad categories. There is little recent research on the causes of debt and it is very difficult to quantify how many debts fall into each category. In the Office of Fair Trading's survey on consumers' use of credit, 14 per cent of credit users said that they had experienced problems in making payments in the last 5 years. The most common reason given (by 21 per cent of those in difficulties) was loss of a job. Eleven per cent said their partners had lost their jobs, 11 per cent blamed other loss of earnings, 8 per cent mentioned sickness in the household, and 7 per cent mentioned marital breakdown. Eighteen per cent thought that they had made too many credit commitments (6).

In our view, whether the main cause of problems is poverty, unemployment or over-commitment, little is to be gained by taking a purely punitive approach to those with debts. We wish to see the court take account of debtors' individual circumstances before taking action against them.

Present court procedures

Money claims are dealt with by a "default" procedure. At present, summonses are sent out by individual county courts. The defendant receives a summons and reply form, which asks whether the claim is admitted or denied. There is a section for the defendant to make an offer of payment, and another for a defence or counter-claim.

Defendants who wish to dispute the claim must lodge a defence. The matter will then proceed to trial or, in the case of a small claim, to arbitration. Where the defendant admits the claim and makes an offer of payment, the offer will be put to the plaintiff. Where the plaintiff accepts the offer, judgement is entered; where the plaintiff rejects the offer, a disposal hearing takes place in which the registrar decides the rate of payment.

In two-thirds of cases the defendant fails to reply (2). The plaintiff can then ask the court to enter judgement by a purely administrative process without a court hearing.

Once judgement has been obtained, it is for the plaintiff rather than the court to decide how the debt should be enforced. There is a choice of methods. The most popular is "sending in the bailiffs" to seize, or, more often, threaten to seize, the defendant's goods. This is known, confusingly, as a "warrant of execution" in the county court or "writ of fieri facias" (shortened to "writ of fi fa") in the high court. In 1987, 1.16 million warrants of execution were issued in the county court although in very few cases (2,882) were goods actually seized and sold (1). In addition, there were 67,054 writs of fi fa in the high court (1).

County court bailiffs are employees of the court, while their high court equivalents, known as sheriff's officers, work for private companies. These companies are accountable to "under sheriffs", who are usually solicitors appointed by the sheriff of each county. In county court warrants, plaintiffs pay a fixed fee, while in the high court most of the fee is levied as a percentage of the debt recovered. Defendants are not informed that a warrant is being applied for, although county court debtors have the right to apply to the court for a "stay of execution". The county court may suspend the warrant on the basis that the debtor will pay the debt by instalments.

The next most common method of enforcing a debt is the attachment of earnings order in which the court orders the debtor's employer to make weekly or monthly deductions from the debtor's earnings. This is only available in the county court but high court creditors who wish to use this procedure may ask for their case to be transferred. Unlike the warrant, an attachment of earnings order can only be made after a hearing before the registrar. The registrar will set a "protected earnings level", fixed by reference to the income support rate, below which the debtor's earnings may not be reduced. In 1987, 103,382 orders were applied for and 53,297 were made (1).

Other methods are much less commonly used. In 1987 there were 32,078 applications for "charging orders", in which the court may make a charge over the debtor's house (1). This means that when the house is sold, the creditor must be paid out of the proceeds. Although in theory the creditor can force the house to be sold, this very rarely happens in practice (2). There were 4,049 "garnishee orders", which require money to be paid out of a bank or building society account, or by anyone else who owes money to the debtor (1).

A creditor who is unsure which method to use may apply for an "oral examination", in which the debtor is compelled to attend court and answer questions about his or her means. In 1987, 93,076 applications were made, resulting in 74,098 examinations, mostly before court staff rather than registrars (1).

Finally, there is the administration order procedure which allows multiple debtors to have all their debts dealt with together. The court sets the amount of the total instalments, which are apportioned pro rata to different creditors. Debtors who make regular payments are protected from other enforcement actions. In 1987, 4,928 orders were made (1). Research for the Civil Justice Review shows that debtors found administration orders a useful way of dealing with several unsecured creditors (2). But administration orders do not prevent landlords or mortgage lenders from taking possession of the debtor's home, or fuel boards from disconnecting the supply. The law permits disconnections without any form of court action.

Where one month after a county court judgment has been given £10 or more is outstanding, the debt is entered on a public register, where it remains for six years. Debtors who have paid can apply to have their debt marked satisfied. The register is run by a non-profit making organisation established by the credit industry. In 1987, 932,721 judgments were registered, and 52,365 were marked as satisfied (1).

Problems with current debt procedures

We are concerned that the court system for recovering debts is more suited to organisational "bulk" plaintiffs than to the needs of individuals, whether as creditors, defendants who dispute the debt, or debtors who need time to pay. The county court system concentrates on single debts, rather than looking at the overall circumstances of the debtor. We look at each problem in turn.

Individual creditors

In *Simple justice* we identified enforcement problems as the most serious weakness of the small claims procedure (7). Consumers did not realise that once they had won their cases the onus was on them to collect the debt. Many found the procedure and terminology confusing and two-thirds were given no help on how to find their way through the procedures. Comments included: "I never received any indication from the court that they had not obtained payment nor that I needed to take further action myself in order to secure payment"; "the garnishee summons is very archaically worded. No-one at the court seemed to know how to fill it in" (7). In all, a quarter of those winning their cases did not get paid. People thought that the court itself should play a more active role in enforcing debts (7).

Individuals disputing debts

Individual defendants rarely become involved in court action, even where they have a valid defence to the claim. The Civil Justice Review study found that almost a third of debtors in the sample disputed the claim, "although they had not generally filed a defence". Altogether, only 7 per cent of cases were defended (2). This is borne out by other studies. A survey of 100 judgement debtors carried out for the Scottish Law Commission found that 24 disputed the amount on the summons or felt that they had grounds for non-payment but only 2 contested the action in court (8). In a study of debtors by Queen Mary College, 17 per cent of defendants said they had refused to pay because of disputes with the lender or dissatisfaction with the quality of goods, although there was considerable confusion among defendants about whether they had filed a defence (9).

Many defendants with valid defences are too confused and worried by the idea of court action to return the reply form to the court. Even where forms are returned there may still be problems. A small study of a London county court found that defendants do not always appreciate the distinction between admissions, explanations about why they have not paid, defences and counter-claims (10). In some cases, defendants put forward both offers to pay and defences, or put the defence in the "admissions" section of the form. The clerk whose job it is to read the defence forms would sometimes place confused forms in the "admissions" category rather than the "defended" category, even where there appeared to be a valid defence.

For example, one defendant was sued for failing to make hire-purchase payments for a television set. She returned a form which offered £8 per month, with the counter-claim and defence section left blank but with an accompanying letter which stated that the set had gone wrong:

> "I do not dispute the amount of money I owe. What I do dispute is the paying of it for the first twelve months while the television was under guarantee. It was in being repaired more than it was being used and every time it was still in the same state" (10).

The letter went on to explain that the set had now broken again and was not in use. This would appear to be a valid defence because the set was not "fit for its purpose". However, by offering to pay £8 per month the customer was taken to have admitted liability. The record card was marked "admission and offer", and judgement was entered for the hire-purchase company.

In another case a defendant stated:

> "When I received the wall units from the furniture shop the glass was broken. I told the salesman and he told me he have to order

the glass. I waited a few months. They haven't come to fix it...
nothing has be done" (10).

However, this explanation was not entered in the correct section of the
form. As a result the possible defence was ignored and the matter was
treated as a routine hire-purchase case: an order was made for the
return of the goods, suspended on payment of monthly instalments to
cover the full cost of the wall units (10).

Individual debtors

The debt system proceeds with very little information about debtors'
circumstances. The Civil Justice Review research found that 67 per
cent of business creditors had no knowledge about a debtor's financial
circumstances at the time of the original transaction, and 77 per cent
did not obtain any further information during the proceedings (2).

Cain's study of a county court found two different types of
institutional creditor using the court she studied (10). The Inland
Revenue, banks, and creditors who pursued mainly business debts
only used the courts where they felt reasonably sure that the debtors
had the resources to meet the debt. These creditors kept in close
contact with debtors and usually telephoned or called on debtors
when the debt first became apparent. They only used the courts as a
small and relatively unimportant part of the debt collection
process.

Most plaintiffs, however, did not expect each case to result in
payment. They brought debts before the court as a matter of routine,
in the expectation that enough debts would be paid to show an overall
profit for the department. They would send a series of demands to the
debtor before taking court action, but would not visit, and rarely
received any information about why payment had not been made (10).
It appears from the Civil Justice Review study that the majority of
plaintiffs use the courts in this way (2).

Most cases are begun as a matter of routine, with no consideration
of the individual circumstances of the debtor and continue in the same
way. Only a third of debtors return the summons form: in the rest,
judgement is given in default as part of a purely clerical procedure (2).
The most common form of enforcement is the warrant of execution:
the Civil Justice Review found that in 605 cases where some method
of enforcement was used, 525 (87 per cent) used a warrant of
execution only (2). Thus in many cases, the first direct contact
between the debtor and the court or creditors is a visit from the
bailiffs.

The joint review of the bailiff service carried out in 1985 describes the warrant of execution in the following terms:

"Strictly, a warrant of execution is a direction to bailiffs to seize goods. But it is not used as such. In the absence of information concerning the particular circumstances of a debtor a warrant is often used as a first step to finding out more about him. It is not really used as a demand to execute, but as a demand to assess a debtor's assets, to levy on them and then to attempt to organise payment to the creditor." (11)

There are serious problems with using the bailiff at the door as the first point of contact with the debtor. Experienced debtors may realise that they have nothing worth taking, and ignore the warrant. Others panic—by breaking into agreed repayment plans with other creditors, or by borrowing more money to pay the bailiff. The Queen Mary College study found that 28 out of 150 debtors tried to borrow money to pay the debt, eight of whom approached banks, finance houses and money-lenders (9). The Civil Justice Review study, which substantially under-represented debtors who had experience of bailiffs, found that 18 per cent of debtors had taken out new loans (2). In the Queen Mary study, a third said that their health had suffered, just under a third said that their family's health had suffered and two debtors had taken drug overdoses as a result (9).

This is not a criticism of bailiffs themselves, who approach their job as good humouredly as possible. The great majority of debtors report that the bailiffs had been as pleasant and sympathetic as they could in the circumstances (2). But the bailiffs' task is a difficult one. The Civil Justice Review research found that bailiffs were confused about their role and uncertain as to how far they should go in advising debtors or collecting instalments. Many bailiffs regretted they no longer served default summons and therefore could no longer meet the debtor, explain the system and encourage payment before the action had taken its course. Morale was low (2).

Warrants are not only harsh, they are also an inefficient way of finding out about debtors. Often vital information does not get passed back to creditors. The 1985 review of bailiffs commented:

"Creditors also complain that they receive inadequate information from the court. Often they get no more than a terse statement that the defendant has gone away or has no effects. Many bailiffs make extensive enquiries and some put full returns on the backs of warrants, giving precisely the details the creditor would like to hear: that the defendant was unemployed, the furniture was in poor condition, the television was rented, etc. However, court offices frequently cut out all this information when making returns to creditors. Sometimes this is because they think it is irrelevant, more often it is because court staff do not have time to write it out. Occasionally it is because court staff believe that creditors seeking such information should ask for an oral examination'' (11).

The Civil Justice Review's research found that though bailiffs would answer creditors' phone calls courteously, written records of visits were brief and stylised. Most of the information was kept in the bailiff's head (2).

The result is a system which does not distinguish between those who can pay and those who can't, does not allow for consideration of the debtor's circumstances and can subject the debtor's family to hardship. The experienced and ''hardened'' debtor is favoured at the expense of the inexperienced and vulnerable debtor.

Concentration on the debt rather than the debtors

A final problem is that the county court deals with each judgement debt separately. The present filing systems do not allow courts to discover if debtors are being pursued for other debts, even before the same court. In fact the Civil Justice Review's research found that over half of debtors did face other debts—typically they had two or three other debts in addition to the judgement debt (2).

Debt enforcement is a case of every creditor for himself. Some creditors have far greater sanctions than others. Landlords and mortgage lenders can threaten to repossess the debtor's home; the gas and electricity boards can threaten to disconnect the supply; non-payment of rates can lead to imprisonment; hire-purchase companies can repossess the goods. The non-secured county court creditor is at the bottom of the hierarchy.

The multiple debtor can face a bewildering array of different creditors using different courts, different procedures and different threats. The county court, the magistrates court and the high court may all be involved. Generally, debtors must negotiate with each creditor separately, and must face the ordeal without advice. Debtors have difficult choices about whom to pay first: often they will pay the person at the door at the time. This can make it very difficult to keep to repayment plans and the loss of home and fuel becomes more likely. It also contributes to debtors' sense of hopelessness because as soon as one crisis is sorted out, another hits them.

The only way in which debtors can have all their debts dealt with together is the administration order. The procedure is relatively simple and informal and is generally liked by debtors—in the Civil Justice Review sample, all 57 debtors with experience of administration orders expressed satisfaction with the procedures (2). But there are problems: the process is burdensome to the court, and staff are disinclined to tell debtors that it is available; it is not used for housing and fuel debts where creditors have other sanctions; and to be used to best effect it requires advice from specialist debt counsellors which is rarely available.

Alternative debt enforcement methods

Before examining proposals to reform the system in England and Wales, we look at other debt enforcement methods used in other jurisdictions.

Increased credit use and increased default does not necessarily result in more debt cases before the courts. In the United States, since the second world war, consumer lending has increased sixteenfold, but the use made of small claims courts and municipal courts for debt collection has remained about steady in proportion to the population, while the number of debt cases before the higher courts has dropped (12). Creditors have developed better systems of credit and debt control. They are better able to spread their losses, and insurance against unemployment or illness is more common. Debtors are more likely to seek relief through more liberal bankruptcy proceedings.

There are some some signs that creditors in England and Wales are making more selective use of the courts. Maureen Cain's original interviews with creditors were carried out in 1980. When they were repeated in 1984, she found that many creditors were actively searching for alternative means of control (10). They were making greater use of new technology in all aspects of credit control and were conducting experiments to see which approach to debtors was the most effective. There was increased use of door-to-door collection agencies and cases were scrutinised more carefully before the summons was issued.

If the costs of enforcement through the courts rise, it is inevitable that large-scale creditors will become more selective in their use of the courts, only issuing summonses where there is a greater chance of being paid. They will turn to private collection agencies. There are dangers if debtors are harassed by unscrupulous firms and we recommend more stringent controls to stop this happening. But if the safeguards against harassment are adequate, and advice for debtors is available, we see advantages to greater use of informal repayment arrangements.

An enforcement office

The problems we have identified are not new. Very similar criticisms were made by the Payne Committee in 1969 (13). They found that creditors proceeded with no real knowledge of a debtor's circumstances, and that the procedures were complex, coercive and inhumane. There was no adequate machinery for bringing together multiple debts.

They recommended the establishment of an enforcement office, which would proceed on the basis of full information about a debtor's assets, liabilities and circumstances. The office rather than the creditor would choose the most appropriate method of enforcement. Money recovered would be distributed pro rata to all judgement creditors. Advice to debtors would be available from social workers attached to the office.

The Enforcement of Judgment Office (EJO) was established in Northern Ireland in 1969, following the recommendations of the Anderson Committee. If a judgement debt is not satisfied within 7 days, the creditor can apply to the EJO, who interview the debtor and decide what means of enforcement is appropriate. If it appears that the debtor has no assets, they can issue a certificate of unenforceability, preventing any further enforcement against the debtor. Unlike the office recommended by the Payne Committee, the EJO may not distribute the money it receives pro rata among creditors. Creditors are paid on a "first come, first served" basis. The second creditor will receive nothing until the first creditor has been paid in full.

The EJO has been criticised for being expensive and slow. In 1985, typical fees on a debt of £100 in Northern Ireland came to £37, compared with £26.50 in England and Wales (14). It also takes an average of 117 days where debts are paid in full, compared with 35 days in the county court (15). This is partly the result of the "queuing" system, in which creditors must wait for others to be paid.

It is difficult to compare "success rates" between Northern Ireland and England and Wales. The EJO will look at the "case" rather than the judgement debt, and the more expensive procedure means that creditors are likely to be more selective than those in England and Wales. Figures produced in 1984 show that the social and economic circumstances are also different. Northern Ireland is the second poorest region in the EEC, it has the lowest average male earnings in the UK and the highest number of social security claimants.

Necessary living costs, other than housing, are higher and families are larger. As a result debt is a more intractable problem in Northern Ireland than in other parts of the United Kingdom.

On the other hand, figures produced in 1982 show that the EJO can work: of cases started in 1979, 51 per cent had been paid in full, 18 per cent had been declared unenforceable, and 27 per cent were still unresolved. In the remaining cases, the debtor had disappeared or died (16). A statistical survey in 1986 showed that 40 per cent of debts were paid in full, and 19 per cent in part. This was not significantly different from the recovery rate in England and Wales (15).

We are wary about setting up a new bureaucracy that may prove slow and unwieldy. We do not suggest a completely new administrative structure. There are elements of the enforcement office idea, however, which could usefully be incorporated within the existing system. These include the emphasis on collecting information about debtors and dealing with all debts together. We wish to see the courts have the power to issue certificates of unenforceability where enforcement procedures would serve no useful function.

Bankruptcy

In the United States of America, individual voluntary bankruptcy is becoming an increasingly important way of dealing with debt. In 1978, American bankruptcy laws were liberalised. Although states differ in the details, most aim to discharge debtors within 6 months, and provide them with a "fresh start" free from all previous liabilities. It is common for debtors to be able to preserve important assets, such as their house and household possessions. The procedures aim to be relatively simple and straightforward so that they can be used by small consumer debtors (17). In an entrepreneurial society, easy bankruptcy aims to rehabilitate credit casualties, and allow re-entry to a market that is generally considered socially beneficial.

We are not suggesting that debtors in Britain should be provided with full discharge of their debts after six months. But there are strong grounds for encouraging greater rehabilitation. The Cork Committee recommended as a first priority a new procedure to offer ordinary consumer debtors relief from their debts after three years of payment (18). The Civil Justice Review research found that courts were making orders requiring debtors to pay instalments for up to 70 years: long orders offer no incentive to pay, and are often no more than an administrative burden for creditors (2). We fully support the administration order reforms proposed by the Civil Justice Review to allow discharge after 3 years payment.

Our proposals for reform

The Civil Justice Review sets out the following objectives for a system of debt recovery:

(i) the system should aim to recover as much as possible of the debt quickly, cheaply and simply;

(ii) creditors should be able to obtain adequate information about debtors' circumstances;

(iii) maximum information should be available about debtors on public files;

(iv) there should be machinery for bringing together multiple debts;

(v) the period for repayment should not last indefinitely, and a debtor should be restored to full economic status as soon as possible;

(vi) debtors and their families should not be subjected to unwarranted hardship, fear or humiliation (19).

We would add a last objective—that the system should distinguish between those who cannot pay their debts and those who will not pay them. It must allow for proper consideration of the debtor's circumstances and provide sensible arrangements for those who genuinely need time to pay their debts.

In making proposals for reform we have looked for a system in which:

★ all consumer debts are dealt with in the county court;

★ debtors are provided with protection against harassment, and have access to advice in negotiating informal settlements;

★ defendants are encouraged to put their defences before the court by well-designed forms, information and advice;

★ court staff scrutinise returned forms to ensure that valid defences are put before the court;

★ debtors are encouraged to provide as much information as possible about their circumstances;

★ courts keep information about debtors, rather than individual debts, and this information is used as the basis for enforcement decisions;

★ the threat to seize goods is used as a last rather than a first step in the enforcement process;

★ the administration order is reformed and expanded, and is made more readily available through the provision of money advice;

★ debtors who show the courts that they have made their best efforts to pay and also show that they were not fraudulent or reckless in incurring debt can be given relief from liabilities after three years;

★ individual creditors are given greater help and advice by court staff.

1. One court

The Civil Justice Review raised the question of whether all debt cases should start in the county court but refrained from making any recommendations while the central computerised claims registry is being established (19).

They recommended that county court judgment debts under £5,000 should continue to be enforced by the county court bailiffs, as should debts arising out of agreements regulated by the Consumer Credit Act 1974. All high court debts, and county court debts over £5,000, should be enforced by the sheriffs. There would be a discretion to transfer county court debts over £2,000 to the high court for enforcement provided that they were shown to be of a commercial nature.

We wish to see all debt enforcement against individuals take place in the county court. The high court is a totally inappropriate forum for pursuing consumer debtors. The procedure is remote, extremely complex, and very difficult for the unrepresented debtor to understand. The defendant is even less likely to take a valid defence to court for fear of legal costs. There is no procedure for making instalment orders and payments must be made to the creditor rather than the court. If a debtor seeks an administration order, the matter must be transferred to the county court. In theory, the court does have a power to 'stay a writ of fi fa'—ie suspend the threat to seize goods—but applications are rarely made. It is not surprising that two-thirds of the high court debtors interviewed expressed dissatisfaction with the procedure (2).

We are not convinced that the high court offers significant advantages to creditors. Enforcement in the high court is more expensive, takes longer and appears to be no more effective (2). It would be possible to make the high court procedure for summary judgement available in the county court.

We recommend that all cases against individual consumers involving less than £25,000 should start in the county court and should be enforced by county court bailiffs. The onus would be on creditors wishing to use the high court to show that the debt was incurred by a company or partnership, or by an individual acting in a business capacity.

The Civil Justice Review did not examine other debt recovery methods, such as those of the magistrates courts' jurisdiction over rates and tax, "distress" for rent, and disconnection for unpaid fuel debts. We wish to see all debts dealt with together by one court, rather than the present system in which some creditors are given priority, and debtors face a bewildering variety of different recovery techniques from different courts. We are concerned that debtors continue to be imprisoned for unpaid rates, which are a purely civil matter, and fear that the switch from rates to poll tax will considerably increase the numbers of people at risk of imprisonment.

An investigation by Stoke-on-Trent citizens advice bureau concluded that magistrates courts were inexperienced in collecting rates and interpreted their duties in an alarming variety of different ways. Several courts did not carry out means enquiries themselves but relied on local authority rating officers' reports. Two-fifths of rates debtors coming to the bureau had borrowed money to pay their rates, transforming a simple debt problem to a complex multiple debt problem. The bureau commented:

"In 1987, 370 people were sentenced to terms of imprisonment for failing to pay their rates. Of these 6 were in Stoke on Trent. A very much greater number of people suffered indirectly from the threat of imprisonment, and in many cases lived in fear of this for many months" (20).

We recommend that the magistrates courts' jurisdiction over unpaid rates and taxes should be abolished and that these should be enforced through the county court in the normal way. Imprisonment should no longer be available. In our response to the Law Commission's report, we recommended the abolition of distress for rent on domestic tenancies (21). Instead, landlords should pursue arrears through the county court. We are concerned that public utilities, such as fuel and water boards, are able to use their position as monopoly suppliers to collect past debts by threatening the disconnection of essential services. If the right to disconnect for past debts is retained, we believe that it should only be permitted on a court order. We repeat the recommendation we first put forward in *Paying for fuel* in 1976, that the fuel industries should also collect their debts through the county court: disconnection of electricity, gas and or water supplies should only be allowed on the express authority of the court, after the debtor has failed to keep to repayment arrangements (22).

Thus all recovery against consumer debtors would take place within the county court, with the exception of criminal fines and maintenance debts. We have treated maintenance debts as a family law issue, rather than a consumer issue, and therefore make no recommendations concerning them.

2. Protection against harassment

Evidence about harassment is difficult to find but it appears from press reports, and complaints received by the Office of Fair Trading, that malpractices continue. These practices included holding social security books, contacting the debtor's employer to create embarrassment and the fear of dismissal, threatening criminal sanctions, making nuisance visits and phone calls, and using abusive and threatening language (23).

It is likely that recorded complaints represent only the tip of the iceberg. Debtors are often ashamed of their debt, or fear that a complaint may deprive them of their last source of credit. Harassment is also likely to increase, as the level of debt rises and creditors turn to private debt collection agencies rather than the courts.

A tough approach is needed. We repeat the recommendation made in *Consumers and debt* for new legislation to strengthen the protection afforded by section 40 of the Administration of Justice Act 1970 (23). The legislation would offer more comprehensive protection, and would place a duty on trading standards departments to enforce the provisions. Where debtors can show that they have been the victims of unreasonable pressure the debt should not be enforceable.

3. The claims registry

The Lord Chancellor's Department has produced plans for a central, computerised county court "claims registry" (24) to replace the current system in which summonses are sent out by individual county courts. It is envisaged that all requests for a default summons for a fixed amount of money would be sent to one central address. The computer would create a case file and dispatch a summons. The defendant would no longer send the summons back to the local county court but would reply to the central address. If the claim were defended, the matter would be referred to the county court closest to which the defendant lived or carried on business. The computer would record all payments, and provide information for the register of county court judgments. Requests for default judgements and warrants of execution would be sent to the claims registry. Local bailiffs would be notified of warrants within 24 hours. All other enforcement would be dealt with by the local court.

County courts would be linked to the central computer, allowing them to view the central case record. All county courts would be able to advise litigants and accept payments.

This major change in court administration has dangers and advantages. The most serious danger is that the defendant will perceive the court system to be even more remote and may be less likely to reply to a central address than to a local court. It is very important that the forms defendants are sent state clearly that advice can be sought at the local county court, and include its address and telephone number and other sources of advice in the area. Again, there will be a need for experiment and research in the design of the summons and reply form. It is important to find a form which encourages the maximum number of defendants to return it. Where defences exist, consumers should be encouraged to put them before the court.

The returned forms must be carefully scrutinised. Legitimate defences must not be missed simply because a defendant has used the wrong part of the form, or put forward an offer to pay. The job must be done by trained staff. Where there is doubt, the presumption must be in favour of a defended action.

There are also advantages to a central computerised system. One is that it allows staff released from clerical duties to be trained to provide advice on court procedures to the public.

The computer would allow information to be kept by debtor rather than by debt. The register of county court judgements, available to all members of the public, would be improved. We recommend that, in addition, judgement creditors have access to the full file on each debtor. This should contain details of their financial circumstances, records of instalment orders made and paid, and details of all enforcement action taken against the debtor, together with the result. Where garnishee or attachment of earnings orders have been made, the file should provide creditors with details of the debtor's bank account and employer. This would meet the Civil Justice Review's objective that creditors should be able to obtain adequate information about a debtor's circumstances so that they can suit the enforcement method to the debtor's individual circumstances.

4. The bailiff's visit

The Civil Justice Review found that bailiffs are often unclear about the role they are expected to play. Although in theory they are sent to seize goods, in practice they are used to gather information about the debtor and collect payments. They recommended that the bailiff's duties should be redefined to include arranging and collecting instalments and recording information given by debtors about their personal and financial circumstances. An account of bailiffs' duties would be set out in a publicly available manual, so that both bailiffs and the public know what to expect (19).

We wish to see the bailiff's duties redefined so as to separate the investigative role from the threat to seize goods. In our view bailiffs' first duty should be to visit debtors (or arrange to meet them at the office) to find out about their circumstances (income, value of household goods, name of employer, details of bank account etc.), and collect money and negotiate repayment by instalment. The present arrangements by which debtors are expected to pay regular sums are inconvenient because they must either visit a court office between 10 am and 4 pm, or pay by post. We wish to see debtors given paying-in books for banks and post offices. Bailiffs would also explain court procedures to debtors and tell them where they could go for further advice. We wish to see them report to creditors by means of a special form. The 1985 review suggested that resources could be found for this by saving on typing warrants (11).

At present, attachment of earnings orders, garnishee orders and charging orders can only be granted after a court hearing before a registrar. We wish to see similar safeguards apply to the authority to seize goods. In our view, seizure should only be used where the creditor has investigated the debtor's circumstances and knows that goods are available to be sold.

The procedure we envisage would involve a court hearing in which the court had a flexible range of sanctions before it—including an instalment order, a custody warrant (taking walking possession of the debtor's goods), an attachment of earnings order, a garnishee order, a charging order and the authority to seize goods. Alternatively, the court could decide that no orders were appropriate and issue a certificate on unenforceability. Where necessary, the court could apply a number of orders (such as an attachment of earnings order and a charging order) simultaneously. The authority to seize goods would no longer be seen as the main enforcement method but only one among many.

5. Exempt goods

Even if the seizure of goods becomes a much less important method of enforcement, we would still wish to see an increase in the categories and value of goods which are exempt from seizure. Debtors and their families must still be given the means to survive and earn a living and debtors should not have to turn to social services or the social security system to replace seized goods.

The Insolvency Act 1986 allows bankrupts to retain "such tools, books, vehicles and other items of equipment as are necessary to the bankrupt for use personally by him in his employment, business or vocation", and "such clothing, bedding, furniture, household equipment and provisions as are necessary for satisfying the basic domestic needs of the bankrupt and his family" (25). We agree with the Civil Justice Review's recommendation that the small county court debtor should be given similar protection to that available to bankrupts (19). The bailiffs' manual could give further guidance on what is "necessary to satisfy basic domestic needs".

6. Administration orders

The Civil Justice Review follows the Cork report in recommending a reformed administration order procedure to act as a 'poor man's bankruptcy' (19).

At present only a judgement debtor can apply to the court for an administration order. The Review recommends that the procedure should be open to all debtors, whether or not they have a county court debt against them. Judgement creditors would also be able to apply and registrars could take the initiative in making an order. At present the administration order procedure is only available to those with debts of under £5,000 but the Review recommends abolishing the monetary limit.

At present registrars appear unwilling to abate debts, but prefer to make very long orders. The Civil Justice Review survey of 98 administration orders found that a third were expected to run for five years, a third for between five and ten years, and a third for more than ten years. At the extreme, one order was expected to last for over 70 years (2). The Review considered that these orders were much too long. They recommended that no order should last more than three years and, where the debtor is unable to pay off the debt within that time, the registrar should make a "composition order" for repayment of less than the full amount. The Review states that this would have "the important economic function of rehabilitating debtors in a comparatively short time and restoring to them their full economic status" (19). Long orders provide the debtor with no incentive to pay and often create more difficulties for creditors than they are worth.

At present fuel boards are able to subvert the effect of the administration order by threatening disconnection unless the debtor pays them more than the pro-rata rate given to other creditors. The Review recommends that public utilities should no longer be able to withdraw the service they provide without leave of the court (19).

This will provide important protection to debtors against gas and electricity disconnections.

The Review rejects the idea of a scheme along the lines of the Northern Ireland Enforcement of Judgements Office (EJO). But they recommend introducing an important ingredient of the EJO—the certificate of unenforcability—into the administration order procedure. This would mean that, where a debtor was found to have no realisable assets or income, the court could make an order placing restrictions on future enforcement. The order would last for a limited time and would be reviewed if circumstances changed. Each court would publish a list of orders in force.

We very much support the Review's proposals. The administration order procedure is a useful way of bringing all a person's debts together, but at present it is rarely used. The recommendations would make the administration order procedure available to more people. We are concerned that many of the long orders currently made do not provide debtors with any incentive to pay, and are often no more than an administrative burden to court and creditors. We support the proposal that debtors who make every effort to pay should be given a fresh start after three years. Where debtors behaved dishonestly, or failed to make any effort to pay, the registrar could withdraw the protection of the administration order.

We are very pleased that the Review recommends that where fuel boards are scheduled creditors they should only be allowed to disconnect with leave of the court. This is an important step towards controlling the way monopoly suppliers use disconnection to seek preferential treatment over other creditors.

The Civil Justice Review consultation paper described administration orders as "a major burden" for court staff, which would be relieved if debtors could be encouraged to obtain assistance from outside agencies, such as citizens advice bureaux and money advice centres (15). These can obtain details of all loans, notify creditors and prepare detailed financial plans. In our view, the provision of specialist debt counselling is crucial to the success of administration orders. Research into administration orders in Birmingham has shown that they are much more likely to be used if the debtor has access to debt counselling (26). Birmingham money advice centre was involved in 19 out of the 31 administration orders made by Birmingham county court in 1978. By 1982, 65 per cent of orders handled by the money advice centre were up-to-date, compared with only 33 per cent of other orders. The centre looked at the whole financial situation of the debtor, dealt with creditors within and outside the order and provided the debtor with encouragement and support (26).

When the Australian Law Commission proposed a similar scheme, it described the provision of expert financial advice as essential to the proper operation of the scheme (27). It proposed setting up a training scheme to allow more people to become counsellors. Where the Legal Aid Board contracts with advice centres for the provision of money advice, it should ensure that advice, assistance and representation are available for debtors who are seeking and paying administration orders.

7. *Advice and representation*

The Civil Justice Review consultation paper commented that: "money advice is proving to be of great advantage to debtors, creditors, and the courts. Assistance with correspondence, form-filling, budgeting and income enhancement may mean that some cases need not come to court at all, while others are well prepared" (15).

The Review commented that lay representation is particularly beneficial in debt cases: "most hearings... are interlocutory in nature, for example disposal hearings and applications to vary an instalment order or to suspend a warrant, and it is recognised that in such circumstances the presence of an experienced money adviser can often be useful to the court as well as the litigant" (19).

The Payne Committee wished to see a 'social services' or 'welfare' office attached to the county court (13). Only Birmingham county court employs a welfare officer to assist debtors. An evaluation of this scheme suggests that a welfare officer can improve the quality of justice (28). The welfare officer is able to take referrals directly from the registrar during the course of a hearing and can negotiate with creditors and put the defendant's side of the case before the court. She approaches people coming out of court where they appear to be confused about the order made. She also ensures good liaison with other advice agencies in the city. One registrar commented "the present system is worth to me up to half a Registrar in the saving of judicial time" (28).

We agree that lay representation should be allowed in all debt proceedings and we welcome the recognition of the importance of money advice. Money advice can certainly keep cases out of court. Some centres even provide their own informal equivalent to the administration order, by opening client accounts into which the debtor pays a regular sum to be distributed among creditors. Where cases do come to court, time can be saved by preparation.

However, recognition of the value of money advice is of little use without adequate resources. Good money advice, whether offered inside or outside the court is a highly skilled task and, as we discussed in chapter 4, resources are inadequate to the task. The Legal Aid Board should take immediate steps to improve provision. In our view, the onus is on both the government and the credit industry to provide funding.

8. *Help for individual creditors*

It is very important that the court provides advice and assistance to individual creditors who do not know their way around the debt enforcement system. The Birmingham experiment of a special "small claims division" has proved particularly effective in helping small individual plaintiffs to enforce judgements (29). We recommend that each court should nominate a member of the court staff to advise individual creditors about the procedures. Where a judgement creditor is unfamiliar with the different methods, the court should propose the steps which appear to be most appropriate to enforce the debt.

The procedures we have recommended, in which a creditor may ask for a full report on the debtor's circumstances, and the court has a choice between different enforcement methods, should be of benefit to individual judgement creditors who do not know where to turn. The court should be able to make appropriate orders, whether or not they have been requested by the creditor. We wish to see hearings in which registrars assist individual creditors.

Not all claims result in payment. Publicity about bringing small claims must make it clear that obtaining judgement is only the first step, and that in some cases a creditor will never get paid.

9. *Plain English*

The terminology used to describe debt recovery is particularly obscure. The Law Society has given the following description of how a reasonably intelligent person might interpret some of the terms used:

"Warrant of Execution—You will be hanged at dawn"...'
"Writ of Fieri Facias—Your fakes will be burnt in a furnace".
"Charging Order—The cavalry will advance"...
"Garnishee Order Nisi—You will be nicely garnished with herbs and vegetables".

"Garnishee Order Absolute—You certainly will be garnished with herbs and vegetables" (30).

We are pleased that the Review body has recommended that plain modern terms should be substituted for those now used in connection with enforcement.

References to chapter 13

1. Lord Chancellor's Department, *Judicial statistics: Annual Report 1987*, Cm 428, HMSO, 1988.
2. Touche Ross management consultants, *Study of debt enforcement procedures*, carried out for the Civil Justice Review, Lord Chancellor's Department, December 1986.
3. The amount of consumer credit outstanding has grown from £18,891 million in 1983 to £36,823 million in 1987. See Central Statistical Office, *Financial statistics*, HMSO, July 1988.
4. The number of default summonses issued has grown from 1,983,815 in 1983 to 2,163,488 in 1987. See Lord Chancellor's Department, *Judicial statistics: Annual Report 1983*, Cmnd 9370, HMSO, 1984, and *Judicial statistics 1987* see above.
5. ADVICE Publishing and Training, *Debt advice in Scotland*, a report prepared for the Scottish Consumer Council, March 1988.
6. PAS Business Surveys, *Consumers' use of credit survey*, Office of Fair Trading, August 1988.
7. National Consumer Council/Welsh Consumer Council, *Simple justice: a consumer view of small claims procedures in England and Wales*, 1979.
8. Adler, M. and Wozniak, E., *The origins and consequences of default—an examination of the impact of diligence (summary)*, research report for the Scottish Law Commission, no.5, Scottish Office, Central Research Unit Papers, February 1981.
9. Cotterrell, R. and others, "The recovery of judgment debts in the county court: some preliminary results" in ed. Ramsay, I., *Debtors and creditors*, Professional Books, 1986.
10. Cain, M., "Who loses out in paradise island? the case of defendant debtors in county courts", in ed. Ramsay, I., see above reference 9.
11. Lord Chancellor's Department, *Joint review with the Civil and Public Services Association of the bailiff service*, January 1986.
12. Kagan, R.A., "The routinization of debt collection: an essay on social change and conflict in the courts", *Law and Society*, 1984, vol.18, no.3, p.323.

13. *Report of the committee on the enforcement of judgment debts (Payne Committee)*, Cmnd 3909, HMSO, 1969.

14. Greer, D.S. and Mulvaney, A., *Description and evaluation of the small claims procedure in Northern Ireland*, The General Consumer Council for Northern Ireland, 1985.

15. Civil Justice Review, *Enforcement of debt*, consultation paper no.4, Lord Chancellor's Department, January 1987.

16. McWilliams, M., and Morrissey, M., "Debt and debt management in Northern Ireland", in ed. Ramsay, I., see above reference 9.

17. Shuckman, P., "A brief survey of empirical research on personal bankruptcy in the USA, with comments on legislative impact", in ed. Ramsay, I., see above reference 9.

18. *Report of the review committee on insolvency law and practice* (Chairman: Sir Kenneth Cork), Cmnd 8558, HMSO, 1982.

19. Civil Justice Review, *Report of the Review Body on Civil Justice*, Cm 394, HMSO, 1988.

20. Harris, S., and Wolfe, M., *Jailed for debt*: a report on the imprisonment of rates defaulters compiled by Stoke-on-Trent citizens advice bureau from information supplied by members of the National Association of Citizens Advice Bureaux, 1988.

21. National Consumer Council, "Distress for rent", response to the Law Commission, working paper no.97, December 1986.

22. National Consumer Council, *Paying for fuel*, HMSO, 1976.

23. National Consumer Council/Welsh Consumer Council, *Consumers and debt*, 1983.

24. Lord Chancellor's Department, *The claims registry: computerisation of county court procedures in debt cases*, consultation paper, July 1987.

25. Insolvency Act 1986, section 283.

26. Davies, J.E., "Delegalisation of debt recovery proceedings: a socio-legal study of money advice centres and administration orders" in ed. Ramsay, I., see above reference 9.

27. Australian Law Reform Commission, *Insolvency: the regular payment of debts*, report no.6, Canberra, 1977.

28. Richards, J. and Sherr, A., *The county court welfare officer; an evaluation*, February 1984.

29. Appleby, G., "Small claims in Birmingham county court", *Civil Justice Quarterly*, 1984, pp.203-8.

30. Law Society, *The enforcement of judgements—a different approach*, response to the Civil Justice Review, May 1987.

Index

Printed in the United Kingdom for Her Majesty's Stationery Office
Dd 289367   C30   2/89